The Invention of the Brazilian Northeast

A BOOK IN THE SERIES

Latin America in Translation / En Traducción / Em Tradução

Sponsored by the Duke University–University of North Carolina
Program in Latin American Studies

The Invention of the

BRAZILIAN NORTHEAST

DURVAL MUNIZ DE ALBUQUERQUE JR.

WITH A FOREWORD BY JAMES N. GREEN

TRANSLATED BY JERRY DENNIS METZ

DUKE UNIVERSITY PRESS

Durham and London 2014

Designed by Natalie F. Smith
Typeset in Scala Pro by Westchester Publishing Services

Cover art: Collage by Natalie F. Smith based on a photograph of
a railway bridge between São Félix and Cachoeira, near Salvador,
Brazil. Photograph © dbimages / Alamy.

Library of Congress Cataloging-in-Publication Data
Albuquerque Jr., Durval Muniz de (Albuquerque Junior)
[Invengco do nordeste e outras artes. English]
The invention of the Brazilian Northeast / Durval Muniz de Albuquerque Jr. ;
with a foreword by James N. Green ; translated by Jerry D. Metz.
pages cm—(Latin America in translation/en traducción/em tradução)
Includes bibliographical references and index.
ISBN 978-0-8223-5770-4 (cloth : alk. paper)
ISBN 978-0-8223-5785-8 (pbk. : alk. paper)
1. Brazil, Northeast—History.   2. Brazil, Northeast—Social conditions.   I. Title.
II. Series: Latin America in translation/en traducción/em tradução.
F2583.A5413 2014   981—dc23   2014015441

For my mother, Maria, who reared me a *nordestino* but also led me to dream of São Paulo, with the same longing I feel for it today.

CONTENTS

FOREWORD JAMES N. GREEN

Sometimes a great historical work can have a seemingly simple yet profoundly complex thesis that appears all too obvious after its supporting arguments are clearly laid out to the reader. Such is the case of Durval Muniz de Albuquerque Jr.'s masterpiece about the invention in the 1920s of the Brazilian Northeast as a distinct geographic region. Albuquerque, a professor of history at the Federal University of Rio Grande do Norte, with a doctorate from the State University of Campinas (UNI-CAMP), Campinas, São Paulo, has shaken up what has become a naturalized notion of how the Brazilian nation is thought of spatially and culturally. The author has forced a rethinking about how intellectual production shaped and crystallized a series of myths, stereotypes, and images of a "backward" and "decadent" region of Brazil, which, according to standard narratives, was caught up in an endless cycles of droughts, hunger, and disappointments.

These nationally embraced ideas about the nature of a region that have been projected onto the Brazilian states that bulged out into the Atlantic Ocean even took on an international significance in the mid-twentieth century. In the aftermath of the 1959 Cuban Revolution, the Kennedy administration (1961–63) launched the Alliance for Progress with its legions of Peace Corps volunteers, agrarian technicians, and economic advisers dispatched to solve the problem of underdevelopment in Latin America as a means of averting other revolutions from sprouting up across the continent. The Brazilian Northeast became a privileged Cold War testing ground for how to combat starvation, disease, and the supposed resulting proclivity to subversion that would lead to the embrace of communism over capitalism.

The U.S. media reinforced this image about how poverty could lead to revolution with feature stories about the region. For example, the headline of the first article, on October 31, 1960, of a two-part series on Brazil published by the *New York Times* proclaimed: "Northeast Poverty Breeds Threat of Revolt." A follow-up story the next day was headlined by the warning "Marxists Are Organizing Peasants in Brazil: Leftist Leagues

Aim at a Political Army 40 Million Strong." The alarmist nature of the pieces, written in colorful prose by veteran journalist Tad Szulc, as well as a stern accompanying *Times* editorial about the perils of Fidelistas, cautioned that a dangerous revolutionary movement was brewing among the starving masses of the region. Conforming to right-wing Brazilian anxieties of the Northeast, the *Times* coverage of this area of Brazil presented grossly exaggerated descriptions of rural workers allegedly disposed to insurrection even though in reality peasant organizing in the region was still rather precarious at the time.

Several years later, Lincoln Gordon, the U.S. ambassador to Brazil during the early 1960s, explained that the *Times* articles were perhaps the first time that American readers had ever heard about the Brazilian Northeast.[1] Washington's response to this theoretical threat was to channel hundreds of millions of dollars through U.S. Aid for International Development programs to prove that American largess could somehow break the Brazilian Northeast's almost pathological inability to climb out of its own stagnation and starvation. The Central Intelligence Agency also directed covert funds to Brazil in an attempt to defeat populist candidates, such as Miguel Arraes from the state of Pernambuco, in the 1962 gubernatorial elections. The fear that the Northeast was on the verge of a political explosion and that somehow the region's poverty might motivate the peasants of the Northeast to carry out the second Cuban Revolution in Latin America was one of many justifications that Washington policy makers offered to explain their support of the military dictatorship that came to power in 1964 and governed for two decades. Thus, a stereotype, fueled by distorted national and international images of the region, led to tragic results.

Albuquerque's skillful interdisciplinary approach to charting the process of the creation of a unique northeastern regional identity challenges historians to reexamine entirely the ways in which proponents of competing visions of Brazil have fought for hegemony for over 150 years. In nineteenth-century imperial Brazil, the nation was divided in the geographical imaginary into two general regions—the *Norte* and the *Sul*. During the national campaign to raise relief funds for the Great Drought of 1877 that devastated Ceará and surrounding states, local political and economic elites discovered that the discourse about chronic climatic disasters and the consequential displacement of starving hordes in the North offered a convenient means to extract additional resources from the central government. In this respect a negative image of the area was turned to the advantage of the regional elites. At the same time, the North became a pessimistic foil for those in the South who considered their area of Brazil to be the dynamic train engine that would pull the impoverished states of the North forward on the railroad tracks toward modernization and progress. In this regard, the "crude" and "backward" Norte became the embodiment of what the civilizing Sul should avoid at all costs.

The shifts in political power during the early years of the republic at the turn of the twentieth century, as well as the economic decline of sugar production in the North, pushed significant sectors of the traditional northern elites to the sidelines. Agricultural modernization in the form of centralized sugar processing plants further displaced "founding families" who had exercised political and social control over localities for centuries. In the 1930s, sociologist Gilberto Freyre emerged as the intellectual representative of the antimodernist elites who clung to an idyllic and glorious preindustrial rural past as a means of combating the profound social and political changes that seemed to undermine their entire way of life. Euclides da Cunha and other intellectuals had previously written about a distinct rural archetype whose toughness, silence, and resistance reflected an adaptation to the harsh geography of the desertlike inland *sertão*. Several decades later, Freyre and the regionalist school that he led created a complex set of images of the "typical" northeasterner, rooted in his sociological and historical interpretations of the patriarchy and the ultimately benevolent traditions of the sugar plantation. Literary production of novelists such as José Lins do Rego in the 1930s contributed to the romanticizing of the region's past and its present, as did the music of Luiz Gonzaga, the paintings of Cícero Dias and Vicente do Rego Monteiro, the theater of Ariano Suassuna, the novels of Jorge Amado, and the films of Glauber Rocha.

The Invention of the Brazilian Northeast artfully analyzes the dialectic relationship between these regional inventions as a defensive measure against the rapidly modernizing "South" on one hand, and the appropriation, creation, and dissemination of stereotypical representations of "northeasterner" by the intellectual followers of Freyre and his nostalgic view of the past. However, the author points out that current images of the inhabitants of the migrants from this region of Brazil are as much a product of the regional elite's creations as they are the chauvinistic prejudices of those from São Paulo or Rio de Janeiro. Drawing on elite discourse, literature, popular culture, music, film, and regional archives, the author meticulously weaves together a complex and colorful tapestry of diverse sources to make his case.

The original Portuguese version of this book, *The Invention of the Northeast*, was the winner of the prestigious Nelson Chaves de Teses Award from the Joaquim Nabuco Foundation for the best historical work on northern or northeastern Brazil. It has sold out two editions in Brazil. Now, with the support of the Latin America in Translation series, Jerry D. Metz has produced a beautifully adapted translation that is designed to make the original Portuguese work accessible to an English-language audience less familiar with Brazilian history and culture.

Albuquerque's original thoroughly documented volume has already become the yardstick for measuring all future studies about "invented" regions in Brazil and their relationship to the nation that it will, no doubt, inspire. As an insightful historical reading of the construction of a significant geographic region of an important Latin American nation, it will also serve as a model for how to write the history of other regions within other Latin American countries.

JAMES N. GREEN
Providence, RI

ACKNOWLEDGMENTS

This book is the product of the tense yet fruitful encounter between two areas of Brazil that were invented, and are often experienced, as antagonistic and mutually exclusive. I myself am also such a product, physically and intellectually. My father migrated from the Northeast to the large city of São Paulo in the Southeast, where, during an afternoon mass in 1954, he met a local girl, and they married soon after. Four years later, my mother left the city to accompany him back to his native region. I grew up feeling deeply the differences that seemed to separate my parents, a sort of implacable distance that was just barely resolved by the love that united all of us. When I grew older I determined to finish my academic studies in São Paulo, a place I seemed to know through a sort of affective geography my mother had sketched many times as she recalled her early life, and her friends and family she had left there. While still small, in her lap, I had traveled with her in her memory along the Chá Viaduct, down the Direita Road, and to the Prestes Maia Gallery, where she had idled happy Sundays away in the easy conversation and flirtations of youth. We went there together, in 1968: a trip of wonder for me. The city dazzled and overwhelmed; its din was numbing. I sought the places and spaces I had imagined over so many storytellings, the narrated geography of my mother's early life. Much that I saw and heard was utterly different than I expected, and yet there were still everywhere familiar traces (even in the cast of light, or the smells) of the city I had dreamed of.

Upon completing my master's in Paraíba, I resolved to undertake my own personal, intellectual migration to São Paulo—more specifically, to the state university at Campinas. There I occasionally sensed that I was regarded as, if not quite an interloper, someone far from where the natural order indicated he belonged. Too many times I endured the comment "But you don't look like a northeasterner!" It is the personal nature of this journey and this book that leads me to begin here by acknowledging my parents and my professors at UNICAMP, who facilitated the encounter between the Northeast and São Paulo (as the industrial axis of the Southeast) that is in my DNA, in my sentiments, and in my thinking. This project was born from the interplay of love and disquiet long provoked in me by the separation of the country into different regional spaces; I grew up with the complicated effects of this separation on the inhabitants of those spaces. But the love was more important. And this love only grew while I was in São Paulo, where along with some raised eyebrows I encountered many friendly people very willing to help me in my efforts. And it grew yet more when I returned to the Northeast, to revise the project.

I would like to thank the staff at the principal institutions where research was performed. In particular, at the Edgar Leunroth Archive, Cleusa provided indispensable assistance. Afternoons at the Cinemateca Brasileira screening rolls of film were made more efficient and enjoyable by Iara. Vera and Teresa, at UNICAMP's Central Library, became friends and provided moral support. I would also like to acknowledge the staffs at CEDAE (Companhia Estadual de Agua e Esgotos), Centro de Estudos Migratórios, Pinacoteca do Estado, Museu de Arte Moderna, Museu de Arte de São Paulo, Museu da Imagem e do Som, Casa Mário de Andrade, Casa Lasar Segall, and the IEB (Instituto de Estudos Brasileiros), who all helped me locate information.

My fellow doctoral students at UNICAMP participated directly in the trajectory of this work, through their collegial enthusiasm, their affection, and their continual engagement in helpful discussion. I must single out Regina for her sweetness, and her sharpness.

Many thanks to my generous professors in the history and geography departments at the Federal University of Paraíba, who went to great lengths to facilitate my transition to São Paulo after the MA. Among these I highlight Josefa, Eleite, Martha, Socorro, Fábio and Nilda. I also thank all my professors at UNICAMP, notably Edgar de Decca, who made himself available to read and comment on early versions of this work; and especially Margareth Rago, who, more than being a teacher, became a sort of accomplice on my intellectual and existential forays. Nothing was better than that in proving that an encounter between "Northeast" and "São Paulo" based on fondness and humor is possible.

To Robert Slenes, my adviser, my deepest gratitude. Above everything else that he is, he is a friendly and caring person.

To my brothers, Carlos, Solange, and Marcus, wherever each of us is or will be, my sincere thanks for the encouragement and support that is so fundamental to seeing through a project such as this.

Thanks to my "secretary" Socorro, who did everything but make it rain on command so that I might finish the book.

Other friends contributed to the completion of this text, and these include Agostinho, Auzirete, Cassandra, and Alarcon.

A warm thank-you to CAPES (Coordinação de Aperfeiçoamento de Pessoal de Nível), who financed my stay in Campinas as well as a later revisions period, allowing me to focus exclusively on scholarly work.

Finally, I would like to convey my deepest gratitude to my professor, friend, and adviser Alcir Lenharo. His presence is sorely missed. This book is a small homage to a person who let no obstacle hinder his drive to spread the seeds of knowledge and compassion. This book embodies fragments not just of my life, but also of his. It offers proof that Alcir is still quite alive and with us.

INTRODUCTION

Around the worlds, our legend. Even if we never learn it. I will teach you to make lacework. What more can I teach you? I have no other talents. I know only how to give life a vain intrigue.   **Caetano Veloso, "Tenda"**

At home in São Paulo, we turn on the television set. A portentous pundit ensconced in an ABC studio[1] stares fixedly at the camera and inquires, "Have you ever seen a *nordestino* reach over five and a half feet in height? Or perhaps an intelligent one?"[2] Of course, this pundit is himself barely five and a half feet tall and also holds himself the judge of what intelligence is. Is there an implied connection between height and intelligence?

We change the channel. In some unidentified northeastern city, the June festivals are underway.[3] Two metropolitan humorists enter the crowd, searching for friends of the long-dead northeastern bandit Antônio Silvino (1875–1944). They spot an older man and buttonhole him to wisecrack: "Old Antônio was a tough old goat, eh? Tell us all about it!" Later, we see someone in a white robe impersonating Antônio Conselheiro,[4] lending the preacher a goggle-eyed intensity as he jabbered doomsday visions and brandished a large stick at passersby. Our hosts also treat us to a group of blind women in colorful skirts singing traditional song, as well as a devout procession for Saint Antônio. Finally, and incongruously, we see a modern-day Lampião and Maria Bonita running through beachfront Rio de Janeiro, shooting at everyone, shooting every which way, because there is indecency everywhere (and, presumably, they really just love to shoot people).[5]

Let's try another channel. The evening telenovela once again is set in the Northeast, with an anonymous yet instantly recognizable interior city, stock types such as the *colonel* (local ranch boss and power broker) and the bible-clasping priest, as well as gunshots, mules, and so on. Everyone speaks in *"nordestino,"* a distinct accent and dialect supposedly characteristic of the region and almost impenetrable to those outside it, based on archaic colonial Portuguese and spiced with curious slang. Scriptwriters rely heavily on folkloric dictionaries.

How about the news again? Ah, a drought once again afflicting the Northeast. The camera seems to savor the cracked earth, lingering over the wilting cactus, the starving livestock, the gaunt children who play dustily with bones in the arid field. The earnest reporter produces tears to verify the tragedy, and to promote yet another campaign of electronic, mass-mediated solidarity with a region defined by its inescapable backwardness. We feel compelled to agree with Rachel de Queiroz that the metropolitan media treats the Northeast with great selectivity: that they look "cross-eyed" at it because the desired Northeast is a place of misery.[6] But is that really true?

Among all these framings, voices, and images, we encounter a strategy to stereotype. A discourse of stereotypes is an assertive one, repetitive and arrogant, a language formulated on acritical stability and self-sufficiency. It emerges from the indiscriminate characterization of a social group whose multiplicities and individual complexities are banished in order to construct a superficial collective identity.[7] So may we concur with Queiroz that the media does not see the Northeast as it truly is? No, because this would be to posit a reality for the Northeast that does not exist. This would be to forget that a stereotype is not merely a crooked gaze or a distortion, it is something that also generates concrete dimensions for those who are made subject to (or objects of) it. A reality is created and accepted as such. We need to avoid the trap of falling into a simple perspective of prejudice—discrimination against the Northeast and nordestinos. What this book attempts to do is not merely investigate why the Northeast and nordestinos are marginalized and stereotyped in national cultural production and by the inhabitants of other areas; but also investigate why, for nearly ninety years, we in the Northeast complain that we are discriminated against with such indignation. Why do we claim, with mingled exaltation and rancor, that we have been forgotten and minimized, that we are victims of our own country's history? What are the mechanisms of power that have seemed to place us in the position of victims, of the colonized, miserable in body and spirit? And how, in our own discursive practices, do we reproduce a set of meanings and symbols that construct us as beggars stuck intractably at the margins? Through what masochism do we take pride in the discrimination that casts us as vanquished? In other words, if the Northeast has itself participated in shaping this balance of power, how? Why and how would our own dominant classes take delight in affirming its own impotence, preferring a national posture of subordination and dependence?

The miserable Northeast and nordestino, whether in the media or beyond it, are not the product of a problem with how power functions in Brazil but are inherent to this system of forces and help constitute it. This Northeast and nordestino are invented by these relations of power and knowledge, and deeply associated with them. We cannot combat discrimination by inverting the direction of the discrimination, nor can we try to determine who is telling the truth and who is lying because this accepts the premise that the marginalized have a truth waiting to be revealed. To proudly assume the mantle of "northeasternness" (*nordestinidade*) with Rachel de Queiroz, and demand that Brazil's southerners revise their ignorant and harmful discourses, is to remain imprisoned within the parameters of those very same discourses. The greater goal is to rise above those stereotypes by examining the relations of power that produce both the discriminated and the discriminators. Both are fruits of truth-effects, born of struggle and bearing its scars.[8]

While nordestinos (among whom I number myself) are accustomed to view ourselves as the vanquished, always set in contrast to the tenacious exploiters in the Southeast, this assumed exteriority in our social relations does not exist. We are agents of our own oppression and discrimination. These are not imposed on us from afar; they circulate within and through us. The best modes of resistance we can construct will be formulated within this network of power, not outside of it. Thus can we shift the trajectory and momentum of the force fields that seem to impose on us a narrowly defined cultural and geographic space (that was shaped by history, but is therefore dynamic). Is it really better, more effective, to allow ourselves to be comprehended as the opposite of powerful—the beaten, the weak, the needy? Would it not be better to refuse that wretched position?[9]

The larger question, then, is whether there actually exists a northeastern identity within us. Is there some truth defining and linking all the stereotypes, within which the swarthy "flat-heads" (*cabeça chata*) of the Bahian, Paraíban, or Pernambucan interiors are merely variations and generically equivalent? Does the Northeast of the media, its images and discourses, actually exist if such a thing is scorned by the actual people who live there? The focus of this book is the history of the emergence of an object of knowledge and space of power called the Brazilian Northeast. Of special interest is the formation of preconceptions, a term that is not necessarily pejorative. How was this archive of images and articulations formulated, this stock of "truths" that made the Northeast able to be seen and spoken, and which directly shaped the attitudes of the media? What is the interplay between concepts of the Northeast and nordestinos, and the use of images and discourses to ostensibly reveal the true essence of the region?[10]

Once we begin to accept the idea of the region as problematic, we might ask: What is a region? What is the best way to measure or capture its identity? What makes the Northeast different, individual, coherent? This book intends to raise for analysis the historical conditions that made possible the diverse discourses and practices that produced the Northeast as a defined and definable space. Rather than consider the boundaries of this region as somehow written into the natural world, or generated by the "development of capitalism and the regionalization of means of production," yet another form of geographical naturalization, this book considers the Northeast as a historical space. It was constructed at a precise moment in history, the end of the first decade and the second decade of the twentieth century, as the product of cohering "regionalist" concepts and practices. The space became understood as having experiences that might characterize its regional identity. These experiences were grouped and categorized and enmeshed in theories that held the promise to offer recognition of the region's essence and defining traits. Yet this did little more than capture and imperfectly reflect diverse quotidian experiences of both the winners and the vanquished, along with fragments of memories of past situations that were reset as heralding the present; all embraced as the "apex of regional consciousness."[11]

Our objective is to understand the diverse pathways along which the Northeast was produced within the larger scope of Brazilian culture. The nexus of knowledge and power that created the nordestino type obliterated it, at the same moment, as a human being. It would seem that arriving at the true Northeast requires whittling away the rest of Brazil from it. Thus the Northeast is pruned to reveal its economic, political, or geographic unity, but also its primordial cultural essence whose production relies on the pseudo-unity of culture, ethnicity, and geography. The Northeast can be born only where power meets language, where the spatialization of power relations runs like a current through images and texts. By spatiality, I mean the spatial perceptions that inhabit language and that through language interrelate with the broader field of forces that instituted them. In this book, geographic, linguistic, and historical forces will all be comprehended within an analysis of the diverse languages that constructed a regional geography, a spatial distribution of feelings, through a given historical period. For this, it is necessary to leave behind the assumed transparency of spaces and languages; spatiality is made through the accumulation of discursive layers and social practice. Language (discourse) and space (historical object) encounter and interrelate. Our work is in a dimension where history destroys supposed natural determinations—where time gives space its malleability, its variability, its explanatory value, and, even more, its warmth and true human aspects.[12]

It should be recalled that *dis-cursus* is, originally, the action to run back and forth, coming and going, *demarches*. And the spaces are networks, webs of images and language sewn into patterns of social relations—reticular "plots" in both senses of the term. The diverse forms of language considered here, from literature and cinema to music, painting, theater, and academic production, are like actions: they are practices indissoluble from institutions. They do not simply represent reality but construct and institute realities. Their discourses are not enunciated from separate and objective exterior spaces, but they create their own spaces, which in turn produce them, presuppose them, and legitimize them. Regionalist discourse is not emitted from some region existing independent of itself. But it is from within its own locution that the region is mapped out, its stage set and enacted and finally recognized and anticipated. The region is part of the topography of this discourse, instituted by it. Every discourse measures and demarcates a space from which it will enunciate itself, in which its truth is embedded. Before regionalism was invented, regions were being produced by these discourses. This book explores how discourses establish the region by seeing and speaking it. Reconsidering region may open our sensibilities to new ways to see and speak it, to feel and know it. However, these regional images and texts are interrelated with other series of practices, notably economic, political, and social, that between them have considerable power but do not determine an end or establish conclusions. They only connect, merge and diverge, forming a web of discursive and nondiscursive practices—relations of power and meaning that we, following Foucault, might call dispositive (*dispositif,* "apparatus") in order to underscore their diversity and strategic complexity.[13]

To suggest the emergence of a new visibility and speakability implicates the emergence of new concepts, themes, objects, figures, and images that permit us to see and speak what was grasped only distantly before, as if by the reflection of faint light. New configurations and problems may in their turn provide new sources of clarity to illuminate other dimensions of the historical and social networks that compose the texture of space. Through visibility and speakability are articulated the thinking and production of space, the discursive and nondiscursive practices that prune and shape spatiality and the forces that delineate its cartographies. To define the region is to conceive of it as a group of enunciations and images that repeat, with a certain regularity, through different discourses and epochs, in different styles; but not to imagine it as a homogeneity, an objective identity present in nature. In this book the Northeast is viewed as an invention, through the regular repetition of determined enunciations that have been taken as defining the character of the region and its people—defining, and limiting, the truths of their personal existence. And this spatiality is itself characterized by a cyclic or pendular movement of destruction/construction, in counter to the quality of eternity that is usually associated with space. In this context, the problematic of power is not to be resolved through an analysis of what appears obscure in the images, or between the lines of texts, but rather through facing what they create in their exteriority—the differences they assert and assume. Discourses are not objective documents "of" a region, but monuments to the region's construction. Instead of grubbing around for artifacts to prove the historical continuity of a place called the Northeast and the identity of the nordestino, this book hopes to suspend and shine light on those assumed continuities themselves. Its goal is to place certain frontiers and identities, which have been widely canonized, in question.[14]

Never should we imagine that regional territories can be situated in a frame outside of historical analysis. They are eminently historical. And their historical character is multivocal, depending on which type of space is called into focus—political, juridical, cultural, ethnic, et cetera. That is, regional space is the product of the relations among agents and vectors that act and reproduce themselves with distinct spatial dimensions. We must perceive spatial relations more clearly, as political relations. What seems to be natural about regions must be recast into political and historical elements. Space does not preexist the society that embodies it. It is through social practices that spatial division consolidates, or changes. Social practices articulate the shearing of space into seemingly disparate parts, cloaking their dynamic relations with the whole—while the whole is also conceived in relation to the separate fragments that constitute it, posing a normative contrast to regional exceptions, an abstract portrait painted in broad brush.[15]

The notion of region, from *regere*, to command, goes deeper than superficial connotations of geography to convey administrative division, fiscal accountability, and military sensibility. Definitions of region that rely on nature or territories of production merely flit on the surface of a concept that is deeply rooted in the spatialization of power relations. A region is space reduced, cut down to manipulate strategically. A commanded space can be controlled and can be analyzed. It recalls the concept *regio* (*rei*, or king). We thus confront a politics of knowledge, a special (spatial) mode of power relations. The region is a point of concentration for the forces that strive to make a large homogenous space knowable and controllable. Historically, regions can be viewed as a manifestation of difference or conflict between different social groups within the same nation. The regionalization of power relations can be accompanied by other processes of distinction, such as modes of production, labor relations, or cultural practices, but these alone do not shape or predict a region's emergence. A region is the product of battle, its segmentation caused by fissures in the conflicted space of litigants. Regions represent the strategic provisioning of space. Space that is fought over is divided, being apportioned differently among various winners and losers. In that sense region is the landscape of internal war, of national conflict.[16]

This book aims to denaturalize regions, to problematize their invention, and to search for their historicity among layers of practices and discourses. They are not fixed, immutable features in the landscape but moving soil—landscapes in transition, engaged by history and engaging history, pushing against and being shaped by history.[17] A region is not a frame of unity containing diversity within it. It is the product of operations of homogenization but is open, transitory, and intercut by power relations; the state may be called on, or not, to collaborate in its sedimentation into perceived reality. The state might be seen as a privileged battlefield for regional disputes. It does not formally, institutionally demarcate political limits of regions but can legitimate or refute the regional manifestations emerging from social conflicts.

It should be acknowledged that this book dwells more on the history of concepts, themes, strategies, images, and enunciations than on the histories of individual men and women. Of course, such personal histories will be present to a degree throughout, because it is people who have articulated the nation and composed dynamic regional realities. But my focus resides more on the history of struggle between concepts of nation and region, particularly as they are in dialogue with historicized notions of regional, national, and international culture. I am concerned with struggle in the articulation of national versus regional identity, especially in the realms of culture.

It was around just such ideas that, in 1920s–1960s Brazil, a set of rules was developed that I call the national-popular discursive formation. The power apparatus that sustained them might be called the *dispositif* of nationalities. My intention is to trace the history of the practices and enunciations that gave shape, visibility, and speakability to these ideas. More specifically, I examine the idea of the Northeast—from how it was invented in diverse images and texts starting in the 1920s, to how it was radically contested among some artists by the end of the 1960s. How did particular audiovisual enunciations produce and crystallize, through representation, the essence of this spatial construct? How did power relations sustain this identity, and how were they sustained within it—an identity preserving the Northeast as peripheral to Brazil's economic and political relations and sweeping its inhabitants to the margins?

The term "identity" is too often accepted on its face, as a suite of repetitions or superficial similarities, without considering its internal tensions. Identity, whether national or regional, is a mental construct. It is an intellectual abstraction that covers an enormous variety of experiences. To see and speak the nation or region is not, indeed, to recognize these "realities" but to create them. They are imagined spaces that are secondarily institutionalized, and that take on the sheen of truth. Such gossamer crystallizations lead us, with so many other contemporary forces, to live by and through images. Our territories are image based. They arrive to us in channels—the media, education, social contacts, habits—cultural channels that encourage an abstraction of the real. In this way, history resembles theater, on which the actors, historical agents, may create their forms of identity only through markers of the past, through accepted and recognized roles, old masks that are forever updated.[18]

This book interrogates the forms through which region has been seen and spoken in Brazil—forms that can seem relatively recent, such as the occasional (and intense) separatist analyses in contemporary history, and forms that have accrued an almost primordial aspect. In particular, the regional discourse surrounding and embodying the Northeast really is novel in the history of Brazil. It affects, informs, and motivates not only the elite levels of society but all segments of society. I reject the category of "regional history" for this work because that type of research stays within the accepted discursive field of region itself. It continues to take region as fixed, a concrete referent, legitimating precisely what I hope to decode. Rather than probing region as a network of power, it questions only determined elaborations of region in order to compare them and uncover supposed truths.[19] In that sense, regional history contributes to the historical continuity of regional space. It is engaged in the maintenance of a referential illusion.[20] It might historicize a region, but takes its existence as writ. But neither region nor nation are valid criteria to impose from the outset, as a sort of rigid frame, on historical investigation. They are entities forged by historical processes, continually shaped by discursive webs whose trajectories and textures can be traced.

The manner in which regional history proceeds—defining a region a priori, accepting its naturalness—evades the fact that neither epoch nor space can exist before the enunciations and visibilities that produce them. Regional history coexists unproblematically with regions and in fact reproduces them. It ultimately validates Brazil's Northeast as a coherent place that can be researched, taught about, and administered, even as its intellectual legitimacy is based on imaginary structures of so-called national consciousness, as well as political forces. The Northeast becomes an object of academic study, a curio whose dimensions are measured and qualities catalogued. But historians, as they strive to produce knowledge, must be attuned to questions of epistemology and the power relations shaping their own research and the wider historiography; basic concepts must continually be submitted to inquiry and reconsideration. In contrast to this ideal, however, regional history accepts the received wisdom that divides "national" (Brazilian) history from "regional" (northeastern), creating a hierarchy within the academy that reproduces the territorialization, unequal power relations, and subordination of space that occurs at the level of the nation itself.

Do regional historians somehow see themselves as incapable of performing national history, or are they disinclined? Why is it that historians from São Paulo (and to a certain degree also Rio de Janeiro) are recognized for doing national history, while historians outside this metropolitan axis are regarded as regional historians? We continue imprisoned in a hierarchy of spaces and knowledges that began to cohere at the beginning of the twentieth century, and that resiliently affirms itself in multiple ways in the present. My interest is not in picking up the flag for the victims of so-called *paulista* imperialism, or arguing that there should be more regional histories to counter the national ones. Rather, I reject the disparate spatialized configuration of knowledge and power and call for the right to perform "history" without further qualifiers.

Methodologically, this approach is amenable to the broadest possible source material. I draw on academic texts and cultural criticism, literature and poetry, songs, films, and theater pieces, all of which have northeastern themes and thus help constitute the Northeast in diverse ways. Works of art, cultural products broadly speaking, are here analyzed as discourses that contribute to making reality. I am less concerned with rarified discussions of aesthetics but will introduce elements of such analysis as they serve the project at hand; however, art will more generally be considered in social context. Works of art are dynamic machines generating meanings, producing sensibilities, and helping create ways to see and speak reality. The point of focus is the creation of the idea of the Northeast, and its relation to the idea of the nation. Because the form and content of cultural practices cannot be separated, I explore how the production of texts, images, and sounds can form an aggregate positing the Northeast as a material space and an identity, a recognizable homogeneity—or that, in contrast, can contest this construction.

I have avoided dense thickets of explanatory notes. References to the literature are kept to a minimum because I did not wish to fall into the trap of using the secondary or theoretical documents as "proof" in and of themselves. The origins of important concepts will be cited, but my engagement with the literature will be, more or less implicitly or obviously, in the main pages and paragraphs that follow rather than buried in notes. I have also not attempted to impose a symmetry or coherence on the whole work that its historical subject matter did not provide. History resounds with incoherence, and the momentum of its energies is to destroy and reformulate discursive identities, not sediment them. And because I am interested more in how the Northeast has been produced than in the personalities of each and every artist whose work contributed to it, I typically do not follow those individuals or refer in detail to their lives except in terms of how this shaped their work in imagining and creating regional reality.[21]

What were the conditions that gave rise to so many diverse cultural expressions of the Northeast at a given moment—inventing the Northeast and, at the same time, inventing nordestinos as subjects and objects? The artists are taken here not as extraordinary, in terms of an aesthetic innovation that lifts them out of history or society, but as deeply knitted into the fabric of an era and perspective that they also help to shape. All around them, of course, are diverse other forces that interrelate with institutions, economic and social processes, politics, mores and norms, and modes of characterization and classification. These are part of the threads that were gathered and sewn into a design called the Northeast, an image of something taken to be real. This history, like that of fine lacework, is composed not only of material interlacings and knots but of empty spaces—lacunae that are part of the design itself, integral to its texture.[22]

I often use metaphor to open a new perspective of historical processes and linkages, rather than insist dogmatically on the strict application of explicable concepts. I believe history proceeds in a manner that defies such rigidity, while metaphor is open to ambivalence, androgyny, the extemporaneous realization of juncture. The poetry within this complexity is richer than pure, abstract rules.[23] The use of metaphors in history can permit an analysis to transcend the familiar artifices of representation to reach a more productive level of meanings. Familiar objects can be cast in new perspectives, new tones. Everything potentially has meaningful implications, and everything is newly surprising. As historians, we are forced to think differently through metaphors, which are indispensable to an anthropophagic history that traces the relation between two different things. Metaphors wink and nod; they double back on themselves, fulgent in their dissonance. They are a means to communicate the totality of the real in its density of signification, beyond the limits of either empiricism or pure theory—resetting the relation between subject and object as they propose new methodologies to conquer "reality."[24]

The explanation of the history of the Brazilian Northeast is in the beliefs and categories that emerged at particular moments, within and surrounding particular cultural venues. We can place in question such basic concepts as identity, culture, civilization, nation, and region without abandoning them as empty husks; indeed, we utilize them to explain the discursive machinery into which they have been recruited as essential parts. Language, too, must be sifted and interrogated within its period conceptualization, while we still have the right to carefully extend the linguistic insights of certain past epochs into the present through juxtaposition and bricolage. All these techniques are necessary because one cannot critique the idea of region by remaining devoted to the trap of definitions and feelings that conceptually justify it. We have to find creative ways to reveal its limits, its evolutionary stages, its deep historicity. The very idea of region is to be understood as a historical invention, not merely the idea of one given region. Behind these masks is not the somber countenance of true origin, but the discordant chuckle of something complex and undefined that made such a conclusion (among others) possible. For instance, if one takes capitalism to be the cause and principal force for regionalization, this assumes a previous unity that capitalism dissolved, when in fact both the idea of a prior whole nation and the idea of its secondary regionalization are discursive effects of particular processes established in the early nineteenth century and that continue through the present.[25]

My approach to the various materials was to strip them of accustomed hierarchy. I applied no distinguishing measure of worth to a film versus a poem, a song versus a journal article. All were produced by a reality to which they were avidly contributing. None were to be forced into the role of evidence per se, but to be seen as complex expressive sources. The idea was to detach and reassemble them, to complicate their claims to truth, to note their importance as nodes of commentary and criticism and acceptance, taking their discursive stream deliberately out of context in order to highlight it.

The book is divided into three large chapters. In the first, "Geography in Ruins," I trace the origins of how the very idea of the Northeast became possible. I had to start with the dispositif of nations, without which the concept of region has no meaning. Then there were changes in social sensibilities with respect to space, and space and the gaze; changes with respect to modernity, bourgeois society, the urban experience, the masses. These developments allowed the emergence of the concept of region, which then made possible the invention of the Northeast.

Second, "Spaces of Nostalgia" looks more closely at the spatial division of Brazil. The Northeast crosscuts older binary notions of Brazil as northern and southern, as preindustrial society undergoes crises and cities take on new powers as emitters and condensers of symbols. Conceptual geographies of the country are challenged, particularly in the North, with the end of slavery in 1888 and the collapse of the sugar economy, while the South is the center of the newly proclaimed republic. Political discourses in the North, previously disparate, begin to cohere in the shared campaign for resources and attention from southern institutions. Thus emerged a vocabulary of need, of problems: drought, banditry, messianic leaders and communities, clan feuds for political control of states. A Northeast begins to be demarcated, its uncertain frontiers also suggestively marking the terrain of privilege to be maintained, on the other (southern) side. But the more compelling elaboration of the Northeast is cultural, rather than political, as the offspring of the newly cast regional elite produced sociological and artistic works implying the past glories of the region, the sumptuous mansion and docile shanties, the deeply rooted peace and stability implanted by the empire. From sociologist Gilberto Freyre to writers José Américo de Almeida, José Lins do Rego, and Rachel de Queiroz, and painters Cícero Dias and Lula Cardoso Ayres, the Northeast takes shape as a place of past glories, of longing for the amiability of the sugar mill, of plantation elites and their almost-family slaves; as well as the contrasting environmental purity and starkness of the desiccated interior, a telluric force in northeastern regional identity.

Chapter 3, "Territories of Revolt," considers how the Northeast was reelaborated by authors and artists linked to Brazil's left. Starting in the 1930s, they inverted the conservative, traditionalist idyll of the Northeast they had received. Their invented Northeast did not idle in the sun pining for the past but suggested bold new futures, including the containment of capitalism itself, in the name of constructing a new national society. The works of Jorge Amado, Graciliano Ramos, Portinari, and João Cabral de Neto reversed the earlier image of the Northeast to cast it as a place of misery and social injustice, of utter alienation. This Northeast maintained, through its popular myths and the strength of its folk, the resolve to constitute a space of active revolt against exploitation and bourgeois domination emanating from the Brazil that was *not* Northeast. However, this new revolutionary Northeast was constructed in direct opposition to the previous formulation and was trapped in its precepts— the themes, images, and sacred enunciations of the traditionalists. Inadvertently, perhaps, the new regional elaboration entrenched even more deeply the subtext of the traditionalists that the region was composed largely of victims, the miserable, those whom time and the country had passed by. The so-called "revolutionaries" thus joined their visions and voices to the so-called "reactionaries" in consecrating a certain marginalized identity for the Northeast that has endured to the present day.

ONE GEOGRAPHY IN RUINS

The Northeast is a child of the ruins of an older conceptual geography of Brazil that posited a national segmentation into North and South. The North was understood as defined by natural attributes, its pastoral essence assumed and its countenance quickly recognizable. But by the 1920s, or even the 1910s, a Northeast was emerging that was identified by harsher natural phenomena and a problematic if ardent embrace of modernity—factories, avenues, the rumbling engines of machinery mobilized in public works against the ravages of drought. Juxtaposed alongside fields of cotton and sugar plantations were now telegraph cables, telephone lines, and railroads. Hudson, Ford, and Studebaker automobiles as well as Great Western railway cars sped commerce but catalyzed its detrimental impacts on the environment, as mountains were scraped clean of foliage and smoke darkened the sky. Traditional modes and rhythms of life were transformed. Cities buzzed with construction, modeled largely on nineteenth-century European urban landscapes of banks and markets, while the new vision for thoroughfares owed much to American sensibilities of flat, straight, and square. These sometimes replaced, but more often coexisted oddly with, the narrow and winding colonial-era carriage streets such as those in old Recife. In city centers, many of the antiquated elite mansions, enormous and faded like shipwrecks, were giving way to hastily built factories crowned by towering smokestacks.[1]

The invention of the Northeast, based on reelaborations of the images and discourses of the older paradigm of the North, was possible only through the crisis of the naturalist paradigm and its traditional models of society. A new way of seeing in relation to space was emerging, and along with it a new social sensibility. There was a growing need to reflect on questions regarding national identity, national character, the national "race," as well as the contours of a national culture that could incorporate all the nation's spaces.

The Regionalist Gaze

The regionalism of the 1920s was different from the regionalism of the previous era, the long nineteenth century (until the 1910s). It was less diffuse and provincial. It reflected the different ways that space was conceived and represented across the diverse areas of the country. Brazil's central South, especially São Paulo, would become a highly differentiated space as a result of such patterned developments as industrialization, urbanization, and immigration from Europe, as well as the effects of the abolition of slavery. At the same time, new forms of artistic and cultural inquiry were fostered by modernism. Modernism and modernization lent a new intensity to the exploration of new codes of sociability. Meanwhile, the old North struggled to cope with deepening economic dependence and its political submission to other areas of the country. It reeled under the strain of new technologies imperfectly implanted and poorly integrated, as well as the lack of skilled manpower to support them. Within the more traditional sectors of its society, especially after World War I, another crisis was brewing that had to do with how the nation was seen, spoken, and represented.

The war had resulted in a global redistribution of power, with the United States in ascension and European cartographies rearranged. With all this, history seemed to have definitively penetrated space itself. If classical epistemology saw time and space as two distinct dimensions, in modern epistemology history became the totality of all things, including spatialities. For Brazil, the war had contributed to hastening the end (already underway) of the belle époque sensibility, which had focused on the tropical environment and exoticness of Brazilian space as factors, alongside race, preventing the nation from advancing in social and cultural terms. The war fostered a new attempt to visualize the nation in its complexity, to reconsider previous categories of thought and space. There was a suggestive new diversity coming into view, and it was the search for the nation itself that led to the discovery of new regions. Different modes of knowledge from art to science were mobilized in the projection of gazes that inspected other areas, measured distances, and weighted discontinuities, but that returned to re-view the nation as synthesizing this very diversity. Every regional discourse would stimulate a diagnostic of causes and solutions for the distances that seemed to separate it from other national areas.

The older proto-regionalism had encountered division as a reflex of nature, and of race. Variations in climate, in flora and fauna, and in the racial composition of populations inhabiting these places explained apparent differences in custom, habit, social practice, and politics. Psychology, along with natural science, could clarify regional types. This intersected with how technologies came to define space across Brazil's vast territory. Unequal development of transportation and communications infrastructure along with the lack of physical human interchange between the North and South helped turn these two spaces inaccessible to and almost unknowable to each other: separate worlds seeking to understand and connect, just as Europe and Brazil regarded each other with curiosity across the Atlantic. Actual visits were limited to a few elites—specialists and intrepid explorers from the South to the North, and the ritual movement of the North's political leaders to the capital city of Rio de Janeiro.

The urge to explore regional particularity was nonetheless still part of a nationalist drive, an impulse to discover Brazil itself, that would take on new emphasis in the 1920s. It is not a coincidence that in this moment, the idea was floated to compile a Brazilian encyclopedia that would contain information describing all the country's diverse realities as a starting point for formulating a politics of unification and nationalization; the stubborn distances that impeded the emergence of the nation might thus be finally transcended. Regionalisms have long been viewed as an impediment to this sort of process of unification, but they are integral to it. They reveal how the nation's constituting was never a neutral or objective process but a deeply political one, which was from the beginning bound up in the hegemony of some spaces over others.[2]

The press played a key role in sparking curiosity about the nation through wide publication of travelers' letters and essays, especially between the 1920s and the 1940s. Already in those discourses a typology of customs emerges: in the North, local habits come across as "bizarre if friendly," while northerners describe the ways of the South as "strange and unscrupulous." These recorded impressions help invent a tradition in which the space from which one speaks is taken as the national point of reference, assumed to be the country's center. Customs here are the national ones; customs we explore as visitors in other areas are regional, the exceptions proving our rule. This creates multiple discursive centers. In particular, Rio de Janeiro, São Paulo, and Recife established themselves as points of distribution for national reference and meaning. The differences and "oddities" perceived elsewhere are marked as primitive and archaic, as affectations and superficialities, or as corruptions attendant on urban metropolitan life.[3]

Such accounts of the strange function to create an identity for the region that is speaking, not just for the region that is being spoken of. The paulista and nordestino participate in each other's construction, agreeing on the spatial boundaries of identity and imposing a homogeneity through text and image that avoids internal difference and complexity. A common subject in this era was custom—characteristic, traditional social practice or attitudes. Writers explore "customs of the North or Northeast" versus "customs of São Paulo," basing their own production on what they have read as much as on what they see. Here are some travel notes submitted to the *Estado de São Paulo* in 1923:

> Before arriving we already knew something through our reading of this land of suffering, whose poor meadows boast only a spindly heather, where there are rough craggy hills instead of mountains, the people live in straw huts without floors, and the sky burns without relent. No dew blesses the ground, and the rivers fade to dust. The Northeast of Brazil received that designation only after the most recent major calamity in 1919, after which it was determined to mount a fight against the persistent droughts. . . . And waves of squalid wanderers journeyed to the bosom of the South to enjoy our infinite generosity, doubtless marveling at the misery there and the abundance here and doubting whether to return.[4]

All at once, the author reaffirms a prior image of the Northeast absorbed before going there and, in counterpoint, constructs a complementary image of the South. He also calls attention to the precise moment at which the Northeast was delineated out of the older North, in a manner that also depreciates the place and "its" people.

Such novel regionalist discourses were accompanied by new regionalist practices that were related to wider changes in social relations along the 1920s. For instance, in 1920, the following assertion was published in a major São Paulo newspaper: "It is incontestable that the South of Brazil, which is the region that runs from Bahia through Rio Grande do Sul, presents a robust aspect of progress in its material life that stands in grim contrast with state of abandon of the North, with its deserts and its ignorance, its lack of hygiene, its poverty, its wan servility."[5]

The cohering focus on social and material differences between North and South is routinely attributed to the presence of immigrant laborers in the South, and their absence from the North. Abolition and the rapid transition to a free market of wage labor, which in nascent form had coexisted with the last years of slavery, were key elements in the new reordering of Brazil's spaces as well as the militant tone of the emergent regionalisms. The regionalization of the labor market, shaped by abolition and the concentration of European immigrants in the South (especially São Paulo), helped induce a host of regionalist practices and enunciations through the early twentieth century.

Some intellectuals, enchanted with the perceived superiority of the immigrants to national stock, highlighted the figure of the nordestino as the principal example of racial degeneration in its physical and mental forms. Oliveira Vianna and Dionísio Cerqueira, for instance, considered the downtrodden misery of the nordestino as the direct consequence of the encounter between a harsh natural environment and a degraded race, fruit of the "crossing between individuals of extreme lineages, a submixture." In contrast, the superiority of the "race" of paulistas was declared in quasi-eugenic terms; they knew how to take advantage of the more propitious environment in the South, and of course they would ascend to national economic and political dominance. This superiority was taken as natural, not historical, and the Northeast was deemed inferior by its very nature. Paulistas' reputation for a navel-gazing obsession with their own city was denied as legend but implicitly justified as well.[6]

Such travel notes and other published essays show how strong the naturalist perspective still was, how it endured across other historical changes—and how modernism, which emerged in opposition to this visibility and speakability of the nation, was far from having immediate generalized impacts. Paulo de Moraes Barros, a journalist for the *Estado de São Paulo* who was dispatched on a trip to Juazeiro, blamed the nordestinos' racial inferiority for the presence of "loutish fanatics across the entire region," including the "crowds of rabble that supplicate and jabber with wild-eyed expressions, grubbing in the dirt to get a hold of the priest's cassock." The acts of "violent, villainous bandits" received the same racial explanation, and an exasperated Barros demanded to know how such a people could possibly serve as the base on which to construct a nation.[7]

Soon after its series of articles entitled "Impressions of the Northeast," this newspaper launched another called "Impressions of São Paulo" in order to construct an image of the city in counterpoint to the Northeast it had sketched. The strategy was to demonstrate the superiority of São Paulo and its population, a superiority residing in the European elements of its bloodline. In these articles, the city appears as an empty space that could be filled by earnest Europeans. Slavery and Afro-Brazilians were barely mentioned; neither were Brazil's indigenous, and even less would racial crossings involving these groups be noted. São Paulo and all its people were ostensibly Europeans. "They arrived crossing the Atlantic, settled in and quickly adjusted to this fertile land, realizing the grandness of their destiny through the production of abundance." Even the oldest generation of locals, who traced their heritage back to the early centuries of colonial Brazil, were described as "always an exuberantly productive race, strong in morals and physically eugenic," in order to distinguish them from other national groups.[8]

The regionalism of São Paulo was thus constructed as one of superiority, rather than misery and lack; but it was based on negative comparisons with other Brazilian groups and the affirmation of European, white lineage. In its discourse São Paulo appeared as the cradle of a proper nation, a "civilized, progressive and developmentalist" nation. It was also boldly, unsentimentally modern. Changes to the urban landscape that included the destruction of old architecture such as the "Church of Carmo, the Piques, and the Santa Casa street" represented the progress of the new. The past made way for the future, in the form of incessant community and business construction, "Americanized, metallic, and sparkling." These were symbols of a modernity and civilization that São Paulo was uniquely able to produce, and to generalize to the rest of the country. The modernist movement was also part of this enthusiastic embrace of the new urban world that seemed somehow to belong uniquely to 1920s São Paulo. Even for most of the modernists, with their interest in articulating national identity, the Northeast would appear as a "vast medieval space" to be dominated by "modernizing influxes from São Paulo." The urbanization and modernization affecting cities across the Northeast were largely unknown, because the Northeast's own regionalist discourse cast it as a rural terrain wracked by disasters: a "regionalism of inferiority," not of potential.[9]

Growing curiosity about this Northeast that was being invented as the opposite of São Paulo is suggested by the success of a theatrical production by Cornélio Pires that was presented to enthusiastic audiences at the Fênix Theater in 1926. Called *Picturesque Brazil—Journeys of Cornélio Pires to the North of Brazil*, the play entertained the public with "odd, exotic, strange, ridiculous aspects of our brothers and sisters in the North." As a dramatic type, the modern nordestino was born as an effective comedic character that was laughed at, more than with, by desirable audience demographics in the South.[10]

This cohering narrative occasionally stood at odds with the earlier conceptions of the North as a place of pleasing natural wonder. Previously internalized archives of images and enunciations could color a tourist's expectations and present a moment of incoherence in face of the sharpening new identity based on harshness and privation. In the early 1940s, Chiquinha Rodrigues, a correspondent for the *O Estado de São Paulo* who traveled to the Northeast, at first struck a tone of gratified marvel. "In the Northeast, such exuberant green growth! Here there is more rain than anywhere else in Brazil. What causes the droughts, or so say the experts, is the poor distribution of these generous rains." But soon after, in the same essay, she reveals more contemporary influences: "We must be pleased for any oasis in this desert. . . . Let us uncover the mysteries of this singular region, where a world of sunlight nearly blinds us and the climate is burning hot before it mellows to gentility."[11] The contradictions mount as she expresses growing interest in the blood-red flowers of the cactus and increasingly reaches to Euclides da Cunha's ambivalent classic *Os Sertões* (1902), written about the interior backlands of Bahia state, for descriptive and analytic support. She seems at times to borrow whole phrases from da Cunha: "The carpet of unyielding, aggressive weeds prevents any genuine contact between a creature and the earth." Or "Like a cruel woman, the *cabeça de frade* [orb-shaped cactus] that lurks in reefs among the cactus flowers to commit harm . . . All of it will burn and sting, all of it will pierce our hands." Still, "At the first rains, everything is transformed; the seething variety of birds and butterflies are like a thousand flowers."[12] This Northeast, then, is one of contrasts and contradictions, of seemingly inescapable confrontations with Euclides da Cunha.

The text makes clear that what it says of region is not a direct reflex of what is seen in, or as, region. Words affect what the eyes see. The two regimes, words and images, are independent. Region thus takes form through discourses, images, and texts that may or may not have interrelations or relationships of representation. The truth of the region is constituted through the negotiation between the visible and the speakable. The visibility of the region that emerges is constructed with the assistance of the speakable, or struggling against it. Of course, not always does the spoken become practice, or does a practice become transformed into discourse. Discourses can make things visible, but the things they make visible might be different from what they say. They are strategies of power that orient parallels and divergences between the visible and the speakable, as well as the contact between them. To speak and see are both methods to dominate the regional object, even if they need not be in strict accordance.[13]

This multiplicity of foci that composes the image of a given space, a given region, is artfully brought to the forefront in the articles by Mário de Andrade that were collected in the volume *O Turista Aprendiz* (The Apprentice Tourist). In these pieces, Andrade reflects on his travels through the North and Northeast in 1927. With great subtlety, he considered the simultaneity of various points of view—urban intellectuality, traditional intellectuality, provincialism, primitivism—and generally avoided describing the places he went from the perspective of the South. He adopts the perspective of an apprentice, hoping to be fully present in and learn from his surroundings. That apprenticeship would lead to his novel *Macunaíma* the following year, in which Andrade imagines the nation as an encounter of different epochs, spaces, images, and voices.[14] His approach was particularly influential on my thinking about region and nation. In this book I am not interested in pursuing the "authentic" history of the Northeast, or crafting its definitive interpretation. Rather, my goal is to comprehend the production of the fundamental concept of the Northeast, and how it operates both beyond and within its boundaries.

The New Regionalism

The first regionalist discourses had begun to appear in the second half of the nineteenth century, precisely at the same time that the nation itself began to be imaginatively constructed through (and as a response to) the political centralization of the empire. Reactions around the Brazilian territory to the centralizing impulse were diverse and intense. Regionalism at the time bore the narrow contours of local and provincial concerns, carrying with them the seeds of separatism.[15]

The regionalism that emerged later, in the 1920s, was different. It transcended administrative boundaries of states and posited a greater spatial unity, at the same time that other forces were weakening traditional frames of spatiality in Brazil. The perception of this new space was intimately bound up with transformations in technology; its primordially natural and geographic definitions, once assumed, gave way under the new gaze to a sense of artifice, of historical construction through social processes. Urban growth and the expansion of transportation and communications sped the denaturalization of space. In the major cities, diverse epochs, classes, meanings, and social customs were increasingly jumbled together. As the traditional equilibrium of spaces was shattered, geography itself seemed to collapse. The "real" lay in a pile of jagged fragments that needed to be ordered again—not in the old ways, but in new ones.

The new conception of region, born of this shifting of relations between space, subject, and object, also reflected transformations in the disposition of knowledges—who should be known by whom, and how. But more fundamentally, a novel way of seeing was also emerging, which we might describe as a new discursive formation. Starting in the 1920s, this would provoke the growth of a generalized regional consciousness, diffused in the national space, that was able to connect both to individual subjective existences and to the life of the collective itself.

Within this discursive formation, however, articulating regions (by dearticulating them from the national whole) was not precisely a desired outcome. It should be seen as a particular embodiment of the influence of, again borrowing Foucault's term, the dispositif of nationalities—a series of anonymous rules and values that increasingly oriented Western discourse and practice after the eighteenth century, which urged people to overcome local loyalties and identify themselves into larger abstract wholes called nations. Charters and negotiations were tools of this dispositif, as were wars. Signs and symbols that connoted the nation and impressed its influence on diverse subjectivities were highly sought and widely distributed throughout national spaces. Within such an atmosphere of pressure to recognize the nation—to form it and integrate it—diverse regional discourses clashed as they strove to make their own customs, beliefs, and social relations the model for the nation and thus expand their hegemony.

If the national-popular discursive formation conceived of the nation as a process of homogenizing identities and realities, it was thus inevitably accompanied by new revelations of a country fragmented into more sharply defined and championed regionalisms. Through internal and external dialogues the materiality of these regions became codified. Images, texts, and practices could distinguish them, even if this also meant reducing the complexity of each region to a few easily identifiable tropes. For the Northeast, elements such as banditry, messianism, and traditional clientelist politics cohered as defining symbols even as other ones were ignored and left in the shadows. But the choices were not random. They were guided by the diverse interests at play both within the Northeast and in its relations with other regions, as national identity was being fervently debated. Determining the identity of the nation would mean that some regional identities would be destroyed or discredited, and others affirmed. In the modernist view, identity was an essence that was opposed to difference, and invigorated by the contrast. In that sense, the image of "region" must be continually reelaborated through changing strategies; it is a dynamic construct. Regionalist discourse does not distort the truth of a given region; it is the engine that produces and institutes such truths in the national context. This takes us beyond the question of mimicry in classical epistemology, in which discourse was a copy of the real. In modernity, such discourse contributes to the creation of their own objects, shaped by political strategies as well as historical forces (including social and economic). The Northeast is such a historical production of images and discourses, and its formulation has proven stubbornly resistant to revisions or new configurations of its "truths." The figures, signs, and themes that have been selectively polished and emphasized as regional markers impose their truthiness through repetition and internal consistency. They can then be used themselves as the foundation for new discourses and theoretical analyses of the most self-justifying sorts: indeed, the enunciations of the Northeast have been factored into and replicated through diverse naturalist, positivist, culturalist, Marxist, and structuralist paradigms.

Regionalist discourse cannot be reduced to something that merely describes subjects; rather, it institutes them. Space is a subjective dimension that doubles on itself, producing subjectivities who then engage in their own production of images and discourses, which enter deeper societal currents. Thus, the "new" subjects of the region become agents and vehicles for those same regional enunciations. Regional consciousness does not emerge or emanate from any one individual but from multiple points that are gradually understood as unified. Intellectuals are especially susceptible to this form of space consciousness, because they tend to be far removed from the actual centers of political and economic power (a distance that is geographic, perhaps, as well as measured in terms of the capability for intervention). A regionalist intellectual chafes at the distance from the metropolis, which dominates and radiates power and culture. Discourses of regionalization that also denounce the intellectual's distance from the center and lack of power take on bitter undertones of lack, and of victimization.

It should be noted that some so-called national intellectuals have praised regionalism. Sampaio Ferraz, for example, argues that a deep connection to one's region of birth does not detract from nationalist sentiment but is a critical prerequisite to the transfer of such feelings to more abstract nation itself. Similarly, the modernists thought that regional consciousness represented the initial stages of national consciousness. But it was therefore an evolutionary stage to be transcended on the way to experiencing the national collective. For Graça Aranha, aesthetic regionalism provided one mode of expression among many others; it should never be a goal of art, which must have universal aspirations (a universe in which the status of nations was secured).[16]

Modernist projects hoped to incorporate the different actual Brazils into one, which would effectively counter the elite mission to camouflage Brazil with the trappings of an imposed Frenchness. Studying and understanding regional variations was an important part of these projects, but it was undertaken ultimately in order to figure out how to homogenize them—to reconcile them into a discovered Brazilian unity. *Macunaíma* is structured around spatial oppositions: distinct and contrasting cultural geographies, most essentially the construction of bourgeois, civilized capitalist space and the primitive, precapitalist, traditional space. The factory or theater versus the virgin forest. Mário de Andrade believed that Brazil lacked a traditional cultural identity, which his generation of artists and intellectuals could help provide. On the whole Brazilian modernism differed from the European vanguard in that while the latter was trying to break with tradition, the former was hoping to create and cultivate it. Even though Brazilian culture was thought to depend on the interventions of erudite specialists rather than the unearthing of raw, elemental popular culture, Andrade was nonetheless enchanted by the suggestive figure of the (occasionally, selectively) cannibalistic Tupi.[17] For him, Brazilian identity had the resilient habit of folding back on the local, and local variability; that was why artists had difficulty in feeling and expressing Brazil in toto, without resorting to regional articulations or references to regional "color."

Also working within this attitude, art critic João Ribeiro argued that aspiring national painters should start by capturing the various regional types and scenes that would "produce the national space." It was important to represent the collectivity of people that "work, struggle, and suffer, in that way knitting the rough solidarity of a Brazilian population without rivalries based on birth, language, or religion." However, the nation here was founded only on the sum of these hoarded images. Naturalist paintings should freeze and inventory these diverse manifestations of the nation, registering them as regional variations with the belief that their distinctions would disappear. They were primitive steps leading to homogeneous, adult nationhood.[18]

Regionalist Literature

Brazilian literature had borne currents of regionalism since at least the middle of the nineteenth century, when there was a subtle shift from describing landscapes with a sort of timeless realism to asserting a genealogical connection between geographical areas and their populations (usually their elites). With time a new narrator was consolidated—the voice of provincial oligarchy, writing the history of their patches of space by reference to dominant extended families. The participation of various period intellectuals in this diffuse enterprise ensured that it was entwined with nationalism by the time of the Proclamation of the Republic in 1889. The clash between these diverse regional-national histories has not received the attention it should because of other more dramatic period segmentations, such as those between classes and ideologies, between schools of art and artistic styles, or between intellectuals and the state (a blunt framework of opposition that has tended to ignore how the processes were manifest throughout society).[19]

Antonio Candido believed that regionalism was a critical step in the definition of local consciousness: "Our nationalism was once forged out of regional postures. But premodernist regionalism was based on myths and legends—artificial, pretentious, creating a subaltern consciousness easily condescended to within Brazil. It was as if a European gaze was invited to scrutinize our most typical realities. The man in the field was viewed as picturesque, whimsical, ludicrous."[20]

The notion that the regional was by definition a parade of relics, rare and in danger of disappearing under progress, underlay this view. The narratives attempted to rescue it from oblivion but by doing so further ensconced it within the bounds of antiquary. Elements of folklore and (particularly rural) popular culture were emphasized as regional content often within an authorial tone of distance and superiority.

Regionalist literature was slightly different in that it aimed to define Brazilianness through its very diversity and the continuing coexistence of multiple social and historical landscapes. From the beginning of the twentieth century, this literature demonstrated a keen interest in the environment—a naturalist/realist approach to comprehending social environments that were becoming seemingly less natural all the time with the expansion of capitalism and bourgeois social relations. But such naturalist literature was also firmly rooted in a tropical, emotional, sensual sense of Brazilian identity and culture that was understood to distinguish it from European literature, which was taken as lacking the basis of environmental and racial influences shaping Brazilian art and psychology.[21]

Euclides da Cunha's *Os Sertões* (Rebellion in the Backlands), published in 1906, is generally considered the seminal example of this national culture production rooted in naturalism. In no uncertain terms it cast off the illusion that Brazil was somehow a European nation and called for a reckoning with its actual American character. For the Brazilian reader *Os Sertões* emphasized both the examination of our own land, customs, traditions, and people independent of European categorizations, and the strong influence of the natural world in shaping the character of our race-in-formation. It sketched out the elements and parameters that future artists and intellectuals would use in trying to explain our national identity; and in later decades, critics attributed to it the quickening tendency among Brazilian writers to search experimentally in their work for the true Brazil.

What *Os Sertões* also inescapably did was furnish a new repertoire of images and enunciations for various regional discourses. Within its pages appears an essential and influential opposition: São Paulo versus Northeast, and paulista versus *sertanejo* (a person from the northeastern backlands, the sertão). Euclides da Cunha both affirmed the dichotomy and provided a solution for it by indicating the presence of paulistas or their descendants in the rural Northeast. São Paulo was thus the provider of national unity, in a formulation of social geography that carefully excluded the Northeast's coast and the problematic potential for interbreeding with Afro-Brazilians there. Despite his own ambivalence marking the text with respect to the character and cost of national progress, da Cunha was widely interpreted as revealing the man of the backlands as a sort of national hero whose essential paulista character would help assure the possibility of constructing a shared nationhood. Of course, he has also been read differently, since his text is rich in curious interpenetrations of myth and history, art and science.[22]

The problem of a polarity between rural interior and the coast in Brazil deserves further mention. This would also be picked up by diverse artists and become a sort of archetypical question surrounding Brazilian culture, because within discussions of nationalism and civilization the coast represented a peculiar space with a history of external connections through the multiple landings of colonizers, and an enduring Atlantic bridge to Europe and European culture. In contrast, the interior appears as a redoubt of nationality, protected from foreign influences. In this context the sertão becomes more an emotional space than an objectively measured territory. It is shot through with evocative forces combining aspects of geography, linguistics, and culture and lifeways, as well as historical elements such as banditry, plantation estates, drought, messianism, migrant exoduses, and so on. The sertão incorporates all these images into a tapestry rich with emotional significations, national yet exotic, defined in contrast to the metropolitan cities and ports along the littoral. In that sense a plausible case could be made for the interior as the soul of the country, even if its roots remain obscured.[23] This construct of the sertão provided a new medium for nationalist intellectuals to develop critiques of what they saw as a culture of importation, the insistence on external cultural models, and the nation's subservience to its coastal developments. The patriotic westward march became a fixation, taking yet another form in the 1930s when President Getúlio Vargas embraced it as a geopolitical strategy to more fully integrate Brazil's interior with the nation.

But early on, and for many observers, the relationship between sertão and civilization was regarded as mutually exclusive. The culture of the sertão is traditional, precivilization, a folkloric bedrock for the establishment of national culture. Nonetheless da Cunha, as well as Monteiro

Lobato, believed that civilization should be carried to the sertão in a way that would both rescue and modernize it. Lobato's *Urupês* (published 1918), one of the first books to take head-on the exotic regionalism of the previous decades, featured critique and sarcasm in deploring the absence of policies to modernize the sertão even as it seemed to cast doubt on the capacities of the people who lived there through suggesting they were by nature lazy and indolent. But he called for a Brazilian vanguard to integrate the sertão into the flows of national, not European-derived, civilization.[24] For him the true Brazil was the Brazil of the backlands: the fields and villages, not the cities. "Brazil is not and could never be an extension of São Paulo, a twig grafted onto the branch of Italy—nor of Rio de Janeiro, which clings to its Portuguese artifices. No, Brazil resides in the interior, where the rugged, simple men dress in crude leather and spend their days breaking ponies; it is in the cactus parched by drought. It is not to be found among the polished, foppish folk in the coastal cities, their emotions and energies drained in the pursuit of imported and pointless distractions."[25]

But this sort of naturalist regionalism was not easily reconciled with how modernism was reconfiguring the relation between space and the gaze, within larger transformations of the spatialization of social relations. Modernism was opposed to naturalist regionalism, in that it desired the integration of regional elements into the national whole. The movement might itself be characterized as a sort of regional or provincial upsurge against the cultural and academic prominence of Rio de Janeiro, and it drew momentum and intellectual ammunition from the competing regionalism of São Paulo—Brazil's economic powerhouse with its own growing political base. Mário de Andrade openly recognized the centrality of a São Paulo aesthetics to the modernist movement.[26] His *Pauliceia Desvairada* (published 1921) sang praises of the maternal city and made it clear that modernism would reelaborate regionalism, not abandon it. The modernists' particular aversion to regionalism was part of a political strategy intended to unify the cultural space of the nation based on São Paulo, and some of their projects even fed into the ambitions of paulista politicians to expand their federal hegemony. The Municipal Culture Department of the City of São Paulo, directed by Andrade, had as part of its mission to "contribute to the formation of the Brazilian man, in general and collective, who will be uniquely able to conserve our national identity." This department's projects and research initiatives went far beyond the boundary of the municipality, since it was created as a sort of trial run for the intended Brazilian Culture Institute, which would serve as a base for the nationalization of the modernists' aesthetic codes.[27]

Ultimately, what modernism did was to incorporate the regional dimension into an unstable visibility and speakability that oscillated between cosmopolitanism and nationalism, while leaving behind the exotic and picturesque naturalist elements. These were reworked in order to efface their difference, or sometimes to reify it, but within a gaze that rejected European subjectivities. Regional signifiers took on new sheen and new depths of meaning through their association with the modernist discourses such that, for instance, the cactus was uprooted from its dry northeastern environment to serve as a symbol of Brazilianness, of primitivism or bitterness in the national experience, and it became part of the visual vocabulary of painters such as Tarsila do Amaral.[28]

Prior to modernism, regionalism operated within a naturalist paradigm of describing landscapes and cataloguing detailed descriptions of the spatialized typical. The Brazilian nation was the assemblage of these, but lacking an overarching structure of images and discourses to lend it unity. The modernists adapted those "facts" and details into signs, rearranging them into a new vision and text of Brazil. They centralized meanings by channeling all that dispersed information through a process of interpretation and redistribution—something Mário de Andrade referred to as "extinguishing regionalisms by decentralizing intelligence."[29] Of course, this demonstrated that Andrade believed that intelligence had been earlier centralized among the modernists themselves. São Paulo is erected as the gateway for modernism into Brazil, since it is a modern city of mass culture, ostensibly the "only non-folkloric and non-traditional city" in the country, even though both Oswald de Andrade and Mário de Andrade would elsewhere point out the contradictions in and limits to modernism in São Paulo.

North versus South

The naturalist regionalism criticized by the modernists, as well as the regionalist sentiment running between the North and South since the latter part of the nineteenth century, contributed to the emergence of a new space called the Northeast. Along with environment, race and climate were other key discursive cleavages in the separation of space. For some time, Nina Rodrigues had raised warnings about the possible forging of distinct national identities between the white civilization of the South and the black and mixed-race civilization of the North. In his account these populations were distinguished by social attitudes deriving from a sort of racial response to the weather: indolence, passivity, and subservience in the North contrasted with the persistence and industriousness of the South.[30] The American Civil War had been accompanied with keen interest by many observers in Brazil because of the possibility it suggested of conflict and separation between two race-coded regions with distinct rhythms of development.

Oliveira Vianna, writing in the 1920s and 1930s, extended the rhetoric. He argued that the South, embodied in São Paulo, was the "polarizing center of the Aryan elements of our nationality . . . home to an aristocracy superior in morals and psychology." The South would provide a foundation to the nation, rather than those areas "dominated by the lower-class, plebian strata, the mongrels, indolent fruit of the mixture of savage bloodlines." In other words, people inferior to the robust and industrious southern stock, with its complement of European genetics. Vianna believed the destiny of the North was to be subjugated by the South, dominated by its influences, its vitality undercut by the South's attractions as a place to live and to work. The more eugenically fit members of the North's population would tend to migrate south, depriving the region of its most active, energetic members and deepening its squalor and degeneration. And indeed the fact of these migratory movements at the time contributed to the reordering of space in Brazil, because it brought populations who knew little of each other into sudden direct contact. Many of the enduring stereotypes that came to mark these different spaces and populations began to cohere and gain distribution in this period.

Vianna worried that such "racial, psychological and moral" divisions impacted the political organization of Brazil, resulting in a chaos of oligarchies and diffuse loyalties. This was thought to leave the country more vulnerable to foreign pressures and inhibit the formation of a national spirit, much less a genuine nation-state to validate it.[31] Rodrigues speculated that while the North's tropical climate and entrenched underdevelopment would favor the persistence of "black" social and cultural elements (including a certain roguish intelligence that was quick yet turbulent and too prone to inertia), in the South the starker climate and more impressive civilization would work to cleanse the darker sociocultural stains that might appear as a result of migration.[32]

Such debates reflected the concerns shared by many: that the North, or perhaps even the entire country, was doomed to a state of backwardness due to the substantial mixed-race character of the population and the influence of tropical climate. According to the disciplines of anthropogeography and biotypology, which had fervent adherents across Brazil, neither were the tropics adequate for the establishment of true civilization, nor were African descendants and miscegenated peoples capable of civilization at all. The heat and humidity wore down both body and mind, especially if the blood was already weak, resulting in society's enfeeblement and superficiality.[33] The North was thus condemned to decadence because of climate and race. Resonant discourses emerged from around the country to explain the country's apparent backwardness, but also to proclaim the "providential appearance of an invigorating injection of European blood, since the denizens of the North are generally small and frail, with notorious skeletal defects especially in the thoracic, cervical and cranial areas that lead them to age prematurely."[34]

Invocations of the weather had taken on political overtones in regionalist rhetoric since 1877, when the first major drought occurred. It was a theme that both mobilized action and touched emotions. It served as the basis to request financial help, to develop infrastructure, to dedicate administrative positions, and so on. Initiatives related to drought and the "drought industry" became a constant and highly lucrative pursuit in the most affected northern states, particularly as these coincided with the decline of the states' traditionally principal economic activities: agricultural production, namely sugar and cotton. Drought became a rallying point around which diverse northern politicians could unify. All other state problems and social questions were interpreted according to their relationship with natural calamity. The various manifestations of dominated groups against their oppressors, from banditry to messianism (even the general state of underdevelopment already affecting the states in different ways) were attributed to drought, with solutions to drought called for as a way to simultaneously solve all such issues.[35]

The year 1877 is of fundamental importance. The drought that year was interpreted as giving a fatal blow to the North in its implicit competition with the South for national supremacy. The balance of power changed, as power shifted southward. Gilberto Freyre analyzed how the drought impacted other social practices already underway to the detriment of the North. Brazil was transitioning away from slavery, with the Law of the Free Womb in 1871, ensuring that children born of slaves would be free. The end of slavery in Brazil was thus visible within a generation or so. But for Freyre, the drought actually hastened the signing of the law of outright abolition since it resulted in the massive transfer of slaves and ex-slaves to the South, regionalizing the labor market and destroying longstanding Afro-Brazilian solidarities in the North. Contributing to this trauma, Freyre noted, was the parallel out-migration of many northern intellectuals to the South after 1877.[36]

The discourse of drought, with its appendices of travails and misery, helped catalyze the unification of regional interests as well as broader political and economic practices conceived as involving "all the states subject to this climatic phenomenon." The horrific descriptions all tend toward the composition of both a mappable space and the image of a region "abandoned and marginalized by public officials." The drought was the point of unity for diverse northern interests to raise their various complaints to the national level, at the cost of converging around a shared vocabulary of weather-based misery and suffering. It also provoked new solidarity among these actors. Suddenly a shared common cause and discourse was found between the landholders in the once sugar-rich interior Zona da Mata and the urban businessmen, between the cotton farmers and the cattle ranchers. What Freyre called the "regional elite" began to coalesce, and it was resolutely able to survive for many decades around these same shared arguments. Of course, not everyone in the South was sympathetic. In 1919, the magazine *Spartacus* published a rebuke of the North's drought discourse, calling it "one of the most awful frauds in even these decadent days . . . an orgy at the nation's expense."[37]

Banditry and messianic movements, long disdained by elites across Brazil, became swept into the drought discourse as social symptoms of calamity. They became yet another reason to argue for intervention, for "investing in the modernization of the North." That connection was rejected by, among others, the journalist Lourenço Filho, who attributed such phenomena to the "innate violence and natural fanaticism of the peoples of the North."[38] Messianism in particular contributed to the construction of an image of the Northeast in the South, in large part due to the developments at Canudos as reported by Euclides da Cunha in the newspaper *O Estado de São Paulo*. Later, in the 1920s, the circumstances surrounding Padre Cícero reinforced the idea of the Northeast as an atmosphere of inexplicable extremes, of fanaticism, a characterization that haunts it to the present day. In 1925, in an exercise of reification, the aforementioned newspaper dispatched Lourenço Filho to Juazeiro to describe what he "sees," and the reporting ardently recirculated images and enunciations borrowed from Euclides da Cunha. The North appears, the journalist wrote, "to be retreating incessantly into the past, at least to the eyes of this southern observer. Life seems to grind to a halt, or even more shocking, to be tending toward the opposite of evolution and progress. Each day of the journey seems to take me back another twenty years. People, habits, aesthetic and religious manifestations, ideas and beliefs, everything disappears into the emptiness of a voiceless echo from times lost. . . . The very language sustains archaic forms from the early days of the colony, forms that have long since vanished from the metropolitan Portuguese that once conveyed them."

The journalist's description of Juazeiro is a direct echo of how Euclides da Cunha had described the region earlier: "All of the people insist on maintaining the same old superstition, the same blind fanaticism, caught in a sickness of the past." Filho also associated religious extremism with lunacy; the title of one of his articles was "In the Kingdom of Insanity." It is against this kingdom, he proclaimed that "reason revolts. . . . All around are people whose faces bear the scars and sunken expression of penitence, their bodies bent and twisted in the intensity of their belief. We feel no urge to laugh, but to make a desperate appeal to reason—to protest, to shout, to bring back to reality these *stupid human dregs* who have been so exploited. Yet the same clarity of reason leads us to understand the danger in doing this, as these poor souls would take it only as a gesture of criticism or condemnation of them, not their pathetic lot."[39]

His startled but rationalizing gaze falls again and again to scenes of "bizarreness, discordance and the off-putting." He carefully selects vivid instances of the strange or exotic, enshrining it as what passes for "typical" there: from the rank cactus flowers, a jarring white or bright red, like a seeping wound pouring out from the very rocks; the women who placidly "pick insects from the children's heads"; the resting of feet on the walls when seated, and so on. All these images fulfill the preconceived notion of the North's backwardness and incivility as compared with the South.[40]

Banditry was another theme that, highlighted in the "discourse of the North" as a testament to the dangerous consequences of drought and the lack of state involvement in the area, congealed into a stigma of violence tainting anyone from the region. This fear of northern unruliness that was long brewing in the South cannot be dissociated from how the South was contending with the movements of at first slaves, then former slaves (a general exodus of Afro-Brazilians southward that expanded with abolition) into new milieus of labor and social relations. These northern slaves, challenged by the different forms of privation they now faced in the South, tended to rebel; and this at a time when consciousness of the possible immanence of abolition was widespread. The image of the "bad Negro from the North" quickly entered into the discourses of abolitionists and anti-abolitionists alike, such as those delivered at the Provincial Assembly of São Paulo. [41] Here was a bipartisan contribution from the South to the North's connotations of savagery and unruliness, still in the late nineteenth century.

By the 1920s, the figure of the bandit (*cangaço*) would reinforce the idea that nordestinos were inherently violent, and the Northeast a territory untouched by law beyond the grubby hegemony asserted by local oligarchies of toughs. Urbanites from within the Northeast itself were participants in the spinning of this narrative. It was they who most ardently and fearfully collected the tales of the outlaws' exploits, tales that nearly always were founded on the same premise: the disastrous contact between bandits and vulnerable enclaves of civilization. A dusty band of brigands would ride into a town somewhere in the interior, and proceed to sack it; they would indiscriminately kill people and livestock with their rifles or machetes. Homes would be invaded, structures burned, property (which at that time was conceived as including daughters and wives) stolen and/or abused. Banditry provided one of the key genres of narrative that received space in the South's newspapers, along with religious fanatics, droughts, and the occasional family feud notable for its bloodiness. Such discourses helped mark a conceptual-territorial line between regions; the South was constructed as civilized and civilizing, moral, and rational—everything the North was not, while the North was an example of what the South could not allow itself to be.[42]

These images would impregnate the region of the Northeast, conceiving of it and laying the foundation for its materiality. This would be the Northeast of the "parched and implacable stretches, where the violent caress of the sun left the earth cracked and effaced of green. All around, desiccation, and its partner death. Not a drop of water anywhere." A Northeast where "even if one seems to be able to flee it the desert returns, arid and mournful, and the grim-faced people wander through it to nowhere leading animals so thin their skeletons squeal as they grind."[43]

Wherever and in whatever guise the discourses of the North circulated—in the southern press, among the naturalist intellectuals, in accounts of the droughts—the North appears as a place whose inferiority seems ordained by environmental and racial conditions, even though it was also maintained that state investment could resolve the problems and modernize the region. The rapid development in the South, notably São Paulo, was explained by its climatic and racial superiority. This superiority seemed to assure its own noble destiny: to be the engine "pulling the derailed train of a tropical and mixed-race nation." By contrast, the North was naturally backward. It was through a reelaboration of the images and enunciations of the North that the Northeast would emerge, as part of a new social sensibility in relation to state and nation and a new way to see national spaces.

TWO SPACES OF NOSTALGIA

Stories of Tradition

TRADITIONALIST RETERRITORIALIZATION

"But there are moments that mark us deeply . . .
Made, in each one of us
From eternities and seconds,
Whose longing extinguishes the voice.
And life goes on weaving knots
Almost impossible to undo
Everything that we love are pieces
Alive, from our own beings."
Manuel Bandeira, "A vida assim nos afeiçoa" (A Cinza das Horas), in *Poesias*, 33

The Portuguese word *saudade* has no direct English translation; applied to a range of human experience it conveys longing, nostalgia, homesickness, the desire for something that was. The central feeling is lack or loss. It is a personal sentiment of one who perceives that she is losing important pieces of herself, or the places that made her who she is. But it can also be a collective sentiment, affecting a community that loses its spatial or temporal referents, a social class that loses its position of power to history.

The region of the Brazilian Northeast, which appeared in the country's imaginary landscape soon after the turn of the twentieth century to replace the older division between North and South, was founded in nostalgia and tradition. This book follows the history of that process, and the continual reinvention of the Northeast through the interaction of multiple practices and discourses. Its origins are not simple and linear, although such an argument is useful in denying that the Northeast is still being actively invented today. For if the Northeast is not a political and cultural production, it must be a timelessly neutral and natural object.[1] But how was it that this "Northeast" became shaped into something adequate for so many uses and applications—academic studies,

museum expositions, themes of novels and telenovelas, films, paintings, plays, political rhetoric, economic policies? Why, and how, was the
region born under the sign of nostalgia? What political consequences
have there been to its immersion in tradition?

The appearance of the Northeast can be explained in part as a reaction
to the nationalist strategies put into motion through the dispositif of nationalism and the discursive formation of the national-popular. It cannot
be attributed to particular individuals, families, or groups. It represented
a new type of regionalism, although one sedimented in qualities of tradition and nostalgia for the past. The Northeast emerged as the construction
of a political-cultural totality that was fostered by the shocking sense of
loss among traditional elite producers of cotton and sugar, as well as the
merchants and intellectuals linked to them through an immense web of
connections. Their economic and social dissolution was connected to the
rise of a larger totality, not dominated by them: the nation. Diverse forces
coalesced around the idea of the new regional space, particularly with
the public works and other policies directed at it as a space defined by
drought. Old competitors who found themselves in this new region laid
aside many of their differences and discovered a new equality, a shared
sense of struggle against the ostensible threats from invading forces. The
discovery of this region was not just parallel with new nationalist sentiment, but a reaction to it and another face of it.[2]

Once beginning to be glimpsed, the new region was researched as-
siduously: analyses based in naturalism and economic and social history
accrued. But the finer texture of regional social memory, culture, and
artistic expressions were also elaborated, as these were central to the
institutionalization of the place. Particular images, texts, and practices
would be mobilized to help shape the way to see and speak the region;
its visibility and speakability had to be ordered through fixed symbolic
codes. The Northeast first began to appear once people looked for it to
find its elements of shared identity and the homogeneity of its space.

FROM NORTH TO NORTHEAST

Initially, the term "Northeast" was used to designate the area of operations of the Federal Inspectorate of Works against Droughts (Inspetoria
Federal de Obras Contra as Secas, IFOCS), created in 1919. In this institutional gaze, the Northeast began to be mapped as a territory within the

North that was particularly subject to extreme dry seasons, and hence deserving of special federal attention. Ever since the great drought of 1877, arid weather has played a key role in the discursive parameters of the area. Those discourses, and the social and political practices related to them, gradually helped encourage the idea that the Northeast was a specific entity outside of the North proper.[3]

Very early in that process, it was droughts that first attracted the attention of journalists in the South regarding the existence of the North and its particular problems. The droughts provided a definitive intervention in the differentiation between North and South at a time when natural environment and race were considered determining factors of social organization. Newspapers and other entities in the South sponsored charity drives, with names of benefactors dignified in publications. Indirect though it was, this provided a form of contact between populations that did not then have much direct exchange because of the lack of transportation infrastructure. Oswald de Andrade, during a visit to Recife in 1925, commented on the ignorance in the South regarding that city even though it was already one of the largest in Brazil. The first series of images of the North that was published in the South focused on visible effects of the drought, notably its human and animal victims. It was through such spectacles and associated reporting, as well as themed parties, lectures and other events to collect charitable contributions, that southerners learned of their "brothers in the North."[4]

In such texts produced in the early 1920s, the terms North and Northeast are used as synonyms, which suggests the consensus idea of a distinctive Northeast had not yet crystallized. Several reports from 1920 show their period interchangeability: "There will be tonight at the Hélio Cinema a children's performance to benefit the victims of the drought in the Brazilian Northeast. . . . Directors of the Harmony Society and organizers of the grand ball to benefit the victims of the north's drought."[5] Simultaneously at this time, discourses begin to appear that suggest a separation between the area of the Amazon and the western reaches of the North. This was provoked principally by the migration of laborers to the forests to work as rubber tappers, a migration that threatened the supply of workers for the traditional fieldwork of the eastern part of the North. Economic interests within the "region" seemed to diverge, although one critic suggested that the end result would harm both places equally: "The Brazilian political attitude with respect to the North of the country represents the formal negation of civilization. It is completely and fundamentally wrongheaded in every aspect, and will only serve to sow gloom and disaster in the Amazon, reducing it to desert, while increasing the desolation and social misery among the populations of the Northeast."[6]

The institutionalization of the Northeast would require a shift in how people in the North viewed space, identity, and power relations. Traditionally, the state was the most important geographical entity, although even within states, independent oligarchies typically held sway over smaller domains. These provincial interests as well as the official state interests would have to merge and unite around (that is, within) the concept of the Northeast region.[7] And it was the South, even more than the "leftover" western territory of the North that the Northeast had separated itself from, that would provide a unifying negative reference point. The South was the counter or other to what the Northeast was discovering itself to be: a subaltern space of defeat, bereft of hopes to aspire to national dominance.

A generalized sensation of exclusion, prejudice, and inferiority in relation to the South was experienced in 1878, when Rio de Janeiro held an Agricultural Congress that was ostensibly national in scope but that snubbed the North by inviting no northern representatives. The next year, in direct response, the North held its own Agricultural Congress in Recife. There, the focus was on issues of regional interest such as the recent drought, crises in sugar production, and the effects of the transfer of slaves from North to South. In addition, participants aired acrid critiques of the discriminatory practices of the imperial state with respect to providing unequal investment, fiscal and labor policy, and infrastructure to the North.[8] But the drought of 1877 (lasting through 1879) resulted in unprecedented media attention in the South, especially as it was detrimental not just to the lower strata of society but to landholders, merchants, and the entire commercial sector. Resources were directed to the North, and more were demanded by the assembling coterie of "northeasterners" in Parliament who recognized they had a new platform to both request assistance and demand equal treatment with the South. Drought-related discourses quickly informed the political initiatives of all the northern states so afflicted.[9]

This northeastern group in Parliament managed to insert an article in the Constitution of 1891 obliging the union to dedicate special funds for the rescue of places and peoples who suffer natural disaster (which would of course include droughts). The institutionalization of droughts would progressively open more administrative spaces within the state for groups from the North/Northeast. Nowhere was this clearer than in the creation of the first dedicated agency, the Institute of Public Works against Droughts (Instituto de Obras Contra as Secas, IOCS) in 1909, which immediately became the locus for the official production of a regionalist discourse that decried the republic's favoritism of São Paulo and Minas Gerais in the spheres of investment and public policy.[10]

Ten years later, in 1919, with the reorganization of the IOCS into the IFOCS, associated politicians and intellectuals were determined to eliminate the disparate meanings that still obscured the contours of the precise area that the agency was designed to assist. They attempted to construct precise (and precisely wedded) images and texts to bring definition to the region. Their stated goal was to do away with the "various Northeasts that clog the newsstands and bookstores, some of them sincere, others not."[11] The Northeast needed to be seen and read clearly, in one direction, so that its truth-effects could produce a more efficient politics.

At the Congress of Sugar Producers in Recife in 1920, feverish denunciations of the "privileges of the South, particularly as regards coffee" took on a separatist tone. During a period of crisis in the sugar market and wider trends of agricultural modernization that put yet more pressure on traditional producers, who relied on subsidies from their state governments, the congress leaders prioritized the creation of common regional ground for their discourses of victimization. Here was diagrammed the basic antipathy between the Northeast and São Paulo that would direct all further discussions regarding nation, region, and national identity. In the Parliament that same year, with the rallying cry to combat political discrimination, representatives from the northern states formed the so-called Northern Bloc in order to bring unity and visibility to their individual states' demands.[12]

Banditry, and the necessary measures to combat it, provided another motive for discourses and practices rooted in a northern solidarity within the nation's congress. Like natural disasters, banditry was well suited as a unifying point because it disregarded state boundaries and called for more collective action and cooperation. The integration of the states into a regional repressive apparatus directly informed how the region took shape, in this context around fear of chaos: hordes of disgruntled poor, and the violent exploits of the outlaws, suggested preconditions of revolt from below. The sensation of economic fragility that tormented the traditional producers of cotton and sugar joined with their fear of rebellion and violent rout. This stirred the regionalized preoccupation with uniting forces to counter the disorder emerging from the popular sector, which also included the messianic movements and their separatist, revolutionary potential. The region was being constructed in a manner to close in on and secure power relations, guaranteeing the maintenance of old hierarchies.

Outside the political sphere, centers of higher education were important loci for the elite development of regional consciousness and regional discourse. The young scions of dominant families from diverse northern states tended to make their way to Recife, the cultural, commercial, medical, and academic "metropolis of the north." They attended university (there or in neighboring Olinda), usually law school. Since the late nineteenth century, these institutions had been important venues for the production of regionalist thought and a new common sense about region. They had produced the region's intellectuals, except for the most elite few who managed to pursue their studies abroad. Here, future politicians and opinion makers exchanged ideas and developed networks of collegiality in a forum that privileged a different vision than mere state loyalty, since numerous states were represented in the student body. These young, ambitious people worked and debated in an atmosphere of solidarity against the national trends of northeastern marginalization—a factor that, alongside the crises affecting traditional modes of economic production, seemed to place their own personal and professional futures in doubt.[13]

Recife was also the center of journalism for a substantial area well outside of Pernambuco state, from Alagoas to Maranhão, dating back into the nineteenth century. A prominent Recife-based correspondent was Gilberto Freyre, both before earning his fame as a sociologist and occasionally afterward. He has suggested that the area of influence of the *Diário de Pernambuco* essentially traced the contours of the Northeast itself. José Lins do Rego noted that the *Diário* was an important introduction to letters for many aspiring young sons of plantation owners, leading them to dream of making the trip to Recife. Over time, this newspaper became one of the principal means of dissemination for the assertions and complaints of the northern states and then of the new northeastern region.[14]

The *Diário*'s regionalist discourse took on a different cast when Freyre submitted a series of articles from the United States, formulating what he called regionalist and traditionalist thought. The *Diário* also published the stories of Mário Sette, such as *Senhor de Engenho*, which helped Freyre in his musings on the nature of regionalist romances. In 1925, as the paper was celebrating its centenary, it produced one of the first cultural (rather than narrowly geographic, political or economic) elaborations of the Northeast as a discrete zone. Entitled *The Book of the Northeast*, and prepared under Freyre's immediate supervision, the text established the region's cultural and artistic content and presented a suite of traditions and memories in a manner that suggested they needed to be rescued and preserved. It was with this book, according to Lins do Rego, that "the Northeast discovered itself as a fatherland (*o Nordeste se descobriu como patria*)." In its preface, Freyre affirmed that it was "an investigation into northeastern life; the life of five states whose individual destinies have merged into one and whose roots have thoroughly intertwined over the last hundred years." This hundred years was also, coincidentally, the age of the *Diário de Pernambuco* as well as of Recife's law school.[15]

In a way, *The Book of the Northeast* anticipated the turn of events at the 1926 Regionalist Conference in Recife, an event that commingled cultural and political interests. That meeting served, according to Joaquim Inojosa, to "unite representatives from Ceara, Rio Grande do Norte, Paraiba, Pernambuco, Alagoas, and Sergipe around a regional patriotism." It stimulated "love for the native soil, of whose salutary enthusiasm and ardor is built the structure of the greatest fatherlands." The congress also intended to protect the "northeastern spirit" from the creeping destruction threatened by influences from Rio de Janeiro and São Paulo: cosmopolitan cities already shot through with foreign, invasive elements that weakened their true Brazilian characteristics.[16]

Still, the origins of this congress might also be said to predate the publication of *The Book of the Northeast*. It had been organized by the Regionalist Center of the Northeast, founded 1924, with the mission to "collaborate with all the political movements that are dedicated to the moral and material development of the Northeast and to defend the interests of the Northeast in solidarity." The center's documentation states that while the unity of the Northeast was already clearly defined, there remained a need to do away with some lingering provincialisms that inhibited genuine regional communion. It called for the manifestation of this unity in realms outside official governmental declarations, such as social movements and projects and cultural expression. The center would have a coordinating and encouraging function to congregate "aspects of northeastern life and culture through organizing conferences, excursions, art exhibits, and a library featuring the production of regional intellectuals past and present; and also, editing the magazine the *Northeast*."[17]

The growth of the autonomist movement in Pernambuco and the rise of the Regionalist Center—developments inflected by troubling concurrent events such as the violent clampdown on messianism just after the Regionalist Conference—evoked a negative response in the South. São Paulo newspapers condemned the apparent separatism of the northeasterners and bristled at their accusation that the republic "did not know how to discipline the quasi-imperial abuses perpetrated by the richest states." The provocative regionalist argument that "Brazilian states should be governed only by men who live in their homelands, not by a professional political class that resides in Rio de Janeiro and scorns their states" was met with stunned disbelief. Indeed, the rhetoric was sharp. The radicalization of northeastern regionalism can be traced in the participation of not only middle-class but labor leaders in the autonomist movement. In *O Moleque Ricardo*, José Lins do Rego reproduces some of the scenes he witnessed as a student of Recife's law school, in which demands of a political and class nature were seamlessly merged with regionalist complaints and regionalist enthusiasm.[18]

As it glimmered to life, the Northeast was not a concept prized by elites alone. A series of disparate events and practices was generating and institutionalizing it even among the popular classes. It would cohere into an idea that oriented cultural production of a considerable range and quality, and that attracted federal institutional attention quite disproportionate to its own actual economic and political authority. At the same time, Brazil's modernist, industrialist, and nationalist policies particularly after 1930 would contribute to the region's subordination in the state power structure. There would be other compensatory but focused gestures, such as the National Department of Works against the Droughts (founded 1909) and the Institute of Sugar and Alcohol (1933), which spoke in the name of the region but accomplished little more than to direct funds into the pockets of large landowners there—a sort of investment in obsolescence. The Northeast would become dependent on these institutional gifts of charity, carried in subsidies, unpaid loans, drought relief, and tax exemptions.

In sum, the Northeast was forming through practices that shaped its cartography through the persistent struggle against drought; violent measures against messianic movements and banditry; and political adjustments by elites to ensure the preservation of their privileges. But the Northeast also surged forth through a series of discourses that affirmed its sensibility, by producing cultural manifestations of a marked regional character.

The Invention of the Northeast

IMPRINTING THE REGION

"Up until now, the Northeast has been sewed out of its own threads."[19] This insight, attributed to Agamenon Magalhães, admirably expresses the processes by which images and discourses invented the Northeast. To legitimate the region's existence, efforts were made during the 1926 Regionalist Conference to normalize its origins. This retrospectively articulated past was intended to give the region a legal framework as well as universal and historical ones. It was described as always having existed, in other words, as being continuous, eternal. Any apparent historical discontinuities resided in the region having been forgotten and ignored until now. The region was written into the past as a promise not realized or fully perceived. From the vantage point these activists created, one could look to the past and recognize a range of facts proving that northeastern identity was already there in the record. Based on this paradigm it became quite possible to create a historical account of the region dating back to at least the sixteenth century, even though it remained to people in the twentieth century to comprehend and consolidate it.

Gilberto Freyre, for example, argued that the influence of the Dutch in Pernambuco during the seventeenth century was a decisive factor in the Northeast's differentiation. The area became a separate cultural, intellectual, and economic unit under the administration of the Dutch, and their partners the Jews. But that was all erected over the bedrock of what Freyre believed was an innate regionalism that characterized earlier Portuguese colonial control, since the colonizers would have been loath to contribute to a national consciousness that might have threatened their dominion. In that sense Freyre both discovered a regional consciousness in the early colonial period and suggested that the brief interlude of Dutch hegemony contributed to coalescing national awareness by staging a viable exception to Portuguese rule. For him, region emerged before nation in the Brazilian experience.[20]

In this mode of thought regionalism is itself a basic element of Brazilian nationality from the beginning, when the territory's vast distances lent autonomy to the "genetic foci of settlements" and the competition between regions would have gone on to coexist with animosity toward the colonial metropolis. While Brazil's regions had different histories and characteristics, they nonetheless converged in a heroic tradition of nationalism.

It is important to observe that while Gilberto Freyre highlighted an 1825 drought as playing a key role in the history of the Northeast, he emphasized less the climatic and economic impacts than its "moral and social consequences." By the 1920s, the natural environment and racial mixture had been demoted as the originating elements and fundamental determinants of regional identity. Increasingly, culture and society were explored for their roles in the development of regional consciousness. Events became central to the origin story—from the Dutch invasion to the foundation of Recife's law school, and the Pernambucan revolts of 1817, 1824, and 1848; naturalist arguments ceded space to historical ones.[21]

In the cultural realm, it was necessary to invent a tradition. Ideally, this would establish an equilibrium between the old order and the new, while conciliating the present region with the social and existential territories of the past. In such a context, maintaining traditions is also their invention for new ends, which would include the continuity of threatened social hierarchies.[22] The fear of not having space in a new order, losing individual and collective memory, and watching one's world disappear stimulated the concern with tradition in the construction of the Northeast. Tradition would provide landmarks to guide the activities of a society in transition, and impede the forces of discontinuity. But as the Northeast's tradition was cast in the mold of defense of a past in crisis, regionalist discourses came to emphasize rhetorics of misery and paralysis that were also associated with drought; it was also intended to protect the privilege of elites linked to traditional landholding, even if this meant an antipathy to modernization.[23]

These discourses were filled with archives of clichés and stereotypes simple to decipher, rooted in preconceptions, alongside newly "discovered" knowledges produced through regional studies. Analogies helped link back to the past and assure its survival, even though history was posed as condemning it. Of vital importance was the insistence on memory, whether individual or collective, as embodying the tranquility of a reality without rupture.

The search for regional identity was a reaction to two intersecting forces: globalization, with world capitalism creating new socioeconomic relations and cultural fluxes linked to modernity; and the nationalization of power relations, the centralization and bureaucratization of power in a cohering state. Regional identity and regional memory provided an origin story that could reconnect people facing a diffuse, uncertain present to an ostensibly shared past, bringing meaning back to existences that were increasingly vacant. The idea of the "traditional Northeast" is a product of modernity that could have been conceivable only at that particular moment.

Lack provided the contours of the process by which northeastern activists became aware of the need to shore up and protect something that was disappearing. The end of the regional character of the economic, social, and political structures in Brazil, and the crisis of their regional cultural codes, invigorated the project to rethink and discover the region itself. It was a place created out of sentiment, of lyricism, of nostalgia (saudade), to embody something that never was. It was a terrain grounded in fable. It is thus not coincidental that "northeastern traditions" are regularly sought in fragments of a precapitalist, rural past. They hearken back to customs of patriarchy, even to slavery. The popular and folkloric are idealized; rustic handicrafts, not schooled art, represent the highest expression of a pastoral social tradition.[24]

The intellectual production of Luís da Câmara Cascudo stands out in this process of idealizing the popular elements of northeastern identity. In his work he adopted a static, museological interpretation of folklore that avoided questions of history or sociology. Rather, his researches consisted mostly of collections of material referring to the precapitalist, rural, "authentic" Northeast, with folklore posed as a shield against the encroachments of cosmopolitan culture. While Cascudo and many other folklorists presented themselves as defenders of folklore, paradoxically, they represented the greatest threat to it by insisting on its permanence and denying it the dynamic creativity to reinterpret contemporary issues. They believed that folklore could reveal the essence of the region because it was a set of emotional survivals: a constellation of prelogical elements based in communal affirmation. Folklore was the repository of the regional unconscious—the expression of the popular mentality, which for its part conveyed the regional mentality.[25]

In this discourse, the notion of the popular became confused with that of the traditional and antimodern. This facilitated the embrace of the Northeast's images and texts by the lower classes, who easily could recognize aspects of themselves within it. The construct of regional culture instituted the idea of solidarity, of a homogeneity between the "popular" cultural codes and those of the elites. But unlike the dominant sectors, the masses (*povo*) were defined as capable of only reacting to modernity.

Folklore could be therefore an interface, an element of integration between the people and the region. It opened channels of meaning, facilitating the absorption of regional identity by the people, and encouraging them to seek meaning in it. Within this traditionalist matrix, folklore took on a disciplining and educating function. It could contribute to forming a sensibility founded on the conservation of customs, habits, and conceptions, constructing new symbolic codes around them that avoided the trauma and conflict of modernizing sociability. It was recruited into inventing traditions—traditional ways to see, speak, act, and feel. In both producing the new and denying its novelty, affirming its timeless continuity, folklore provided another important hinge between past and present. It permitted the "perpetuation of states of spirit."[26]

This traditional Northeast was explored, described, and disseminated by diverse intellectuals and artists along the twentieth century: from Gilberto Freyre's "traditionalist school" in Recife, uniting authors such as José Lins do Rego and Ascenso Ferreira in the 1920s and 1930s, to the music of Luiz Gonzaga, Zé Dantas, and Humberto Teixeira starting in the 1940s. Ariano Suassuna contributed theatrical pieces in the 1950s. While there are significant stylistic differences among them, painters Cícero Dias and Lula Cardoso Ayres, the poet Manuel Bandeira, and novelists Rachel de Queiroz and José Américo de Almeida all share this vision of the Northeast and participated in its construction.

REGIONAL VISIBILITY AND SPEAKABILITY

Traditionalist artists and intellectuals gave substance to the visibility and speakability of the Northeast in their work with memory—efforts that might also be defined as the meticulous organization of the present, while the past was characterized by glories in remission. Discursively and artistically arranging such memories was a way to organize and give meaning to their own lives. To conceive of a new identity for their space was to conceive of a new identity for themselves. It was an elite in crisis, brought to the brink of effacement by history, and as such it became doggedly focused on subverting this history.

Traditionalist discourse grasped historical elements selectively to make history produce memory, as a discourse of reminiscence and of recognition. This memory would help subjects in the present recognize themselves in the facts of the past, and recognize a region already present there as well. Memory would link to history to become a process of affirmation for an identity, for continuity, and for tradition; it would uncover eternal truths that would in turn reveal the subjects as a regional community. The disruptive aspects of history were effused. Instead, history was incorporated into an ahistorical regional identity made of stereotypical images and texts of a moral character. Politics were viewed as destabilizing, but space was understood as stable, natural, above politics, and marked by only two dimensions: internal and external. The internal must be defended against the external, which connives to corrupt it. The internal must not plagued by contradiction.

This doubling in on itself of the Northeast in search of its own identity, soul, and truths proceeded apace alongside the unfolding of the dispositif of nationality, which posits as a necessity the extinguishing of regional differences and their integration into the nation. Within the Northeast, to call in protectionist language for the "survival of this space" was actually to call for the maintenance of threatened forms of domination. The region forms as a space defined by its closure to forces of change that come from outside it—from its "other," the urban-industrial space captained by São Paulo. The Northeast was a walling up of national space by an alliance of forces hoping to barricade itself from the processes of national integration emerging from the central South.

The Northeast of the regionalists and traditionalists is a place formed by and of depressing, decadent images. Change evokes existential bitterness. This quality runs through the work of José Lins do Rego and Manuel Bandeira. They devise evocative scenes of a traditional past slipping away, as in Bandeira's poem "My Land":

I left my land, a child
And spent thirty years away
Sometimes they would tell me
Your land is completely changed

It has avenues and skyscrapers . . .
Now it's a beautiful city!
My heart withered.
Finally I see my Recife
And it is utterly transformed
It has avenues and skyscrapers . . .
Now it's a beautiful city.
The devil take those who made my land beautiful.[27]

The romance writers of the 1930s made memory a principal theme. They constructed the Northeast through the lens of youthful memories of social relations now under duress. Their approach to narrative itself was to assert it as a traditional, popular cultural manifestation expressing regional reality, and likewise under threat from the modern world's machinations. It was very different from the modernist movement in São Paulo, in which writers attempted to transcend orthodox narrative to confront the crisis of the traditional novel in the modernist present. In the Northeast the movement was a retreat, an entrenchment. It looked back to "restore" popular narrative as a life-giving force for people facing the upheavals and social disarray of modernity. As an exploration of memory it would offer a preserve for identity. Traditional novels aspired to guarantee the continuity of what they narrated by suspending generations of readers in a world of regional memory.[28]

A region sewn together with the diaphanous threads of memory implicates a coexistence of extremes: on one hand, the idea of survival, and on the other, of the void. Images and texts of the past make it appear suffused in the surprised delight of rediscovery, to provoke both relief at its continuity and the sad awareness of its vulnerability. The romances of the 1930s revel in the celebration of memories, but the happiness is chilled with the dark undercurrents of awareness of time lost. The emphasis on memory was born of the urge to prolong the past, to extend it into the present and perhaps even the future. Traditionalist writers despised history because it established a split between dimensions of temporality. Recognition of the historicity of everything, its fleeting and mutable character, caused considerable anguish.[29]

This spatial memory, aesthetically rescued, would inspire the creation of a better future, one free of affectation and the South's drab bourgeois values. A region, made of memories to last forever, could be brought to life with the production of books and monuments, "typical" landscapes and characters, symbols. It would be a space without gaps or room for doubt—filled up with the images and texts that provided density and texture. Nothing would be transitory and everything would appear as solid as the old stone mansions, the ornate furniture carved from heavy native jacaranda wood; tranquility was in the breeze that made the hammock sway, in the slow social rhythms, in the families of affectionate grandparents and uncles and parents and infants.

A sentimental visibility based on the vaguely remembered childhood gaze characterizes the regionalist literature. It runs through the poetry of Ascenso Ferreira, who was also a pioneering artist interpreting modernism in Pernambuco. His vision of the Northeast, in his own words, "developed slowly as I came into contact with the many regional transients passing through or working the ranch of my uncle. There, men from many different places met and intermingled, bringing their field songs, their songs of the backlands, the dances of the coast or the interior, their guitars, their tales of haunted mansions and of hunting and fishing and of wandering the fields."[30]

Ferreira would recall his experiences later, his formative years between the frontier and city, when the works of Gilberto Freyre "awakened in me the love for our rural traditions." His take on modernist expression would ally itself with a traditional, popular vocabulary to constitute what he would term "a poetry communicating regional truths." He saw the Northeast as the place of genuine Brazilian sociability at risk from the incursions of "foreign civilization." His poems were intended to contribute to the preservation of the "waggish and pungent spirit of the Northeast, its festivals, plantations, the backlands." One will not find in his works, nor for that matter in the paintings of Cícero Dias, any suggestion of social critique or argument for social justice. They wanted instead to "comprehend the totality of northeastern life, distilling its pure essence, its soul as yet undefiled by modernity."[31]

To comprehend the "soul of this land" and discover his own identity was also the mission of José Lins do Rego. For him, organizing personal memory involved the same sources as organizing regional memory, and vice versa. The discovery of "regional psychology" was precisely the same as the discovery of the region itself, which implicated the discovery of his own identity as a person and an intellectual. The Northeast was an image of space and symbols internalized from his infancy in the Santa

Rosa plantation, property of Carlos de Melo and the dos Ricardos. A melancholy space full of shadows, a space of nostalgia.[32] Rego's initial impulse was to record the memories of his grandfather, to help ensure that new generations would not forget the men who had contributed to the glory of the region. That idea transformed into a series of novels whose themes were worked out under the influence of his friend Gilberto Freyre. It is in the pretension to be spontaneous revelations of truth that such writings on memory abandon their critical capacities. The author pretends to be impartial, when all the time his books expressed a specific way to see and comprehend reality (based on the ostensibly clear gaze of a boy growing up on a plantation). It was from the perspective of standing on the veranda of the main house, just as his grandfather did, that he would look and he would see the fields, "his land," the Northeast.[33]

A similar preoccupation with understanding the soul of the land and its spirituality, in all its supernatural and religious complexity, characterizes the poetry of Jorge de Lima. Regarding himself a regionally Catholic poet, Lima tried to unearth the darker roots of a northeastern mysticism that connected the sacred, the natural world, and the social sphere. His was a Northeast with a black soul, its spirituality transcending oppression in search of God's redemption; a place where mixture was the norm, in bloodlines, spiritualism, and social roles.

> There reside in my blood
> Three runaway maidens, two bandits
> One *candomblé* priest, two rogues, one machinist
> Two roustabouts.
> An Indian girl was born,
> A Brazilian girl,
> One with blue eyes:
> A first communion.[34]

Rachel de Queiroz, another regionalist writer, was concerned with the dichotomy between time and space. For her, space was stable while time was not. What happens in time disappears forever. Her work is weighted with the dour vision of the past as a finite, limited substance, a past that disappears over the course of one's life. Time is distressing for her because the only marks it leaves are memories; and the witnesses to those memories themselves are transformed and pass away with time. Humanity does not control time but suffers with it. Time walks through people, but people do not walk through time. The same time that makes people grow uses them up and deforms them. But space can serve as a repository of memory, she thought—a dimension easing time's continual sense of vertigo. Space could gather and conserve, stabilizing the human experience and defying time.[35]

Even in the danceable songs of Pernambuco's "king of the *baião*," musician Luiz Gonzaga, can we discern this modern sense of time's destructive character. But here it is sometimes carefully displaced or juxtaposed with a different idea of time, a regionalized, cyclical idea of time based in the supposed proximity of the Northeast to nature. Rather than cutting a straight line, time in the Northeast describes arcs, say between the hot droughts and the return of the rains with winter. The entire natural world, from people to livestock, plants, and minerals, participates in this cycle. Even for the migrants who abandon the Northeast, it hovers in the mind as a fixed space suffused in nostalgia. The migrants' vision clarifies this aspect of the Northeast's identity: it seems to exist in the past, in memory. It is a place everyone hopes to return to one day. A space that stays the same while everything around it transforms maddeningly, incessantly. Locales, loves, family, a favored horse, the fields, all are suspended in time awaiting the migrants' return, waiting just the way they were left. In the backlands, bonfires warm the passions of the heart in contended ignorance of the news and squabbles of "civilized" places.

Ah, if I could I'd return
To the arms of my sweetheart
This longing gnaws at my heart
More bitter than the tartest fruit
But nobody can attest
That they saw me sad and crying
Longing, my medicine is to sing.[36]

Ariano Suassuna, in his literary and dramatic works, also participated in the construction of the Northeast as a place of tradition. There memory was sacramental. There "a rustic aristocracy and the simple folk lived with each other in time and outside of time, occupying the same plane of particular, immediate interests." For Suassuna, time was a destructive dimension, a force like death, aridity, disease, and poor fortune that threatened the region he hoped to preserve. But inescapably, since the region was held as being outside time, its opposite, death, accompanied it everywhere. Death was its insignia, its brooding coat of arms.[37]

Suassuna's focus was the backlands, the "enchanted kingdom of the sertão." Neither the urban landscape nor the old plantations captivated him the way they did Gilberto Freyre. He located the authentic Northeast in the backlands, where there existed a regional "nobility, and not only crude prophets, lunatics, and filthy, bloodthirsty outlaws." He claimed this backwoods nobility was equal to that of the sugar aristocracy, but crucially lacking the latter's "malice and haughty affectations." It was a brutal and distressed kingdom that Suassuna identified with and devoted his writing to, making it a theme of his own existence as well as that of his imaginary, hardscrabble protagonists.[38]

In his fight against history, Suassuna envisioned the Northeast as a land of myths where the sacred held sway. Making use of the epic genre, of mythic narrative structures and the magical realism of popular *cordel* literature, he crafted his Northeast as an "epic, sacred, flag-bearing kingdom." He also drew on youthful reminiscences and a considerable amount of folk material to forge a space shot through with mystery, where the marvelous intermingled with cruel reality and thus heightened its meaning. But this was also a place that was directly linked to the medieval past of the Iberian Peninsula, with its exaggerated baroque flourishes and anti-Renaissance, antimodern attitudes. The speakability of this Northeast, the language that composed it, could be found in medieval Iberian theater as well as the local popular expressions that embodied its "archaic" forms. Suassuna's incorporation of cordel influences, its archaic language and fantastic assertions, provided yet more texture to his representation of the Northeast as a place where there was no barrier between the real and imaginary, between divine and pagan, between tragic and comic, between madness and rationality.[39]

The authors and artists I have addressed above developed distinct, highly individual bodies of work. But each in their way collaborated in fashioning a Northeast whose visibility and speakability were centered in memory, in a negative reaction to the modern, in a turn to the past as a temporal dimension spatialized. This Northeast would become its own generator of images and discourses that ultimately repudiated autonomy and inventiveness for custom and submission. Even if its authors did not see it as such, their discursive paradigm would function to prevent nordestinos from taking control of their own history, to face it and transform it. Instead, it imposed a ready-made history that naturalized the present injustice, discrimination, and misery. If the past was better than the present, and also represented the ideal for the future, the most obvious form of social action is to run from the present back to the traditions of a territory that advances of history seem able only to corrupt.

TRADITIONALIST REGIONALISM AND MODERNISM

The regionalist and traditionalist movement in Recife had its origins in the foundation of the Northeastern Regionalist Center in 1924. This brought together not only intellectuals steeped in art and culture but additionally those focused on the more pragmatic stuff of politics. But after the 1926 Regionalist Conference, at which Gilberto Freyre was a principal influence, the movement definitively took on the character of an artistic and cultural initiative dedicated to rescuing and preserving northeastern traditions.

Freyre's regionalism was of a different type than I explored in the previous section. It went beyond ideological justifications for conserving a threatened memory-based imaginary to create a new way to see, know, and speak reality, and it was possible only with the emergence of the nation as a major problem demanding a response. Regionalism was redefined and amplified: it brought together the picturesque artistic representation of local experience and the political struggle for territorial legitimacy, connecting the projects and transcending the limitations of each. Cultural production would shed its preference for the exotic to lend the region a coherent cultural formulation that could, in turn, engage political meanings. Traditionalist intellectuals would need to recast their activity as a mission to raise regional awareness and unite the people around it. In this paradigm, regionalism would integrate not only images and texts related to the space of the Northeast, but also its currents and forces, channeling them into an entity that was culturally, aesthetically, and politically united.

Before the 1920s, regionalism was not in dialogue with sociology. Put another way, the sociologically instituted region had not yet appeared. The region would only come to be viewed as a social and cultural reality within a new discursive formation, and it was at this moment that Gilberto Freyre's sociological definition of regionalism became possible.[40] It was still impressionistic in outline, its forms assimilated between a dimly glimpsed past and a confused, agitated present. It aimed for a poetics of space that could reduce actual spatial-sociocultural diversity to a series of semblances of type and characteristic realities. Freyre hoped to establish a set of truths through assembling representative figures (for example, the sturdy landowner in the spotless suit, the simple seamstress, the robust ox driver). He staged the contemporary region as historical drama, a theatrical synthesis of the entire social structure, including culture and nature. This Northeast was not a static catalogue of natural descriptions or of social evaluations but a qualitative elaboration, a suite in many movements resolved harmoniously. A Northeast that was a cultural being, an attitude, "a personality, an ethos."[41]

This new regionalism was described by José Lins do Rego as a search for the unity of everything, based on a close examination of component parts. It emerged from the political practices that had sketched the region as a weapon to be marshaled against the excesses of political and economic centralization in Brazil; it was a reaction to the centralizing processes of capitalist development itself. It asserted the fact of diversity, although in a reactionary way, because it summoned the return of the past and hence the paralysis of history. It called not for creativity and for distinction based on invention, but for a conservative statement of difference, an enclosure of difference.[42]

For Rego, this was a truly innovative enterprise. Its novelty was not founded on the trick of mere linguistic extravagance, nor on the hayseed sentiments of Monteiro Lobato, nor even on superficial nostalgia. It had a vision. It would be, on the political plane, contrary to state-centric federalism. In the artistic realm, it would "plumb the depths of the soul of the people, in the fonts of folklore." It would be an organic regionalism, revealing truths, stimulating the vitality of "Brazilian character" and hence strengthening true Brazilian unity by helping form a collective that recognized its differences.[43]

Traditionalist regionalism did not have the same preoccupation with research that the modernists did. José Lins do Rego justified this apparent weakness or simplicity by affirming that the movement sought to address the public more directly in terms they could understand. He condemned what he called the "artificial language" of Mário and Oswald de Andrade, their pursuit of idiosyncratic brilliance, because it made that much more complicated the production "of something permanent and lasting in terms of modernist literature." Oswald de Andrade, himself a vociferous critic of northeastern romance writers including Rego, retorted that this so-called new regionalism was a regrettable step backward in terms of literary concept and expression.[44]

Freyre did not steer clear of this debate, although his interjection was somewhat odd. He accused the modernists of having abandoned any anthropological, sociological, or historical concern with the Northeast (and even with Brazil itself). He suggested that they "scorned Brazilian traditions" and "showed disregard for the things of the nation's past, such as colonial art." But the modernists had been deeply engaged with the question of tradition. They perceived it in a more multiplanar form as something not yet systematized, something that modernism could help vitalize and reelaborate, rather than what they implied was the sort of "tradition" Freyre preferred: a host of musty folkloric artifacts enshrined in a museum.[45]

To Freyre, nationality was rooted in tradition; hence he regarded the modernists as a denationalizing force, perhaps even contrary to the nation, since they did not seem interested in "national tradition" in a form he concurred with. José Lins do Rego, whose own thinking was intimately influenced by Freyre's (and whose literary inventions of the Northeast were parallel to and resonant with Freyre's sociological ones), argued that the modernists had essentially done little more than make a lot of noise, gratify some elite cosmopolitan snobs, and knock over a few sacred cows to be quickly replaced with others. They were a bunch of "mundane Parisian fops." Modernist fiction, "writing turned inside out, to be savored by a thin erudite stratum," was nothing like Northeast fiction: fiction that was "vigorous, that comes from the earth, from the soul of the people, simple and direct the same as they are. A production that links the modern to the eternal, to the strains of an old melancholy song."[46]

Both Rego and Freyre strove to assert the authenticity of the regionalist and traditionalist movement, in part by articulating its autonomy from the modernists in São Paulo. They denounced the centrality of the 1922 Modern Art Week in recent Brazilian history and the mass media, which were too keen to identify every interesting new cultural development as a consequence of it. Rego flatly denied that his own writing had been influenced at all by the modernists, citing instead his close working relationship with Freyre as formative. He queried how a movement he characterized as a "transitory agitation" could have such broad and deep consequences. He went even further, referring to the movement as "rubbish, a bit of knavery that the genius of Oswald de Andrade devised to entertain his millionaire partners." Leaving aside the arch tone from one who was himself the son of a (ruined) millionaire, what was driving the dispute was also a regional confrontation stirring between the Northeast and São Paulo. After all, while regionalism was claimed as the patrimony of the nordestinos, a central South regionalism was also clear throughout the modernist criticism of northeastern fiction—a genre Oswald derisively referred to as "buffalo stories from the Northeast."[47]

To Freyre, the Northeast would become culturally fertile and creative if it could recuperate its genuine traditions and focus on regional unity, not the arbitrary divisions of state boundaries. But implicitly, and sometimes openly, his intentions were to unify regional discourse around the base of his native Pernambuco. Nonetheless, he argued that regionalism was a reaction to the processes of standardization afflicting daily life, processes that were a symptom of imperialism; and a medium of resistance to the supposed cultural superiority of these foreign but homogenizing influences. Regionalism was therefore important to the nation, an attitude of defiance toward the cultural colonization of Brazil. The processes of modernization and their bourgeois flavor had the sheen of nationalism but were in truth corruptors of Brazil's national identity. Because cultural debate and cultural influence were stronger at the level of region, it was there that the concerted defense against colonialism ought to be mounted, and not at the level of the nation—because this was an artifice, a political abstract without a foundation in cultural reality.[48]

Freyre employed the term "modernist" to classify all those intellectuals and cultural practices he believed were transforming Brazil into a poor copy of Europe and Westernizing its customs. Parsing a distinction between modern and modernist, he maintained that his vision of regionalism was modern, but certainly not modernist (which would imply the reification of one moment of modernity). The modern could change form although its content was maintained. Brazilian culture should integrate not just a rarified variant of Europe but extra-European elements; here he had in mind Portugal, a place where people and culture were miscegenated, embodying a bridge between East and West, between Africa and the Americas.[49] The Northeast would be this region that was not specifically European, as São Paulo was becoming, but a place of mixture, genuinely Brazilian. From the Northeast would emerge a movement to renovate Brazilian arts and letters, a movement with its own ecological properties. The traditions that developed in the shadow of the plantation big house and slave shacks, and within the churches—the traditions rooted in ostensibly affectionate coexistence and social contact between whites, blacks, and Indians—would prove the true national substrate of Brazilian culture.[50]

In this traditionalist view, the region would provide the matrix or interface through which the popular sectors would connect to the nation, providing the forms of expression of a noncolonized culture to underwrite national culture. This is not too different from how the modernists conceived of how the nation would emerge culturally. But rather than concern ourselves with byzantine discussions over which movement was first with what argument, or which movement influenced the other and how, we might simply note that each was dealing with the same field of visibility and speakability and the same codes of sensibility regarding both national space and the function of culture and the arts. They were trying to respond to the same cultural problems. From that perspective, the furious scuffle between Pernambucans Joaquim Inojosa and Gilberto Freyre over the origin of the modern influence in Pernambucan arts (that is, over the greater prevalence of São Paulo–based modernism versus traditionalist regionalism) is understandable but not overly important.[51] In the 1940s, when modernism seemed to have won the internal battle over degrees of prominence and influence—but was also, notably, a thing of the past—and the regional questions intersecting it were displaced politically by the nationalist interventions of the New State, struggles over the spoils of modernism in the Northeast were heating up. It was a carnival of personalities and egos battling over the construction of a memory of modernism, grounded in regional space.[52]

It does appear that Inojosa made an early maneuver to translate paulista modernism for people in Pernambuco with his publication there of an article called "What Futurism Is."[53] He had been involved with São Paulo's Modern Art Week in February 1922 and had participated in the First International Student Congress in Rio de Janeiro marking the centenary of Brazilian independence. As a journalist for *Klaxon* magazine in Pernambuco, Inojosa intended to "preach the new creed among the local savants." He also wrote for Recife's *Jornal do Comércio*, which belonged to the Pessoa de Queiroz family; they were critics of the Republican and Autonomist movements and rivals of the oligarchy led by Maoel Borba. On the other side of the political front, José Lins do Rego founded the serial *Dom Casmurro*, a pamphlet dedicated to overthrowing the Pessoa cartel and supporting autonomist efforts in Pernambuco. In this atmosphere, cultural movements intersected with political questions at the national as well as local levels. While the modernists had been in favor of the federal government's "moralizing" intervention in the states, the traditionalist regionalists hearkened back philosophically to the founding of the Regionalist Center and its concerns with "the strengthening of autonomy, the defense of the region against excessive political centralization, and the rebuke of economic favoritism shown to other areas."[54]

In 1923 Inojosa founded the magazine *Revista Mauriceia*, with a name recalling the title of a poem by Mário de Andrade. That publication was the venue for a range of articles from new adepts of modernism such as the poets Austro-Costa and Joaquim Cardoso, who made Recife the basis of their ideas. Inojosa also communicated his views in the nearby state of Paraíba through a letter written for *Era Nova*, a magazine there later relaunched to great success as *A Arte Moderna*. Influential modernists in Paraíba such as José Américo de Almeida made a few criticisms of his text but received it with great enthusiasm. Almeida is often mentioned as an important pioneer of northeastern modernism through his books *A Paraíba e Seus Problemas* and *Reflexões de uma Cabra*.[55] Inojosa went on to write for *Brasil Brasileiro*, where he more openly admonished the traditionalists for being absorbed with past glories rather than confronting contemporary Brazilian circumstances. He also emphasized the need for a nationalist culture without internally imposed cleavages given the threats to solidarity between nations that were associated with the First World War.[56]

Gilberto Freyre, almost the minute he returned to Recife from his studies in the United States in 1923, dashed off a rebuke of modernism from the perspective of traditionalism to one of Pernambuco's main papers. His stature grew with the Regionalist Conference of 1926 and the Afro-Brazilian Congress of 1928. The press in São Paulo gave prodigious exposure to both events and Freyre's role in them, although that exposure was sometimes inflected by a journalistic urge to incite controversy. Still, the national press record disproves the assertion made by paulista critic and historian of modernism Wilson Martins that the traditionalist movement linked with Freyre had no profile or repercussions beyond the "frontiers of the province."[57]

But even before that, Freyre had published pieces lauding Pernambucan tradition from his vantage point in the United States; his series "From the Other America" was written between 1918 and 1922. Paradoxically or not, it was the precise period that Freyre spent far away from Pernambuco that lay the foundation for his coalescing Pernambuco-centric regionalist thought. During his studies he encountered the regionalist work of Japanese-born Lafcádio Hearn, whose influences merged with those of the Portuguese integralists, the French regionalist Maurras, Franz Boas, and the modernist painters Joaquim and Vicente do Rego Monteiro (whom Freyre met in Paris). Far from home, the young Freyre was wading in deep intellectual currents that would help him reformulate his relationship to it. Freyre had also admired the Recife-born writer Mário Sette, whose books *Senhora de Engenho* (1921) and *Palanquim Dourado* (1923) he praised for their "regionalist spirit" in his 1923 submission to the *Diário*. Inojosa, ever watchful for opportunities to detract from Freyre's reputation as a pioneer, also warmly extolled Sette for instituting the regionalist and traditionalist vision in northeastern literature.[58]

The regionalists and traditionalists were different from the modernists in that they embraced the past as a simple spectacle, avoiding the fact that selection of any one tradition over another as more worthy of rescuing and following had an inherent political dimension. The (ambiguous) distinction between modern form and traditional content, and the criticism of bourgeois ethics and sociability, were not the intellectual domain of the regionalists exclusively; they also were present in the more conservative wing of paulista modernism. If we believe that these two movements were independent of and antithetical to each other, we accept the false image they hoped to construct for themselves as intellectually air-tight entities rather than perceiving how deeply interactive was their dispute over cultural hegemony at both the regional and national levels. They were cultural movements that defended the dominance of different regional spaces, but using the same discursive field. They revolved around the same themes, assumptions, strategies, and problems.[59]

THE NORTHEAST AS SOCIOLOGICAL INSTITUTION

To the same degree that the naturalist paradigm with its biological and evolutionary bases was entering into crisis, sociology's focus on social and cultural problems rose in importance as a mode of inquiry to help define Brazilian identity including its regions and regional types. Imperialist expansion and World War I stimulated research into "exotic," non-European societies. The problems of acculturation and cultural identity received new prominence, sparking studies by not only sociologists but anthropologists and ethnographers. The goal was to understand the psychology of these diverse peoples and the presumed "laws" that underlay their societies.[60]

It was within this context that Franz Boas developed his cultural formulations as a counter to the racist naturalism of Arthur de Gobineau. He strongly critiqued the use of race-based methods such as biopsychology and anthropological geography to arrive at some general characteristics of a given people. Boas also stressed the implicit ethnocentrism of most European studies of non-European and nonwhite peoples. He brought to sociology a keen sense of cultural relativism.

Gilberto Freyre is understood to have been a disciple of Boas, although the former's sociology was perhaps less relativist than Boas might have preferred. Freyre occupied something of a middle ground. He believed there were characteristics of peoples that emerged through the interactions between races and nature; but whether or not these represented a sort of environmental determinism, it was their expression in the social and cultural spheres that interested him. He thought that Brazilian society could be characterized not by racial mixture alone, but by the particular manifestation of cultural miscegenation that followed from it. It was in the area of culture that he hoped to comprehend Brazilian national identity and the contribution of region to the Brazilian national formation.[61]

For Freyre, region was the basis for beginning to think about the nation. The regional perspective should guide studies in sociology and history because region was the spatial frame most approximate to the natural environment, shaping a society and its customs. Region was the initial building block of social space, its genetics. Freyre even referred to his discipline as genetic sociology, and he made region—alongside tradition, understood in regional terms—the parameters for interpreting Brazilian society. His work would represent the extension or amplification of a personal memory and experience, as well as the memory and experience of a given group in a given space.[62]

Freyre's sociology was an attempt to understand Brazil's differences with respect to the civilizing processes of the West. He used what he called "authentically regional, traditional, and tropical" evidence to unearth the processes of Brazilian uniqueness as well as show how Brazil was integrated into a larger, non-European world. He structurally opposed the tropics to Europe and sought within Brazil the social dynamics that fostered its singularity. It was in this larger construct of ideas that he would adopt the region, specifically the Northeast, as the substructure for sociological analysis.

His approach was experimental, transitional between paradigms. For this reason, he was in constant dialogue with older systems of knowledge—announcing his departures from them while also reproducing some of their themes and perspectives. For instance, even as he rejected the use of racial objectivism or ethnic atavism, he also fell back on that rhetoric (as with his claims of the Jewish origin of the mercantile impulse in Brazil). His principal argument, that of the superiority of the mixed-blood *mestiço*, is also an attempt to reconcile an emerging theoretical apparatus with received, established concepts.

A sociological approach to the Northeast would have to question the hierarchies ostensibly imposed by nature and race, and as part of that, deconstruct the assumed superiority of "white" nations and regions over "nonwhite" ones. Freyre's strategy was not to come up with entirely new ways to conceive of these categories, but to invert the formulation so that mestiços were given pride of place over races imagined as constrained by their purity. This was a solution to the fact that Brazilian nationality could not be associated with a single race because Brazil incorporated numerous races and their hybrid offspring. From that angle everyone in Brazil was a mestiço, including the Portuguese who initiated this civilization in the tropics.[63]

Freyre inaugurated a discourse that, by revalorizing the mestiço, at the same time gave new value to his particular space that was so evidently marked by miscegenation. He firmly contested the allegation of mestiço inferiority—that they were inept at mechanical or fine technical work. He also denied that any innate limitations fed into their apparent troubles adjusting to new global economic exigencies, attributing that rather to an educational system that was insufficient in content and that urged the maintenance of troubling aristocratic social systems. The fact that Brazil existed at all, its agriculture and its cities and its generally harmonious social relations, demonstrated the true capacity of mestiços starting again with the Portuguese colonizers.[64]

Freyre maintained that racial differentiation was only meaningful in terms of how it expressed a division based on class or on regional differentiation, since the hierarchy of colors and classes could vary according to the internal dynamics of each region. Regional circumstances could modify interactions between or expressions of race and class, as they had done since the colonial period; regions were cultural and mental configurations that reached deeper and had a greater determinative power on society than any environmental influences.

In that way, Freyre gracefully skirted debates around class or racial conflict to reframe the problem as regional conflicts between cultures. Although he never denied the existence of class struggle in Brazil, Freyre tended to deemphasize race and class as meaningful signifiers or subjectivities. For example, he took the historical fact of slave uprisings as expressing something beyond racial conflict, or class conflict: it was a struggle between mentalities and cultures. If race could be conceived as dynamic, culture was even more so. Culture could never serve as a static foundation on which societies grew. It was in the social and cultural fields that resided the distinctions and antipathies that generated attitudes of rivalry between regions, which could be exacerbated by regional imbalances in technological progress. Industrial development, at least as much as ecological atmosphere, accentuated difference and inequality.[65]

Still, Freyre was among the founders of a novel discursive regime that attempted to modify the negativity associated with the environment in Brazil, especially regarding the Northeast. In emphasizing the impact of the Portuguese in the tropical new world as a civilizing one, he inverted the naturalist declaration that the tropics were antagonistic to the development of civilization. His initiative was not roundly hailed, however. Paulo Prado countered with an argument that the inherited effects of the environment were responsible for the Brazilians being taciturn, melancholy, suspicious, and nervous. Where Prado argued that its tropical environment condemned Brazil to weakness as a nation, Freyre believed the environment lent Brazilian civilization a distinctive identity and robust character.

A significant contribution of Freyre's thought was in recognizing the importance of the participation of Afro-Brazilians in the processes of "national formation." While he seemed to constrain their role to that of docile assistant, he still asserted their importance to Brazil's economy and culture and did not try to deny that slavery was a violent institution that had had deleterious effects and stimulated resistance and revolt. He had to address slavery and race relations in one form or another, since for him the cradle of Brazilian civilization was the sugar society of the Northeast that had relied on blacks' forced labor. He suggested that the structure of this "rural and patriarchal society" guaranteed both perfect control of the black population, and the "docile" relations between master and slave. It was thus in other milieus—the cities, or the coffee plantations in São Paulo—that there were conflicts between slaves and society. This idea was based on two factors: the presence of more mixed-blood people, who were agitated and unstable, lacking a clear role in the traditional patriarchal system composed of masters and slaves; and the nature of forced labor in the central South, described as more mercilessly mercantilist and violent than it was in the Northeast.[66]

Working in a juncture in which the scientific, naturalist discourse had not been separated off from literary discourse (following from the reduced division of intellectual labor in the country), Freyre reached for images to help convey the fragmentation, hybridity, and disorder that Brazil's circumstances implied. They were symbolic, not allegorical images, and intended to resolve the lack of fit between form and content— between the empiricism of daily life and its extrapolation to national interpretation.[67]

This flexible vision of reality resonated with Freyre's essential political posture: to defuse conflicts with harmony, and transcend conflict through a conciliating interpenetration of opposites. Far from conceiving of a dialectic in which synthesis would mean the negation of one side or the other, he prized the establishment of an amiable continuum through concrete logic that would function to dissolve abstract antagonism.[68]

This search for accord was of a piece with the search for permanence, the mutual maintenance of order, and it is in this way that the contours of Freyre's work were shaped more by space than by time. He was obsessed with the divisions and constitutions of space, as well as space's transformation—an ecology of space's dominion and occupation. He was constantly attentive to the relations between power and spatiality, and to the imbalances in harmony between the natural, social, and cultural elements that composed this dimension of the real.[69] For this reason, he elevated patriarchal society as the ideal example of sociability in which conflict was avoided, and power relations based in the relations among individuals instead of impersonal classes, groups, or social institutions. It was not a depersonalized system such as that characterizing bourgeois sociability: conflicts were organically defused rather than integrated into the texture of life. The city was revealed as a den of hedonism and moral laxity, of the celebration of imported and artificial customs, of the embrace of elements corrosive to the national character and traditional codes he understood as Brazilian.[70]

Modernization and "progress" are viewed by Freyre as forces that disrupt social equilibrium. Capitalism, the relations of production and consumption, bourgeois political and social institutions, and bourgeois sensibility and culture are considered destructive to nationality. For Freyre, the nation was not a capitalist, rational space to be improved on but a space of traditions to be cultivated, that offered the promise of progress along the deep grooves of time-worn order. It was a space that connected past, present, and future in a single continuum, or that assured the construction of a future that had a commitment to the past; in other words, a commitment to those parties and interests dominant in the old regime. His emphasis was always on the necessity for smooth, measured transitions between the different temporalities without any harsh edges, an accommodation of the present to the past and the future. His sociology was ultimately the search for historical constants that intersected Brazil's processes of formation.[71]

One of these would be the patriarchal family, which existed throughout the country's history and its regions. The patriarchal estate as an economic enterprise and a social and cultural organization, based on the leadership of the white aristocracy and the decisive participation (starting with their labor) of the blacks, was responsible for the formation of the unique "Brazilian personality." Freyre called attention to the fact that across the regional differentiation of colonization and Brazil's ensuing history as a republic, its familial character was the only shared constant, the most consistent mark of unity. As a primary institution of power, of economic, political, and moral influence in the nation's history, the family had a civilizing function. It provided the sociological element to Brazilian unity, through its articulations of diverse regional pasts into one "comprehensively national past, characteristically *luso-afro-ameríndio* in its principal traits of cultural composition and social expression."[72]

In a trilogy of ambitious books including *The Masters and the Slaves* (*Casa-Grande e Senzala*, 1933), *The Mansions and the Shanties* (*Sobrados e Mocambos*, 1936), and *Order and Progress* (*Ordem e Progresso*, 1959), Freyre delved into the history of sugar production in the Northeast—more specifically Pernambuco—and generalized from it a social and cultural analysis of Brazil's entire colonial experience. In Pernambuco's sugar society he encountered the original genetic material of Brazilian civilization, as well as a framework of social constants that continued to characterize and orient contemporary Brazil. In his view, it was the collapse of this paradigmatic society that gave rise to the process of disequilibrium among all Brazil's regions. The sociological thrust of his project was to explain and denounce this lack of consonance between regions, as well as to make a case for the necessity of reestablishing the harmony lost. The collapse of original society made possible other potential new markers of regional differentiation, such as differences in the soil, landscape, and weather, as well as patterns of economic activity. He saw regional division as more than a physical or geographic boundary, or rather, prior to those visible "proofs"; region is first made possible by specific ways of life, culture, and sociability.[73]

For Freyre, the nation emerged as a pact among regions agreeing to establish its reality, although it should guarantee the continued existence of both the distinct spaces within it and the dominant groups within each. Consciousness of difference is not effaced or ignored but subjugated to the logic of shared identity. Nation provided a new way to restore the equilibrium lost, a solution to the fragmenting of Brazil's original society.[74]

Freyre addressed the sociological institutionalization of the Northeast more directly in Northeast (Nordeste, 1937). His preface made clear his political objective: "To make Brazilians aware of a spatial entity that began to be sociologically corrupted. To provide a warning call against the unraveling of the federation" through the unequal concentration of power and investments in a few favored states.[75]

He also outlined the physiognomy of the agrarian Northeast, "center of Brazilian civilization": The relations between man and the soil, the natives, the water, plants, and animals; the adaptation of the Portuguese and the African to the new environmental and social milieu. It was a historical approach intending to reveal the region's processes of formation, which would also explain to a greater or lesser degree the other states in the union (as they fell away from or degraded its model). The region was portrayed as based on the monoculture of large estates worked by slaves, and in that sense monosexual—it was the noble man of the plantation who more or less by himself produced economic benefits and established the web of amiable social relations. The region had an aquiline profile, aristocratic and chivalrous, even if the aristocracy included elements of the sadistic and morbid.[76]

The Northeast's psychological unity was fostered by life on the plantations, a life of extremes. The Northeast as Freyre imagined it had a landscape ennobled by chapels and crosses, by the stately big house, by horses of fine breed, and by statuesque palms. But at the same time it was deformed by monoculture and the forced labor of slaves, its grassy meadows devastated, its waters dried up or polluted. The Northeast was a vortex, in which the disappearance of fine soil by erosion and of native plants by burns to expand sugarcane seemed to contradict what was ostensibly its greatest mark of permanence: nature, the landscape of the space itself. For Freyre, the physical degradation of the Northeast was one of the indices of the decadence of traditional society. The search for social equilibrium, for permanence and stability, thus had a component of natural conservation. The state of the rivers had symbolic power. Freyre extolled the presence of rivers once untouched by dams, diversions, or waste, constant in their flow, friendly generators of natural motion and of sediment for early families of sugar cultivators. But the rivers had been fouled by new generations of senhores with their filthy factories and disrespect for nature; the suffering waterways became for Freyre both symbol and proof of social decadence. These men with their backs to the river, with their disregard for the region's proud past, threatened to definitively impoverish the Northeast. Freyre wanted to restore the Northeast as it was before the expansion in scale of the smoke-belching sugar factories with their reeking cauldrons, the "progress," the destructive affectations that were changing traditional social relations. Against the stark image of a Northeast rotted out by capitalism, Freyre posed the primordial image of Northeast as garden, as orchard, a space where man and nature cared for each other and protected each other among the fragrant fruit trees and affable tufts of sugarcane.[77]

Freyre recognized the environmental and historical diversity within the Northeast, notably its dry interior, but emphasized the visual and discursive unity of the coast and its sugar economy—even though it was precisely the "other" Northeast of drought and inhospitable terrain that would be adopted by those whose strategy was to denounce the region's social conditions. The Northeast of the sugar plantations served more prominently in the project to rescue a past of power and harmony that would compensate for, and provide a way out of, the growing social problems and decadence afflicting contemporary Brazil. It was a space that withheld its traditions and sense of self, that did not radically break with the past but maintained possible the idea of a society internally governed by older values. A space that maintained networks of traditional domination that should not be altered. Yet it was accommodating, integrative; it did not vex or provoke conflict. The sweetness of preserved domination and lifeways on the littoral was contrasted with the earth's grating and the bellicose disorder in the searing interior. There, amiable relations exemplified along the coast were strained by the excesses of capitalism, and the stern senhores in the patriarchies exploited masses of the poor and enslaved. Clearly, Freyre's idealization of a particular Northeast required considerable maneuvering to separate it out from all the other geo-conceptual possibilities.[78]

Freyre's sociological construction of the Northeast is oriented by a political goal: the defense of conciliation, and the condemnation of bourgeois society and the conflicts it provokes. His Northeast was based on a speakability and visibility intended to dissolve social, regional, and cultural contradictions by first making them explicit, then diluting or annulling them aesthetically. He indicted the cultural alienation introduced by modernity, defending the integrity of the great house (and even of the slave quarters) as more authentic than skyscrapers. His utopia was the return of an idealized society in which technical advancement was not necessarily an enemy of tradition, if it was diligently controlled; in which tradition and modernity strolled together, the latter supported and guided by the firm masculine arm of the former.[79]

IDENTITY AND THE OTHER'S GAZE

The sociological and historical institution of the Northeast did not arise only internally, from among its self-defined regional intellectuals, but it was also elaborated as part of a discourse about itself and its opposite, the South. The Northeast was invented with considerable input from the South, where intellectuals avidly disputed their regional neighbors over hegemonic title to historical and sociological discourses.

The origin story of Brazilian nationality was sought within the history of each of these spaces. Regional tensions can be traced across the historiography of the nation, which was compiled to establish the prevalence of one area and one "regional type" in the construction of Brazil and its people. It is remarkable how this literature tends to step lightly around the questions, problems, and characteristics of each region's present-day situation to focus on its identity as grounded in the past. Far from producing generally empirical arguments, it generated instead a mythology framed around each region, salted with historical events and individuals that were affirmed as precursors of nationality, the founding heroes of Brazil. As mythologies they have a wide grasp, drawing on historical memory, folklore, popular narrative, and the personal recollections of their authors. Each region is an ensemble of imagetic-enunciative fragments that were assembled around an initially abstract spatialized idea.[80]

In the South, starting in the 1920s, national identity began to be conceived around several antagonistic poles. São Paulo, Pernambuco, and Bahia were regarded as each having claims to being the initial cellular material of national tissue. Historiographical discourse centered on the history of these three areas to compose the history of Brazil. Origin myths were created and diffused by intellectuals from each pole, affirming and explaining their regional differences from the national whole—deepening the contours of each case of regional distinctiveness while still placing it in the center of Brazil's historical processes of formation.

A shared theme in this literature was the opposition between nomadism and sedentariness. Colonial Brazil was sketched according to this framework, with the perspective changing according to regional position. If São Paulo is raised as the dynamic center of colonial Brazil, nomadism is emphasized, while the opposite is true from the point of view of the Northeast. But each pole also explored nomadism in another, centrifugal sense: the dispiriting tendency of Brazilians to move around and leave no roots, without creating anything solid, complicating the realization of national potential.[81]

For Freyre, the plantation owner (*senhor do engenho*) provided one of the few examples of sociocultural concentration that lent density to nationality. The notorious bandits, even if some of them conquered riches and land, still compromised the colony's economic health and might have destabilized political unity if it had not been for forces linked to the large estates, especially the church (since Catholicism was understood as part of the cement of Brazilian unity). But critically, Freyre suggested the origin of banditry lay outside the Northeast itself. There, the Portuguese and their descendants regressed to a form of feudalism through their aristocratic methods of colonization, leading to a greater attachment to settling on the land; whereas in São Paulo it was the adventurers and explorers, feeling no sentimental connection to the land, that ultimately gave rise to the modern bandit.[82]

If those restless southern adventurers, the famous *bandeirantes*, had widened Brazil's frontiers through their nomadic impulses, it was the sedentary northeasterners ensconced in their estates that gave those frontiers meaning. The northeasterners gave content to the country, constructing its social and political territory, laying the foundation for "houses that were nearly forts, where they felt so self-sufficient that it became nearly possible to create their own country with its own set of borders and frontiers—all born of the desire for stability and permanence." They would have crystallized the country out of slabs of cane sugar if they could have. Both the empire and independence from it drew sustenance from these families led by noble agricultural men, "barons of a feudal lifestyle, patriarchal, devoted to God and the emperor."[83]

Not surprisingly, the supposedly exclusive nature of the northeastern plantation elite's aristocratic character was a point of discord between northern and southern intellectuals. For instance, Oliveira Vianna argued that the same pomp and finery of Pernambuco's colonial mansions could be found in São Paulo. He maintained that there was a paulista aristocracy and that it derived from noble Portuguese families as well as some plebeians who had made their fortune in the colony. Freyre would have none of that, however. He countered that São Paulo's population derived from ranks of humbler Portuguese, their bloodlines mixed with Moors and Jews. Unfortunately for Vianna, his thesis of a noble origin in São Paulo was not unanimously embraced by his fellow paulista intellectuals. Cassiano Ricardo and Alcântara Machado were more focused on the centrality, and complexity, of the figure of the bandeirante for São Paulo. These were "poor men, of rustic or even crude manners, living nearly in indigence, hard on themselves and demanding of their fellows." São Paulo's present wealth was thus opposed favorably to the poverty of its unsophisticated origins—a construct that usefully reinforced the image of a decadent, fallen Northeast where the riches of the past stood in contrast to the crisis of the present.[84]

Ricardo believed that the Brazilian "type" emerged through the biological democratization that transformed the patriarchal Christian family in São Paulo. This racial democracy led to a wider tendency toward social democracy there, unlike in the Northeast, where the family maintained the rigid air of aristocracy. Reversing Freyre's trope of aristocracy as a positive trait of the northeastern past, Ricardo attributed the origins of Brazilian democratic individualism to the more open, democratic nature of family life in São Paulo. Where aristocracy emerged or held out, he argued, it was contrary to the salutary democratic trend. Thus where Ricardo cited the traditional patriarchal family as facilitating the onset of a "bourgeois spirit" in Brazil, Freyre had argued the opposite, that it was a bulwark against that very spirit. Depending on the nationalist project of each intellectual, and the space they represented, the history of Brazil could be read and interpreted in diverse forms.[85]

For his part, Roger Bastide, a French intellectual, also pondered the history and identity of Brazil from the perspective of a scission between São Paulo and the Northeast. He regarded the Northeast as characterized by archaic norms of social relations, of affectionate solidarity and community labor, and the maintenance of a prebourgeoisie sensibility and ethics. This was not a derogatory judgment. The region's work of conciliation, of harmonizing technological development, of integrating capitalist modernization with communal patterns of coexistence, were for Bastide highly original and important contributions of the Northeast to Brazil. As he does throughout his oeuvre, Bastide described the situation in terms of sharp contrasts, but when he praised the Brazilian capacity to reconcile polarities he was praising what he understood as a primordially northeastern trait. He admired the nordestinos for their ability to found cultures and races, to transcend barriers between the past and present and between the archaic and the modern.[86]

Brazil was therefore a double country: the South boasted intelligence, practicality, and a commitment to reality, while the Northeast was imaginative and sensitive, prone to fantasy and mysticism. Reason and emotion, the basic dualistic dilemma of Brazilian national identity, became embodied in regional division. For Menotti del Picchia, the legacy of the bandeirante in São Paulo ran deep. Paulistas were adventurous, autonomous, rebellious, the perfect traits to explore and dominate new territories. They had discarded the known, including the familiar coasts, to plunge into the unknown interior. However, the nordestino's cultural heritage resulted in a poor copy of this robust, productive vitality. Denizens of the Northeast's interior were engaged in a constant battle with the environment. Their hardness was based on bitterness, on the inability to dominate; they wandered, unable to put down roots, lacking the organic capacity to institute enduring civilization. Freyre saw in the nordestino, or more specifically the Pernambucano, the same taste the paulista supposedly had for initiative, discovery, innovation, colonization. But of course, his interpretation of the character and civilizing influence of the sugar elite's activities was not broadly embraced. None other than Sérgio Buarqe de Holanda disputed Freyre's assertion, claiming that the limits of the "adventurous spirit" of Freyre's plantation master were reached in exploitative agriculture pursued carelessly and wastefully, along with a marked aversion to physical or otherwise productive labor.[87]

In the vast majority of cases in this literature, São Paulo is seen as the area of modern, urban-industrial culture, a reading that omits its strong foundation of traditional culture as well as the social-cultural reality of the vast fields and agricultural regimes linked to it. And for the Northeast, that scheme is reversed: it is imagined as a rural region, a state of nature whose cities (among them some of Brazil's oldest and largest) are neglected outright in terms of both their scientific and artistic production. When northeastern cities are discussed, they appear to have frozen, not in the colonial period exactly, but in some later dollhouse concept of it—they are folkloric, picturesque, placid, happy cities, full of sunlight and talk of horses and of the harvest, cities composed of exorbitantly baroque architecture painted in fading blues, pinks, and yellows. São Paulo is again the opposite; it has sloughed off the decrepit relics of the colonial-era burg it might once have been and now exudes modernity, wealth, movement, polyphony, potency, electricity, a kaleidoscope of contemporary luminosities.[88]

The southern intellectuals, who may have felt vindicated and inspired by Roger Bastide, affirmed that the Northeast was a place "suffused in history . . . in which the drive to have everything new and make everything new, to modernize, to be contemporary, does not inspire anyone. Its very stones sing of the past, telling proud tales of ancient Brazil, when the Portuguese roamed the earth." São Paulo was another reality, the embrace of the new, of change, of ambitious development, of being unlike the Northeast "that God made, not the people." One was the region of memory; the other expressing the passing of time. One was nature, the other culture.[89]

Some modernists, notably Mário and Oswald de Andrade, viewed the Northeast as the last redoubt of Brazilian culture—understood as essentially luso-afro-ameríndia, a primeval entity that did not experience the effects of mass immigration the way Brazil's central South did. Oswald, contradicting his endorsement of cosmopolitanism in other writings, practically reproduced the rhetoric of northeastern traditionalists when he praised the Northeast for being the only part of Brazil where "capitalist machines do not noisily churn out cloth and lace and embroidery, the things we once shared that were sacred in authenticity and human beauty." Perhaps he had absorbed a slice of Freyre.[90]

Fernand Braudel, a French historian who worked in São Paulo in the 1930s and also had a stay in Bahia, contributed a series of texts that reinforced the vision of Brazil as a dichotomy between the modern-capitalist and archaic-feudal. He admitted that his long experience in São Paulo left him feeling "a little paulista," and his gaze does seem influenced by the particular visibility of the Northeast that was being mounted in the South at the time. Braudel mused that Bahia was an old society, with a hint of Europe, while São Paulo reminded him of Chicago and New York. He saw paulista society as fluid, letting itself be battered by the waves of economic imperative ever since mass immigration had submerged the older realms of sociability. But in Bahia, his only taste of what might be the "Northeast," society was traditional, fenced off, internally coherent, and capable of heading off any threat from external forces of change.[91]

The selective nature of Braudel's sensibility is obvious, not least when it comes to perceiving Europe in Bahia, something that might be a historical exception to the widespread perception of Bahia as a Brazil's most African place. And to claim that European migration gave paulista society an American character is bizarre. He apparently had a highly individualistic interpretation of Oswald de Andrade's idea that São Paulo was "the engine pulling the old, empty boxcars of the rest of the federation."[92]

As early as 1920, Amadeu Amaral had denounced the rise of a new outbreak of regionalist practices and discourses. While he rebuked the perceived separatist character of the North's regionalism, he acknowledged of paulista regionalism merely that it was "rather blustering and superficial, of no real consequence." But he suggested that the lack of a cohesive identity emanating from São Paulo was due to the presence there of so many people from elsewhere (in Brazil or the world), but if there was a certain palpable paulista identity it was a response to the "anti-paulista sentiment" coming from around Brazil, helping to shape and reinforce an identity there.[93]

But the only "regionalism" that managed to transcend state barriers, uniting intellectuals from across various states, was that of the Northeast.

That region, a space of longing and nostalgia, defined by the past and tradition, was also invented by and through fiction, music, poetry, painting, and theater.

Northeastern Pages

THE NOVELS OF THE 1930S

We now turn to a literary machine that was produced through the representation of a referent it assumes to be fixed: the region of the Northeast. The Northeast is taken in these books to be a preexisting object, a natural thing that could serve as the basis on which to build a whole new literary discourse. But in truth, this literature was not merely reflecting the Northeast but actively participating in its invention and its institution.

The last years of the 1920s and the decade of the 1930s witnessed the transformation of regionalist literature into "national" literature in Brazil. The emergence of sociological analysis of Brazilian identity, with an urgency provided by the discursive formation of the national-popular, gave to northeastern fiction the status of a literature preoccupied with the nation and its people, mixed-race, poor, rough and primitive in their social manifestations. This literature came to be regarded as destined to offer meaning to the various realities of the country—to unmask the essence of true Brazil.[94]

Literary criticism, an important site for the institutionalization and regulation of forms of speakability, adopted the regional as a legitimate way to think about Brazilian literature. Viana Moog described regionalist literature as "an expression of the different local temperaments and talents that compose the national character." Analysis of literary works could be accomplished through frameworks of stereotypes ostensibly characterizing each region. Cyro T. de Pádua proposed mapping the geographic divisions of Brazilian literature, reinforcing José Américo de Almeida's idea that it was the "spontaneous expression of its native soil [terra]." Thus literary critics also acted to legitimate the connection of literary production to spaces understood to be natural, fixed, and ahistorical.[95]

Roger Bastide concurred that the best way to approach Brazilian literature was precisely to consider it an expression of the "diverse cultural islands that formed the harmonious archipelago" of Brazil; his was also a criticism that nominated and reified the region as the producer of national literature. But as Merquior astutely noted, the "literature of the Northeast" never existed. It is a body of work that is viewed as such, grouped in an identity that was created by critics as well as assumed by its authors.[96] But what he did not fully grasp is that this identity was gestated in struggles both within the literary field and beyond it. The northeastern fiction writers, while stylistically diverse, shared common ground as representatives of a cultural area of Brazil that was declining in various aspects. They also all chose the politicization of culture as the means to make themselves present at the national level. From the strict literary point of view, northeastern regionalism does not exist, but it does exist as a literary discourse that sought to legitimize, artistically, a regional identity that had been shaped by diverse regionalist practices and given sociological coherence by Gilberto Freyre.

Critics came to explain the style of northeastern authors by using the images linked to that space: these authors supposedly had styles that were arid, dry, sharp, and craggy, all qualities recalling the desert and the cactus. The identity of the authors is established based on their and their works' relations with the northeastern space, although some, such as Graciliano Ramos, went deeper by affirming in their expressive style and the texture of their language the image of the region they drew from and constructed.[97] The growth of what came to be called the "fiction of the 1930s" had developed with the complete identification of authors with their landscapes and environments, coming to feel, see, and speak it as they had never done before. Paulo Cavalcanti believed this fiction expressed a collective reality, loyal to the tendencies of the people and to regional characteristics, creating an interweaving of the authors' memories with what was most essential in the structure of society. It was truly a Brazilian literature because it was connected to region, which suffered less foreign influence. And it was the synthesis of all its contradictions, its social and natural contrasts, embodying this rich complexity.[98]

Once the Northeast was acceptably defined as a "literary province," what was legitimated was not only the identity of the fiction as being essentially northeastern, but the region itself as a place "possessing its own literature that expresses its truths." Regionalist literature conveyed the "spirit" of each region: paulista literature was one of adventure, conquest, the bandeirantes, while northeastern literature was "rustic, crude and strong, just like its area of origin."[99] Northeastern critics characterized 1930s fiction as meeting the demands of the physical and social environment that produced it; as an "expression of its space." It was interpreted as an "innately northeastern reaction to the ancient canons, without losing the universal meaning of Brazilian culture," or as an encounter of the differentiating traits of Brazilian prose and customs with models of European reality.[100]

Whatever its sheen of the past, this literature was made possible by the growth of a complex, modernizing society. Poetry, which dominated the national literary realm until around 1914, gave way to fiction that was directly linked with the nationalist necessity to understand and explain both the nation and its people. The other modes of knowledge that focused on the question, such as sociology, history, and ethnography, would furnish data, suggestions, and norms to literature. Nationalist practices in the cultural field, such as the creation of universities and institutes; the realization of congresses, symposia, and debates on national culture, language, and problems; all would stimulate literary production directed down the same path, toward the authentic essence and truth of the nation. Inquiries into the national character and the Brazilian "type" found in novels and other fiction offered a whole new dimension for psychological characterization, regional discourse, and confrontations with miscegenation.[101] This fiction was guided by the mission to form a critical consciousness and become a participative activity in the historical transformations of the country—whether impeding them or engaging them to direct their momentum in certain directions.

To the extent that the national-popular discursive formation had as a central problematic the idea of the nation, and to the extent that the diversity of Brazil's social conditions was growing more accentuated, 1930s fiction developed with the preoccupation to recognize and define the human types and social characteristics that composed the nation. It was able to vividly explore the intersections between psychology and sociology. Northeastern fiction in particular contained the tremors of numerous crises affecting traditional sociability and intellectual paradigms, as well as families of landholders and sugar producers. The construction of these "regional problems" had to contend with Freyre's sociological production and all the discourse that went before it.

These authors' success throughout the decade was due in large part to a significant expansion of the editorial industry and the commercialization of books. Still, the industry was concentrated on the Rio de Janeiro–São Paulo axis, meaning northeastern writers typically had to move there for a real chance at exposure. Their fiction had as a principal base of reader-ship the urban middle class, which was then in a phase of growth and for whom the nationalist imperative to "discover the problems of the country" had profound resonance. That sector, considering itself "mod-ern, polished, civilized," was also curious to learn about the "exotic and rustic." This would be a way to mark off and emphasize their own dif-ference and at the same time join the collective project to recognize "our problems, our fears, our miseries, our traditions."[102]

The discourse of 1930s fiction was concerned with elaborating sym-bolic characters, whose individuality was expressed in actions; characters who transcended the laceration of identities suffered at the moment by their authors. They are characters who want to assure the maintenance of an essence, to eliminate virtuality. They are "typical," fixed types who, even with all the conflict and drama they confront within the story, never come to doubt themselves or fundamentally change. They offer the guar-antee of continuity of a regional "way of being" and "way to think" and "way to act."[103]

The central theme of the literature of the 1930s is the decadence of pa-triarchal society and its substitution with logics of urban-industrial society. Its actors vigorously engage in battle among the various national projects swirling about in this moment of transition, from the most conservative to the revolutionary. That is why they strive to get nearer to the "people," adopting forms of expression of popular origin as a way to denounce the social conditions they experience. The authors, in the majority middle-class descendants of traditional families that have fallen on hard times and were enduring new circumstances of marginalization, felt little com-mitment or loyalty to the dominant groups. Along with its profession-alization, the literary field acquired a certain autonomy, leading it to (as Candido put it) "de-officialize." In their independence the writers identify more with the popular sectors, feeling marginalized like them and uncon-nected to the bourgeoisie. The fiction of this period was imagined to be made for the people, for the public, rather than for a class. But the authors' sensibilities and values existed in tension. As they newly identified with the suffering of the masses, many fostered the populist pretension to be the people's spokesmen even as they felt lingering support for the old par-adigm of paternalist domination that their families had once enjoyed.[104]

This production used the conclusions of the sociologists as a spring-board to arrive at a nuanced depiction of the "various realities of the

Northeast," leading ultimately to an abandonment of the dichotomous structure of naturalist regionalism and its cleavage between coast and interior. The man of the backlands is no longer viewed as an exotic rube who is flustered by cities, and who also threatens cities. He is explored for his psychological and sociological constitution and meaning, fixing him in a social-cultural totality rather than excluding him from rarified "civilization."[105]

However, the work is not monolithic in emphasizing a vision of the Northeast as a space of nostalgia and tradition. Only some of its authors contributed to this idea, among them José Lins do Rego, José Américo de Almeida, and Rachel de Queiroz. And each of these distinguished themselves further in their choice of particular area that would serve as the basis for how they thought and wrote about region. For Rego (as well as other writers who do not fit into this group, such as Ascenso Ferreira, Jorge de Lima, and Manuel Bandeira), the traditional Northeast was the part that was covered in sugarcane, with patriarchal and slaveholding society around it—especially the intermediate coastal plain referred to as the *zona da mata*. Almeida and Queiroz, on the other hand, gave some attention to the coast but tended to focus on the dry interior as the traditional space par excellence that gave the Northeast its originality and identity.

If we say these authors invented a traditional Northeast, that does not mean they started from zero and created something new. They chose carefully among recollections, experiences, images, clichés, enunciations, manners of expression, and facts to select those they considered essential to the regional essence and regional "type." Their selections aligned with the concept that the Northeast was a place where an identity threatened with effacement must be conserved. The truthfulness of what they wrote about the region is not really based on the "Northeast" itself and hardly depends on it. What is of interest are their techniques of representation, and how these render the place visible, clear, and apparently "there" geographically.

This literature operates through elaborating "typical" characters who speak of what they regard as fundamental social experiences. The constitutive power of their identities is engaged in mutual constitution with the regional frame. It is intended that the reader identify with their behaviors, values, ways of thinking and feeling. These characters should function as revealing the essence of a regional way of being. Creating the "typical" is part of the mechanism that will produce regional subjectivity. But to become credible subjects, the typical characters must also embody experiences, modes of speaking, and social practices that can be recognized by the reader. Rather than being "discovered," the characters actualize elements that have already been consecrated by the codes of meaning and perception of their era. To be comprehensible, their strangeness must be to an extent familiar.[106]

Although the repertoire of types is rooted in repetitive tropes that recall a dominant social and cultural order established before a given work was written, this project was not exclusively conservative in that it functions to incite new production. In the identification with types there is room for invention, and an identity is never guaranteed or fully predictable. These are the two faces of the type: a model to be serialized, and raw material for the new. The regional types in this oeuvre, for example, have a tendency for repetition but are still creatively displaced, reset, and reconfigured.[107]

With its implications of romance and fantasy, fiction writing fit smoothly into the project of rescuing a tradition of narratives, images, and discourses that would be "representative" of the regional space. Fiction was a predominant narrative form in both the oral and written realms, and was embraced as the best way to recreate the lives and history of the region. Roberto Ventura has shown how, by the late nineteenth century, elements of popular literature and popular song were absorbed alongside more austere juridical arguments into the debates of northern intellectuals with their southern counterparts. Sílvio Romero, Joaquim Nabuco, Araipe Júnior, and others interpenetrated evolutionary assumptions with an honor code ostensibly characteristic of rural, patriarchal society and that was the richly explored theme of such popular production.[108]

Cordel literature also furnished elements of narrative structure, language, and values to northeastern fiction. Cordel had been itself an important diffuser of images, texts, and themes about the Northeast, its production based on the repetition, variation, and reactualization of collective forms. It represents a sort of grassroots text in which popular narrative and enunciative models interweave and imbricate. It has functioned as a repository of expressive forms from which other "erudite" cultural production has drawn, not only literature but theater and cinema.[109]

As a popular manifestation, cordel goes beyond representation and the idea of an author's workmanship. It produces its own language and a "reality" that derives from how it allows popular memory to intersect with contemporary events and references. Its discourse is presented as being beyond the corrosive effects of historical time. As a practice that invents and reinvents tradition, it was appealing to diverse intellectuals preoccupied with both popular identity and spatial-temporal stability. Its narrative structure operates according to paradigms embodied by a narrator speaking with the voice of the people, and it is thus vulnerable to deformation caused by excessively individual impositions. Of course, its traditionalist vision allowed it to dialogue with many other realms of cultural production about the region. The "primitive" character of its oral structure appeared to be the natural outgrowth of a region whose general content was taken as primitive (if not barbaric), the opposite of modern. The authentic stories of the Northeast were understood by the 1930s generation of author-interpreters to be similarly oral, and effectively anonymous in their collectivity—the narratives of ex-slaves and people with no last name, half-remembered tales heard in infancy of bandits, saints, miracles, droughts, lost women, and unhewn men. This displacement from time and authorship contributed to the vision of the purity of the interior, a nostalgic space that had not yet suffered the denaturalizing effects of bourgeois social relations.[110]

As noted, however, cordel did not reject novel or surprising contemporary interjections. But they were reset and defused. Modernity's power to perturb a daily life immersed in regularity and tradition was subjected to an interpretative matrix giving the novelties a traditional cast, diluting their capacity for difference and knitting them into the absorbent substrate of similarity and continuity.

The fiction of José Lins do Rego clearly drew on the circular popular narrative processes of storytellers and story singers. He eschewed the linear imposition of centralizing arguments and explanatory, conversational dialogue, preferring internal deposition and reflection. Various voices, popular or not, melded into the shared vision of a world not yet lacerated by the cleavages of self-aware class identity. The great house looming over the estate was depicted as a place where people might exist in hierarchy, but that hierarchy was implicit, and their voices were not essentially differentiated. In Rego's writing the various voices speak in harmony to affirm a cordiality, a deep familiarity, rather than assert dissentions and critique (although Rego does use discord when he gives voice to urban people, or trade professionals such as artisans working outside the rural sphere).[111]

In order to see, speak, and write the region "as it was," all these authors attempted to establish a regional style based in such popular sources. But northeastern literary regionalism formed also in opposition—to academic styles, and to the alleged artificiality of modernism. The goal was a quotidian manner of expression, a language that could sketch a world that was a direct representation of reality. It sought a feeling of veracity, immediacy. But the language also sought to be the basis for re-creating and reinstituting a reality that was disappearing. As it maneuvered to close the distance between object and meaning, its thrust was to reestablish old codes taken as "natural" and essential.[112]

While they rejected the modernists, these authors were still making works based on a modern gaze. But they were nostalgic for the clarity and substance of the naturalist vision with its sense of a true reality, clear, fixed, and stable, its hierarchies secure. One of the sources of greatest tension and anxiety in modernity is atomization and the resulting conflict over a place and space experienced, up until then, as natural and eternal. It must be related to this that 1930s fiction has as a regular theme battles over land and power. The mechanized plantations and their insatiable hunger for land, leading them to invade territories and ecosystems that had been sacred to earlier generations, were the greatest symbol of the process in which land was no longer a fixed repository of traditions and power relations but merely "cheap merchandise."[113]

Another indication of the naturalist nostalgia of these authors is their negative posture toward the city. If the earlier regionalism looked from the perspective of the cities rather scornfully to the rural areas, the regionalism of 1930s fiction reversed the point of view and saw in cities the ultimate symbol of ruin and disgrace. The ideal Northeast in this work is thematized as rural, pure, and robust, posed against the cities, which are places of sin and degradation. Although the Northeast has its own cities, critically important in the history of Brazil, these are mostly ignored by its literary and artistic production. Being that the Northeast was the site of one of the first manifestations of industrialization in the country, industry is viewed with suspicion as an invasive, foreign force in an innately "agricultural" region. "To view the Northeast from the big city is like looking through binoculars backward—everything distant and entangled."[114] The region is symbolically rooted in both its own rural dimension, and the performative folkloric "survivals" of it carried by migrants to the big city. Some of the works seek to assure the superiority of bucolic life over urban life, as well as that of traditional patriarchal relations over the bourgeoisie relations of the metropolis. Rural sociability is generalized to the regional scale, averting the fractures and complexity of the region itself—much as the earlier split between the coast and interior provoked camouflaging strategies. What is constructed is the image of a society profoundly involved in itself, in a state of self-absorbed serenity that can be disrupted by the interventions of nature (droughts, floods, births, deaths, hunger, passion) or of modern capitalism.[115]

When the Northeast's cities are dealt with, it is in the style of Ascenso Ferreira or Manuel Bandeira: the contemporary city is not confronted on its own terms, but what is sought is an antiquated essence underneath the modern concrete overgrowth. These writers prioritize "the old Recife that lingers behind the clangorous streets, of the river easing along the quay, of the slumbering mansions." In the preferred cities, "the streetcars are pulled by burros, and are outnumbered by wagons carrying brush or produce." Cities "that are small like the people that live in them, always the same, never giving more or less than they always gave, whose only gestures of grandiosity were in the church or the great house of the coronel." The principal urban features of the fictionalized Northeast were the markets, pungent with fruit and gossip, and the complacent market towns "where if an improvement happened to come along it would leave things worse than they already were."[116]

The Northeast invented by the traditionalists might in some senses be called "the land of Ascenso Ferreira," such was the influence of his poetry that he spun out of popular verse. He crafted a Northeast where everyone had a simple life, where needs were met by fishing and trap setting and sleeping soundly at night. The Northeast where men are born sinewy and tough, men "for whom struggle is destiny: Cabeleira, Conselheiro, Lampião." Yet regardless of the wider contexts surrounding these men's controversial activities, the Ferreiran Northeast had no social problems. It was lyrical, ideal, poetic, unsullied by contradictions and struggles over power.[117]

This Northeast appeared hazily like a dream only barely recalled, but summoned forth in the evocative names of idled sugar plantations—Esperança, Estrela d'Alva, Flor do Bosque, Bom Mirar—and in the colonial great houses, now softly falling to ruin. A Northeast of the mansions where senhores had been obediently fanned or intimately embraced by their fond slaves, a Northeast suffused in sugar and that ornamented its daily life with products of sugarcane: "*mar de canas, cana-caiana, cana-roxa, cana-fita*, each sweet morsel more delightful and tasty than the last."[118]

In this Northeast the backlands were "the other side of the world, from whence emerged gaunt fugitives of the droughts and coarse fugitives from justice." But the Northeast was the domain not of lawmen but of families, who owned everything and everyone. These families were extensive, incorporating concubines and bastard children. Grandparents were patriarchal but generous and tender, with considerable social power. Their poor literacy had not impeded their participation in the political accords leading to the end of the empire and the beginning of the republic. Their offspring were the rich senhores, arrogant perhaps but obligingly accessible to the throngs of indigents who sought their attention and favor. It was a noble, ordered world being destroyed by Machiavellian forces from beyond its borders.[119]

But the traditional Northeast could also be that of the backlands, the sertão, the "naked landscape broken only by withered, leafless trees, perforated by thorns like Jesus's forehead and riddled with deformed rocks suggesting monsters that had been rejected passage on Noah's ark." The sertão belonged to the "cowboys, the herds, the aging churches, the convoys of tangerine carts, bandits and prophets; while above all the red sun scowls like an ember." It was a world "soaked in blood, the blood of God and the blood of men." The land of a "damned race that desired revenge, the land of bullets, fire and death." A place of environmental brutality, where "hard, ascetic, brown-toasted men concentrated themselves around little islands of water, surrounded by seas of dry earth on all sides." A "no-man's land of wanderers" sewn out of the whips used by cowboys and by penitents, choked with misery and mysticism. A region "whose signature was the cadaver, where honor and vindication guided people's lives rather than laws or rights." In the Northeast of the backlands, "man's suffering was the suffering of the land itself; both were identified by and mired in the same state of disgrace."[120]

The mythic centrality of the sertão to the Northeast was already present in cordel literature and in the nineteenth-century fiction of Franklin Távora and José de Alencar, and it was systematized by Euclides da

Cunha in his account of Canudos. But in the 1930s it was extended to represent the region as a whole. It was no longer an abstract space defined only as the "frontier of civilization." It was identified specifically with the Northeast and adopted by a set of writers as the true Northeast, a land defined by drought and outlaws and political bosses and wild-eyed prophets. This meant "the negation of the green and aquatic Brazil, of the Brazil of scented gardens. Here was a Brazil brutalized by the sun, violently decomposing, grated by dust and dissolving in the whirlwind."[121]

The Northeast was taking on a visibility and speakability, its diversity worked and polished into recognizable forms and genres by poets and fiction writers. Such a reality needed to be spoken (and spoken of) in its own language, and the traditionalist regionalists had as one of their goals to restore and institute the regional language, the "northeastern way of speaking." It began to take shape in the literature of this period and later would become the topic of study of folklorists, linguists, and ethnographers. It cohered as a single entity, implicitly rejecting the variations in pronunciation and modes of expression across the Northeast. The 1930s fiction both created it as something distinct and endeavored to diminish its exotic character by adopting it as its own material.[122]

This was not done in a cultural or symbolic vacuum. Gilberto Freyre had already pointed to the importance of the "sociocultural complex of the great house and slave hut" for the formation of a Portuguese who was becoming Brazilian, more rural in outlook, with its own language adapted to the tropics—conservative in its maintenance of archaic references to the 1500s and before. This language was both sharpened and smoothed by the pronunciations of the Africans and their descendants, which tended to minimize the "s" and the "rr" in words. For Freyre, as for José Lins do Rego, this linguistic development would present a manifestation of regional identity that was rooted in authenticity. The region was the locale of the most authentic, the most Brazilian language since it was based in oral contemporaneity and the real life of people.[123]

It was under the direct influence of both Freyre and Rego that philologist Mário Marroquim determined to study the "Northeast" as a region per se, to analyze its regional dialect. He believed that the region's particular ethnic and historical formation would have produced a distinct, shared dialect within its boundaries. That is why his study, called *A Língua do Nordeste* (The Language of the Northeast), extrapolated from his research in the coastal plains of Alagoas and Pernambuco to make claims for the region as a whole.[124] Freyre would then praise Marroquim's philology since it allowed analysts to get to know nordestinos better through understanding how history and context had shaped their words. It was taken for granted that language had an implicit regional content that could be revealed. To speak of the Northeast, and to speak it, required a northeastern language. Because of the territorial expanse of the country, and the contact with diverse ethnic and linguistic groups, the Portuguese language had segmented into different colonial-regional variations with the Northeast being the original. To study the northeastern dialect meant to return to the past and explore the memory of a society that seemed to only now be revealing its primordial secrets to earnest artists and scholars.[125]

Marroquim characterized the northeastern way of speaking as being marked by a slow, apparently tired attempt at clear pronunciation. All the vowels were emphatically open, and lingered over, giving the impression of a half-sung speech. The locution of *de* in *de manhã, de tarde,* and *de noite* would ring out as the more sonorous *di*. However, a hard "l" sound was systematically substituted for "r," which demanded more artistry from the tongue. The vowels "a," "i," and "u" were nasalized by the addition of an "m" or "n" afterword, such that a bull's *cogote* (scruff of the neck) transformed into *cangote*.

This schema of a "northeastern language" was at times based purely on the manifestations of a single city, such as Água Branca in Alagoas, where there was the habit of adding a letter "i" to a word ending with "l" or "r": *soli* for *sol*, *doutori* for *doutor*, et cetera. But Marroquim also forefronted diversity among states, such as *coma* in Paraíba versus *cuma* in Pernambuco. In Alagoas, an article was used before the words for mother, father, aunt, and so on, whereas that was not the case in Pernambuco. This begins to suggest the fundamental incoherence of his approach to a "northeastern language" that would be taken as "the expression of the character and traditions of the region, a language giving voice to the soul of the people."

The origins of this dialect were explained as archaic Portuguese, leavened by the contributions from Africans and the indigenous. Since there was not a notable history of migration to the region (unlike to Brazil's central South), this language had been able to stabilize long ago; in Pernambuco, some of the native peoples still spoke the pre-Renaissance Portuguese they had learned and carried into the interior. Words with slight variations from their contemporary forms, such as *alifante* (*elefante*), *amenhã (amanhã)*, *apus (apos)*, *antão (então)*, *coidado (coitado)*, *distruí (destruir)* and *rezão (razão)* advertised the ancient Portuguese roots.

Fiction of the 1930s would give the Northeast a visibility and speakability that involved language itself, and the centrality of memory to the present. The past was scrutinized for meanings that could help invent the present. The leather-clad bandit one may have glimpsed long ago, the starving wanderer, the poor and shuffling peasant, the saint carried in devoted procession, the *coronel* in his white suit riding a horse, all acquired a unifying meaning as they were considered manifestations of regionality—indexes of the regional essence. Region explained them, while at the same time region was implied by them, and traditional continuity was mutually underscored in an era of change: "A region of people obsessed with the past, in a life that was all death."[126]

REGIONAL THEMES

This literature used regionalized language to institute a number of basic themes: the decadence of sugar society; piety as a counterbalance to banditry and savagery; the power relations surrounding the coronel (the favors, the clientelism, the hired goons); the drought and the wandering in its wake. These themes had been present in popular literature, in the songs and improvised poetry duels, and in the political discourse of the oligarchies. But they took on a new form and a new reach in literary production, which heralded them as emblems of regional essence.

These traditional and folkloric motifs would take on new life as they were incorporated into both implicit and explicit political strategies to denounce regional conditions. Their dimensions of want and misery were configured into indices of discontentment with the new society forming around them. While they had the power to impress viscerally with their strong tone and imagery, they also conveyed to middle-class readers that the Northeast was opposed to capitalist modernization. They synthesized a regional social reality. Their manifestations of popular revolt provoked gestures of solidarity from diverse intellectuals who were also concerned with changes affecting traditional society and threatening its proven mechanisms of control.

Dichotomies provided the foundation for constructing this regional identity: God and Devil, traditional and modern, sea and backlands, drought and starvation versus ardent prophecies of salvation.

The theme of drought was certainly the most important, because it had first given rise to the idea of a Northeast as a separate space from the North, defined by the reach of this climatic occurrence. The discourse of the drought was transformed into a regional rhetoric addressing a variety of questions and themes. This was accomplished through the simultaneous and diverse practices and methods of the drought victims, of strategies to control starving populations, of the relocating of wandering indigents to grim labor camps, of the institutions organized to gather and send charitable contributions, of the mechanisms to devise and control drought-related public works. Among the representatives of the drought-afflicted area there was a need to unify the discourse at the national level. Drought was decisive in helping Brazilians think about the Northeast as a natural territorial division, encompassing a homogeneous environment that had also given rise to a homogeneous society.

Drought encouraged the embrace of an image of the Northeast as desert, an image that ignored the humid regimes within the region. The wandering, the migration, the exodus sparked by drought established its own narrative structure: a ritualistic formula of people cast out, recalling the biblical exodus of the Jews from the desert. In this case, the waves of wretched faithful would keep roaming until they reached the coast, or even better, the promised land of the South. But there was also a secular, timeless aspect of the story, since droughts were a natural phenomenon. If they had always existed, then by definition the Northeast, "land of the droughts," had always existed. This was the guarantee of continuity, of the reassuring eternity of the regional space (even if it was hellishly associated with catastrophe and hardship).[127]

In literature, drought appears as the phenomenon that catalyzes radical transformation in the lives of individuals and society. It disorganized families physically, socially, and morally. It is also given the responsibility for the social conflicts in the region, embodied in the dual symbol of priest and outlaw, naturalizing social problems. If the Northeast was catching on fire, whether or not a desperado's torch or anarchist's bomb was involved, the merciless sun was ultimately to blame.[128]

Fiction of the 1930s instituted in cultural production a series of bold images derived imaginatively from drought that became classic. They gave the region a visibility that proved nearly impossible to avoid or to change. This was the Northeast ablaze, seething with charcoal and ashes, the livestock skeletal and dying of thirst under a cloudless blue sky; of aggressive vegetation, spiny and rigid, with only some scant inedible weeds daring to flush green; of the beaten wanderers pulling donkeys and the death-mask women pulling wispy, filthy children along from somewhere to somewhere. The Northeast of so many painful farewells, farewells to the land and to family members and to a favorite horse or dog that must be eaten. The Northeast of polarities between drought and winter's offer of rain, between fields in scorched ruin and the paradise of color, sound and smells the rain could bring. Nature, circular nature outside of time, defining a region whose history was not linear but caught in perpetual motion between extremes.[129]

Everywhere one might look this image of the Northeast is marked by the presence of the sun: "The indignant sun shimmering in its fiery rings, boiling the waterholes to nothing, the moon red and morose reflecting it. The sky burns and the very horizon turns to smoke." These writings create a "portrait of inferno," an arid landscape singed to lifelessness. The Northeast appears condemned by nature to this desolate fate, and characters in books will be assigned inescapable destinies that parallel the world of fatalities and ruination—but it is a world also of social injustices committed by society's new dominant groups who, reflecting callous modernity and the corruptions of centralization, turn away from the paternalist protectionism that the old senhores had always provided. The Northeast was victimized by the indifference of a federal public authority controlled by politicians from other regions, who did not comprehend the "problem of the drought," the "problem of the interior," the problem that annihilated men and women and transformed them into beasts. Fiction writers would denounce this reality by making this Northeast relentlessly present and in sharp contrast to the image of the Northeast as paradise, drowsily basking in the past glories of the sugar epoch.[130]

Coexisting with the infernal image of the sertão was the idea among some traditionalists that it was actually the best place to live since it was free of the contagions of civilization, and home to strong, noble men and honorable women. For Rachel de Queiroz and José Américo de Almeida, the sertão presented a repository of genuine national traits including salutary communal, family-rooted traditions that contrasted with modern capitalist society's individualism and commercialization. In their works dissolution is a constant theme—the physical and moral degradation of people submitted to bourgeois social relations, the atomizing loss of meaning, the lack of a language to express the experience of the new reality, and the madness resulting from not being able to assimilate it. This is as much the case for José Lins do Rego, who focused on the old sugar aristocracy as the prototype of traditional society, as it is for Queiroz and Almeida in their construct of the backlands as a holdout of pure community values.[131]

The desperate contemporary circumstances of the Northeast were effacing the naively utopian version of the Northeast that was grasped in the authors' childhood memories of song and fable, and held to the mind's eye as they wrote: the terrain of plantation estates ordered through patriarchy, not yet corrupted by smoky mills and Ford trucks and rumbling turbines. That was a Northeast where the central authority of the grandfather was assumed and expected, "where no one was an idler but neither did anyone go hungry, where waltzes were played as lullabies for the slave shacks." It was this society that "created the greatness of Brazil, its power and authenticity," where slaves and their masters lived together "harmoniously" and the town bosses and their hired enforcers had the affection for each other of "fathers and sons."[132]

This literary discourse tended to valorize hierarchy, a system in which "each knew his proper place" and social differences were carefully obscured by paternalist mechanisms and personalized power relations. In that sense traditional northeastern society was more sentimental and hot-blooded, less rational. It was not a natural substrate for the rise of rational political ideologies and abstract arguments, which were regarded as prerequisites for class conflict. The white author, educated by the black nursemaid who also cured his illnesses and accepted his first searching caresses, was the "racial democrat" who proclaimed solidarity with those lower on the social scale as long as they "showed their respect" and stayed in their place.[133]

This literature had and has a resilient effect on readers' subjectivities, creating an idealized vision of slavery that masked its cruelties and thus reconciling the present with a past (of the region and the country) that would otherwise be embarrassing and potentially contentious. A more critical attention was paid to the world of the bourgeoisie, its individualism and exploitation of laborers, in a manner intended to further emphasize the value of patriarchal slave society. The literature hoped to foster antimodern and anticapitalist perspectives by revealing traditional society as sacred, a refuge. The Northeast, as the region defined by this sociability, must be preserved against the chaotic whirlwinds from the metropolis, the discord, the clangor of machines. It would be the place where the mixed-blood Indian (*caboclo*) still merrily sang the time-honored work songs, where "even the misery was pleasant" and "the very mud itself spoke of love." It would be the locale of perpetual order, where the artificially tempting world of impersonal capitalism was recognized as the perdition it was. Where the traditional enslavement of men and women actually allowed them to live in greater freedom, better clothed and fed, than bourgeois social economy would ever permit.

The actual manifestations of revolt, violence, apocalypticism, and desperation that shook the Northeast were not ignored in this literature but given a particular set of explanations that translated popular discontent largely into a grassroots agitation for the old ways. There were droughts as a cause as well, and the incapacity or unwillingness of authorities to address their impacts, but underlying it all was the sense of diverse popular rebellion against the encroachments of modernity. The collapsing of traditional power structures, the patriarchies that dispensed favors and protection, left people newly helpless at the same time that economic shifts destabilized once-coherent agricultural practices and alliances. Even the bitter disputes within aristocratic families and the feuds between them were taken as verifying the degenerative effects of new individualistic, mercantilist strategies that challenged the ethics of the region's social world to the core.

Traditionalist fiction spun the vision of an ancient equilibrium in the use of violence between the elite class and the poor, endowing it with the sheen of an accord among equals. This was to contrast it from the new patterns and modes of violence deployed by the state and its associated ranks of bosses to impose their will on the region. Popular cultural production also contributed to this interpretation by helping to mythicize some of the region's most notorious outlaws as valiant activists avenging the poor. This merged with a long tradition of medieval narrative focused on crimes of honor, on violence to defend the family and society's weak. The reinterpretation of a preexisting moralizing function in popular narrative to cast bandits as heroes chafed with the new dominant morality, which would quickly make the apparent popularization and glorification of criminals into a crime in its own right.[134]

In a society defined by middle-class values, the crimes of the poor retain a certain base power to fascinate, but they are drained of meaning. They become drab repetitive acts, an annoyance to be stamped out, rather than sources of pride and solidarity. Criminality loses the sanction it enjoyed in a range of circumstances within traditional patriarchal society. The press played a key role in interpreting crime, cleansing it of the mythic depth and tones of admiration it enjoyed in popular discourse. The press described it in terms that did not admit that it could be just or proper or accepted. The ambiguous and symbolic power it retained in popular narrative, of overlapping the human dimensions of violence, bravery, and heroism, was all rationally wiped away. Crime appeared as a mere disturbance to be dealt with by appropriate means.

The overthrow of popular heroism was viewed by traditionalist writers as another revelation of how the people's world of honor, bravery, and redistributive derring-do was giving way to an abstract, ineffective, and oafish state. The great bandits of yore had aspired to claiming power and glory through their wits and fearlessness; they wanted their crimes to be retold and sung and recounted in area papers as well as by the "people." They savored publicity. Antônio Silvino read the newspapers regularly to ensure that they had not skimped on details of his exploits. Lampião wanted pamphlets and posters to be produced about him, just as he was gratified by popular tales and song. All of these different versions of the same people and events helped to compose a mythic figure, a complex, multiple "bandit" whose identity drew equally from God and Devil and who would be embraced as the emblem of a degenerating society that needed to be rescued.[135]

For the writer José Lins do Rego, there were further distinctions to be made. He saw Lampião, known for outlandish feats of cruelty, as symbolizing the social degeneration of the Northeast. But Lampião's contemporary Antônio Silvino represented another type of lawlessness, the sort that avenged the poorest classes by reestablishing their identity and their rights and defending the traditional code of honor against a powerful but clueless state. Silvino was part of a world that included the local political boss (coronel), two bookends of authorities who were just and paternal but who could become equally violent and terrible when their rights, honor, or confidence were betrayed.[136]

The urban sectors of the Northeast, as well as the urban sectors elsewhere in Brazil, viewed banditry in the blunt oppositional terms of littoral versus interior and civilized space versus primitive space. They fashioned archly negative narratives emphasizing the outlaws' brutality, often with connotations of an animal nature (wild, savage, plague). The crimes were depicted as pointless and gratuitous, linked to archetypes sure to muster public opinion—the torture of the elderly, gleeful rape and castration, forcing mothers to watch their children die. Banditry was stripped of any social meaning, becoming instead the product of a sadistic instinct to pillage and destroy. The possible social motives of the bandits were obscured in order to dilute popular support as well as denounce the traditional regional power brokers (*coroneis*) who put up with or even used them. Much as the bandits themselves, anyone who lent material or cultural support to banditry was castigated as a symbol of the region's backwardness.[137]

The discussion of outlaws was unfurled into a broader discourse of the Northeast as untamable and menacing, a place peopled by macho brutes who might become professional assassins with just a little polishing. The peasants, who took pride and inspiration from the bandits' bold exploits, were stigmatized by southerners as dupes who were profoundly uncivilized themselves. As that reputation solidified, migrants to São Paulo or Rio de Janeiro found themselves regarded with wary disdain, believed to be trying to mask an innate viciousness: "sometimes they did not even appear to be human beings." The Northeast unfolding in southern newspapers became a land of blood and rough leather, of arbitrary violence and gratuitous murder, the kingdom of the bullet, torch, and machete.[138]

The fiction writers provided a sociological context for the rise of the bandits but went a step further, suggesting that as a response to moral degeneration they represented a sort of destiny, an inescapable outcome. Bandits were valiant rebels launching a counterattack against the myriad injustices unleashed by the region's changing power relations. The books even followed a narrative pattern established in popular literature, which starts with the poor and simple but happily ordered existence of a peasant family cast into confusion by new, greedy leaders who exploit them and steal their land. Violence ensues; family members die; vengeance is sworn. Enter the bandits, who would fight the corrupt authorities to the death or risk imprisonment and the firing squad. They embodied the peasants' desire for justice and the restoration of the past. Their persecution by an abstract, merciless state was drawn with considerable detail to imply that the new forces of modernity and centralization were far more relentless and bloodthirsty, and socially destructive, than the modes of traditional rural justice.[139]

The bandits were adopted as a symbol of the struggle against modernizing processes that threatened to disfigure the essence of the "region," including by resetting its traditional webs of power relations. Fiction depicted them as battling the delivery of mail, ripping out telegraph wires, pulling up train tracks, kidnapping visiting investors and entrepreneurs, and defying the state in general even as they deferred to the local, traditional coronel and padre. The bandits were portrayed as tragic figures caught up in the maelstrom of losing their world, but who responded quixotically to shore up a vanishing society. They were no less tragic than the prophets and their pious followers also wandering through the pages of the books, who promised that sinners and innovators would be tortured and who saw in bourgeois society the lurking promise of apocalypse. Traditionalist fiction explained them too as products of a social degeneration that had roots in natural causes (the droughts) but more substantially in the introduction of new, impersonal and rationalizing social relations.

The literature enshrined messianic movements as a regional trope, linked to the image-concept of the Northeast, even though they were a national phenomenon. But this had already been accomplished in large part through Euclides da Cunha's 1902 *Rebellion in the Backlands* (*Os Sertões*), a hybrid narrative account and analysis of the rise and destruction of the alternate community of Canudos in the interior of Bahia. This event, what da Cunha called the "massive disgrace that wounded the Brazilian fatherland," also stayed alive in a range of popular cultural production that embraced the figure of the community's religious leader Antônio Conselheiro as a symbol of resistance against bourgeois values. The ideal of dying in defense of an imaginary, sacred world came to be absorbed into the sense of self of the dry Northeast as a whole.[140]

Mysticism, a spiritual vision of nature and of society, was a fundamental part of a traditional sphere that commingled diverse religious influences from Catholicism and millenarianism to indigenous and African-derived practices. It possessed an internal value system contrary to materialism and to rationality, which were associated with the modernizing society of urban centers particularly in the South. The Northeast came to be seen as a sort of laboratory for "primitive" beliefs and devoted sects that were opposed to the rational faith in political-social utopia emanating from beyond its borders. The Northeast represented a space where modern society, with all its logic and iniquity, might be evaded.[141]

Messianic movements delineated "sacred" territories led by prophets who, like the most charismatic bandits, devised their own laws independent of society's structures of authority. The assemblage of poor, hungry, racially diverse people in their communities caused panic among nearby landowners, who feared a violent takeover of their property despite the ecclesiastical undertone of the leaders' mutterings. These religious communities appeared to have a hallucinatory atmosphere born from the members' collective madness that seemed to contain forces both of good and of evil.[142]

The fiction strove to normalize these movements as characteristic to the region. They deployed considerable contextual detail, from biblical images and phrases to discussions of saints, from examinations of the martyr Sebastian to the adventures of medieval knights. But the literary force of the movements was still in their power to startle: Prophets in filthy robes bellowing and gesturing, followed by straggling lines of bearded men and gaunt women, all of them tugging at crosses or beads and chanting incomprehensible prayers. The rule of social life in their camps was that of the stern old saints, who could demand corporal punishment, torture, or death for determined infidels. On the day of the millennium all believed they would be purified to gain entrance to the glorious kingdom where pain and misery would cease, and rivers of milk and mountains of grain would welcome the righteous famished.[143]

One common element in the narratives of banditry, messianism, drought, and the stresses on traditional society in general was the local political boss, the coronel. He could be described as an ambiguous combination of secretive, cowardly, violent and miserly with paternal, wise, sympathetic, and selfless. He oscillated from the grandfather figure in the work of José Lins do Rego—a vibrant and sage leader of the people, champion of a way of life—to the character of Dagoberto created by José Américo de Almeida, an exploiter and a cheater, an obstinate conniver who aspired merely to benefit from the ruination around him.

Taking the genre as a whole, Dagoberto is understood to be a degraded, later form of the essential wise old grandfather. However, the division was never really so simple. *Coronelismo* arose as a symptom of the decadence of rural patriarchies and the growing dependence of landowners on public officials. This was to maintain their own privileged position, which was built on the latticework of dependency of the popular sectors under them. As a form of brokerage, coronelismo emerged from the new need for compromise between urban groups and rural economic interests and was formed around the manipulation of an electorate that had grown significantly since the declaration of the republic. It developed as a mediating zone between the diminishing mechanisms of private power and the progressive strengthening of public power.[144]

Like religious movements, coronelismo was a national phenomenon, especially common in rural society, but it came to be seen as a marker of the Northeast. This is explained in part by the active role of the local oligarchies in defining the region itself at the national level. Their images and discourses were aimed at creating the Northeast in order to avoid the economic marginalization and political submission of traditional rural power structures. The region would be an instrument of preservation for traditional mechanisms of power and domination, providing a basis to undermine the local effects of national processes deemed modern and radical.

Fiction of the 1930s consolidated these tropes into a persuasive, influential concept of regional identity. However, as has been noted, the authors were not working from one monolithic perspective, and there was variation in how they wrote the region. That is an important point, because readers who assume that the traditionalist fiction writers were unanimous and interchangeable unwittingly play into a deeper political strategy that casts the region as an organic reality and its cultural production as essentially the discovery and revelation of truths, rather than as mythmaking.

JOSÉ LINS DO REGO

José Lins do Rego was born in 1901 in the municipality of Pilar in Paraíba State. His father owned a sugar mill, and his mother died when he was very young. He pursued university studies at Recife's law school, and it was there he met Gilberto Freyre, a future friend and colleague. Inspired by Freyre's sociology and regionalist traditionalism, Rego would become one of the most well-known and prolific of period Brazilian authors.

While the work of both men was concerned with northeastern society during the heyday of sugar, and relied on personal as well as collective memory, there was a slight difference in focus. Freyre's analysis centered on the social frameworks that sustained such memories, while the novelist explored individual lives and modes of experience during the onset of change threatening rural landowners in Paraíba. His fiction did not derive from sociological research but from stories he had been told, in the formal sitting room of the great house or the kitchen staffed by black servants. His books attempt to both record and imaginatively explore the world of his infancy, writing it into an existential but recognizable landscape. Sketches of true events melded with hazy reminiscence, all shot through with a sense of suffering and woe for what was lost. Each book was the account of a process of destruction and, at the same time, an effort to reconstruct his internal and external space with fragments of the past. His goal was to bridge the past to the present and provide a witness's testimony of a receding world that should not be allowed to disappear. Reestablishing the continuity and unity of regional space meant for Rego also the reaffirmation of self and personal identity.[145]

Rego's stories were stitched from threads of the past as well as the filaments of dreams of continuity. His objective was reached, at least in part, because his work contributed decisively to the creation of a Northeast steeped in tradition and described in terms of sentimental nostalgia: a region that was desired, a place more absent than present. This affectionate desire to return to a dream grew stronger the longer one stayed outside of the region itself. But despite all his idyllic overtones, Rego's fiction also contained the unpleasant poignancy of human experience, represented largely through his own history and interpretations. Idealized plantation life was darkened by psychological torment caused by the loss of his mother, as well as the guilt, confusion, and fear associated with the onset of puberty. He wanted to show all of this, to be as real as possible in order to make the truth of the narrative "as present as a handful of earth."[146]

His utopian project was to rebuild the social and cultural world of his grandfather's era, to escape the chaos of the present. But his consciousness was riven between the desire for deep continuity with his ancestors and the knowledge that he was different and his time was different—that such hoped-for continuity was impossible. He was a city dweller who dreamed of settling at the head of a sleepy but ordered plantation, the breeze stirring the sugar fronds to soothing murmurs of patience and permanence, even though he knew that the social transformations had been too profound and the plantation great house lived on only as a literary setting. Because of this, his prose was judgmental of the forces of change and often dwelled on the dissolutions—pain, disease, melancholy, deformity, madness—that change had unleashed.[147] This stands in sharp contrast to his soft, nostalgic tone in describing the society of his infant years, before the ruin. His youth and the plantation were vibrant and colorful, defined in opposition to the new circumstances of reality. Only in those idealized spheres were his characters able to recognize and understand each other, just as he was, himself.

Throughout Rego's writing the psychology of his characters emerges not through abstract characterization but through actions. It is traced "from the shadowy speculation that coheres into strategy, the thoughts that harden into form." Analysis of the human spirit was directly based on tactile interventions in the natural and social environment. It is by their deeds, phrases, and gestures that his characters reveal their personalities, including their regional qualities. His method was a form of documenting a civilization, revealing a "northeastern psyche" and "northeastern personality." But in this effort Rego avoided making the interior dimensions of his characters overly complex. They were "primitive souls," spontaneous and natural, with an openness to the unconscious and irrational. They were better understood by what they did than by what they said or thought. They were persecuted by obscure forces, which gave them a fatalistic vision of the world.[148]

Rego's style eschewed dialogues, which gave him as the narrator (son and grandson of rural elite) considerable power to command both the gaze and the power of explanation. The space is thus illuminated by single beam of light, perceived through the same framework that imposes consistency and truthiness and an implied verisimilitude. Only in a later work, *Fogo Morto*, does he depart somewhat from this structure by introducing a multiplicity of visions and voices; but this is in the context of directly depicting the shattering of the traditional world and its traditional consensus. Various characters discuss the same problem but they see it in different and conflicting ways. These people have lost the shared sense of reality that bound them together, and they are suspended awkwardly between the bourgeois and traditional worlds unable even to communicate effectively any longer.[149]

Before it is overthrown, the intermeshing of traditional society had appeared tight and coherent enough to present a closed system, impervious to outside forces. All the characters' diverse actions are oriented by the implicit goal to reinforce the old order against gathering threats. But the sense of isolation this connotes is echoed at the human level, as individual people become locked inside their internal frontiers and are rendered unable to describe or engage a system that seems designed to make them suffer. They retreat from reality to reminiscence or imagination, as their world withers and shrinks. They come to avoid this painful world and deny it through desperate embraces of anachronism, hallucinatory dreams, madness, sexual indulgence, and crime.[150]

Rego also draws from the earlier literary trope of naturalism. The attitudes of his characters appear at times to have been determined by the environment, if not through outright hereditary transmission through the blood. He explores "human nature" in a specific sense: to forefront emotions, appetites, and primitive tendencies, the irrationality that modern civilization is not able to suppress. Civilization was a layer of affectation overlaid superficially on people, incapable of expressing their full truth. Rego saw in bourgeois social relations a series of artificial masks intended to confound how people really live with each other and their environments, particularly the environment of the Northeast. His work is divided between natural, genuine life, the life of the region, and the invasive attempts from outside to mischaracterize and corrupt it. He sought to find an element of northeastern humanity that was resistant and oblivious to historical processes, locked in the eternal return of a stable identity and fixed social relations.[151]

This approximation of human and nature is most visible in Rego's treatment of popular-class characters. His animalization of blacks, mixed-bloods, and the poor reflects his adherence to traditional social hierarchies. It also shows how Freyre's analysis of miscegenation, which Rego championed, was at root something other than the basis for instituting a racial democracy in Brazil. In fact the miscegenation Freyre praised was a stark symbol of traditional power imbalances in Brazil, since it was the result of white masters choosing to couple with female black slaves they controlled while white females were never placed at the disposition of male black slaves.[152]

The Northeast Rego constructed was ruled by the coroneis, who "scrutinized their underlings with the arrogance of a lord," but who were loved and respected by them because of established relationships of favors and protection. The Northeast of droughts at the onset of modernity was a place of dire insecurity. Its living cycles of harvests and seasons were replaced by successions of death—death of people, of animals, of families, of plantations, of societies. The conversation and sung folktales of yore had given way to laments and muttered prognostications of apocalypse. But the marshes and meadows, the green plantations, were a paradise sought by hordes fleeing the dry interior; they were "a retreat from the blistering sky, the thing of a fairy tale, a child-fable kingdom." The plantation societies were a Shangri-la overseen by wise grandparents that functioned through the warm understanding between master, slave, and the aggregate of peasant hangers-on. They offered patriarchal protection against drought and hunger.[153]

This was the region of the poor but content submissives, accepting of their place: "sheep, but sheep on whom you could count for the roughest of labor and a doglike dedication." They were miserable without any hope of improvement, but it was fundamental that they should see themselves as "blessed by God for not having died of hunger, and for having the sun, moon, river, rain, and stars as playthings that will not break in their rough hands." They were haggard and coarse but took pride in their apparent confidential relations with the bosses. Any sort of conflict was understood to be personal, not systemic, and was dealt with resolutely through fisticuffs or the knife.[154]

Rego, in his consideration of the poor, oscillated between a social and human comprehension of the injustice of their situation and the assumption that it was frankly inevitable. Indigence was most often seen as an irremediable fact attributable to the natural inequality of men's capacities, and as a state that should be endured with the proper dignity and deference. For their part, the rich enjoyed a wider palette when they confronted the poor, being permitted to behave with either humane goodness or the most arch cruelty. Even as he recognized that the socioeconomic extremes in the region were monstrous, Rego suggested that the local well-to-do simply could not provide more than they had already done. It was the new example of bourgeois social relations that made the long-standing structure of patronage appear heartless and insufficient. In his book *O Moleque Ricardo* (Ricardo the Kid), Rego drew a counterpoint between plantation and city. He denounced the lack of solidarity and compassion between bosses and laborers in cities, as well as the absence of structures to assist and protect the poor there. He declared that in the plantation, "even the cry of 'Stop, thief!' delivered by Colonel So-and-so had a different sound and meaning than the same phrase shouted by an urban boss, because the latter really was just trying to offend and cause trouble."[155]

Rego developed a critique of Recife's modern labor movement that implied it was a deformation of how laborers and bosses had related in the idyllic past. In *O Moleque Ricardo* the workers did not have true leaders but callous and calculating chieftains who insisted on blind subservience. These chieftains were not motivated by political ends, or dedicated to structurally improving the lot of the workers, but merely corrupted the mutually beneficial relationships of traditional patronage to foster passivity among the urban ranks. Political leaders came in from outside the factories to exploit the laborers' amassed voting power and recruit their support for public demonstrations, including the inevitable brawls among campaigns. Weighing this degeneration, Rego noted wanly that the circumstances of the simple plantation folk were preferable since their "only utopia was rain for the gardens, and the weekend festivities." With his gaze cast ever backward, Rego did not attempt to consider nuances of contemporary political militancy.[156]

Throughout Rego's work, the city appears as a hive of confusion and uprootedness, the point from which plantations were viewed nostalgically. The misery was greater, the pain more anguishing, the injustices more extreme there than in the plantations, with their traditional moral codes. Cities were places of treason, impersonal laws, and harsh discipline. Woe unto the poor northeastern migrant in the city who no longer had the guidance, support, or gentle paternal control of a wise old coronel. Urban life was riven by conflicts and social contradictions, especially among bosses and laborers—the essence of capitalism's destructive force. Rego attributed the harsh attitude of the bosses also to the fact that they had grown up as the plantations were fading away; they had no experience of plantation life and its ways, its rules and hegemonies. This was the case with Lula de Holanda in *Fogo Morto*, for example, a modern boss who had never learned to lead. Men of this ilk demanded obeisance and asserted command gruffly. In their off hours they abandoned rural pursuits for idle conversing in foppish clubs.[157]

The principal theme uniting Rego's fiction is the decadence of the world, expressed in various forms. One of these was the onset of sex as a problem to be either hidden or scientifically studied, rather than as the spontaneous passion of men and women. This new psychology of and around sex was part of a cohering subjectivity: that of the bourgeois individual. Traditional societies had not seen sex as a problem. Certainly there had been some taboos, but on the whole sex was understood implicitly as a natural act and a transcendent ritual that was larger than any one individual and that linked a society internally. The new anxiety around sex was a reflex of how traditional life was destabilized. Communities linked by blood and custom became in the cities patchworks of strangers obeying capitalist rationality. Its natural character now leaving it open to association with disease, sex was catalogued into forms such as "normal," "abnormal," "aberrant," and "sick." The great house with its effusive populations of concubines and bastard children had given way to the bourgeois family dwelling where individuals fretted and judged in the darkness.[158]

These changes in the understanding of sex were linked by Rego to not just the loosening of communal blood ties but the weakening of blood itself. Perverse products of miscegenation—children born frail and ill, deformed, half-witted—were a sign of the dissolution of patriarchal society. Homosexual practice also symbolized the withering of a society founded on the patriarchal family. Relations that were "not reproductive" took away the essence of a world based on identity roles defined from the grandfather on down.[159] Male homosexuality effaced the central figure of the virile man, indicating a society feminized, a society allowing itself to be violated by new bosses. The younger generations were degenerate, impotent, dominated. In the plantation, the "homosexual" as such did not exist. There were acts of sodomy, associated with either brute youthful curiosity or the practices of odd cults, but not modern homosexuality, which would be classified into an abnormality or a disease or the result of unfortunate destiny—but in all of these cases an index of a fallen society.[160]

Another aspect of Rego's fallen society was madness, such as that afflicting Captain Vitorino Carneiro da Cunha in *Fogo Morto*. Madness expressed the social alienation of people who belonged to a prior sociability, who could not come to grips with capitalist rationality or the impersonal power structures of the new world. Their lack of understanding bloomed at every new encounter, every new development, until they were left psychologically paralyzed and unable to communicate. But at the same time, it was their stoic rejection of the obscenity and fetishized mercantile character of modern society that bourgeois society classified as insanity. From Vitorino's (and Rego's) perspective, the men that accepted the new order in which everything was out of place and constantly in motion were the senseless ones. As Rego contextualizes it, Vitorino's madness had more to do with the irrational nature of the bourgeoisie themselves.[161]

As his writing reveals, José Lins do Rego was perhaps, as he once wrote of someone else, "a body trembling with passions but a soul much older than its body. . . . A lost boy, a boy of the plantation."[162]

JOSÉ AMÉRICO DE ALMEIDA

Born in 1887 in the Engenho Olho d'Agua in the municipality of Areia, Paraíba, José Américo de Almeida is best known for the novel *A Baga-ceira* (1928). This book is deeply transitional, pivoting between the natu-ralist and modernist aesthetics, just as its subject is the transformation of a patriarchal society to a bourgeois one. It is thus inescapably replete with ambiguities. It interlaces the regionalist proclamations of Gilberto Freyre with Euclides da Cunha's naturalist metaphors and positivist phi-losophy, in a dense writing style also derived from da Cunha.[163]

In fact da Cunha was a profound influence on Almeida, who adapted the former's treatment of the dichotomy between littoral and dry interior into his own polarization of the semi-humid marsh terrain (*brejo*) and the backlands. Almeida also reworked da Cunha's mythology of the sertão into a critique of plantation society, recently having emerged from slavery and falling to degeneration. And da Cunha's eugenic overtones echo through Almeida, appearing in his racial prejudice and his grim view of the racial miscegenation that was part of the slave-labor regimes of the Northeast's temperate sugar zone. The sertão was embraced for its distilling environ-mental harshness, and Almeida regarded the inhabitant of the sertão, the sertanejo, as an ideal racial specimen for his lack of black blood. The ser-tanejo was for Almeida the perfect regional type, uniquely capable of deal-ing with the region's defining climatic feature, the droughts.[164]

Beyond its discussion of natural elements, *A Bagaceira* contained a sociological undercurrent: the (false) premise that slavery did not exist in the sertão while it defined social life itself in the sugar zone, which created two distinct societies. The presence of slavery was linked to es-sential attitudes and emotions: where there was slave labor there was a thick atmosphere of brutality, a heritage of savagery. A man who grew up in sugar society had violence in his blood. He was devoid of sensitiv-ity; he could not love his land or his region. Meanwhile, the "flotsam of negroes in the shanties, products of the arbitrary crossings of racial mix-ture, with their tumult of pigments," were servile creatures, incapable of fighting against regional subordination or of being proper regional citizens. Slavery and the presence of blacks themselves were cited as sources of the region's present state of decay. But at other times the natu-ral environment of the plantation area joined them as a cause of what was deemed a pathetic debacle.[165]

While *A Bagaceira* was written as fiction, its author was an essayist at heart. But he sensed the efficacy of writing a novel, a more attractive and accessible form than nonfiction, in order to convey impressions that in a set of essays would have lost both appeal and symbolic thrust. Almeida had also initially seen *Coiteiros* and *O Boqueirão* more as documents of "northeastern reality" than as works of fiction. But fiction (the evocative term *romance* in Portuguese) provided a convenient facade behind which the author could still endeavor to utter truths about the region without restriction or counterargument. Almeida's strategy was dissimulation, not simulation, which allowed him to alloy fictional and scientific discourse. He made clear in a preface that his goal was to call the attention of Brazilians "from more civilized regions to grave problems that still are not well known or understood." He wanted to make the Northeast known through its predicaments, which were forgotten or unobserved by others.[166]

A Bagaceira follows the journey of a group of sertanejos from the backlands to the sugar zone, where they would labor in the cane fields and await the return of the rains, but a series of conflicts with the dwellers of the temperate region naturally ensued. This book inaugurated the literary tradition of the northeastern social novel, emphasizing how misery was spatialized in the region but also removing any indication that there are more powerful interests at work benefiting from the situation.[167] But the construction of the Northeast in *A Bagaceira* also contains contradictions because Almeida, unlike Rego, was less adamantly opposed to the intellectual influences of modernism. He thought that some of the region's traditional political elites were corrupt and ought to be replaced. Bourgeois rationality should not be rejected but adopted, as the best way to protect and maintain the Northeast's characteristic social relations. A conciliation with modernity would defend against drastic ruptures with the past. Modernity should be introduced from the top down by an elite vanguard able to orchestrate technical change and fortify paternal power structures, thus minimizing the chances of open social conflict.[168]

Almeida's regionalist work was centered in the uncertain nexus between the past, which he believed slavery had debased, and the new bourgeois sociability, which alarmed him. It was his impulse to reconcile traditional modes with modernity that led him to focus on the sertão as the model space for northeastern society, a natural substrate where technical advancement could occur without transforming traditional social codes. However, the conclusion of *A Bagaceira* reveals that the author harbored doubts about the viability of its premise: nature might accept modernity's impositions with docility, but men were neither docile nor predictable, subjecting their beneficent reformers to rough ingratitude.[169]

There is a proximity between Almeida's political vision and Gilberto Freyre's theory of the plasticity of northeastern society. Almeida believed it was necessary for the Northeast to adjust to the changes affecting the rest of the country to avoid polarization, open conflict, and the loss of control of the region's own future. He regarded with pointed disdain the contemporary coroneis who seemed incapable of promoting new economic and political structures in the region, ignoring the needs of their humble dependents while swilling voraciously at the federal trough.[170] Because of this, the messages in Almeida's fiction were more moralizing than social. In the novel, Lúcio, educated son of a plantation owner, represented the disjuncture between a romantic attachment to the land and traditional values and an intellectual, rational interest in improving the place where he lived. Lúcio dreamed of modernization, but not modernity, and he regarded social inequality as accidental since "branches from the same tree can turn out differently." The type of change that he championed were more targeted to the activities of plantations than to the interests or endeavors of society as a whole.[171]

Almeida thought the Northeast could be unified around the model of the sertão, and modified by targeted modernizing efforts directed from above. In this, his vision was fully in accordance with the authoritarian attitude of the federal government of the 1930s. Improvements to workers' conditions were understood to derive from paternalistic leaders, not to be something won by the workers themselves through political action. While Almeida did lament the indolence of the people in the sugar zone, and praise the rugged heartiness of the sertanejo, he did so in a framework that individualized the sources and instances of conflict. And yet the popular sectors in his writing do not possess individual voices or subjectivities. Their speech has been corrected by the narrator, who makes them recite civilized words rather than their feelings or hopes.[172]

Unlike Freyre, Almeida never separated civilization from culture. While he constructed the Northeast as traditional and steeped in memory, it was still part of history, which was why to him technology did not represent a threat but an opportunity. What was needed were more machines and greater techniques to tame the droughts and generate a truly Brazilian civilization. He thought traditional values could not only coexist with but take new life from technology. He wanted nothing more than the introduction of the automobile to the sertão, which would bring with it a new velocity of change in the region's economic and political spheres.

O Boqueirão is a novel depicting the shock between forces of modernization that arrive in the interior, and the traditional structures that resist them. Modernization is portrayed as compelling in its dynamism, but still superficial compared to the deeply rooted customs and attitudes it confronts. The book shows the automobile being driven into the sertão, but forced to stop and wait for an indignant cow—a metaphor for the stubborn resilience of the region. Reformist efforts are met with resistance, less an active resistance than an idle, sleepy one; and nature always seems to win out over civilization because the people themselves do not care for change.[173] The civilization Almeida desired would not antagonize or wipe out nature, but the two would exist together within the true traditional characteristics of the region. It was an ambitious idea. Northeastern civilization would unite the people within a single mechanism, with the same objectives. The landscape would be transformed, and tamed; rivers dammed, their energies channeled. This Northeast would be "the terrain of organized labor. A docile and loyal land, concerned only with its well-being and beauty. It would require a constructive sensibility to order and educate nature in this way." In his fiction, Almeida accepted technology-inspired change to the Northeast as long as it accommodated the structures of order already present in the people's lifeways.

RACHEL DE QUEIROZ

The last author addressed here, Rachel de Queiroz, was born in Fortaleza, Ceará, in 1910, to traditional families in the Quixadá and Beberibe districts. She has claimed that her writing was heavily influenced by the regionalist fiction of Antônio Salles and by the sociology of Djacir Menezes, her principal companions in Forteleza's literary circles. She had been partial to the Communist Party in the 1930s, and was—alongside Bahian author Jorge Amado—one of the first fiction writers to take up revolution and the "social question" as themes. Her handling of these subjects differed from Amado's in that she allied them to an extremely traditional view of society and its values. Almir Andrade has noted that Queiroz sought to discover a "natural" man, wild, free of any intellectualized codes or systems of belief. Her concept of revolution involved a romantic view of the artificiality of the modern world and the masks it demanded people wear. What she wanted was a social upheaval that would bring back the true man, restoring him from the degenerative toxins of civilization.[174]

Her basic framework was similar to that of Almeida although she had a very different notion of how the utopian Northeast was to be realized. When she idealized the sertanejos and the myths of the sertão, when she denounced the social transformations and mercantilist ethics wrought by capitalism, she was arguing for a new society in the Northeast that would rescue the human purity, the communal links, and paternal relationships that were traditional traits of the region. Her socialism was melded with Christianity and patriarchy, and it drew intensity from her displeasure with how new capitalist relationships and the growing power of the cities had degraded her own family's fortunes. Her characters are "subversive" to the extent that they contest the onset of the capitalist regime, but her utopian vision of the future was anchored in nostalgia for the sertão, where there had once existed "liberty, purity, sincerity, and authenticity." In that sense the "revolutionary" activists in her books do not fight for social change so much as against it. They are seeking humanity's irreducible truth, untouched by the "lies" and "contrivances" of the modern world.[175]

Queiroz's idealization of the sertão confronted a significant obstacle in the droughts. In O Quinze, her most influential work, she describes the personal and collective dramas of people caught up in the 1915 drought in Ceará. That event is interpreted as fatally disorganizing local society, devastating its traditional relations of production and of power, as well as enervating its social and moral codes. Its excess was an intrusion on the natural order, of environment as well as of society understood as rooted in an essential human nature. Her characters bravely reject the artifices of decadent society in the name of their own truth. Nothing in the social world is permanent, but human nature is universal and eternal: "only chance and the quirks of fate can displace people from their own selves." These characters affirm life in the face of misery, searching for the ultimate truth that will one day be reencountered and reestablished. They struggle for the end of history itself, when being and appearance will converge and people can comprehend themselves without masks or deceit.[176]

Vicente, in O Quinze, is an example of the ideal man who is himself almost a state of nature: "pleasant to see and hear like a charming landscape, of which nothing is demanded but beauty and color," a virile sertanejo "of nearly animal strength." He was capable of living in harmony with nature, by reconstructing it according to his own pure image and pushing back against the effects of modernity. He understood nature and was understood by it: a good man, a traditional man who respected his family and protected the weak. His place was the sertão of kind bosses who loved their underlings as their own children, whose wives were carried on palanquins by adoring villagers. The sertão that inspired a sort of quiet sensual passion for the land, but that also bore threats—the droughts, hunger, gloom, disease, and drudgery.[177]

In *Caminho de Pedras* we get a clearer look at the ambiguity of the social transformation Queiroz had in mind—a progression toward the past. This novel, set in Fortaleza, examines the relations between a middle-class intellectual (not unlike herself) and the labor movement, in particular their disputes for control of the local Communist party. Queiroz uses classic Marxist statements awkwardly but knowingly, in order to critique the affectedness of some Communist characters, and she denounces the way the party machine winds up reproducing society's unequal social relations. The author had already distanced herself from the party when she wrote the novel, which portrays the tension between an intellectual vanguard in control of "revolutionary wisdom" and the laborers who complain that they are treated as tools of the intellectuals' secret agendas.[178]

If the book evades clear engagement with the realities of factory life in Fortaleza, it also looks back ideally to a past that does not acknowledge slavery. Her characters seek a return to moral and ethical codes from a utopian antiquity that are being undermined, including by leftist militants; they strive for a traditional, prebourgeois state of being. Cities embody the corrupt present afflicting the Northeast, so they are cast as islands of filth, isolation, captivity, and fear obtruding on the landscape.

Queiroz condemns how the intellectuals' generalizations and abstractions denied the humanity of the workers, transforming them into "masses" of people with somber faces and dirty hands, but no names. For her, the theory of "class" displaced the workers' human side, ignoring how their communitarian and personal dimensions influenced the struggle for a new (old) order. She responded with colorful portrayals of flesh-and-blood people, willful, incoherent, and superstitious, who were torn between the disgrace of daily life and the noble fight for a better future.[179]

By rejecting the idea that the labor movement was a product of intellectuals' devising or even of bourgeois society itself, Queiroz gave it a different connotation and significance. She saw it as offering the possibility to return to a more harmonious human and natural state, such as that of the traditional sertão communities. Her Christianity gave her an additional vocabulary with which to critique aspects of bourgeois society, from the place of women to poverty and social injustice. This new society, based on rationality and impersonal discipline, was not only drearily oppressive but it degraded the traditional safety nets that had given security to the popular sectors. They were viewed as raw material, fodder for industrial processes they should embrace in the name of progress but that denied their true human nature, their "animal side." Still, her fiction, in its disgust with the present and yearning for an idealized past, was paternalistic in its solidarity with the poor. She articulated a populist condemnation of intellectuals as competitors, not allies, of the workers—stuffed shirts who, rather than helping the "masses" frame and understand the revolutionary project, actually created more obstacles in the way of a new society that would reconcile nature and the past.[180]

In her construction, the Northeast's natural integrity was threatened by the interactions of the impacts of extreme weather with the encroachment of cities, and their ripple effects of capitalist social relations. But the region continued to represent the county's best and last space where people could live their lives according to natural rhythms. The nordestino, and especially the sertanejo, offered the greatest hope for a decisive counteraction against modern society's conflicts and corrosive denaturalization. They maintained the dream of a future society that would reweave the bonds of communal responsibility and personal honor, a society that fostered the coexistence with nature. These were regional traits but universal in scope, providing the outlines of a goal for revolutionary social change.[181]

In her writing Rachel de Queiroz formed a link between two Northeasts—that of tradition and longing, and that of social upheaval and mobilization against bourgeois injustice. She experienced in her own life the anxiety of a generation suspended between the fading of traditional social landscapes, and the diverse reterritorializing projects emerging in the 1930s. The new society seemed hell-bent on destroying the natural world, a world that Queiroz "watched disappear into the night's golden mist, slipping away like a phantom between the doleful gnashings of the handsaws."[182]

Northeastern Brush Strokes

The institution of the Northeast as a space of tradition and nostalgia was carried out not only in sociology and literature, but in painting. This visual art provided a fundamental contribution to the Northeast's visibility, giving vibrant form to the more conceptual sketches written into traditionalist sociology and 1930s fiction. It would help crystallize a suite of "typical regional images" that had enormous influence on later regionalist production, such as cinema and television. Its trove of symbols became the way the region was visualized.[183]

Produced on canvas were not straightforward representations of empirically real things, but novel ways of seeing, and new angles from which to perceive. Regionalist paintings fractured the sense of common visibility and shared identity to emphasize subjective difference. They demanded that the region be "seen," not as an objective demonstration of material trappings (such as those exotic items domesticated into curio-cabinet shelves) but according to its own distinct aesthetic synthesis. Through their colors, lines, and scintillating light, these paintings constructed the Northeast's imagetic space, lending it a "true and definite" form that expressed both its visual texture and its soul. The works did not merely display regional markers but taught how to perceive and design them, even how to imagine them, as timeless iconic symbols.[184]

Gilberto Freyre, whose writing was strongly influenced by these images, had long called for a regionalist/traditionalist school of painters to help "fix" regional forms. He noted that the constant presence of the sun in Brazil, but especially the Northeast, generated a unique landscape with its own light, its own color range, its own ways to see and modes of expression that were different from any in Europe. The natural world, such a part of the northeastern experience, demanded a distinct artistic language to convey it—one that would meld the tropical essence with foundational Portuguese elements, since it was they who had first attempted to describe Brazil authentically, in its own terms.[185]

Freyre thought that regionalist painting had the power to reflect "the true scenery and life of the Northeast." In the tone of his own art criticism, he attempted to fix a certain regional visibility characterized by deep ochre and umber or tropically exuberant greens and yellows, in contrast to impressionism's more abstract and carnivalesque mélange of hues. In preference to Recife's surging cityscape, Freyre admired the Northeast's pleasing rhythm of natural verticalities, in its trees—the regal palms and slender, bulbous papayas, the colossal mangoes, the cashews hunched and writhing in voluptuous lagoons. It was a landscape seething with natural color, and that still "seems to contain something historical, something ecclesiastic and civic." Within this prolific environment Freyre depicted scenes of past plantation life: black slaves working in the fields or along wooden aqueducts, ox-driven carts laden with cane; or moments of repose and recreation, slaves dancing and singing in a meadow observed by the amiable senhor.[186]

Freyre looked toward a truly regionalist painting with its own forms and techniques that could transcend the lingering colonial subservience to Greek and Roman mythology. It would show blacks, Indians, and *mulatas* rather than pink-faced European models, and it would capture the sensuous heat of the climate and of physical work—half-naked black men portrayed in movement, sweating and sunburned as they toil. If it subverted the European past, it would forefront another, that of the Northeast's environmental and social history. Freyre was thus a champion of the work of painter Manoel Bandeira (not the poet Manuel Bandeira), choosing him to illustrate *O Livro do Nordeste*, which Freyre edited and which also was concerned with past civilizations of the plantations and of old Recife. He wanted images that contributed to his text's goal of describing the landscape, "the most color-rich of any in Brazil: greens, reds, yellows, violets, all bursting in effusive tufts, clusters, florets, and leaves." But it was important not to demonstrate the mere picturesque quality of the landscape, but to penetrate it, revealing its essentially "regional character and composition."[187]

Another artist who shared this way of seeing was Cícero Dias, whose work concentrated on lyrical views of sugar society, the great houses, the "black and Africanized plebes," the social harmony. He emphasized that harmony technically, through careful use of lines, forms, and color, resulting in images of a space that was soothing to gaze at and consider. He also used juxtaposition, combining snippets from different time periods (for example, train tracks near the cane fields) to suggest that at its firmly rooted best the Northeast could absorb multiple temporalities without conflict. Dias also depicted family scenes, urging the familiarity of objects, animals, people. He painted entire households, from formally dressed aunts and eyeglass-wearing young college men and scads of children to the ever-patient black help; outside, dogs cavorted

2.1 *Família de Luto* (Luto Family). Oil on canvas.
Cícero Dias, 1929. Fundação Gilberto Freyre.

near milk cows and oxen. He lavished reds and blues on his canvases, colors borrowed from folklore. Dias emphasized the link to popular art by evading studied precision, substituting the union of bold colors in an aesthetic evoking the visual palette of traditional cultural life— festival parades, women's ornate dresses, paper flowers, the heaped tables of street vendors, the angel-embellished wooden coffins of the deceased.[188]

Dias helped codify a collection of regional archetypes: trees corresponding to each environmental zone (the coconut palm for the coast, the cashew for the intermediate temperate area); the church, and the padre delivering mass; pregnant women; children playing in the street; vivid handicrafts; popular dances, such as the fandango and *bumba-meu-boi*. He painted a past of dense hybridity, with English details of the priests placed alongside food characteristic of the plantations and all further joined with festivals, bastard children, rural toughs, nuns, the smiling senhor. It was a patriarchal worldview that perceived inequality but praised the absence of conflict, and saw artistic beauty in the activities of slave labor. Dias created a multiracial space whose contrasts were harmonized into idyllic hues, a bright past of typical people and practices. His landscape was the product of dreams and sublimations, and careful historical sequestrations. But it offered, in the words of Mário de Andrade, "a particularly northeastern complex of music, religiosity, and family essence."[189]

Another set of visual representations of the past came from Lula Cardoso Ayres, who focused on the relations between people and nature and the degrading impacts of civilization they suffered. For Ayres, traditional man had not attempted to dominate the tropics but had learned to live with them, through love and symbiotic identification. But the modern world was imposing artificial, damaging forces, and nature was in remission. In response, Ayres's early painting constructed a visibility of the Northeast forefronting what he considered the apex of human-environmental harmony, the plantation society.[190] The work that he generated in the 1930s added expressionist touches to portrayals of daily life working on the plantation, or of festival revelry. But by the 1950s, his subjects had shifted to surrealist takes on fantastic beasts from the regional popular imagination, such as the half-man, half-animal *jaraguá*, *foiará*, and *caipora*. Even in his backgrounds to apparently innocuous folkloric images, the vegetation took on a queerly human aspect, regarding the viewer with its own melancholy inquisitiveness. This later work attempted to express nature's revolt against depersonalizing capitalist social relations, and modern man's decreasing affection for the environment. The encroaching bourgeois rationality stripped the region of its marvelous dimension, of the poetic possibility to transit between dream and reality.[191]

During the 1930s Ayres had performed studies of the region's folklore to mine themes for his magical realism. The centrality of the ox in his work recalled both bumba-meu-boi and cordel literature; other influences included the humanizing of nature and the existence of phantoms. In context, the presence of ghosts often signified the death of the society he portrayed, and longed for. His work called up childhood memories of the tactile solidity of existence—the clock in the family house's visiting room, his grandfather's high-backed chair, the great staircase to the bedrooms—and filled them with hollow-eyed wraiths. He painted the past as haunted dreams that could actually scare the inhabitants of the present.[192]

Both Cícero Dias and Lula Cardoso Ayres participated in making visible a region defined by tradition, patriarchy, folklore, and harmony, col-

2.2 *Os Tuchauas do Carnaval de Recife* (The Tuchauas of Recife Carnival).
Oil on canvas. Lula Cardoso Ayres, 1942. Archive of Lula Cardoso Ayres.

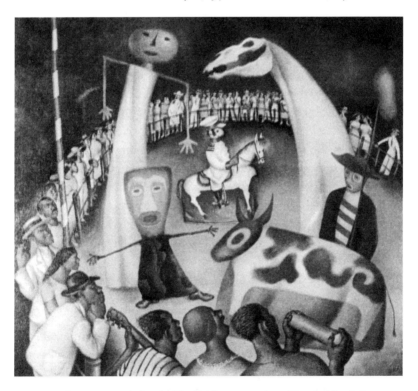

2.3 *Representação do Bumba-Meu-Boi* (Representation of Bumba-Meu-Boi).
Oil on canvas. Lula Cardoso Ayres, 1943. Archive of Lula Cardoso Ayres.

ored with a tropical vitality that was tempered by longing and hazy reminiscence. Their painted Northeast was primitive, rustic, unpolished, a place where the integration of man and nature appeared complete and the relation between them unproblematic.

Northeastern Music

It was not only the children of traditional families in decline who constructed the Northeast as a space of nostalgia. In this project they were joined by the thousands of poor nordestinos who were forced to migrate from their native northeastern territory to the commercial agricultural fields or the rapidly expanding industrial parks of Rio de Janeiro and São Paulo. These peasants were abandoning a region in crisis whose traditional economic activity and social customs were unable to keep pace with national and global transformations—a region whose climatic problems and entrenched power relations seemed to remove any possibility for improving the lot of the rural poor.

Thus, despite the ambivalence and uncertainty of migration, it also offered the promise of liberation from misery and exploitation. Nordestinos responded to the idea that material progress and security were available in Brazil's urban south, if they abandoned their native lands (as well as their positions as subservient dependents or desperate roamers). Especially by the 1940s, as the Northeast's economy weakened but its traditional power relations entrenched, São Paulo and Rio de Janeiro hovered like captivating mirages, dazzling the peasants' imaginations and insinuating that their lives could be better there.

A decade earlier, in the 1930s, improvements to and expansion in transportation and national mass communication, from mail and newspapers to radio, helped disseminate what was essentially propaganda from southern governments and businesses anxious to attract laborers. Nationalist discourse regarded this process favorably, praising its contribution to "national integration" and the interpenetration of the "two Brazils" that seemed always threatening to cleave irreparably. And the major cities in the South, serving as bases of social consolidation, would provide the cradle for the authentic national culture so ardently sought.

Radio, the most modern and potentially most accessible form of communication at the time, was understood as fundamental to helping produce national integration, shortening distances and homogenizing differences between regions, and divulging national culture across Brazil. While 1930s radio was a commercial entity, underwritten by advertisements, it took on complex relations with the state following from the context of populist politics as well as the censorship efforts of Getúlio Vargas's Estado Novo after 1937. But the nationalist mandate proved unstable in practice: to the extent that radio was encouraged (politically or economically) to address the nation and reveal its unity, radio also inescapably reflected the cultural diversity of performers and audiences. Stations in the South such as Rio de Janeiro's Rádio Nacional served as magnets for artists of all sorts, but especially musicians, from around the country; they were the first to concentrate, distill, and divulge what would be called Brazilian popular music (*música popular brasileira*). Up until then, the basic generic separation in music was between a large grouping of popular song (*canção*) and erudite music, usually European classical music. But at this moment the music of the nation's various popular sectors took on a new importance, as preoccupation with recognizing the authentic "national" and "popular" came to redefine artistic and cultural production.[193]

The nationalist project, and the power structure that sustained it, invested heavily in changing people's tastes—not only, even perhaps not so much, the lower classes as the elites and the middle class. It was they who needed to learn to recognize and value genuine "national and popular" production, which should transform their cultural attitudes and consumption habits. Something similar had been occurring in erudite music during the 1930s, as modernist writers urged the exploration and development of specific Brazilian themes in national compositions, whether in timbre, rhythm, melody, or form. Such classical music would turn to the people and authentic Brazilian tradition for its raw material, mounting a self-affirming bulwark of Brazilianness against the tide of foreign influences. The music, whether classical or popular, that resulted from this process should embody notions of civic values, faith, work, and hierarchy—indispensable elements of the "construction of a civilized nation." But while it would converge in and radiate back out from the cities, the urban milieu was too dissonant and shot through with foreign influences to provide its foundations. Those were sought in the rural areas, the regional territories, repositories of Brazilian identity. Popular music traditions in the Northeast that, like the modal singing of blind beggars in country fairs, could be traced dimly back to European Gregorian chants but were newly regarded as manifestations of authentic Brazilian music.[194]

In the 1940s, popular, radio-friendly northeastern music became principally associated with the *baião* of Pernambucan musician and singer Luiz Gonzaga. He had served as a cornet player in military bands between 1930 and 1938, and, after acquiring an accordion in São Paulo, made his way to Rio to try to launch his own music career. Gonzaga was born in 1912 in Fazenda Caiçara, a municipality of rural Exu, Pernambuco, to poor peasant parents. Growing up, he had observed his father, Januário, an amateur accordionist who also worked in instrument repair, playing at animated weekend dances. So it might have been an intuitive move for Luiz to begin playing in cabarets. Still, it was not in Rio's noble dance clubs where he could find work, but the shabby bars of Mangue in Estácio, a red-light district. He performed tango, waltz, bolero, polka, mazurka, all the favored international dance forms of the period. Gonzaga also appeared on the amateur music shows held by famed composer Ary Barroso, where he received only modest recognition until his 1940 performance of "Vira e Mexe" earned him the top score from the judges and a contract from Rádio Nacional.

In 1943—and through the influence of a musician friend in the Rádio Nacional stable, Pedro Raimundo from Rio Grande do Sul—Gonzaga determined to base his professional identity on the Northeast. He created a "typical" costume combining the leather garb of the horsemen of the interior with the wide-brimmed leather hat favored by bandits. That year, he would make his first recording as a singing artist, and his visual packaging would reinforce his thematic style. Persuading skeptics in the RCA Victor offices, who doubted the appeal of his unusual voice with its strong (perhaps cagily exaggerated) regional accent and mannerisms, Gonzaga was determined to "give a northeastern direction" to his music. He was not a writer, though, and needed someone able to render his childhood memories and regional ideas into the deft poetry of popular music. The composer Lauro Maia indicated Humberto Teixeira, and the Teixeira-Gonzaga partnership would quickly yield an impressive number of national hits and lasted until 1949. That year, rising on his wave of celebrity, Teixeira entered politics. Gonzaga replaced him with the writer and physician José Dantas, who composed lyrics until his death in 1962. In 1951, at the height of his popularity and influence, Gonzaga signed a contract with the private firm Colírio Moura Brasil, who sponsored him on a tour to every city in Brazil with a minimum population of four hundred thousand people.[195]

Gonzaga's music was discursively and strategically directed at two main audiences: northeastern migrants in the South, and the record-buying public of the cities of the Northeast. His radio presence in the South was rooted in relationships with Rádio Record in São Paulo, and Rádio Nacional in Rio; the latter carried his program *No Mundo do Baião* (In the World of the Baião). Other programs he hosted were *Alma do Sertão* (The Soul of the Sertão) for Rádio Clube do Brasil, and *No Reino do Baião* (In the Kingdom of Baião) for Rádio Mayrink Veiga. While Gonzaga had a sharp entrepreneurial instinct, he was also a Christian, a fact that both led him to emphasize Christian traditions and references in his songs, and inflected how he saw and critiqued the circumstances of the Northeast in general. At the same time, it is difficult to find a consistent political voice in his songs because they were written by various collaborators, at different points in his career.[196]

In its own way, Gonzaga's music was representative of the regional identity inscribed in Freyre's sociology and the 1930s fiction. He leant it an audible and commercial quality, steeped in folklore. The creation attributed to him, the baião, hybridized elements of the Northeast's traditional guitarists and dueling singers with the urban samba and other contemporary influences from his present milieu. What he achieved was a national replacement for the dance music that came to Brazil from other countries, but also, at a particular nationalist moment, his "music of the Northeast" was the first to speak and sing of that place on the radio. Gonzaga used the radio to reach a targeted public, a public that had the Northeast in mind already. And it was to a large extent the fruit of a regional sensibility that had cohered in earlier decades.[197]

Gonzaga's complete delivery, from lyrics and dress to the sound of his voice and overall rural sensibility, cohered into a message that signified the Northeast. His accent was familiar to some listeners and strange to others, and Gonzaga became a powerful index of both identification and stereotype; through it he linked to other aural, discursive, and visible associations that could provide comfort or trigger prejudiced judgment. More than anything, his accent helped consolidate the idea of the nordestino migrant, with his own culture and values, as a figure to be incorporated into the world of the southern listening public. His speech generated a new recognition of the group of people who were understood or presumed to speak in that way by the dominant regime of listeners.[198]

For the most part, northeastern migrants brought with them a participatory sense of what music was and what it meant: Music was to be danced to, it was to be sung, it was to be used to coordinate the flow of physical labor. The reality in the South was different, however, with its rationalized work routines and its emphasis on the radio as a "source" of music to be heard and consumed. Migrants' embrace of the radio would symbolize their integration into their new social and cultural milieu. By its nature, the concentration of musical practice in professional, commercial institutions such as the radio and recording studios diminished the space for legitimate popular music production, although northeastern street musicians struggled to maintain it. But the value system predominating in the urban south disciplined both the body for industrial work and the ear for industrially produced music. The nordestino that sang, danced, and played instruments should be reduced to a being that listened passively and obeyed orders.

Everyone had to learn to consciously hear the Northeast, to discern its sounds—not only southern audiences but Gonzaga himself, first challenged in a Rio cabaret by students from Ceará to play something from "the backcountry," and his migrant audiences who grew increasingly aware of how different northeastern music was from other broadcast genres. Gonzaga became an artist known for his capacity to produce something familiar for the migrants—a music that recalled their land, their infancy, the texture and color of what they missed. His fame was materially assisted by the contemporary expansion of both music criticism in the newspapers and specialized music and radio magazines, which in their analyses of or interviews with him all assumed the veracity of his regional character and took to debating the niceties of it.

The proliferation of discourse around the baião established its reality. The magazines and radio programs contributed to the institutionalization of the voice, Gonzaga's voice, as his own identity and that of "his" region, and by extension that of the nation. But control of the national voice was a disputed field. After 1930 and especially after 1937, the federal government sought to control the voice of Brazil; Vargas's New State wanted to establish the parameters within which the nation would speak and be spoken of. But the participants and their motivations, as well as their audiences, were too diverse to be homogenized. Gonzaga's success derived from, on one hand, the generalized appetite for ludic dance music—but on the other, the growing consumption of regional culture as symbols of national identity. His greatest popularity was among the northeastern migrants, because he spoke both to their longing for home (mingled with fearful ambivalence of the big city) and their pride in taking on the challenges of relocation while maintaining such traditional regional values as religion and family.[199]

Luiz Gonzaga fully assumed the character of the "voice of the Northeast," even with all the dimensions of political consciousness raising that implied. His music and the business strategy underlying it "wanted to make the Northeast known around all of Brazil," with songs full of local detail, intimations of strife, and "celebrations of the positive." He willingly accepted the position of mediator between the people and the state, helping make the realities and the dilemmas of the Northeast both visible and audible. And the principal problem of the region in his music was the droughts. After all, this was the main cause for the exodus of nordestinos to the South. In 1950, he and partner Humberto Teixeira composed "Asa Branca," his most well-known song, a beautifully sad statement from the distant perspective of a migrant that he conceived as a sort of "Christian protest" of the droughts that uprooted and displaced people. Later, in 1953, he and Zé Dantas cowrote "Vozes da Seca," a song that incorporated the suggestion of state solutions for the droughts' effects.[200]

But Gonzaga was also deeply concerned with the recognition and acceptance of northeastern music in the South, which betrays a sense of inferiority widely shared with other northeastern intellectuals and culture producers. This encouraged him to target his act, to strategically create and reaffirm a character that was both emblematic of tradition and easily recognizable for southern audiences. His popular sensibility, rooted in his own rural experience, merged with the effort to create musical forms and images that could be urbanized to fit into the professional market of recordings and performances.[201] Gonzaga's generation of artists was involved in a phase of Brazilian popular music that was not so much created by the popular sectors as created for them. It was thoroughly commercial music that relied on radio to reach communities of listeners. At the same time, since nationalism was a major concern of the period, regional and folkloric music received attention not only from private entrepreneurs but from the state apparatus.

It is an intriguing paradox that while on the whole Brazil's cultural economy was increasingly homogenized along the strategies of capitalism, the

Northeast would be hailed as one of the country's most culturally rich and resistant regions. How was it that the Northeast, its society subordinated both politically and economically, its people regularly displaced, managed to "preserve its origins and maintain its cultural traditions"? This was possible precisely because "northeastern culture" was like the Northeast itself a recent invention, largely created by the processes of uprooting. The shaping of the space, and its culture of memory, legacy, tradition, emerged in counterpoint to the urban reality in the South confronted by migrants. Migration made possible the invention of such culture and reinforced its connection to the place left behind. In a manner distinct from reading literature or viewing paintings, listening to music (which is perhaps more visceral and immediate) was a principal mechanism for imagining a new territory and perceiving its symbolic and organic coherence. Hearing the Northeast offered more than explanatory power—it helped produce the region as a place that was both consistent and predictable.[202]

In that sense, Gonzaga's music, which forefronted the experience of the poor nordestinos and their "marginalized culture," did not so much reproduce some sort of traditional peasant discourse as help make such an identity plausible and compelling. His music embodied a vision not of the past but clearly of the present, of a marginalized regional group resisting the immanent destruction of its traditional territory by constructing an imaginary one that would always stay the same. While often interpreted as a form of cultural resistance, his music actually reflected a thorough engagement with the new social conditions migrants confronted in the big city. Gonzaga's Northeast was composed to nourish the memories of these migrants, tailored to address their fears and desires. While his musical identity was also influenced by southern conceptions of northeastern regionalism, the audience for his music (both during and after his period of greatest commercial success, roughly 1946–54) was overwhelmingly northeastern in origin. Part of what detracted from his crossover appeal was the establishment of samba, another music form reflecting the lived experience of urban popular sectors, as Brazil's national music. And Gonzaga's own definition of his music as "regional" limited its broad embrace, particularly as the Northeast was often seen by outsiders as crude backcountry whose economic marginalization offered proof of its primitivism.[203]

Indeed, the success of his music among migrants was one aspect of the solidification of a regional identity among individuals that were framed by stereotypes in the South, such as the so-called *"baiano"* of São Paulo and the *"paraíba"* of Rio. It was only in the urban south that migrants from diverse parts of the Northeast began to perceive themselves as equals and countrymen, "speaking with the same accent," possessing the same tastes, customs, and values—an act of recognition (of self and other) that did not occur back in the Northeast itself. Whatever the direct or literal messages of Gonzaga's songs, his work was directed at the urban nordestino listeners' unconscious minds to make them aware of regional space in new ways, how the Northeast and the South interrelated or contrasted, how they *were*. He revealed how the Northeast could emerge as a subculture in the South, or how the South looked from a northeastern perspective. He also showed how the Northeast could recognize itself in Ceará, Paraíba, or Pernambuco.[204] Gonzaga's music contained audible signs intended to provoke a sensation in the listener of being close to regional authenticity. These were in his accent and vocalizations, his individual words and phrases, his arrangements and instrument selection. All were guided by the desire to flesh out the distant, abstract space of the northeast.[205] His songs gave the Northeast a power to affect listeners' bodies as well as their imaginations, summoning them with rhythm, exulting in the happiness and sensuality of regional couples dances (from *forró* to *xote*). He orchestrated a range of visual, audible, and corporal experiences to give the Northeast human texture.[206]

The center of Gonzaga's Northeast was the backlands, the sertão. His texts referred with intimate familiarity to the lifeways there, the drought and the wonder of rain returning, the wandering, the suffering, the devotion to saints, the bandits and bravery, honor, respect for the elderly. He contributed to crystallizing the portrait of the nordestino as a victim of nature, with a rough temperament, but capable of grand sacrifice and rich cultural production. Gonzaga wove his material from the variegated strands of traditional regional culture, incorporating verses from popular poets ("Chegada de Inverno," "Perfume Nacional"), cowboy song ("Algodão," "Feira de Gado"), festive *coco* rhythms and choruses ("Siri Jogando Bola"), children's melodies ("Xô," "Povão"), circus music ("O Circo"), oral literature and proverbs ("Cintura Fina," "Café," "Vou Casá Já"), legends ("Lendas de São João"), bonfire customs ("Qué que Tu Qué"), beliefs and superstition ("O Xote das Meninas," "Acauã"), and popular humor ("Derramaro o Gai," "Forró de Mané Vito").

At various moments Gonzaga seemed to comment wryly on rural life, adopting the role of the self-deprecating nordestino chuckling at his traditions and innocent foibles. This image of the rustic buffoon could also suggest an oblique criticism of how urban "sophisticated" audiences saw Gonzaga and his audiences. But it also resonated with the familiar stereotype of the country bumpkin that had been a standard Brazilian type in radio and cinema since the 1940s, and would later be absorbed into television. Over time the visual and cultural trappings of the non-regional-specific hayseed character were narrowed to, and equated with, the rural nordestino in mass media.

However, the main impulse of his work was to reaffirm the perception of the Northeast as a homogeneous space defined in opposition to the South. His audience was understood as people living "far from their homeland," and he sketched that homeland in terms general enough to be recognized by migrants from across the region, allowing them to associate with it in their own ways. Its topography, the stage for so many climactic extremes, was cast as fixed and stable, although intercut by long roads that carried nordestinos away to the South and sometimes back again. His Northeast was timelessly rural, its own cities ignored for the essential nature of the interior and nordestinos' relations with agriculture. In "A Volta da Asa Branca," the singer is gratified to be summoned home to "his sertão" by following the white-winged dove who hears the thunder that portends rain for the crops.[207]

Gonzaga made nostalgia for the Northeast, for its people and customs and scenes, a constant theme. The region's most dynamic incarnations were those from the past and in the memory, for listeners in the cities of the Northeast as well as the urban south. He praised the peasants' rugged purity and moral depth, even if at times expressing their anger at the new regime of authority that disregarded traditional relations of protection and assistance.[208] Gonzaga affectionately embroidered the sertão as the site of not just regional tradition, but authentic Brazilian values and rituals. Conversely, the city represented loss of traditional knowledge, of family, and of the empathetic coexistence with nature. Cities were impersonal and monotonous, offering only work—and even then in degraded forms of activity. The sertão was characterized by its studied but proud rejection of the social and economic changes transforming other parts of the country. Its abundant simple pleasures offered respite from vapid modern civilization, a place "where there's none of this at all" (*onde não se tem disso não*).[209] In his 1955 "Riacho do Navio," Gonzaga implicitly recognized the power relations between Northeast and South but declared that if he were a fish he'd rather be in a stream heading back to the sertão, swimming against the current, than in the wide ocean. At home in the interior, after a day tending to livestock from atop a horse he could "sleep to the festive rattle / and awaken to the birds / with no radio imposing news / from civilized areas."[210]

Luiz Gonzaga's music reflects the ambiguity of the combination of traditional content and modern form. While his lyrics affirmed a traditional, antimodern attitude, his rhythms and harmonies were inventions of the urban milieu of the South where he worked. He sang of a space that rejected bourgeois capitalist relations, but he was a professional artist with a product targeted to urban audiences. His self-defined "regional" music, called baião, reached national success for nearly ten years and seemed to some critics to ably reconcile the mandates of traditional and modern. But rather than transcending these axes of cultural production he emphasized their coexistence and irreconcilability. He proclaimed their separation, not their consummation.[211]

Gonzaga was an innovator. The way he rejected standard vocal technique and operatic, romantic traditions for a rural aesthetic rooted in regional popular culture was unprecedented. That was also true for his accordion playing, characterized by an until-then uniquely distinctive rhythmic approach featuring rapid and propulsive fingerings quite unlike the standard lyrical approach for performing waltzes and other smooth dance music on the instrument. This allows Gonzaga to join an elite group of musicians who introduced new ways to interpret Brazilian popular music in the first half of the twentieth century. His name must be inscribed alongside other period inventors and modernizers such as Noel Rosa, Dorival Caymmi, and Jackson do Pandiero.[212]

Thematically, Gonzaga presented a core of tradition whose delivery was being continually updated, similar to cordel literature. He recounted daily life in the Northeast emotionally but warily, as though he were observing the circling threats of modernity with apprehension. But even here it is difficult to generalize, because during the 1950s he celebrated the developmentalism of Juscelino Kubitschek and the Sudene initiative (Superintendancy for the Development of the Northeast) as solutions for what public and private interests viewed as the "problem of the Northeast." It was only by the late 1960s that Gonzaga, influenced by the

Tropicalists, who had praised his contribution to the modern-trending evolution of Brazilian popular music, began addressing more contemporary aspects of northeastern life.[213]

Still, Luiz Gonzaga was the popular artist who most effectively instituted the Northeast as a space of longing and nostalgia—not in the older, colonial-era frames of slavery and sugar plantations, but as a place that living people had physically abandoned, that they remembered fondly, that they missed. The distance here was more geographic than temporal, although those dimensions intermingled. The Northeast of Gonzaga's songs was ordered by patriarchy and a symbiotic relationship with nature, its society marked by hierarchies and suffering as well as rich cultural expressiveness. Gonzaga's work aligned with the projects of other writers and artists described in this book because it endeavored to demonstrate the reality of the Northeast, to conquer recognition of it at the national level and declare its importance as a bastion of authentic Brazilian cultural identity against the globalized and cosmopolitan southern cities.[214]

Northeastern Dramas

By midcentury, the Northeast was the theme of plays that gained national attention. Foremost among them were the works of Paraíba-born playwright Ariano Suassuna, and perhaps the most notable of those was *Auto da Compadecida*, which in 1955 earned the gold medal from the Brazilian Association of Theater Critics and two years later was staged at the First National Amateur Festival in Rio de Janeiro by a group of young actors from Recife. Suassuna's success in the drama world of the South was due in some measure to timing as well as the content of his craft. In Rio and São Paulo, the theatrical tradition maintained long-standing generic divisions between drama (of mainly Italian influence) and comedy; Suassuna's plays intersected and reinterpreted those separations. But he also was there at the right time. Since the 1940s political enthusiasm to foster a native Brazilian dramaturgical tradition had been growing, expressed in the creation of the National Theater Institute, and Suassuna offered plays that answered the call to foment "national spirit." They avoided gratifying bourgeois tastes to focus on ostensibly national topics, places, and realities. His theater suggested the opportunity to not just gather an audience but to shape a people around his subject matter.[215]

And the Northeast was an ideal theme, according to Pernambucan critic Hermilo Borba Filho, because "it already contains a grand historical and national drama, with the tragedy of the droughts, the sugar distilled by slaves' blood, the wealth of popular legends." There was also a rich tradition of popular puppetry in the Northeast, as well as colorful religious pageantry, storytelling, and oral literature. These raw materials all presented the opportunity to mount a "serious theater" that would surpass in national import anything achieved by the mass-culture plays that sold tickets in Rio or São Paulo. Ariano Suassuna benefited from these and other analyses that cast him as the creator of a genuinely national Brazilian theater, since he incorporated an abundance of popular drama, song, and tale-telling from the Northeast that all had some Iberian roots.[216]

In fact, Suassuna leveraged the traditional explanation for the fall of Europe's Middle Ages and adapted it into a schema to explain how the "loyal society of the sertão" was being demolished. His basic framework was the opposition between urban merchants, who supported modernization and increasing state power as tools to weaken traditional social bonds in the Northeast, and the people (povo) who valued honor, bravery, respect, and mutual assistance. All of his works are seasoned by a populist vision in which the people expose their misery and suffering but denounce modernity and capitalism, as well as the collapse of customary paternalism, as the causes. These were people who benefited from the old hierarchy as it was, who followed local chiefs or bosses but never impersonal "leaders."[217]

In his critique, Suassuna ultimately revealed the limits of the progressive politics of traditional regionalism if carried to their extreme. He would become an eager supporter of the national military coup in 1964 and with the new regime helped found the Federal Culture Board (Conselho Federal de Cultura) in 1967. His antipathy to foreign and cosmopolitan culture was so great that he proclaimed the Catholic Church and the military the only institutions capable of protecting an independent Brazil from such corruptions. If the empathetic coronel of the sertão was dying off, the military was the best substitute, providing unity, hierarchy, and discipline to a society threatened on various fronts. Suassuna applauded military intervention, characterizing it as salvation—notably in his play *O Rei Degolado nas Caatingas do Sertão*, which used as background the national response to the 1912 droughts to depict the military and state apparatus as national saviors, fighting for the popular class against newly cruel, degraded elites.[218]

Suassuna's fondness for order, which can also be discerned in his poetry and other writing, derives from his nostalgia for a time before the Northeast entered into crisis, when the sertão was peacefully ruled by aristocratic families. His work is a form of memorial for the lost, gentle kingdoms he imagined, coloring their society, daily life, and popular culture with hues of feudal and medieval anachronism. The basis for his conception of the Northeast was European history and legend, which he transmogrified with the addition of African and indigenous elements, situating it all in the environment of the sertão. Castles, chivalry, and honor coexisted with pagan rites, toothless prophets, and bandits lurking among the cactus. It was a rich, dense space, mystical, brutal, and picturesque, which he both posited and hoped to decipher.[219]

Still, Suassuna's politics were not simple. He regarded warily the left's most ardent progressives, who clamored for modernizing the traditional society he wanted to preserve. But while he could be sympathetic to military intervention, his deep Christianity led him to distrust the right's use of anticommunism to legitimate the imposition of a capitalist regime that was clearly unjust and inhumane. The result of that hypocrisy was, he argued, greater human misery and a society moving further away from God.[220] In contrast, the profound religiosity of the sertão, with its medieval accoutrements of insignias, banners, lances, duels, and horsemanship, offered the vision of a space rooted in history and the sacred. He envisioned a space where all were equal before God, if not here on land; where the consciousness of divine equality gave people hope and resilience as they faced adversity. The extremes of happiness and despair were reframed as the forces of God and the Devil, as they battled to control the region. In Suassuna's Northeast, institutions were imperfect, and as the feeble creations of men grimly accepted as such. It was a place, and a people, defined by faith and the search for mercy.[221]

This sacred world was contrasted with the bourgeois, modernizing South, which had rationalized God out of the discussions of meaning and value. In the Northeast, traditional people both poor and aristocratic still sought out the internal, spiritual dimensions of life, unlike in the South, where a society of disconnected consumers were swayed by external superficialities. Truth and loyalty, hallmarks of the religious Northeast, were countered with treason, selfishness, and the idolatry of merchandise in the South. In the play *O Santo e a Porca*, for example, Suassuna presents a critique of bourgeois materialism; like many of his works, it was a moralizing tale of how capitalist society perverts "human nature."[222]

This theological impulse drove how he envisioned scenes of northeastern life, as well as his selection of source material. He depicted simple, unpolished people struggling for transcendence and seeking answers to life's ontological questions. He created a theater in which human society was a farce, a circus in which everyone was a clown. Puppets represented the controlling hand of God in people's affairs, while society's actions were little more than a parade of masks. Modern public space was an ambivalent stage for antiheroes who cowered before the force of the "Terrible" or the "Light." To construct this world where humans and nature are part of mysterious divine creation, Suassuna harvested the numerous biblical images in popular Catholicism—images mingling Iberian medieval ritual with indigenous and African beliefs and practices, including animism and fetishism. He wove them into dramas in which nordestinos fought epic battles against the "diabolical power" of secular institutions. His Northeast was harsh, but across its parched soil lay the path leading back to the divine.[223]

The setting of his Northeast was always the cactus-choked backlands, or the small dusty towns bordering it where the only building of note was the church, and the only authorities the coronel, padre, delegate, and judge. Suassuna felt it was the "civilization of leather," not the "civilization of sugar," that gave birth to Brazilian identity and the national personality. To enact the genealogy of the region—its families, dreams, madnesses, adventures, tragedies—was to perform the history of the country itself onstage.[224] He unfolded the Northeast like a map, bringing forth its stony ridges and mountains painted with nut trees, rivers and streams crosscut by dams, flagstones burnt by the sun to quartz mirrors. He spun his plots from the destinies of his characters, their individual passions, and their spiritual fatalism. His nordestinos were animalesque in their exaggerated physical degradations: big-bellied, sweating, wounded, reeking, tattered. They were haggard from droughts and injustice, but they maintained their regional pride. They were still able to dream visions of an idyllic past, of a paradise lost and the return some day of a millennial king.[225]

Suassuna wanted to forefront the vigorous beauty and poetry of the sertão in order to counterbalance the way regionalist sociology and literature had emphasized the importance of sugar society, and the way those genres had devised a corresponding perspective of the sertão as ugly and dismal as part of a political strategy to denounce capitalist society. He did not wish to refute outright the regime of traditionalist images and discourses of the Northeast, even though they made the sertão synonymous with misery. He accepted the point but shifted the terms, such that in his work the sertão could be hellish but also a paradise of brooks and orchards. It was a dry land bristling with thorns, but it also had colorful songbirds, inspiring moonlight, and delicious breezes. He sought a resolution that would be neither ideologically right nor left, but a reconciliation, a sacred and "divine vision" based in aesthetics of popular Catholicism. In the religiosity of the backlands, good and evil did not occupy opposite polarities but coexisted.[226]

Similarly, man and nature did not live in separation or false distinction. In Suassuna's sertão the patriarchal clans had animals as their insignias and as their ancestors. People understood, felt, that they were descended from beasts and had kinship with them, that they all shared instincts of cruelty, savagery, resistance, cunning, and appetite. All were divine creatures whose nature was treacherous, unpredictable and dangerous. This sertão was the stage for epics in which warriors from mixed-blood clans brawled in the name of honor or vengeance under a fiery sun.[227]

Suassuna hoped to decipher the grand enigmas of this society, while at the same time absolving it, its people and its memory, of all the condemnation unleashed on it by outsiders and encroachers from civilization. The reality of the sertão could be grasped only in the feral eye of "Onça Caetana," a character from *História do Rei Degolado nas Caatingas do Sertão*, who could shape-shift from woman to jaguar and back. The society of the backwoods was so close to the state of nature that only a cat's eye could take it all in and comprehend it.[228]

In his totalizing account of the sertão, Suassuna ignored the rationalist division between the real and the mythic. He made a cut in space to define the parameters of the locale, and he asserted the unity of all the disparate elements it contained. In that way, his work can be distinguished from the 1930s fiction writers who maintained an attitude of realism. He started with the idea that the proper capacity of art is not merely representation but the presentation of a new reality as the artist sees it. His Northeast adopted the previously crystallized regional images and themes—drought, misery, banditry, the messianic priest and coronel—but reconfigured them into a medieval society with knights and heralds and insignia. He ennobled the sertão, rendering its past into a dream of the future in which epochs lost to time return transfigured by beauty and grandiosity, rescued by their own heroic essence.[229]

Suassuna's drive to explain the sertão ultimately clashed with his desire to construct it as mythical: unintelligible in the present even if it had been fathomable in the past, and perhaps graspable again in the future. He wanted his work to stand as a monument to its particular order, rooted in patriarchy and faith. He wanted to be the prophet, priest, astrologer, and wise man of this Northeast where the sun flamed so intensely that the real appeared as a mirage and the mirage, real. He wanted to be at once praise singer, scriptwriter and harbinger of an archaic society, one that ran with blood and bore scars of its innumerable past tragedies. His concern with the bloodiness of the sertão is part of his exploration of how its essence has often been bound up with racial preconceptions, just as he also interrogates the naturalist concepts of psychological and cultural inheritance.[230]

He believed that art could make the insanity of life bearable, neutralizing or alleviating in its own way hunger, degradation, despair. It would be art in which laughter "is the horse, rude and undomesticated, that courageously manages to unite the injustices and atrocities of real life so that they undertake the gallop of a dream and keep lit the candle of heroism, of permanent insurrection against the iniquity of the real." He put to use comedy, farce, and magical realism, all characteristic elements of popular culture such as cordel literature, in order to provoke surprise and laughter, dreams of alternatives, and the brief glimpse of a society resacralized. But his art would reflect the sertão "in spirit, not in form, because the artist should elevate the people to his perspective and not stoop to theirs." Suassuna reworked Iberian and popular models, as well as elements from classical Greek and Roman theater, striving to find a "northeastern and Brazilian way to do theater"—something avoiding the psychological indulgences of contemporary bourgeois theater to express the authentic "mindset of the race . . . the musings of kings, pamphlet scrawls, romances." The sertão was traditional, so modern theater had nothing to offer its baroque sensibility. It would be peopled by rustic characters who used bawdy language to satirize modern society's effete niceties and denial of carnal truths. But their irreverence was not chaotic, it was ultimately constructive of another worldview. They used laughter, jokes, and taunts as a mechanism of social control and Christian moralization. In this sertão, the power of carnival was not only to invert order but to create and reaffirm order.[231]

Suassuna's oeuvre takes language as a mode of institution, of the invention of a world. He thought language in its very texture should be able to express the reality it presents. That is why he wrote his works using "the mulatto, stony, near-unintelligible Portuguese of the scrublands." His manner of writing, as well as what he wrote, became another denotative dimension of the Northeast region.[232] He did not see language as a neutral code, as the realists did. He contributed to the invention of the Northeast as a space of nostalgia and tradition but nonetheless saw his work as fictional rather than documentary (as the regionalist writers in fiction and sociology did). Although Suassuna denied modernist influences in the theater, this aspect of his production was thoroughly modern. His medieval Northeast linked to the earlier phase of traditionalist regionalism, including regionalist painting, and the music of Luiz Gonzaga in the (re)invention and actualization of a series of themes, concepts, images, and enunciations that defined the Northeast as a space opposed to the modern, the bourgeois, the urban and industrial. His Northeast had no public sphere, and there was no clear distinction between humans and things. Nature was sacred. It was also a place of traditional forms of domination, of patriarchal social codes and values. Suassuna's Northeast could only react to the present, marked by the entrenchment of capitalist society in the South, as the cause of all its ills. It dreamed of a return to the glories of its past and disregarded history for the charms of memory. The Northeast that these intellectuals and artists helped create was a sophisticated machine, designed to appear primitive and organic. And it generated images and discourses intended to conserve and curate particular views of the past, deploying them as reactions to the new.

THREE

TERRITORIES OF REVOLT

The Inversion of the Northeast

"The other day I bade farewell to my comrades. The breeze caressed the fields, and for the first time I felt the beauty around us. *I looked without sadness at the great house. The overwhelming love for my own class, for the workers and laborers*, did away with the trivial affection I had for the daughter of the senhor. I had good reason to think this way. At the curve of the road I turned back. Honório waved good-bye, and on the veranda of the great house the breeze played with Maria's blonde hair. *I departed for the struggle clean of heart, and happy.*"[1]

During the 1930s the Northeast was not only invented as a place of longing for the past, but also in a distinct parallel movement "discovered" as a region uninterested in either the past or the present. Rather, this Northeast looked to the future with utopian dreams and hopes for new tomorrows, even if revolt was necessary to counter injustice and clear the way for progress. It was a place where the discursive projects of nation as well as region had to contend with the realities of the people (povo), that is, the laboring class. It was less concerned with memory than with making history, or remaking history, through the conflicts for power between social groups. Rupture and revolution were prized over tradition and continuity. This Northeast's fragmentations and instabilities indicated not doom through the entrenchment of chaos but the active search for new connections with universal causes. It sought a new cultural and political identity, one that only a "revolutionary aesthetic" could properly express. It was a territory whose future would be created not only by the arts of politics but by the politics of the arts.

If Freyrean sociology had been largely responsible for the visibility and speakability of the traditional Northeast, this other, revolutionary Northeast bore the direct influence of Marxist thought in both its politics and its artistic production. The Marxist paradigm, which offered this Northeast more than theory—it was an interpretive method into national reality as well as a political roadmap—was after the Russian Revolution a principal cultural influence also, through the official aesthetic of socialist realism.[2]

The images and texts of this Northeast were elaborated according to the strategy of denouncing the injustices suffered by the popular classes, while simultaneously recuperating and redeploying the traditional discourses and practices of popular revolt that characterized the region. These territories of popular revolt were cast as harbingers of a wider, inexorable revolutionary transformation. Images of the region's ghastly, miserable present were taken as the starting point to construct an imagined future, a spacialized utopian tomorrow.

This movement showed that, while negating the present can be accomplished by fixating on the past as the traditionalists attempted, it can also be done by focusing on the future and trying to bring it to life in the present. Revolutionary reterritorialization was a way to imaginatively construct a future space to substitute society's immediate travails and discomfort. Leftist intellectuals who adopted the Northeast as theme described the region exactly as the traditionalists did: as a place that negated modernity in its forms of bourgeois society, capitalism, and modernist sensibilities, but that could be the site of a new "communitarian society" with the reconciliation of the separation between people and nature. But the ideological infrastructure of their analysis of how this was to be achieved was, of course, quite different. Taken as a whole, the generation of the 1920s and beyond was suspended in these two sociabilities; they believed in the immanent transformation of the world, but in distinct directions. This was a moment of intense anticipation of change and awareness of the need to guide it to a desired end. Their zeal to interrupt history's ostensible one-way motion makes clear the fear that the acceleration of change was provoking among them.

Marxism's messianic appeal, its secular connotation of "priesthood and dogma," was embraced by a subgroup of the era's insecure middle class in Brazil. Marxism offered certainties based in the myth of science and technical progress, a myth that helped ease the anguish of those who felt the world had lost meaning. These people—like the children of northeastern landowners who found themselves in a newly unstable, politically impotent middle class, grasping at the past for survival—turned to the future, a future of hope and improvement. Revolution hovered like a messianic mirage, one of the most tantalizing possible paths for the disaffected left to reencounter its lost identity.[3]

Modernity's explosion of the whole into shards of difference vexed these leftists, who sought in the revolutionary future a reestablishing of unity. Their political rhetoric denounced bourgeois democracy as a fraud, since it admitted the existence of democracy among equals only through the elaboration of consensus, not as the productive coexistence of differences. Hegelian dialectics, one of the fundamentals of Marxism, was concerned with the dominion of the whole over the parts; the totality suppressed full representation to implement the identity of all. This line of thought contains skepticism of representation, even in language. Worlds made of images and words were distrusted in preference for a concrete, real world outside of discourse. Marxism saw itself as the last of all discourses, the ultimate discourse. It would be the regime that facilitated the union between words and things, between representation and referent, transcending and repairing the lacerations wrought by modernity.[4]

Marxist thought also assumed the existence of a multiplicity of social gazes and voices that would ultimately be transcended by revolution's dialectic synthesis. Revolutionary theory, to be embodied in practice by the proletariat, would shatter the artifices and superficialities impeding the true understanding of both people and objects. By freeing themselves from alienation, the proletariat would make it possible to comprehend social relations and historical processes. For its part, the party would provide guidance and orientation to the working classes, as well as consciousness raising in a manner adequate to their capacities. The party would weave unity out of theory and practice, joining concept to action, mediating man and history. Its goal was to both turn social relations transparent and control them, remaking them according to man's image.[5]

In Brazil, intellectuals came to Marxism somewhat later than the militants linked to labor movements. The academy began to be influenced by the Communist Party in the 1930s, as shown by their incipient production of some sociological and historical analyses. By the following decade, Marxism was being embraced more systematically. In 1948, one of the first courses on Marxism to appear in Brazilian higher education was offered by George Gurvitch at the University of São Paulo. Coincidentally or not, that institution was also beginning to engage problems of Brazilian society more directly.[6]

The developing Marxist theory of both the leftist militants and the academics in this period bore strong traces of positivist, evolutionist thinking. In many cases this reveals an ignorance of classic Marxist texts but also suggests the context into which Marxism was being introduced—one in which militants and intellectuals were seemingly predisposed to seek theoretical bases for either naturalism or anarchy. Take for example a 1940s text by Nelson Werneck Sodré, a former militant who entered the ranks of party intellectuals and whose highly influential *Formação Histórica do Brasil* was one of the first serious attempts to use historical materialism to interpret Brazilian society. Sodré's reading of Marxism was deeply positivist:

> The sociologist is charged with establishing the *main lines of human evolution* and marking its *stages*, noting its critical moments and, with the power of his analysis, establishing the *necessary differentiations, fundamental correlations, and absolute connections* that combine to make the history of facts, social history, and human developmentalism in general *an indivisible unity*. This must be shown to be *coherent and in a perpetual state of becoming*, constantly shifting and containing new aspects but *always under imperative reason that the past explains and facts of order clarify.*[7]

Even before Sodré, in the 1930s, Communist intellectual Caio Prado Jr. published *Evolução Política do Brasil*, perhaps the first application of Marxism to Brazilian history. In 1942, with his *Formação do Brasil Contemporâneo*, Prado brought Marxist analysis to a study of contemporary Brazil in a form that dialogued with the period intellectual focus on Brazil's national-popular discursive formation. His preoccupation with economic factors as decisive in Brazilian history also revealed a sensitivity to issues of the day, as the nation chafed under the transformation of its economic structures. At that time, too, as they coalesced and became more systematized, both social and economic studies were tending to leave behind racial and environmental determinisms as well as moral or religious interpretations. The late 1930s in Brazil witnessed the foundation of the Ethnographic and Folklore Society, the Brazilian Sociology Society, and the Brazilian Society for Economic Study, with the last focused narrowly on economics.[8]

It might be noted that while Marxism represented a new paradigm for Brazilian social science in this era, in Europe it was among a range of theoretical schools that since the nineteenth century had been shown to be finite or insufficient. Recognizing this, George Gurvitch suggested soon after the end of World War II that many of sociology's classical theses had been revealed as bankrupt:

> The positive state did not succeed the metaphysical and teleological states as Comte predicted; the industrial regime did not bring liberty; instead it revealed problems with Spengler's law of integration by differentiation; *nowhere was class society replaced by a society without class, and class struggle, far from heading toward triumph, everywhere deepens in capitalist societies in opposition to what Marx supposed*; and mechanical solidarity or the force of identity was never substituted by organic solidarity or the force of differentiation, as Durkheim predicted.[9]

Still, in the 1940s, Florestan Fernandes emerged as one of Brazil's leading sociologists through publications on such subjects as folklore and the Negro in Brazil. Fernandes strove to construct for his sociology a theoretical apparatus that was international in character, and hence it is not surprising that he would vehemently criticize the sociologists later associated with the Higher Institute of Brazilian Studies (Instituto Superior de Estudos Brasileiros, ISEB), such as Guerreiro Ramos, who took as their mission the development of a "national sociology."[10]

The influence of Marxism in Brazilian sociology was decisive in the elaboration of two classic studies of the Northeast that inverted the traditionalism embedded in Gilberto Freyre's discourse. Djacir Menezes's *O Outro Nordeste* (1937) offered a compelling vision of the Northeast's socioeconomic problems that proved influential not only in later sociology but as an artistic theme. Menezes focused not on the plantation regimes or the backlands per se but on a third milieu, the "civilization of leather," the sertão's cattle culture that was falling into squalor and needed assistance from public authorities. The other book, Josué de Castro's *Geografia da Fome* (1946), utilized geography as well as sociology to explore the Northeast's problem of hunger.

With the redemocatization of Brazil in the 1940s, interest in fostering a national popular culture expanded from the intellectuals associated with Vargas's New State to middle-class sectors often connected to the left. As state centralism eased, it would be institutions of civil society such as the Communist Party, ISEB, Popular Culture Movements (Movimentos de Cultura Popular, MCP), Popular Culture Centers (Centros Populares de Cultura, CPC), the National Students Union (União Nacional de Estudantes, UNE), and other movements in theater, cinema, literature, and music that took up the work of exploring and disseminating national culture. To the extent that these diverse initiatives intersected with Marxism, the theme of revolution also became incorporated, but this was less the classical, international idea of Marxist revolution than one reshaped for a nation not traditionally concerned with class struggle but instead that saw imperialism as a primary threat to its identity. Accepting as it did the nationalist imperative, the Brazilian left was unable to conceive of a revolution that abandoned the nation altogether. In contrast, the left took revolution as a mechanism of defense, to empower and free the nation. Their conception of revolutionary process was a reaction to the transformation of traditional territoriality fostered by the internationalization of capital and of mass culture. It was along this circuitous path of national defense that Brazil's midcentury "revolutionaries" encountered the "traditionalists" on the same footing.

In this context, national-popular discourse was tending to reconfigure the very idea of "popular" culture, introducing a revolutionary element to what was claimed would best represent the interests of the people. Popular culture became a synonym for "nonalienated culture," aesthetic manifestations built from discussions of power and politics. In truth, of course, this so-called popular culture was increasingly the culture of subgroups of the middle classes, who were exasperated with their diminishing participation in national politics. The growth in this social group, especially in the sectors associated with liberal professions and services in Brazil's cities, rendered them not just a principal cohort of consumers of national culture but a dominant participant in its creation. In that way the "popular" and the "people" were bourgeois through and through.[11]

This nationalist-populist Marxism intended to study the people and the nation by inverting the focus of the bourgeois gaze. It claimed to perceive society from the bottom up according to its economic structure and economic relations, thereby explaining reality objectively and exposing truths. It was assisted by the conception of empty, homogeneous time that historians and other analysts could fill with their narratives. This history was a rational process, historical coherence attained as contradictions revealed and reconciled. It was a history dominated by internal obligations and with a predictable, inevitable end. The necessity to anchor history to conceptual schemes, which turned it into a fixed game of marked cards, derived from the fear of history's destructive, sacrificial character, its capacity to branch into new and surprising openings. But the pretense of turning history predictable and rendering reality controllable was essentially a desire for power, for truth, for the control of interpretation, and hardly an objectively attainable condition of history itself.[12]

It was precisely the sentiment of fragmentation, of deterritorialization, that socially conscious art combated. Such enlightened art would maintain a critical posture before the shattering of reality, denouncing the absence of totality, avoiding pretty diversions to postulate new meanings for human and national life. Aesthetically, the obscure, fanciful, and irrational in human existence should be displaced by bold light, and unforgiving clarity. Marxism brought with it a strictly realist conception of art, and in a sense was stuck with literalist mimicry, even though it simultaneously distrusted all forms of representation and simulation. But artistic realism could extend from human gestures and social practices to the characteristics of a person, a place, an era. The artist should choose the most relevant profiles of the "original," those best revealing essences, and transform them into fixed depictions. Art as mimesis must by definition reflect reality. It would then become part of an ethical discourse (not an aesthetic one), capable of being adapted into a political pedagogy to form "revolutionary subjectivities."[13]

Within this worldview, art's only acceptable diversion from the natural form would derive from the style of the artist, a function of period training combined with individual personality. However, art must also be undertaken as a contribution toward creating universal conscience. The particularities of any given work must be contained in a universal matrix that contextualizes and extends them. Art should demonstrate the social processes that gave rise to it and should espouse general truths. In that way it could be taken as the reflex of a given social psychology and not the idiosyncratic vision of an individual. And that social psychology would be determined by the circumstances of production. For Georg Lukács, art would form part of what might be called the lifestyle of an epoch, involving both the conception of a world and an action taken to transform it.[14]

Underlying such art, the philosophy of materialism should be able to surmount subjective fantasies and defeat mythic apparitions. This art would be the objective face of an unquestionably real world—one made of rationality and not beliefs, given weight by the seen and not the imagined. A prominent theme would of course be the economic base of society, since this was the determining factor in how people live their lives. Artists must never forget what is at stake. The struggle between labor and capital should be depicted with blunt realism, without indulging in the colorful distractions and frothy dramas of bourgeois private life.[15]

This project was not without contradiction, and one of the more notable voices raising critiques of it was that of Mário de Andrade. Although Andrade had also argued for the need for art to have a social commitment, he nonetheless was wary of how artists were contending aesthetically with the unpleasant aspects of Brazilian life, especially in the Northeast. He condemned the 1930s romances in particular for transforming "the terror of drought, the human suffering, the misery of the Northeast, into hedonistic enjoyment and damnable beauty; turning the awful awareness of our obligations to the Northeast into an equally beautiful sensation."[16]

A broad range of artistic production—the fiction of Graciliano Ramos and Jorge Amado in the 1930s, the poetry of João Cabral de Melo Neto and diverse "socially conscious" painters along the 1940s, New Cinema from the late 1950s into the 1960s—enshrined the Northeast as the most representative example of Brazil's problems with hunger, poverty, subdevelopment, alienation, and despair. Accepting without question the spatial existence of the Northeast, these "leftist" works ultimately reinforced a series of images and enunciations of the region that had emerged through the discourse of the droughts by the end of the nineteenth century. They combined the idea of the Northeast as victim, as a place of ruin (product of droughts), with the idea of the Northeast as poor and wretched (product of entrenched oligarchies), adding to the mixture a jarring dose of stern Marxist topicality and aestheticized realism. They created their own mythology of the Northeast, although it came to them embedded in the raw materials of previous discourses. This new mythology inverted the old model to give it a Marxist reading but in so doing still kept it imprisoned in the exact same texture and logic. From the Northeast of traditionalist conservatism we come to face it conversely, inside out and from the left, but yet we find that the very same threads compose the fabric of the region. The essential warp and woof is still there, recognizable. The only difference is that exposed now are the knots, the rough cuts, the mismatched patches, the rough side of the cloth. But the side of the Northeast we were not supposed to see before, here emphasized or exaggerated by the leftists, is just as much a part of the Northeast's imagetic-discursive tapestry as the intricately archaic designs of the traditional regionalists that overlay them.

As with any space, the visibility and speakability of the Northeast are composed principally of products of the imagination, to which reality is attributed. "Facts," once seen, heard, recounted, or read, become fixed through diffusion and given the aura of consistency. They take on the presumption of certitude, even as they abstract into general themes, stereotypes, and preconceptions. They become a necessary vocabulary for the authors, painters, musicians, or cineastes who want their art to have the ultimate representative force of being "lifelike." Their discursive regularity crystallizes them into typical and essential regional characteristics. As Graciliano Ramos observed, it would be nearly impossible to capture on canvas the northeastern summer without rendering the plants' hopeful shoots as burned and black, and the water hole dry. The Northeast becomes defined by drought, its indispensable attribute. To be authentic, the image of the Northeast needs its cast of coroneis and padres, bandits and saints. The tropes become obligatory through repetition and acceptance. Even when the political strategies giving rise to particular works of art conflict, each side utilizes the same mythology in order to be recognized as legitimate and to advance its own ideological argument.[17]

The theme of the Northeast, whether in the realm of academia or art, is never neutral. The region is shown to be populated by people that, like mythic figures or myths themselves, are able to survive the destruction that time seems to have foretold for them. But these people remain enigmatic; they are objectified if never fully contained. They are portrayed as questions demanding a response, wounds that periodically bleed and demand new medicine and new explanation. They are defined as incomplete and always in need. In mythical narrative, historical information is applied to create a truth-effect. The narrative follows a predetermined course, and new or challenging information can be submitted to its ritualizing operations that minimize surprise. Of course, myths are not necessarily the opposite of history. Myth can be used to construct an idea of the past that should guide the future, as the traditionalists attempted. It can also be used to valorize the discontinuity between present and past, making the idea of history more plausible and appealing. The discourse of the Brazilian left leveraged various myths of the past either to demonstrate the superiority of "civilization" over "barbarism" or to choreograph visions of history as fundamental steps toward a revolutionary future.

Differences in interpretive shading could be subtle but significant. Consider the familiar figure of the backlands bandit, with his or her machete and sidearm, leather clothes to protect against slicing thorns, and leather hat casting a precious pool of shade. The traditionalists took the bandit as a sort of Robin Hood character, not quite *of* the poor but valiantly providing justice *for* them as the traditional structures of society were weakened by bourgeois encroachments. But the left saw the bandit as either an image of the salutary revolutionary capacity of the proletariat itself, or more negatively as proof of the lack of political consciousness among the dominated who wasted their energies in unorganized, individualist, anarchic rebellion.

For many leftists who believed in the dichotomy of a savage past versus a civilized future, bourgeois society represented something of an advance over traditional social relations. Others, like Graciliano Ramos, regarded it as a relative decline while still arguing that future social advances would transform the injustices of each. However, all of them concurred that the bandits represented a distasteful form of violence that was illegal as well as primitive. Indeed, their discourse tended to valorize the concept of society based on laws, on written codes that helped depersonalize conflict into the impartial judgment of the organized public sphere. "Primitive revolts" were chaotic and shocking, insufficient to true revolutionary practice and the opposite of the disciplined utopia imagined by the left.[18]

The urban middle-class artists and intellectuals who invented the Northeast as a territory of revolt were thus unable to rid themselves of a certain attachment to bourgeois society because of the order it represented. Even those who called for the transformation of bourgeois society wanted to retain aspects of it, as they gazed from the perch of "civilized Brazil" toward rural, traditional, archaic Brazil. The rebellious Northeast should be dominated and disciplined, through bourgeois mechanisms if necessary, as a stage toward socialist society. Leftists concurred that a true Brazilian nation could be created only through transcending the country's internal differences, whether that was through generalizing bourgeois relations or the integration of prebourgeois spaces into the market and bourgeois power structures (to secure them for future revolutionary enlightenment).

But traditional codes of meaning and values must be adjusted, and regionalisms abolished, in the name of a homogeneous and "organic" nation.

The left's diverse production is marked by an ethnocentric vision that regards the "other" as exotic and curious, and always from a careful distance. The narrator is from civilization and implicitly loyal to it, speaking of the past as something either extinct or as a warning example of what should not be done in the present. There is little of the empathy and (paternal) affection of the traditionalists for regional characters, with the possible exception of novelist Jorge Amado, who seemed fond of traditional patriarchy even as he defended the need for a new world of socioeconomic relationships. The bandit, coronel, and other stock figures took on the role of representing a dying society, a barbarous society that had to collapse to make way for future civilization. Lampião, Antônio Conselheiro, and Padre Cícero were demoted by the leftists in preference for Delmiro Gouveia, pioneer of northeastern industrialization who brought electricity to the sertão and battled against English imperialists. He was the symbolic precursor of a new, strong, rational Northeast, one free of the "pagan deliriums of mysticism, ancestral fantasies, morbid feelings of guilt; the manias of sex, humility, gloom, and pointless violent exploits fueled by delusions of grandeur."[19]

Marxist discourse contextualized phenomena such as banditry and messianism according to social determinants, mainly reducing their analysis (as Graciliano Ramos did, for example) to economic explanations. The left used these traditions to criticize the miserable conditions in the Northeast, but also to overthrow them as popular myths and distractions that should be desacralized so that the povo would come to understand the true forms and meanings of revolt. It was necessary to teach the people to abandon their spiritual vision of a world trapped between the powers of God and the Devil so they could begin to construct a world based on rationality and human action. In related artistic production the lower classes serve as both pretexts and mouthpieces for the leftists' discourse, their complaints to the dominant classes, their demands for power. They took the voice of the people for themselves, to convey and legitimate their own goals. This reveals the limits of the artists' and intellectuals' own supposed integration with the people. Since they position themselves as the vanguard, as best able to formulate what the people want and want to say, as the solution to the people's problems, they reaffirm their inclusion in the dominant strata and their concern for its continuity.[20]

During the 1950s, the rise of the Peasant Leagues made the Northeast a yet more popular subject among leftist intellectuals, who pointed out the widening gulf between abject northeastern reality and the necessary conditions for radical social change. Viewed as primitive and feudal, with its plantations and foreign economic dependence, the Northeast emerged as a principal obstacle to Brazilian development and independence. Through the tactics and alliances of the Communist Party the Northeast was given priority status as a target for structural change. This initiative counted on the participation of the "national bourgeoisie" in the South. The expansion of bourgeois space, the generalization of bourgeois power from the South along with the proletarianization of the northeastern peasants, were considered fundamental preconditions for revolution in Brazil.[21]

It was understood that the spark of change would come not from the rural people, but from the cities, from the South. True, the nordestinos and especially the sertanejos were famous for their traditions of chivalrous bravery and their organic sense of liberty and justice, as well as their irascible tendency to revolt; but they were believed to be rather politically witless and therefore reliant on the urbanites' enlightening revolutionary leadership. The Northeast was a powder keg, but it needed a steady, wise hand to light the fuse and rescue the population from the intellectual limits of its social universe. This view was in alignment with the Leninist premise that conscience was most effectively raised by agents from outside a given milieu. But to arrive at the people, to communicate with them in ways they understood, it was necessary to adopt their forms of expression while adapting the content to desired revolutionary themes and meanings.

Over time there were differences in tone. If in the 1930s and 1940s this cultural production had an attitude of censure mingled with proselytizing fervor, in later decades culture was seen as a form of direct intervention into the reality of the people. For example, the Popular Culture Movement came to use stock images such as those of the bandit, cowboy, coronel, and valiant rustic in order both to make them contemporary symbols of social action, and to reinforce their identity as "heroes" among the lower-class audiences. They were linked to important formative myths of the region. The identity construction of the exploited group, of a group united by class and domination, was allied to reaffirming tropes of regional identity. The region itself took on the personal characteristic of being wronged and abused. The Northeast and the peasants living there were mutually defining, nearly interchangeable: it was the weak being exploited by the strong, the poor by the rich, in a context of past heroism that needed to be reconfigured, redeployed, and recuperated into the present for future transformation.[22]

There were other reasons for the Northeast's appeal to the left. It was both the country's most underdeveloped region, and the most "national" from a cultural point of view in that the depersonalizing, alienating influence of mass culture had not yet penetrated and diluted its popular traditions. The left, fascinated by developmentalist discourse, believed that the true sovereign nation of Brazil would emerge from the reconciliation of its two primary regions: the South, providing technical, economic, and political infrastructure, and the Northeast, with its resistant cultural traditions. They envisioned bringing a paulista rationality to irrational nordestinos with no conflicts or negative cultural side effects. But in constructing this Northeast they carefully excluded the pastoral aspects of its landscape, the green breeze-swept hills of the littoral, the verdant marshes, the quiet pastures. They tiptoed around the rich religiosity and warm family life of the people. Instead they emphasized the arbitrariness and fatalism of life, where even dreams withered in drought and all human existence had to offer was to work slavishly hard, generate doleful offspring, and truck the dead off to the cemetery.[23]

This would be the reverse of the romanticized Northeast, a region of grim proletarian suffering in need of outside help. A region where the traditional sugar aristocracy was irrelevant at best, corrupt and parasitic at worst, but where the popular heroes of gossip-turned-folktale provided inspiration—Lucas de Feria, Lampião, Zumbi, Zé Ninck, Besouro. Its people were weathered and bent by adversity, struggling to maintain dignity as they scrabbled for favors and a handout or wandered southward in search of employment. Altogether, a region constructed from the outside in to appeal to the sensitivities of those not in the Northeast, indulging in picturesque suffering and misery, combining fact, recollection, invention, adventure, and romance like any good fiction.[24]

The result was a curious space, balanced between the perpetual need to beg for help from public authorities and a proud, rebellious nature, denouncing Brazil's social injustices. In any case it was constructed as the shame of Brazil, the opposite of São Paulo, Brazil's pride. The discourse of the left operated along the same strategies of that discourse inspired by the droughts, or that of the traditionalists, which was to generalize determined images, enunciations, and facts as permanent and unquestionable traits of the region. Internal differences or contradictions were ignored, contributing to the idea of a timeless but struggling place. Drought and starvation, which afflicted certain parts of the region at certain times, were made a permanent, inescapable fixture of the entire space. From real but limited social-environmental problems they were expanded into totalizing regional explanations.[25]

Not only did regional power brokers benefit from the establishment of this characterization, but it also appealed broadly to southern audiences. With remarkable consistency, the promised land for wanderers forced out of the burning backlands, or for the poor fleeing their decaying towns, was to be found in the South—whether the sugar mills of southern Pernambuco, the cacau farms of southern Bahia, or the coffee plantations and industrial parks of Rio and São Paulo. This idealized South offered the promise of stability and an escape from poverty, as well as the circumstances for alienated peasants to become enlightened workers. Southward movement was the path to liberty, even if it also meant, at least initially, being imprisoned in bourgeois labor schemes. But it was the South that was posed as responsible for the capitalist development of Brazil, whether that would lead to the ennobling of a class society or to the revolutionary implementation of a socialist society. In all these discourses the "northeastern people" are always marginalized from the capitalist system's power centers, even when they are shown debating the labor movement and the progress of the revolution. They are artisans, fishermen, street vendors, outlaws, roamers, religious zealots, accepted as social types to populate and animate the narratives. More critically, they are shown believing themselves to be outside the system and powerless, accepting their vulnerability to conniving capitalist and sympathetic intellectuals alike.[26]

The Northeast is portrayed as a mythic space in which history seems suspended and requires a shocking intervention to awaken and proceed on its course. This Northeast is a social desert, a place to be conquered. Its people lack faces, names, identities, individual voices: they are merely more wanderers, more unemployed ranch hands, more bead-worrying nuns, a haggard parade of specimens. This discourse is driven by the impulse to enclose the space and give it meaning, to apply human action and dreams to it from outside, to root the wanderers in place and start constructing the civilization that does not exist there. It maintained that the people, living almost in a state of nature, were nearly themselves animals yet they were too submissive to be animals. They had *learned* to quiver before God, before nature, before the smiling local boss, before the government. The men were devoured by a society they could not transform, while the women hunched under the weight of bitter sorrows, their age guessed only by the number of children they have borne.[27] But none other than Graciliano Ramos called into question this account of the Northeast, which exaggerated it as a sort of hopeless Brazilian Sahara. "Truly, the fiction writers of the last century spun so many strange tales, spread so many bones in the parched sertão, painted the sun and sky so fiercely red, that a few overly sensitive politicians actually considered moving the entire population out of so damned a place."[28]

The Marxist discourse, with its emphasis on the struggle between social classes, is often cast in the blunt Manichean terms of good versus evil. The bourgeoisie represented a clear source of villainy, but more immediate was the figure of the coronel, an embodiment of all the primitive forces holding Brazil back. The timeless schematic of the coronel lacked humanity and any interior, reflective dimension. Accompanied by his loyal platoon of toughs (the *jagunços*), he battled against his mythic archenemy the bandit while contending with the artful strategems of rival coroneis. These figures and their rustic power plays compose what we might call horse dynasties—society's dominant group, at the top of the hierarchy, get to ride and gaze down in gentle, affectionate disgust at the masses who follow obediently along on foot.

This scenario contains the basic division characterizing agricultural society. A city or town invaded by horsemen (a pervasive scene in Brazil's banditry film genre) symbolizes the invasion of urban space by a rural threat. The standardized barbarity of the depictions speaks to the fear the average city dweller had for the forces from the wilds. But this symbolic world was expanded by popular narrative and folk literature, which had medieval influences, and were absorbed into 1930s fiction. As these symbols get more widely diffused, the very figure of the nordestino comes to be identified as a vector introducing threatening elements of chaos into civilized regimes. In response, to contain the threat, the nordestino was redrawn as an oaf, ridiculous and childlike, in the *chanchada* films produced by such southern studios as Atlântida. Later, New Cinema would transpose the image of rural horsemen out of the low register of simple pillage, refashioning the bandits into serious, noble people on an ideological mission to transform society.[29]

What emerges from this discourse is a Northeast containing both a warrior ethic and a salvationist ethic—the former deriving from local currents of power and ambition, the latter from the ingrained culture of subservience and mysticism. The dialectic tension between these two attitudes would produce a third that synthesized and transcended them: the humanist revolutionary, who craved power in order to help the oppressed rise from their dusty knees. Both warrior and savior, the heroic leftist was a harbinger of social transformation, substituting revolutionary weapons and enlightening texts for the crucifixes clutched in humble nordestinos' hands.

The paragon of the enemy here was the coronel, drawn as a gluttonous, authoritarian type holding sway in brothels and taverns. All he cared for was the ability to command, to rule over his women and children and the maudlin circle of dependents who hovered nervously at the margins of his favor. Jorge Amado was among the authors who, while explicitly decrying the coroneis' exploits, barely masked their fascinated admiration for this breed of strong man with his complex identities and appetites. The coronel's temperament could cycle between sentimental or wrathful, sometimes managing both at once. The coronel was the ultimate source of both aggression and protection. There is an intimation deep in Amado's work that he found the stout old coronel morally superior to the new generation of sons and grandsons, young men who abandoned traditional virility for the polish of university education and the idle frettings of city dwellers. The figure of the coronel has been absorbed into both the political imaginary of the region as well as a range of academic production, such that it seems difficult to consider the possibility of a Northeast without coroneis even today.[30]

To say that the coronel has taken on a mythic existence similar to the Northeast's bandits is not to assert that they never existed or are devoid of present significance. Rather, it is to call attention to the fact that even the sociologists or historians who evoke coroneis in order to critique them contribute decisively to their survival. Another example of the interpenetration of myth and reality resides in the encounter between the particular Marxist messianism of the Brazilian left and the religious messianism of northeastern social movements. The left adapted from those movements the preexisting belief in the possibility of constructing another world, a new world purified of the errors of the past and present. Rural mystic tradition was channeled into an archetype of readiness for the dream of a better future to come. The Christian background of many militants worked to ease the contradictions, and contributed to a sort of revolutionary metaphysics in Brazil that sought the return of a primitive communality of believers. The left's Marxist formulations operated on both the rational and spiritual planes and carried a sense of the sacrifice of human existence. Many intellectuals produced analyses of the Northeast that conveyed a penitential vision of their own militancy in a form that would be familiar to any Christian community.[31]

If bourgeois morality tended to demonize and criminalize the poor, presuming them a threat, the left regarded the poor as martyrs and heroes of the revolution. The association between messianic and socializing practices was first established in 1936, when the Ceará state police and military used extreme violence, including air attacks, to wipe out the alternative religious community of Caldeirão de Santa Cruz. This community, under leader José Lourenço, fostered communal labor patterns and had been increasingly attracting peasants from the area. The bloodiness of the state crackdown had to be justified to a stunned country, and local leaders, aware of the growing national anti-Communist movement, fell back on the claim of Communists in Caldeirão to explain the slaughter. Later, these processes were at work in a different way in the reinterpretation of the Canudos massacre in Bahia (1896–97). In the 1940s the left took that conflict, especially the willingness of some inhabitants to fight back, as an important example of popular resistance to capitalism in Brazilian history. They cited the highly unequal patterns of landownership and the cruelty of coroneis as factors leading to the creation of the alternative communitarian society of Canudos, also noting the encroachment of urban threats to traditional values and lifeways as reasons for peasants to organize.[32]

But although the left explicitly appropriated messianic themes, and implicitly bore a certain sensitivity to them as aspects of a widely shared Christian background, Marxist doctrine required leftists to identify religiosity and spiritual faith as partly responsible for the misery and subservience of the northeastern underclass. Irrationality was condemned as an impediment to the utopia of an ordered, logical future. The collective madness associated with messianism provided a clear measure of its alienation. Even if a messianic community managed to shift the balance of power, as in the instances above, it was a temporary coup leading to their own destruction since they were theoretically and materially unprepared for genuine revolution. They had given themselves over to "waiting for angels with swords of fire who would defend them on land, or carry them in glory off to heaven."[33] Only politicization could help these unfortunates understand the cause of their misery and bring true hope. If mainstream condemnation of Antônio Conselheiro, apocalyptic leader of Canudos, called him a degenerate, the left viewed him as a flawed popular commander—unable to liberate the people, he contributed to their decimation. Graciliano Ramos described him as "a lunatic, an idiot who tried to change the world with a force of illiterate clodhoppers. . . . Men with an unhinged look, festering with fleas, crying for an end to an unjust world." The assurance of leaders such as Conselheiro that the end was nigh fit hand in glove with the certainty of the left that capitalism was burning itself up and a new, better world was on the way. Of course, the left maintained that the architects of this more just future would be those with enlightenment, reason, and education, which excluded nearly everyone in the popular sectors they were taking it on themselves to save.[34]

In the early 1940s, the end of the scourge of northeastern banditry was declared. The death of Corisco (Cristino Gomes da Silva Cleto, 1907–40) from bullet wounds he received even though he had resolved to turn himself in was widely accepted as the symbolic close of an era. The standard explanation is a greater police presence in the Northeast, along with changes in the relations of production. But beyond those factors, the New State was diligent in trying to help Brazil forget about bandits. The press had been encouraged to stop publishing their exploits and instead to proclaim their obsolescence. Bandits were degraded to common criminals, and treated to a regime of recuperation: the government offered jobs to any who "left the profession" and served their time. And the shining cities in the South were emphasized as the modern way to flee the misery of the droughts and the oppression of the coroneis, offering proper paths to conquering individual power and riches. The status of the bandit was quickly shunted to that of a symbol of the past, a colorful one certainly, but one routed by order and civilization.

Bandits became a myth as soon as they were no longer regarded as creating history. However, they stayed alive in popular memory and popular cultural production. During their last decade of activity, the 1930s, they received the almost unanimous condemnation of intellectuals. For traditionalists, the ideal bandit was a dead one, for he had lived in an idyllic past defined as just out of reach. Graciliano Ramos saw bandits as no more than ruthless villains, even genuine monsters. He thought they did not fight to transform the property rights of all Brazilians, only to take from their enemies. Their violence was shown as helping mire the Northeast in underdevelopment, and its causes postulated as simply economic. The end of banditry was commemorated as a step toward the pacifying of the sertão, a close to the senseless anarchy. This was either the victory of order, or the possibility of constructing a different order from the ashes of the vanquished one.[35]

Whether fictional or academic, works on northeastern bandits all wallowed in savagery, sadism, gratuitous death, and vengeance. This became its own classic popular film genre with the national and international success of Lima Barreto's *O Cangaceiro*. That movie, the product of an educated man and a professional at Vera Cruz studios (a formidable bourgeois cultural establishment in São Paulo), inspired a raft of knockoffs in the 1950s and 1960s that also incorporated elements of Hollywood westerns. Their stereotyped image of the bandits' milieu, devoid of historical or social analysis but brimming with horses and gunfire, led the films to be grouped under the hybrid category "*nordestern.*" They show banditry as destabilizing and disorderly; bandits are bad guys that must be and will be beaten. The bandit is violent by instinct, or by a sort of fatalistic regional destiny, but never for reasons that could be socially and culturally explored.[36]

The films of directors Carlos Coimbra, Osvaldo de Oliveira, José Carlos Burle, and Wilson Silva all equate popular revolt to brutality. Bandits are depoliticized, their myth and their space alike stigmatized. (In that sense they might be said to provide a cinematic vocabulary that later New Cinema would use to diametrically oppose its initial meaning.) Chanchadas were also made to lampoon both the bandits and the films that portrayed them seriously if two-dimensionally. In films such as *O Primo do Cangaceiro* and *O Lamparina*, the bandit is grotesque, an ignorant and clownish buffoon. Many of these were made after the military coup of 1964 and carried the clear subtext of affirming existing authority and respect for the law. Ridiculing the figure of the bandit was a way to delegitimize recent political mobilizations among rural northeastern peasants.[37]

The influence of clichés from the Hollywood West can be seen throughout the genre. The shooting location, almost always in Itu, in the interior of São Paulo State, was chosen to emulate the familiar western panorama. Cactuses, large brooding cliffs, and dust-choked wagon roads are staples. Curiously, the 1953 film *O Cangaceiro* included scenes of a river and an indigenous Brazilian, for no apparent reason other than generic atmosphere. The figure of the solitary avenger, used notably by Glauber Rocha for his Antônio das Mortes, was of obvious western lineage. Scripts followed a basic plot: a throng of bandits invades a house, from which the resident male is usually away; they kill the male's wife and children and/or his aged parents. The soon-to-be hero returns, buries his dead and pledges to settle the score. He pursues the villains, picking them off, until a final duel with the leader. Such films never attempted to understand the logic, culture, or rationality of rural society and instead applied a superficial reading according to the values of an urban culture that held itself superior.

In the 1940s, when the demise of the bandits was announced, leftists changed their opinions of them. They grew appreciative of the bandits' raw rebellion, as an index of possible future revolution. Their mythification of the bandit derived in part from their own superficial comprehension of the social and historical circumstances of the phenomenon, rendering the bandit strictly a victim and product of the region's pattern of large landholdings. But this had a logic. As the bandit disappeared he could be effectively substituted by the worker. The labor movement would take over the struggle against capitalist oppression, carrying it from backlands to shop floor. The collapse of banditry, sung from a thousand headlines, was to the leftists merely a necessary step on the way to utopia. The individualist, egotistical, lavishly costumed bandits of Barreto would be transformed by Glauber Rocha into a dourly epic, baroque symbol of future revolution.

Academic, literary, and artistic production of the 1950s and 1960s adopted the approach to bandits Jorge Amado had taken in the 1930s. In *Jubiabá*, Lampião appears associated with a black dockworkers' strike. Both are viewed as instances of popular resistance, even if qualitatively distinct. There is already the idea that the myth of the bandit might be an instrument of consciousness raising across borders and spheres of existence. The bandit was the hero of the street children in Salvador in *Capitães da Areia*, who know that Lampião had once been a poor boy like them. Pedro Bala aspired to rule the city the way Lampião controlled the sertão. He wanted to represent the armed and noble contingent of the poor, to be their avenger.[38]

The rise of the bandits had been one more indication of the crisis afflicting patriarchal society: sons of slaves and indigent men rose up to attack the scions of the plantations, burning buildings, destroying property, raping white women, hanging the rich from nooses strung on trees. Bandits were the mortal enemy of the coroneis, the only adversary that left the region's bosses sleeping lightly, and even then with a revolver under their pillows. The bandits symbolized the future power of the poor—but a collective social power, not individual. They were men that could be like Corisco himself, the descendant of a ruined plantation owner who returned to take vengeance on the new bourgeois order and sow the seeds of a future society. This at least was the dream of middle-class leftist intellectuals, who saw themselves as taking part in the myth of banditry and the myth of the rebellious territory, commanding and guiding them both toward genuine transformation for the advancement of the humble people.[39]

Controversy and Indignation

NORTHEAST, LITERATURE AND REVOLUTION

The initial inversion of the Northeast's traditional texts occurred in the 1930s in works of authors such as Jorge Amado and Graciliano Ramos. While Amado constructed social types intended to represent broad collectivities, personalized emblems of groups or classes, Ramos focused on the withering effects of the new bourgeois sensibility on individuals. But both authors concurred that a revolutionary reterritorialization of Brazil was necessary. Both were sons of rural regional elites in decline, and while their works occasionally revealed traces of nostalgia, they were committed to rejecting both past and present to make way for the new society promised by Marxism. As active members of the Communist Party and skilled writers, they had a fundamental part in recasting the Northeast as a place of revolt and revolution.[40]

Since the nineteenth century, Brazilian literature had encompassed two basic themes or discourses: politics and the scientific study of society, including philosophy and other human sciences. These had been the tools used to describe and understand culture. It was only in the 1940s that authors began to experimentally liberate literature from social sciences and doctrine, focusing more intimately on language itself. The so-called

Generation of 1945, including poets such as João Cabral de Melo Neto as well as various fiction writers, became known for their greater concern with aesthetics rather than the realist approach to content that had oriented literature for decades.[41] Their path had been opened to a large extent by developments in the 1930s, a period wracked by ideological and intellectual disputes over the nature and future of Brazil. Organizations such as the Brazilian Integralist Action party (AIB), Communist Party, and National Liberator Alliance (ANL) as well as the church and state engaged in debates around the meanings of history for the country, the nation, and the people. Literature took on a new importance as a medium not only to speak of the real but to offer interpretations of it, often formed around the strategies of these interest groups and targeted to the collective subjectivities of audiences they hoped to create as well as awaken. Social fiction, influenced by modernism and socialist realism, provided a vehicle for artists and activists to confront the extant order.

The literary social function emerged as an imperative at the moment in which bourgeois fiction began to be contested, and when new technological methods allowed both the diffusion of literature into serial form and the expansion of print media, from illustrated newspapers to brochures and pamphlets. This allowed the intersection of literature with contemporaneity, topicality—the immediacy of social action, commentary, and solutions. Fiction of the 1930s participated in the effort to understand and respatialize a society in crisis, shaken by the transition between old and new sensibilities and sociabilities. Of course, as demonstrated in the previous chapter, this literature was often rooted in political objectives.

In realism, social representation is limited by the circumstances of experience of each reader. The potential of the word is channeled or narrowed into the frames of visibility and speakability already crystallized, or else it is rejected as incomprehensible. Realist fiction's contours are thus shaped by the forces of political and intellectual hegemony of its place and time; meanings tend to be restricted to an already consecrated field of knowledge. Meaning and signifier are also assumed as inseparable from each other. Denotative language imposes a meaning as the obvious truth, and the reader is offered little space to create alternative readings of that meaning. The prose is based less on dialogue than on monologue by characters tightly knitted into closed symbolic language.

On the whole this literature is intended to portray the Northeast as a victim of Brazil's capitalist development. It hoped to show the ugly truth,

asserting the opposite of the honeyed proclamations of those who mercilessly dominated the region. It wanted to export misery into the hands
and minds of readers, to perturb their consciences and make them experience the Northeast as it really was. Its declamatory character could
be strident as it extended the region's anguish to the nation as a whole,
blaming the nation for it and demanding resolution.[42] Its authors are uneasy with regional power plays even as their works forefront them. Sérgio Milliet accused northeastern fiction of constructing a sort of veracity
effect containing only a partial vision of reality, a vision southern readers
could not easily share since it sentimentally emphasized death and despair rooted in archaic regional settings. He argued that it was unable to
ask genuinely national, much less universal, questions. In contrast, he
claimed paulista prose was affirmative, not negative, since it dealt with
life, health, family, national heroes, with the nation in ascension.[43]

Along the same lines, but much later, Roberto Simões criticized northeastern fiction's strategy of insisting the region was subjugated. He argued
that this distorted reality, shamelessly exaggerating the fear and helpless-
ness of the people, the bloodthirstiness of vengeance, the oppressiveness
of the dry seas of cactus. But northeastern critics such as Ademar Vidal
praised the genre and countered that the reality of the region was even
worse than the laments of its fiction indicated. The written word could
never convey the fullness of experience there. Realist fiction could hope to
approximate it by emphasizing the misery and hopelessness, the wanton
suffering, the corrupt politics, the cruel feudalism. What becomes clear
is that the discourse of such leftist intellectuals winds up reinforcing an
image of the region that is conducive to their own strategies as well as
helping reproduce the power and fortune of a dominant class that benefits from the misery and exploitation.[44]

These are some of the contradictions of a literature that is locked into
a dispositif of power, subsumed in its logics, even while proposing a progressive social project for the Brazilian people. The Northeast was enshrined as the place where the perverse consequences of capitalism are
most explicit, and the impositions of the dominant class most arbitrary.
If southern cities flourished with capitalism's marvels, the Northeast was
the gaunt, sickly cousin trotted out to shame the consciences of those
enjoying wealth and power. Northeastern fiction asserted a generalized
national alienation—the poor, who did not understand the basis for their
oppression; the bourgeoisie, captivated by greed and gratification. With

all its complexity, the genre hoped to construct the Northeast as a territory that could stimulate not only local but national revolt and revolution.[45]

This Northeast bore no fond memories of the sugar plantations worked by slaves. Rather, particular memories of slavery were evoked to feed a new struggle against modern forms of slavery. It was a space divided not only into those that owned and ordered versus those that begged and obeyed. The fiction depicted a cleavage between whites and blacks, going beyond class oppression to suggest endemic racial prejudice that was as old as the colony but unfolding into terrible modern forms. Given such conditions the struggle to fight against misery and injustice required special courage from the ranks of the poor and exploited.[46]

This fictional Northeast was drawn as innately artisanal. Industry, capitalist discipline, and routine were cast as ugly and antithetical to the traditional ways of life of local street hustlers, vendors, fishermen, and informal workers. This is also a paradox, given that the authors hoped to find here a proto–laboring class with revolutionary discipline to undertake a radical transformation of Brazilian society. The contemporary bondage of the factory worker found its counterpoint in the idyll of small-scale work in direct contact with natural materials and conditions. The artificial was to be rejected. Characters asserted their right to live free in misery, but in touch with the cultural, natural, and social traditions that embodied the soul of the nation. Cosmopolitan cities represented the negation of true Brazilian sensibility and sociability, drawn as affectionate, communitarian, and spiritual. This reveals how the authors themselves struggled to leave behind a naturalist sensibility and coexist with modernity.[47] But while the works of Ramos and Amado are broadly similar, there are substantial differences. Each saw the Northeast, and the Northeast's future, distinctly.

JORGE AMADO

Jorge Amado was born in Ferradas, a municipality of Itabuna, Bahia, in 1912. His father, once a businessman in Sergipe, bought a series of cacao farms there in the Bahian South. At its most essential, Amado's writing contended with the questions that had been circling around Brazil since at least the First World War, animating the debates of the modernists and fueling the literary movement of the 1930s: Brazil's national and cultural identity, the character of the Brazilian "race," the influence of foreign capital, and how to speed the move from a present mired in the past to the future. His first book, *O País do Carnaval* (1930), examined Brazilian identity through the nation's relationship with carnival. Although Amado was not a supporter of São Paulo's modernist movement, and in fact was associated with the antimodernist magazine *Arco e Flexa*, he still engaged some of the same questions. He depicted the lack of a true Brazilian identity by emphasizing the use of European harlequins and colorful masks during carnival season. From this book on through his diverse oeuvre, Amado strove to capture the essence of Brazilian cultural identity through the recuperation of its popular character and popular roots. He himself said that what drove his work was the search for solutions to problems facing the nation and its people, as well as the conviction that a new world was coming in which Brazil should play a central role. He believed that of all intellectuals, writers were in the best position to perceive national problems and both create and communicate solutions.[48]

Amado hoped to discover internal truths of the Brazilian people, and convey their vision in their own words. He wanted to integrate the people (povo) into national culture without losing their originality, and he believed in particular that the nation needed to see and hear from the people of the Northeast. The nation needed to confront their sweat and their work songs, their mysticism and prostitution, their diseases and their misfortunes. Starting with his book *Cacau* (1933), this popular vision of the country would be allied with Marxist concepts and dogma, adding the theme of revolution to the mix of nation, people, and region. His production had a clear objective: to denounce social injustice, to condemn the way the majority of people in the country lived, and to propose socialist revolution as a way out of the morass.[49]

His characters would develop into emblems of social conditions, of the values and aspirations of an entire class. As if to rebuff the lacerating effects of modernity on identity, he created schematic personalities and molded them into enduring types. They had limited psychological sophistication, opting more often for action than subtle contemplation, although social class and political position were key factors in the choices they made. Their attitudes symbolized an ideological posture, and they had but a single message of truth to express. This truth centralized the narrative and attributed universal meaning to their actions. His early work has a strong undertone of Manicheism, posing the proletarian characters on the side of good. As poor people, they proclaimed their moral superiority over the rich, who knew only how to steal, pray, and cheat.[50]

Amado's proletarian fiction, which emphasized the psychological flatness of the "exploiters," encompasses his early work up until *Terras do Sem Fim* (1942). With that book, which explores the transition of patriarchal cacao plantation society into new mercantilist logics, characters in the dominant class begin to exhibit more humanity and complexity. They are placed in a historical context that helps explain their attitude and behavior. As Amado eased away from strict socialist realism, the "exploiters" gained more texture, as is clear in the figure of Ramiro in *Gabriela, Cravo e Canela* (1958). This coronel was capable of monstrous evil and despotism, but he was also able to love; he was able to extend emotionally from giving lashes, to giving roses.[51]

Unlike José Lins do Rego, Amado brought a universal dimension to the region, but he did it by submitting local expressions to international Marxist schemes of interpretation. Aesthetically, his work balances lyrical views of country, people, and nature with the social concern to emphasize ugliness and grief, a project undertaken to help advance the onset of a new and better world. His early fiction bore a firm connection to descriptive naturalist aesthetics, which the elements of socialist realism only affirmed. In this phase he aspired to paint sociological portraits, to create fictionalized scientific documents that would justify revolution—bringing an end to capitalist exploitation and a return to the idyllic society lost.[52]

By the time of *Gabriela, Cravo e Canela*, Amado's critical sensibilities had matured. He no longer indulged in the satisfying but relatively simplistic, pamphlet-like denunciations of the bourgeoisie, opting instead for the more insidious corrosive force of humor and chiding. His work came to develop more gently incisive lampoons of the new middle class, desperate for social climbing; of the decadent families of puerile aristocrats; of the foreigners who arrived in Brazil barking orders. The demarcation between classes was no longer drawn with assertive ideological lines but teased out through the observation of codes of sociability and sensibility, through the "false and hypocritical" frontiers mounted by the bourgeoisie between themselves and the popular sectors. Popular spontaneity and robustness clashed against artifice, convention, and the false moralism and maintenance of appearances valued by the middle classes. With *Bahia de Todos os Santos* (1945) Amado was implicity critiquing bourgeois rationality by including rich passages on the invisible, marvelous aspects of existence. His popular characters take on new depth. While they are still reflexes of their social environment, they take in human experience in differentiated ways that not even social class can fully explain.[53]

His proletarian fiction attempted to assimilate popular rebellion as a precondition for awakening revolutionary consciousness. That is, uprisings of the poor against the changes attacking their traditional world were interpreted according to Stalinist Marxism by a middle-class intellectual, who was ambivalent about capitalism in Brazil and tended to distrust modernity but favor a naturalist vision of society and space. What Amado had in mind was a radical transformation of popular nationalism that would be both antibourgeois and antimodern.[54] But he had expressed doubts about this, starting with his first book, which concluded that Brazil had a carnivalesque core that rejected order and restraint and would need considerable persistence to attain revolutionary discipline. He reflected that only the genuine love for humanity, which Communism signified, could bring happiness. Only the end of the people's stunting preconceptions, the end of the church and idols and the beginning of the people's rational certainty of materialism would bring the happiness they craved. Brazil would be the stage for a battle of international import between those on the side of human happiness, and those against it.[55]

Amado's work published between 1944 and 1954 featured militant characters who saw the Communist Party as the ultimate source of truth and the reason for being. Amado's own identity at the time was based on being a voice of the party, a voice of revolution, a summons to the fight for a better destiny for all. The party's growth depended on the individual successes of its members but was still above their individuality and reflected the authority of their collective will. Because of this, prior to middle age Amado the author felt his life belonged to the party and its objectives.[56]

His attitudes changed over time. With *Tenda dos Milagres*, completed during the late 1960s, Amado began introducing critiques of what he saw as the rigid, prejudicial discourse of the leftist militants. The character Pedro Arcanjo made a declaration that might have been spoken by Amado himself: "If I have changed, if inside of me some values have been sundered and substituted, if a part of my old self passed away, I renounce nothing. . . . My heart has made its reckoning, and I want only to live, to understand life, and to love the people, all people." Materialism was no longer sufficient to explain everything; rationality had its limits. To reduce all of human experience to one set of theories was by now inadequate to Amado's curiosity.[57]

Amado's early work offered little in terms of formal experimentation. It was basically literary regionalism encased in the rather high-minded descriptions and artificial dialogues of naturalism. His fundamental stylistic change came with abandoning socialist realism to embrace (in his reading as well as subsequent writing) the comic and fantastic. He found in cordel literature a model of the genuine public voice, a linguistic source for intellectuals who hoped to reach the people's imagination. But it also offered a popular vision of society and social relations, of cities, of the rural environment. It was a reservoir of regional legends, tales, myths, and traditions. It influenced Amado's conception of the Northeast, shifting his emphasis from political and economic circumstances to popular knowledge and experience often conveyed in the wry, colorful, grammatically incorrect dialect of the people.[58]

For a time, the result of this widened appreciation was the coexistence of two discursive regimes: one popular and poetic, rooted in the oral narrative of dockworkers, the mutterings of blind fortune-tellers, the exuberant slang of the street and bar; another political, and deliberately artificial in comparison. In books such as *Mar Morto*, these approaches chafe, and Amado seems to want to maintain his authorial voice outside them, in a third space. But in *Capitães da Areia* he effectively uses official rhetoric regarding criminality to show how it manipulates and obscures reality and impedes meaningful reform, especially for street children. He creates a narrative of actuality by using fiction to denounce the fiction of official discourse. His fictional language serves the imperative to tell the truth and reveal the falsehoods of bourgeois ideology—a more creative and balanced method to fulfill his theoretical values.[59]

The simplicity of Amado's popular discourse contrasted with the verbose sophistry he attributed to the elites and dominant culture, whose clouds of words were intended to confuse the people. The popular classes spoke from the bottom up, in the fullness of disregard for grammatical rules or social norms. They could reveal the truths obscured by lattices of rhetorical codes. Amado engaged the stereotype of Bahian prolixity by showing the power of what lay in those words, striving to carry that popular wisdom to the decorous halls of national literature. The Northeast, and Brazil itself, would turn more visible in their own essential truthfulness when the people spoke them.[60]

If there was a unity in the voices of narrator and characters in *São Jorge de Ilhéus*, centered on the intellectual Sérgio, by the time of *Gabriela, Cravo e Canela*, Amado was exploring the possible simultaneity of different voices, of distinct interpretations and testimonies of a given situation. He calls attention to the relative, subjective character of eyewitness accounts, and finally even of "truth" and of history itself. His previous position of absolute rationality that would do away with gaps and shades of meaning had transformed under the influence of popular literature, and he began probing how discourse was subject to constant rereadings. Truth was formed historically and collectively, not in the sense of a monolithic Communist Party will but through the mixture of voices and interpretations. In this new vision, everything could be at once; no contest between viewpoints was fatal, and no form of inquiry was prohibited.[61]

As Amado himself was aware, his work brought a visibility to the Northeast and especially to Bahia that was highly reminiscent of that in the music of Dorival Caymmi and the visual art of Carybé. All three artists shared a taste for the picturesque, organic, and sensual aspects of local culture. Theirs was a naturalism rooted in the exotic, and a vision of the popular that embraced the area's substantial African-descended population with its customs, beliefs, and lifeways. Caymmi and Amado both were intrigued by the voice of these people, not just what they said but how they said it. They, like Carybé, were focused on showing Bahia as a place of baroque spirituality and vivid color, a place that was poor and yet still allowed human beings to live in harmony with nature and natural impulses.[62] They superimposed a romantic view of Bahia's past, with innumerable references to colonial sugar society and its supposedly gentle patriarchal slavery, onto its present. Especially in the case of Amado, the evocative nostalgia and idyllic natural environment they drew often sat uncomfortably alongside their awareness of cities grown squalid with hunger and poverty.[63]

When Amado began his writing career in the 1930s, the coalescing idea of the Northeast to which he was responding did not yet incorporate the state of Bahia. It was seen as its own territory, politically, economically, and culturally. To be baiano was thought to be something different from nordestino, even though ironically it was the term *baiano* that would be used in São Paulo to refer to migrants from the Northeast without distinction. Within Bahia itself, there was often thought to be a division between the interior, centered on the Recôncavo, and the capital city of Salvador, Brazil's first colonial capital and also called Bahia. Amado's work began to imaginatively recruit and unite the spheres of the state, from the once sugar-rich interior to his familiar cacao plantations in the South, joining them to Salvador. Although there had long been resistance to seeing the sertão as part of Bahia, in large part because it mostly belonged to the captaincy (later the state) of Pernambuco, Bahian politicians came to understand the advantages of appealing for federal help based on drought. It was during just such a campaign in the 1940s that Amado made the sertão the setting for his *Seara Vermelha*. In his own way Amado, like Caymmi, was rendering Bahian identity and culture into a part of the Brazilian whole. But this was done by expanding the contours of the Northeast to include Bahia, or a collection of Bahian signifiers—fetishism and trance, African rhythms, the culture of fishermen, a spirituality both richly syncretized and pervasive. If literary critics of the 1940s were slow to accept Bahia's status in the Northeast, Amado and Caymmi captured national audiences with their portrayals of a place where the people were good-natured but eccentric, as prone to fighting as to amorous encounters—a coastal territory with its own particular melancholy, where the blacks recalled Africa in their songs and tales and chants as daily acts of resistance; where the belief in liberty ran in the blood.[64]

Amado's most explicit attempt to formulate a definition for Bahian identity came with his *Bahia de Todos os Santos*, an exploratory guide to the city that was modeled on an earlier book on Recife by Gilberto Freyre. As we have seen, the traditionalist regionalist movement was largely ambivalent about cities, usually seeking the source of northeastern identity elsewhere. But Amado embraced Salvador as the portrait of a multivocal and unequal Northeast, where beauty nearly masks the suffering and pain and the people understand that much of their world needs to be transformed. He painted it a liberal and libertarian city. As an important subtext to a postwar book, Amado implies that fascism would be impossible in Bahia, even though its nostalgia and focus on its own past could take on reactionary overtones; it was simultaneously affirmative, progressive, revolutionary. By cultivating its past it projected diverse options for the future. Profound mysticism lived alongside militant anticlericalism.

Although his conclusions and attitude were different, Amado reveals the influence of Freyre's work on Recife at nearly every turn, starting with a consideration of the historical creation of the Brazilian Northeast through contact between Portuguese and Africans. He does not avoid contradictions but seemingly revels in harmonizing them through literary images, an approach that somewhat dislocates his periodic discourse of class struggle from the baroque social and cultural reality he constructs.[65]

If Amado synthesized an identity for Bahians that was based in reality, it increasingly became reality as it was processed by large numbers of readers and audience members (for the movies and telenovelas derived from his books). As with nordestino identity it was developed out of contrast with that of São Paulo and Rio de Janeiro, but Amado's innovation was to show a popular civilization flourishing in an urban milieu. The city of Salvador represented harmony, tradition, and conciliation, while the cities in the South remained superficially cosmopolitan, ridden with conflict, and rootless.[66]

If for Freyre the ultimate source of regional customs of amiability was patriarchy, Amado countered that it was the popular character of the region. One saw from the top down, one from the bottom up, yet they agreed that authentic traditional society was being threatened by modernity and bourgeois relations and needed to be rescued. The world of capital and routinized labor was condemning Bahia's diverse cast of popular characters to a sad end, while once widely known songs, prayers, tales, and folkloric practices were disappearing. Amado saw Rio and São Paulo as emitters of both extreme scientific rationalism and decadent mass culture, weakening the unique personality of Bahian cultural identity.[67]

Once a committed Marxist author with little patience for mysticisms, by the 1950s Amado was convinced that western rationality was limited in explanatory power, and dangerous to popular knowledge and lifeways. In *Tenda dos Milagres* he explored the confrontation between bourgeois and popular logics, spatialities, and temporalities. One senses he was siding with the black and mixed-race popular classes, with their alternative territories and power sources, as they challenged the empire of white civilization. He showed their good humor, their cultural strength, and made the conflict political without resorting to blunt political discourse. He also called attention to how the dominant sectors attempted to co-opt and contain popular knowledge, bleeding it of its critical capacity and freezing it into a sort of standardized folklore. His commitment to the idea that popular beliefs and practices should remain "pure" reflects his view that these reflected the national conscience, although it does approximate him stylistically to the traditionalists. He regarded it as a miracle of the Brazilian soul that such a poor, diverse population could form itself into deeply organized cultural groups, the samba schools, *ranchos*, *ternos de reis*, the *afoxés*, each with its rhythms and song styles and dances. He came to believe that only Brazilian miscegenation could explain this richness, this talent for creativity wedded to resistance. He thus took a different intellectual path to ultimately concur with Freyre that the mestiço, the mixed-race individual, represented cultural superiority and reconciliation. The mestiço would lead the way to a future universal civilization more innately equal, in which racial prejudice was absent.

Of course, both Amado and Freyre merely inverted the naturalist discourse that gave negative connotations to races other than white, especially blacks. They maintained established concepts of race, but revalorized (mixed) race both culturally and psychologically. Miscegenation would be the basis for a syncretic culture, capable of easing tension between extremes. For Amado the presence of the black contribution in the Northeast and in Brazil was fundamental. His work reinforced a variety of white myths about black people, even as it has been praised as an important source for the preservation and divulgence of black culture. The myth of blacks' instinctual, voracious sexuality, a notion at some level intended to compensate for the history of sexual exploitation of slaves by their masters, is a constant presence in Amado's writing. This is one reason he found carnival so compelling a symbol of Brazil's miscegenated culture, because of its voluptuous and Dionysian side. Even if blacks were being recuperated into participants in the formation of Brazilian national culture by social scientists such as Thales de Azevedo and Arthur Ramos, they possessed a sexuality still regarded as bordering on savage and uncontrollable, impervious to bourgeois morality.[68]

If this involved the paradox that blacks, especially black men, would seem to be eternal slaves to their own instincts and appetites, Amado ameliorated the problem with consistent moral and ethical codes ensuring that blacks might be poor and carnally voracious, yet they were good and noble, the opposite of the rich and cruel whites. To refute racist theories Amado forefronted the cultural strength of blacks, who called on a legacy of resistance and fortitude their ancestors had shown under the most appalling circumstances. He saw the fight against racism and the struggle for economic justice as two sides of the same coin, both of which social-ism could help advance. Amado believed the left always tended to engage the class issue first, leaving questions of race a distant second. Meanwhile, racist discourse served to justify bourgeois domination of a doubly sub-jugated population. That is why he insisted on showing blacks as fully capable of assimilating into Marxism's rational, progressive project.[69]

But there is a lingering tension in Amado's work between material-ism and spirituality, between rationality and irrationality. He regarded the philosophical profile of the black and the mestiço as the antithesis of bourgeois materialism's clutching greed for money and property. In both Balduino, the poor youth in *Jubiabá*, and Gabriela, the simple hero-ine of *Gabriela, Cravo e Canela*, we find popular characters able to be con-tent in a state of poverty. They are intended as national representatives in their emotions, affection, spirituality, and human values, characteristics opposite to what a cold capitalist required. For his part Pedro Arcanjo in *Tenda dos Milagres* was a sort of universal intellectual, capable of found-ing new and enlightened sciences; he understood the rational yet racist bourgeois reality as well as the baroque, hybridizing science of the Bra-zilian popular personality. He would work to elevate popular knowledge to new levels, forming intellectuals who (perhaps following the example of the author himself) would work for the well-being and advancement of the people.[70]

The conflict between Amado's latently rational discourse and the ir-rationalist content of the popular culture in his fiction erupted into the text of *Tereza Batista*, rendering itself explicit. Amado pauses the nar-rative flow to give context and justification for the *orixás'* supernatural intervention, explaining that the Bahian people believe in these things and that they live their lives in daily contact with fulgent realms of the divine. His use of a sort of documentary magical realism here was likely a conscious move to try to preserve and communicate these traditions at a time when the forces of consumerism, propaganda, and shock art were spreading rapidly in Brazil, and popular culture was being rendered into staged "folklore" shows for tourists.[71]

Still, it is difficult to deny that Amado ultimately maintained a pa-ternalistic posture toward the people and popular culture, much as one might expect from a man who came from an elite family in decline and who identified with the people strongly but narrowly, in their antibour-geois sentiment. The overarching theme of his writing is the transition away from traditional cacao plantation society, and the submission of local senhores and coroneis to the new mercantile relations controlled by international capital. The new, rationalized cacao farm denounced in its very layout the exaggerated social differences between strata, as workers were pushed further out into simple huts and housing units—a coldly explicit division mirrored in the changes to cities, with business and elite districts consolidating in the core versus a distant indigent periphery of the underpaid and underemployed. Social relations were increasingly depersonalized, being weighed, measured, and transacted with money. Ilhéus lost its tranquil, rural character and became a business town. The last generation of farmer owners was being replaced by its sons, young men polished to an obsequious shine by university educations and city living, men with no sense about dealing with the land or the people who worked it. They were incompetent to maintain the traditional relations of patriarchy and patronage that had accompanied the glory days of cacao in the sunny Bahian South. Similar to José Lins do Rego, Amado tended to attribute the decadence of cacao society to the new generation's incapacity to keep up their grandfathers' paternalistic system of control and conciliation on a regime rocked by the surging waters of capitalism.[72]

Amado's *Terras do Sem Fim* narrates the epic trajectory of the turn-of-the-century coroneis who had conquered Bahia's southern territory, typically by force. Within two decades the area was generating fortunes, which by the 1930s had shifted fill to the pockets of the exporters. A timeless story of feudal conquest was dissolving tragically, subsumed by imperialism. Traditional family names disappeared to make way for the logos of businesses printed in foreign tongues. The old face-to-face way of doing business was replaced by impersonal forms, telegrams, and telephone calls. The cacao plantations appeared to be going the way of the sugar society of the Recôncavo, a place now populated by ghosts and memories under the arching telegraph wires. The coroneis had paid dearly for choosing to keep outside the changing dynamic of politics. By digging themselves in to try to safeguard their lands, they ultimately marginalized themselves. Amado delved deeply into the concerns and contradictions of the northeastern rural aristocracy who fought their obsolescence while refusing to change.[73]

Amado was also a constant critic of bourgeois sociability and morals. He used prostitution to comment on the hypocrisy of bourgeois morality and the commercialization of social relations, but he did not spare the left from critiques of their own biases and supercilious attitudes, which he regarded as another form of oppression. However, Amado was more conservative in his position on homosexuality. He tended to view it as an index of bourgeois moral decadence, a relatively novel threat to traditional society that a proper moral and economic revolution would do away with. He associated homosexuality with the middle classes, with artifice, with feminine and passive spheres of society, thus opposing it to the robust popular sectors, the brave and virile men of the people. Clearly in his view, the revolutionary class was masculine, as the future utopian society would be. The psyche and strength of Afro-Brazilian men in particular would open the path to freedom from bourgeois moral repression.[74]

Amado's rejection of bourgeois ethics leads to another tension in his work, between valuing the world of labor—fundamental to Marxist theory and the goal of revolution—and the contrary popular world of avoiding work and routinization, of living by one's wits, of surviving marginalization to construct alternative territories of resistance. Amado consistently viewed the factory as a symbol of modern slavery, and industrialization as an antiseptic force threatening to wipe out Bahia's diverse artisanal traditions. If São Paulo and Rio de Janeiro appear at times in his books as the source of both hope and enlightenment for the proletariat, Amado could never accept that Bahia should be made over into a northeastern version of those cities. Popular lore and wisdom offered its own liberation, and men could graduate from the universities of the street to become "orator[s] for the beggars, for the blind scrounging for small change, for the handicapped, the prostitutes, the sailors, the homeless children." These men saw the world not only from the bottom up, but from all sides, understanding its difficult options, its surprising opportunities, its permeable borders. Such characters could be instructed in Marxist revolution, but they already carried with them a deep-seated tradition of rebellion against bourgeois models of work.[75]

Amado's construct of popular knowledge and spaces distinctly emphasized the alternative, or what some critics might call sordid, aspects of urban cultural life; this introduced a new visibility and speakability of the region (and nation). It depicted a place suspended between the real and the magical, a place of fervent religiosity that was shot through with hivelike warrens of illegality, a place where life was still made by people with their own hands and the alienation of capitalist labor had yet to penetrate. From his earliest writings in the 1930s he was sensitive to how Brazilian labor patterns were shifting after the end of both slavery and the era of greatest European mass immigration. Around the country, alternative forms of survival and community life were newly threatened by the spreading logic of the labor market, as well as by state initiatives to discipline, modernize, and cleanse cities. Amado was a champion of northeastern popular cultural traditions yet vacillated between praising the popular ethics of "alternative" idleness and denouncing it as not leading toward any concrete change or improvement for the sector. There were territories of revolt all around, but they lacked the spark of ideology to transform them into true territories of revolution. The discourses of the left and the right tended to converge around the conviction that the *malandro*, the iconic Brazilian layabout who shunned work and defended his honor with a straight razor or *capoeira*, was a doomed species—either he would march off to the factory lunch pail in hand to produce consumer goods, or he would be recruited into the ranks of soldiers to produce the revolution.[76]

In response Amado, like Caymmi, deployed a selective vision with respect to work. Both of them typically referred to work only in the form of activities that showed people in harmony with the natural world. They both also tended to valorize nature, placing it above humankind, leaving its secrets unattainable. They condemned modernization for its destructive effects both on nature and on people, who became independent and resentful of nature; people were left confused, becoming more predaceous yet fearful of their animal side. The city itself was preferentially treated in their works according to its natural elements—the sea, the breeze, the coconut palms. Nature appears at times as the very source of the slow, easygoing Bahian way of life, as well as the storm-like surges of bravery and violence that punctuate it. While Amado in particular was obviously concerned with the influence of social factors on lifestyle, he still could join Caymmi in offering an antimodern perspective that accepted nature as holding the ultimate sway on human affairs.[77]

Beyond the paradoxes and tensions of Amado's novels, one of the more consistent and affirming aspects of the Northeast he wrote into being was the inclusion of a Bahia where popular culture, especially Afro-Brazilian and mestiço culture, was central to identity. It was a place where poverty and beauty intertwined and fed off each other—a place of natural charms, but civilization was a noisome curse. The warmth of human interaction, of festivals and mass prayer, countered the cold and depersonalized supermarkets. This Northeast was a flurry of color, in motion, not moving in desperation to the South but to and from the ships, along the downtown streets, an infinitude of items, flowers, clothes, foodstuffs, carried in baskets and in carts or on turbaned heads. It was a sweaty, smiling, singing, African-descended Northeast, the reverse of the white bourgeois Europeanisms of São Paulo. It was a newly black face for Brazil to contend with, regarded as barbarous by the European elite even in its carnival celebrations in ornate costume, chanting of love and memory and devotion.[78]

Amado's Northeast was conversant with all the existential problems and universal questions of mankind. His Marxism allowed him to view the region as deeply ensconced in global social processes, including exploitation, although in response he crafted it as oppositional to bourgeois discourse and schemes: the oppressed, the hungry people on the periphery, defiantly enjoyed life as much as possible and maintained a keen solidarity. This Northeast had an internationalist politics even as it attempted to resist global flows of culture to preserve the authenticity of its popular craftsmanship. Although in some respects Amado turned the traditionalist Northeast on its head, in the realm of culture he participated in inventing another remarkable tradition: that of the black Northeast, anchored in Bahia. But it was still a Northeast that could only react to modernity.

GRACILIANO RAMOS

Graciliano Ramos was born in Quebrangulo, Alagoas, in 1892, to middle-class parents with roots in the sertão. His childhood was spent between several cities in Alagoas and Buíque, Pernambuco. He attended high school in Maceió but never finished college. More than many of the contributors to the concept of the Northeast we have examined, he was well traveled in the region. The thrust of his work would be to create an image of the Northeast reversing Freyre's premise—rather than the accomplishments of sugar society as the core of regional identity, he would emphasize the grim world of the sertão. This meant inverting the language, discourses, and visions of the traditionalists. He would contrive native narrators who did not and could not know how to speak "properly." Ramos was sensitive to how language intersects with perception, and he followed in the steps of modernism to further link dialogue and expression with power. Unlike Jorge Amado, Ramos made form as well as content a stylistic priority, since form could help produce and reproduce a given reality. He denounced the alienation latent in the language of modern society, the gulf between words and things, the disappearance of original language, and the fading of reality behind looming fog banks of representation.[79]

Ramos's literature hoped to call dominant language into question by recontextualizing it and displacing it from the center. He probed it for the uncertainties within its affirmations. His irony and sarcasm helped deconstruct conventional textual reality at the same time as it expressed anguish over the lack of correspondence between language and reality. He attributed the lack of one unifying truth in the world to social alienation. He believed that in a better future to come people would discover the truth of the world and of themselves, and their language would reset and align to reflect that clarity. He was preoccupied with how the dominant classes robbed the oppressed of their voice, dehumanizing them, leaving them with only screams or empty silence.[80]

In his work, power relations determined who should be able to speak and under what circumstances. Silence was the absence of speech, and its presence denounced the exercise of power on the lower classes. Ramos saw the northeastern peasant as a being defined by continued enclosure in silence, reduced at times to animal-like grunts. The notion of silence as an imposed lack kept Ramos from exploring the strategic dimensions of silence in social interaction, and from offering alternate interpretations of how silence could be read (or heard). His writing rendered silence into a discursive deficit among northeastern popular classes, making it another indication of their characteristic privation—they were eternally in need, in need of means of verbal expression as well as of economic and political assistance. His work would ultimately convince the next generation of leftists that what the nordestinos needed were classes in literacy, which would provide a basis for their politicization. Breaking the chains that imposed a poverty of language, a poverty of life and power, would be the project of the Popular Culture Movements as well as the basis of Paulo Freire's adult education methods.[81]

The verbal concision marking Ramos's style was designed to evoke the region's indigence and misery. There was a shortage even of words, leading his nordestino characters to resort to animated gestures and simian-like mimicry. The poor nordestinos had their rights to speak taken away by others, and they live on the margins, on the frontier of speakability, within the void of silence. The region itself is a terrain of silencing, in which only certain ways of speaking are available and then only with the permission of others. This experience would have been familiar to some of the working poor, for whom keeping their job meant holding their tongue, swallowing complaints and opinions. Ramos enlarged it to make the region as a whole a place where more laments and sobs were heard than words, where the most common phrase uttered was a plea for help. The Northeast of his images and discourses was a place of quiet suffering broken by prayers and cries for support, support from God, the state, the South, the bosses. In his Northeast, nordestinos mutter and rasp meekly, ashamed of their degraded position and the dusty, hungry, sepulchral voices they are allowed by the powerful to speak with.

In the very language he employs Ramos constructs an image of the region that is destitute, nervous, bitter, and parched. He wanted this image to be known and to trouble the consciences of readers around Brazil. He wanted them to feel a sense of responsibility for the cowboys who felt better around their horses than around other men, because on horseback there was no stressful engagement with the social phenomenon of silence, or the frustrating inability to express ideas. He wanted Brazilian readers to wonder about a region where the people used few names to refer to few objects, who didn't know how to come up with names for others and could not even conceive why they were unable to do so. He created a stark division between those who spoke or yelled orders, and those who silently obeyed. The region's vast spaces and humbled popular classes were prime for exploitation and dominance by an uncaring elite.[82]

Ramos wanted his language to flee the traps of dominant discourse, so he had to police it to avoid falling back into the speakability and visibility produced by those in power. He wanted to avoid their basic tropes and stereotypes, and even to mock their literary affectations. He regarded the bourgeois tongue as flabby, weak, and awkward, like raw lard. But Ramos also maintained a critical eye toward his use of popular narrative and expressive forms to free them of the elite influences they sometimes contained. If his writing were merely to recreate the actual division between haughty, ornate bourgeois rhetoric and a popular voice that was indigent but freighted with elite mannerisms, he would be reproducing a set of class-based relations he hoped to abolish.[83]

In *Vidas Secas*, the transformation of peasant life comes with attaining the ability to shape and use words: in the conversation that opens between Fabiano and Sinhá Vitória, through which they construct a new reality and a new set of goals. The establishment of a new world begins with the capacity to express a dream, a desire for change. For the poor, dominion over the word was a decisive step toward utopia. But Ramos did not go so far as Guimarães Rosa would in exploring the sertão as the basis for a whole new, enlightened popular discourse. Rather, Ramos remained locked into preconceptions that to attain wisdom, the city or the littoral were preferred milieus. He saw the sertanejos as mostly without the opportunity for intellectual growth, mired in incomprehension of the socioeconomic relations that marginalized them, unable to move from thinking and feeling to articulation.

Like so many of the writers and artists we have considered, Ramos was impelled by an anguish wrought by the collapse of the patriarchal northeastern society he remembered from his youth. He described his life and northeastern society itself as being characterized by processes of slow decomposition, and he bemoaned the reterritorializing forces changing his familiar landscape through internal threats, existential hazards. His characters can be observed falling apart in myriad ways, self-destructing like the region itself. Physical death and spiritual agony are constants in his oeuvre, and characters are deeply ambivalent about their own memories as bittersweet connections to people and places that are no more. But nostalgia for the past was made more urgent by the disorienting present that brought pain as it unfolded in hues of burnt ash. This desperate sentiment led Ramos to utopian revolutionary ideals as a way to transcend the present outright for a new order. In such a new world, life would once again have meaning, and truth would be reestablished as something knowable and speakable.[84]

As he wrote stories of the region, Ramos was simultaneously lamenting his own social position. Most of his characters were either sons of once-proud rural property owners who had witnessed the end of family stability, and who now survived through public employment, gained through personal favors; or representatives of the bourgeoisie, sons of merchants and provincial intellectuals, who also get by through relations of patronage. These are the godsons of coroneis who become officers in the military or occupy new positions such as judge, police delegate, doctor. Surrounded by this bland rationality and the cratering of aspirations, Ramos longed for the rugged, vivid world of his grandfather, which his father had been unable to maintain. Humiliation was what his father represented to him, along with subservience to the wealthy. The old farms were themselves embodiments of his family's collapse—afloat in a sea of weeds, termites devouring buildings from the inside out, the once stately ox-cart disintegrating under a dead tree.[85]

Before such degradation, Ramos looked keenly to the future. The past seemed completely beyond recuperation. His memories were constructions of the present, far less re-creations of the past. Traditional society, with its bandits and coronel-centered patriarchy, was gone forever; its sons lacked protection and orientation. Old senses of honor and community had been fractured by new patterns of sociability. Noble peasants lived on only in popular literature, and the folktales rehearsed before skimpy campfires. Life itself seemed to wither, to dry up and shrink inward in Ramos's literature. There were never any silver linings. The end of slavery and changes to labor patterns had worsened poverty and indexes of misery, confounding many senhores and driving them to an early grave. Meanwhile, the slaves suffered the end of what stability they had known, going hungry and without clothes or shelter in their new state of so-called liberty.[86]

Ramos channeled his personal woe into a range of characters who were equally traumatized by the decadence of the world they confronted, with its imposing cities, its smug merchants, its officious public servants. Childhood memories were persistent but brought no satisfaction; in Angústia (1936), the dead seemed to be governing the living. It would require snuffing out those memories to clear one's head for dreams of a new life. If reality was a nightmare, the real must be transfigured into a dream where lost stability and tranquility were in reach. The new world Ramos desired was not a re-creation of the past, but it would be contoured along well-worn grooves of the familiar.[87]

For Ramos, memory (and literature) represented eyewitness testimony of ruin, not a program for preservation as the traditionalists had it. His memory did not ebb and flow as in Proustian fiction but was fragmented into isolated patches by traumas, deceptions, broken confidences. The act of writing was necessary to destroy insupportable memories of a life's overthrow. Only the profoundly frustrated could produce literature. It was a form of reckoning for the wretched, a way to come to terms with the past and present in order to try to move on to the future.[88]

In his own way, Ramos exposed the conservative use of memory by the dominant classes as a linear construct of facts and heroisms that justified their position of power. Historical memory in his view had everything to do with power relations. Like history, the memory of power is an accessory of the dominant. Whether built according to hegemonic strategies or jigsawed together as an individual, personal narrative, history vexed Ramos. He aspired to a relation to the truth beyond it, beyond ideological discourses. History and memory would only retake their vitality with the end of class society, of alienation. Only then would people possess the full detail and veracity and potential of their past, as well as their present and future.[89] For both Ramos and his characters, history surged as a catastrophe that could wipe out the weak, destroying those who were incapable of taking it in their hands and changing its trajectory. Or one made history, or one suffered it; but it was impossible to freeze it or to reverse it.[90]

Ramos transformed memories into libel against one epoch, and the epitaph of another. He felt little pity for, but much animosity toward, people of the modern age. His innate skepticism overpowered any nascent romantic impulse, and he regarded the people with an abiding lack of faith in their capacity to transform themselves or the world. At times his writing appears to try, even to strain toward hope, but he never achieved the calm optimism that Jorge Amado seemed to command effortlessly.[91]

But his work also sensitively expressed the plight of the new regional middle class, which was caught between the traditional but decadent regime and the growing bourgeois world to which it was not yet permitted to belong. This was a suffocating dynamic in a region in which modernization coexisted alongside primitivity, and economic changes could mount without altering the basic balance of power. This was the petite bourgeoisie, who to survive needed to operate according to regimented scripts. They detested surprise. Their lives were repetitive, proper, predictable, competent, tractable. They had to ignore everything but their functions and proper roles and class aspirations. Of course this was another face of Ramos himself, who through his characters deplored the simultaneous instability and monotony of this life, and who dreamed for a new order in which everything was secure and assured.[92]

The regional space he constructed was riven by discontinuities—historical gaps, diachronic differences, landscapes re-created and jumbled by human subjectivities. He accepted as a premise of his work that nature was already dominated by humankind. Space itself was also viewed as a human construct, a fiction that gave limits, organization, and meaning to nature. Landscape also was an objective expression of social relations, particularly related to production and inequality. Space was an intellectual construction, a product of how the various narrators contend with fragmentation. In *São Bernardo* (1934), Paulo Honório represents the bourgeois endeavor to constrain space by work, making his own jail out of propriety and the hunger for power. Space for him was merely an object to be determined, manipulated, used. But space thus loses its stability, as it is submitted to strategic maneuvering and changes of shape and velocity. Honório was the emblem of early capitalism, refitting or destroying territorialities. He was the prototype of the bourgeoisie who lacerate traditional spaces and take full advantage of the people who happen to be living there.[93]

Ramos spun his regional space out of the attitudes, vocabularies, and subjectivities of his characters, but it was anything but narrow. It contained and expressed the full universality of problems afflicting the human condition. The region was produced by his characters, but it also was the backdrop for their diverse dreams, ambitions, and hopes for the future. Throughout *Vidas Secas*, the external effects of drought are given less weight than the internal consequences for the spirit of the characters. In its multiplicity, space takes power both from human construction and from the mysteries of nature that support or thwart people's endeavors.[94]

Ramos believed modern humankind needed to be transformed, because their morals and ethics were jumbled. For him, the transformation of society would come with a change in human values and the reestablishing of clear boundaries between good and bad. But he did not believe a return to some idyllic primitive state was possible. His first book, *Caetés*, included a satirical treatment of modernist primitivism, arguing that it would be impossible for moderns to understand and represent that paradise lost. The essence of the past was gone, and if anything, men's contemporary savagery was such that we ought to move further away from primordial origins and not risk sinking deeper into them.[95]

In *São Bernardo* Ramos focused on the parades of social representation characterizing modern society, critiquing bourgeois society as fostering relations between masks rather than psychological essences. He also noted how easily a false politics can spin out of such a society that prizes images and truth effects. He saw the public sphere as a translucent shell of opinions about opinions, with no substance. Grasping for something solid underneath it all, he created characters that strive to maintain their simulated appearance in the face of withering diversity, and fail; they bleed their truths out before an uncaring society. They live with great discomfort. At least patriarchal society had been based on firm, unanimous notions of reality, even if it also had entrenched inequalities. The future society Ramos seeks would have such unanimity restored.[96]

Neither Ramos nor his characters can handle contradictions or ambiguity well. His resort to Stalinist Marxism and its emphasis on definite truths, as well as on transforming the falsity of the world of commerce through discipline, is perhaps comprehensible in that light. The collective space for the poor to engage reality, to assert their voices, to prepare for revolt, was shrinking into atomized nodes of bleak survival.[97]

He considered the contemporary Northeast to be yet more intolerable because it was suffering the effects of the implantation of new market rationality while preserving the form of traditional domination and power relations, which left the popular classes marginalized by depriving them of the reciprocity embedded in the fading paternal structures. It was a place where no one was satisfied. The bourgeois machine encountered innumerable impediments and crises, making their own transformational project seem aggravatingly suspended, broken, incomplete. Ramos's position was that modernization was at fault for the Northeast's unhappiness and complications. Before its onset, people were less frustrated and shaken. They did not have automobiles or radios, and they slept on simple straw mattresses or hammocks, but they had worked hard at good, simple labor on the land and slept well when they laid their heads down.[98]

Ramos alleged that according to bourgeois ethics, the accumulation of wealth justified any abhorrent act. Violence or injustice were valorized in that code as long as they lead to conquest and individual advancement. The greed of this class, along with their general urban experience, made them crafty. Paulo Honório, the pragmatic exploiter, was able to outwit and displace Luis Padilha, a representative of the old unassuming regional elite. Padilha's generation was doomed to lose their holdings because they were unprepared for capitalism's innovations. They used their money to seed future favors or to indulge their own pastimes, never accumulating it in measured accounts, and they looked on the land with affection rather than detached rationality.[99]

On the other hand, in Ramos's work the bourgeois wasted their lives without knowing why, because they had no ideals. They were suspicious, voracious, egotistical, cruel. Social relations were a mechanism for acquisition of land, stuff, men, women. Honório's jealousy of Madalena was an expression of his sense that she was his property, a condition she refused. Honório cannot understand his spouse, nor the humanistic sensibility she represents. He took on the outward aspect of an old coronel without the genuine amiability and concern for protecting the weak. He was actually more like a slave master, who demanded everything and gave the minimum for survival, if that.[100]

In this northeastern society, the poor were regarded as things, as animals, and subjected to brutality. Ramos appears constantly torn between contemplating the theoretical beauty of a new, more just world, and fretting over the sorry state of the men and women who should put it into practice. But he was often able to aestheticize them effectively, demonstrating his urge to participate in their suffering, to render their misery visible and legible. He wrote them as witnesses to a hostile region, and he wrote their lives in blood to indict their corrupt oppressors.[101]

According to Ramos, he tried to make his fiction more lifelike by studying the region's relations of production but eliminating nonessential aspects; by carefully selecting themes, images, and ideas and forming characters from them to give them a dynamic texture. He wanted to avoid what he saw as the trap that snared many leftist intellectuals of his day—getting lost between nationalism, and romanticizing the poor. To advance an agenda for change, he would not merely write for pamphlets. He would boldly reveal the monstrous face of the region, its nightmares and hopeful dreams. He wanted to bring Brazilian reality to the forefront for intellectuals who were more interested in Europe, and for a government that was abstract and distant. But he rejected turning his fiction into political theses because he distrusted such discourses and their language, even when it came from the left. That is why he developed a style that was dry, lean, and tense.[102]

Ramos critiqued regionalist fiction for its lack of attention to language and its romanticism. He jeered its embrace of the exotic and contrived spontaneity. He did believe that literature obeyed historically defined norms, which applied a speakability to each author, including a set of images and enunciations without which their work would appear untruthful or incomprehensible. In his case, the context and the norm seemed to call for realist fiction. But he felt that in an atmosphere of profound alienation, not everything that is true has the aspect of truth; speaking them risked their appearing absurd. Meanwhile, enunciations derived from the dominant discourse might appear truthful while being no more than lies. Ramos's entire oeuvre grapples with the relative nature of truth with respect to society, history, region. He strove to find a language to break through it all, a language free of ideology and hence capable of expressing the Northeast as a place of brutality and sadness, of the poor and ugly, of individual and social decomposition.[103]

The inhabitants of Ramos's Northeast were so different from the people of the littoral that if they went to the coast they were lost, lacking recognition of habits, objects, words. It was a place where votes were bought with a new pair of sandals, or a fancy buffet sponsored by the candidate. Its elites were pragmatic but coreless, ever willing to abandon their moral conceptions to accord with whoever was the winner of the election or the business deal. Its poor were people who thought little, and desired less, but obeyed effusively. The peasants had inferiority complexes and evoked the dream of the promised land of the South like a ritual hallucination. Theirs was a race condemned to disappear if it was not awakened from its torpor of ignorance. Their occasional revolts were pointless displays of fury without the intervention of a project that would enlighten their understanding of their own reality. Ramos's memories were of a society unjust and unbearable, his hopes for the future too brooding to risk optimism. As if dragging a plow in parched earth, he composed crooked lines about people and places throughout the Northeast—each a microcosm of a world he wanted desperately to see rejuvenated and transformed.[104]

Portraits of Misery and Pain

The inversion of the traditionalists' Northeast to expose its ragged underside can also be found in painting, which adopted the region as a theme in the 1930s. Through their symbolism and modes of visibility, these paintings of the region help us understand what was troubling to society at the time about not just the Northeast but Brazil as a whole. The criticism that mushroomed around the works helped fix a certain reading and a certain gaze, to clarify their "messages." As a subject the Northeast provided another way to interrogate the limits, problems, and possibilities of national identity, as well as the place of the people—especially poor people of a marginalized region—within the nation.

These paintings emerged at a time when art was becoming more politicized, and many painters believed their art could attain the momentum of a sort of socially transformational act in itself. They were also all deeply concerned with realism, even if their representational styles were different. With such concerns, they avoided what might be considered imaginary excesses since these were thought to be false, illusory. The idea was that, in order to participate in transforming reality, the representations had to partake of themes, visualities, and textualities that preceded them. Of course, such so-called preexistent real referents were politically oriented constructs. Realist painting added a new visibility to crystallized commonsense concepts and stereotypes, helping reduce the strange to the known. It was born from the skepticism attacking art from both the left and right at the time; fascism considered any nonrealist art to be a form of degeneration, while Stalinism decried any non-socialist-realist art as fascist.[105]

Subordinating the production of images to an ideological discourse blocks certain expressive possibilities and raises others as genuine expressions of reality. The northeastern paintings tend to emphasize content over formal experimentation. They used known, accepted formal languages to more easily construct and deliver a message to the public. In that sense, while the messages were often thought by their artists to be revolutionary, they were conservative in being crafted accorded to canonized forms. They presented messages of transformation in a manner pleasing to dominant aesthetic taste. Such a dichotomy of radical politics and conservative aesthetics characterized all the cultural production of the left during this period. Painting was inflected by the subjugation of the visible to the political impositions of the speakable. Its imagetic universe was limited to what could be concretely fastened to a political-social totality, a theme with its own representational dictates. As a genre northeastern painting was innately conventional since it emerged within a project to configure a reality that was already a convention.[106]

Between roughly 1930 and 1945, years of considerable political upheaval in Brazil as well as globally, discussions relating to art and especially painting tended to revolve around questions of decorative versus functional character; national or regional content and dynamics; erudite versus popular/national content and style. Realism was surging as a means to portray the nation, in response to the internationalism of modern art. Nationalism encouraged painters to adopt traditional themes and narratives with a modern sheen. During the New State, government sectors dedicated to fomenting culture attempted to define rules for producing national images. That preoccupation was carried to the extremes of prohibiting the exposition outside Brazil of paintings that were held not to depict "a civilized image of the country." Proper paintings would show Brazil's popular face without sinking into vulgarities, which included acknowledgments of the country's deeply mixed-race population.[107]

Brazilian painters engaged social and political questions more directly during the war years. Collective, socializing forms were militating against artistic individualism. It was in this period that the Mexican muralists wielded a significant influence over Brazilian artists, especially those associated with communism, since the murals were viewed as legitimate and effective public art capable of speaking to the Latin American masses, conveying a message of revolution, anticolonialism, and antiimperialism. While those on the right in Brazil were rejecting modernism in preference for traditional classical forms (often inspired, it might be noted, by Nazi aesthetics), the left responded by embracing modernism as "revolutionary," humanist, and antifascist.[108]

After the war, Brazil experienced redemocratization, and with it came a feeling of euphoria. A new country and new world seemed to be at hand. Mexican muralists continued to affect Brazilian painting, which increasingly emphasized exaltations of the nation and its people and disregarded dominant internationalisms. Abstract art was regarded by the realists as cosmopolitan frippery, depoliticized, an arm of cultural imperialism. Particularly among intellectuals and artists linked to the Communist Party, who could express themselves freely at the time, abstract art represented individualism and bourgeois alienation. Realist art saw as its mission to either celebrate or denounce national reality, and it was understood that denunciations reflected more progressive political engagement. Rather than applaud Brazil's developmentalism, it was more valid to reveal the country's underdevelopment as a necessary step toward transforming it.

In this context, as painters considered social questions such as misery, poverty, and unequal patterns of development, the Northeast appeared as an ideal theme. Critics went further, suggesting that artists from the region themselves possessed the greatest capacity to see Brazil with a social perspective. One of the most prominent regional painters, Emiliano Di Cavalcanti (1897–1976) was born in Rio de Janeiro but was embraced by critics as being nearly nordestino himself. Milliet praised his capacity to render the landscape and "*mestiça* race" of the Northeast with a "Brazilian style . . . expressing the peculiar character of our people, of our life, of our natural environment." Di Cavalcanti painted a Brazil that was mixed-blood and poor, but of voluminous curves, hot colors, and unpredictable angles. This was attributed to his "northeastern gaze," an ability to see social truths under surfaces. He drew popular figures affectionately, not rationally, using them to visually embody the region's misery and marginalization.[109]

His paintings were truly national, according to Ibiapaba Martins, because they showed Brazil's world as northeastern with its rainbow suite of race mixture. His paintings represented the monumental synthesis of the country, continued the critic, because he revealed national colors, forms, and symbols; he penetrated the Brazilian soul to show the Lusitanian, African, and indigenous elements that commiserated sadly, or leapt forth in carnival merriment. Di Cavalcanti avoided the ruts of the exotic, of naturalism or impressionism. He generated a perceptive but romantic interpretation in which the national could be seen through the regional.[110]

Di Cavalcanti himself attributed his artistic sensibility of rhythm and full, sensual color to Rio's carnival. His political concerns manifested early, when he worked as a political cartoonist for *O Malho* and other papers. Family in Paraíba and Pernambuco stimulated his travels and his regional curiosity. He had discovered the Mexican muralist movement during a trip to Europe in the early 1930s and quickly incorporated aspects of how they posed authentic human sentiment as oppositional to bourgeois society and values. His energetic, sensual, celebratory, carnivalesque vision of Brazil was balanced by a critical sense of social concerns, making him a perceptive observer of the nation and its people. He spun his reflections out on the canvas, affirming Brazilian culture as he reinvented its national imagery.[111]

Although politically engaged, indeed a militant of the Communist Party, Di Cavalcanti did not emphasize images of suffering and despair for the Northeast, or the country. In urban scenes his human figures were simple but appeared thoroughly, even contentedly integrated in their spaces. He painted the cordiality between people, and between people and nature, accentuating Brazil as a place of harmony and coexistence. In this he was similar to the traditionalist poet Manuel Bandeira, who described a Brazil suspended peacefully between rural tradition and folklore, and urban sociability. Di Cavalcanti was not interested in depicting the urban reality of the proletariat, or exposing class conflict. He wanted his paintings to create pleasure for the viewer, not shock. His aversion to the bourgeoisie may have been based more in a bohemian ethic than a socialist one, but there is a distinct nationalism in his attentive use of both natural colors and recognizable tropes such as *mestiçagem*.[112]

Di Cavalcanti's work is also reminiscent of Carybé's images of Bahia, in that it focused on the artisanal, happy, festive, folkloric aspects of daily life and popular culture. Both artists shared a fascination for Brazil's syncretized culture and the heroism of humble people, and they showed nordestinos at work and at play in a variety of regional settings from the sertão to tobacco fields, hills of sugarcane to rows of cacao, improvised fishing boats to cobbled city streets. The depth of field of some of their images gave a nobility and complex mystery to popular scenes, encapsulating in subtle ways the baroque history, mysticism, and cultural mingling of Brazil as a whole.[113]

In terms of influence on the visibility of Brazil, however, the painter who dominated the 1930s and 1940s and some years after was Cândido Portinari (1903–62). His paintings were able to simultaneously appeal to those on the left, and to the modernizing conservatives in Vargas's government. Portinari was a Communist and was nearly a party candidate for office in 1946, yet his work attained a remarkable establishment prestige. This was because he found ambiguous ways to address concepts such as the nation and the people, lending his art to diverse readings but also making it easily appropriated into official discourses.

Portinari's painting created its own reconciliation between classical and traditional visibilities of Brazil, and modern form. Perhaps this was why he became essentially the official artist of Vargas's New State, since that regime was itself dedicated to integrating forces of the past and forces of the new. In a way, Portinari introduced classical equilibrium to

3.1 *Figuras* [Figures]. Di Cavalcanti, 1957.

3.2 *A morte de Alexandrina* [The death of Alexandrina]. Carybé, 1939.

the vastness and human intensity of Mexican murals to craft an expression of Brazilian identity. By focusing on regional and rural scenes he also lent a literary, mythic imagescape to Brazil as a whole.[114]

Portinari worked against modernism's valorization of fragmentation and details to produce emblematic figures, images of people who represented synthesis and social integration. In the 1930s, much of his work was influenced by childhood memories spent in the interior of São Paulo. By the 1940s, and his rise to state prominence, he had discovered the murals. He created enormous panels exalting the Brazilian nation, work, and racial and cultural harmony. Some of his images were placed on buildings in Brazil and in other countries. Although in this phase he had left behind much of the specific visual world of rural São Paulo State, he would still introduce several iconic rural images to his works (for example, the scarecrow and simply fashioned teeter-totter) that came to be adopted as symbols of the national essence.[115]

In turning away from idyllic São Paulo as the symbolic center of Brazil to call attention to social issues in the country at large, Portinari cast his gaze to the Northeast. The curves of his human figures gave way to rigidity and harsh lines suggesting tension, hunger, the prominent bones and stilted gait of the poor. Desolation and desiccation took the place of trees full of fruit and children, or men working together on the harvest. His canvases became peopled by gaunt, wrinkled wanderers.[116] Even before this, when he was completing murals rooted in universal themes for illustrious buildings, visions from the Northeast served as a source of inspiration. Skeletal northeastern horses such as he included in his 1930 series *Os Retirantes* were later rendered into the Horsemen of the Apocalypse in his painting *A Guerra* that was placed in UN headquarters. Portinari's changing view of the Northeast, a transformation suggestive of the influence of 1930s fiction, can be traced by comparing his early and later representations of nordestinos. His *Os Retirantes* series was initiated in 1930 as an expression of a childhood memory of Bahian migrants fleeing the drought to find work in the coffee fields of São Paulo. The figures bore serious expressions but were not reed-thin or bent; there is a sensuality to their posture, and they seem merely to pose for the painter without calling attention to hunger or pain. But such figures are starkly different in his later phase, in such works as *Enterro na Rede*, *Menino Morto*, or *Família de Retirantes*. These feature wraith-like figures, their faces masks of pain, lined with dry tears. The regional

3.3 *Retirantes* [Migrants from Drought]. Oil on canvas. Cândido Portinari, 1944.

drama of drought has by now been raised to the condition of a symbol of social injustice and the need for dramatic intervention.

In Portinari's expressionist gaze, the wanderers have taken on an emotional vehemence, externalizing the agony of their souls. Their deformations indict the deformations of society and the perverse national reality it accepts. They appear within a host of northeastern signifiers: parched earth, dead children, bones bleaching under the merciless sun, vultures haunting black trees—and, perhaps incongruously, folkloric details from the stage design of the 1942 ballet *Yara*. That show, featuring music by Francisco Mignoni and lyrics by Guilherme de Almeida, was considered the first Brazilian ballet to combine indigenous folklore with a national social conscience of regional misery since its characters were all nordestinos. This reveals how Portinari was shaped by the literary and cultural vanguard of the 1930s and 1940s as he transitioned from the nostalgic, rural São Paulo regionalism of his childhood to a politicized regionalism based on the Northeast.

Portinari is today one of Brazil's most well-known painters. His contributions to the visibility of a harsh Northeast were embraced by a range of later artists. His wan, vacant-eyed migrants leaning on sticks and accompanied by famished children would prove difficult to forget and came to be accepted as the visual essence of the human effects of regional reality. They were scenes in which nature was in remission, providing a background to the image of utter poverty, but still threatening to catch fire under a loose spark. When Geraldo Sarno opened his documentary film *Viramundo* (1965) with shots of Portinari's later paintings in the *Retirantes* series, the director was implicitly placing a seal of veracity on his own filmic regime derived from visual material Portinari had created. It was intended to tell the audience that they are about to get the "real thing." The paintings legitimize the documentary, which had the goal of expressing "the social scandal and tragedy faced by nordestinos who must migrate, tortured into exodus by fiery drought."[117] The influence of Portinari's work has assured that the Northeast continues to be glimpsed around Brazil as portraits of horror mutely begging for help—images of "othered" phantoms that inspire solidarity and revolt, but also evoke repulsion and fear. The viewer wants to help, but also to turn away.[118]

Images That Cut and Pierce

"One rooster alone does not weave the morning: He will always need other roosters. . . . From many other roosters will he interlace the threads of sunshine, taken from their morning cries, so that the morning, fragile and fine, is woven among all the roosters."[119]

João Cabral de Melo Neto was born in Recife in 1920, and spent his childhood among the interior Pernambucan sugar mills of Poço do Aleixo, Pacoval, and Dois Irmãos. His early studies were completed in Recife, but he did not go on to college. He is an example of the so-called Generation of 1945, a diverse group of modernists who, satisfied they had won the battle against academicism, engaged in new internal debates regarding their own premises and aesthetics while attempting to recover their literary and poetic discourses from the politics they had been submerged in since the previous decade. Of all the 1930s fiction writers it was Graciliano Ramos who had moved the boundaries of linguistic experimentalism, carrying forward the early modernists' research program; his interrogation of language and forms of speaking would have great influence on Cabral, who praised Ramos's arid approach as a "model of destitution." Both writers endeavored to find a language appropriate to the theme of the Northeast, a language that derived from the place itself and was not imposed on it. They concurred that the Northeast should be taken as a way to speak, to see, to organize thoughts. The Northeast would reject metaphor as a florid distraction from its own compelling essence.[120]

Cabral believed that language should imitate reality, not obscure it. Thus to criticize reality implied a critical relationship with language as well, a vigorous search for the expressive core—the sinews and bones of language that sustained an understanding of reality. His poetic form, particularly in the case of the Northeast, was distilled of excesses—the "space of bright midday," with the subtle texture of a wasteland of dry emptiness broken by small bright blossoms. It was from a "desert of sheets of paper" that he would cultivate his poems, aspiring to coax his bitter, sharp, "clear-cut, precise verse" from the hard earth of the Northeast. He tended his poems like an improbable desert orchard, with shallow roots straining to pull life from torrid soil. He saw the Northeast as fundamentally desiccated and contrived an equally parched compositional style and symbolic universe to convey it.[121]

While Cabral understood that language was affected by numerous social forces, he never discarded realism outright because all his critical energy, his distrust of words, were based on the desire to find a language adequate to reality. His artisanal attitude sought the imitation of form, not its invention. In his poetry, language was not independent of its referents. He believed there was an actual Northeast outside of language, but his mission was to find the words to express it in all its truth. Guided by tactile research in the region's substances and contours, the exercise of aligning words with things would be a contribution, Cabral thought, toward stripping language of the artifices that aggravated social alienation.[122]

Cabral's Northeast arose from his technical and aesthetic drive to extricate reality from the extraneous discourse that covered it in fraudulent tangles. The region should shine forth from the page undiluted, like a ray of sunshine awakening a slumberer. His words were intended to open readers' eyes to reality, in part by inviting them to join his suspicion of words as vehicles of domination, alienation, and perjury. He wanted his language to duplicate the poverty of the real, not as metalanguage but as semiological realism that equilibrated construct and communication. He challenged the false opposition between form and content to show their inseparability, believing that if the content of poetry could reach and distress a reader, the form ought to do so as well. His Northeast was content and form that cut, punctured, that hurt and drew blood. His region was a seeping gash in the flesh of Brazil.[123]

In Cabral's poems lyricism and formal liberty are substituted by rigorous engineering of words. It was a poetry produced by the heavy labor of measuring and construction, not inspiration. He worked words like stones, polishing and fitting them; he cleansed images of emotional frill to expose their principles and arranged them to offend bourgeois sensibility. It was impersonal poetry, crafted to vex, not mollify. An aggressive poetry, verses of contention, of vinegar and blackened flowers. It was generated in direct response to what he considered the thick, lazy, and self-satisfied prose of the "important, spiritual families of Recife."[124]

Cabral was preoccupied with the materialization of sentiments, ideas, and images, making the abstract tangible. He emphasized object, not subject, because he was still locked into the objectivist illusion and believed comparison could open the essential significance of words. To reconstruct the unity of world and language, it was necessary to accentuate the fractures caused by modernity, but also to avoid using new multiplicities of verbal meanings to try to repair them. Thus his verse was impelled inward like a drill, penetrating, excavating discursive layers that distanced readers from reality. His poetry was not confessional or romantic. It was intended to be like a bright light shone into a deep mine, unfiltered by sentimental lenses or the gauze of ideology.[125]

He recognized that the modernity in his poems was fundamental because of the theme—the Northeast, not an object of classical poetry but antipoetic, antilyrical. It was a tactical move against the traditionalist poetics of a nostalgic, idyllic Northeast. He fought against the image of the comfortable old Northeast, with its plucky poor and content slaves, the affectionate image of a society sweetened by sugar. In reversing the image he was battling against conventional rules for what could be said or not. He wanted to destroy those invented regional traditions by submitting them to the antiseptic of reason, exposing nostalgia as a hoax because in the longed-for region there was never enough to eat and the poor faced constant fear and asperity.[126]

Cabral's poetry, as with Guimarães Rosa's prose, constituted a critical reply to the relations of determination that existed in regionalist literature between material poverty and cultural poverty. Both writers attempted to show that material poverty could be accompanied by cultural riches, and that, while in a world characterized by contradiction and mixture not everything could be resolved in synthesis, the resulting tension could be fruitful for popular knowledge and resistance. Cabral leveraged regional popular culture not for its rhetorical value, but for its grassroots logic. He searched the cordel literature and Christmas dramas avidly to study their direct modes of communication. Borrowing widely, he carefully combined words in novel ways, turning them bright and new as if by the chafing friction of contact within his lines. In particular cordel, with its formulaic recitative structure, lent him an appealing form of expression. Its rhythmic diction seemed to naturally evoke the region of drought, of uncompromising natural cycles, where so many popular discourses recalled laments and death chants.[127]

From popular literature and narrative Cabral also absorbed a cutting irony, using it to mock the pompous speech of regional elites. Where some observers might find only rude simplicity in this popular language, Cabral discovered a reservoir of bruising insights. Its dryness was not a limit or constraint, but a defining feature of linguistic strategy and its inseparable political strategy. In its own way it represented Cabral's greatest aspiration, which was to circumvent rhetorical excess to bear down on words that provoked the consciousness of a different reality, a harder world just under the clutter. He used it to create a poetry that sliced routine from tradition, memory from dream, hoping to isolate all the forms of illusion that bank up in dusty drifts atop the reality of life.[128]

In addition, Cabral's poetry established a critical dialogue with the sociological enunciations and images used by Gilberto Freyre in constructing his traditional Northeast. Cabral's default position was to reverse Freyre's vision, such that he made the sertão the paradigm of northeastern identity rather than the littoral and the sugar plantations. But in doing so Cabral fell into his own trap of assuming a homogeneous sertão with no internal differences, and he offered no major distinctions from other preexisting generalizations of the backlands. He claimed the region's corrupt intermediate zones, prized by Freyre and others, were responsible for the primitivity and misery of the Northeast's most characteristic place, the sertão. It was there that the violence and revenge, the depravity and inequality of sugar society, had their greatest human consequences. But the possibility for resistance lay in the strength and cultural depth of the sertanejos.[129]

Cabral often used the opposite qualities of wet and dry to characterize the differences between the traditionalist Northeast, which he regarded as a construct of decoys and rhetoric, and his own Northeast, which presumed to represent reality. The swamp symbolized the traditional regional elite of the coast, sunken and rotten, a dank place of stagnating mud. It was a place of extinction, defined by the past yet clamoring to stay alive, a place he longed to cleanse with the pure harsh sun of the interior.

> Whoever wants to see the dead
> Having dealt with them in life
> Should think: every kind of marsh
> Fits here in this basin.
> Leftover bathwater, waste water
> From the tubs of the salons,
> Its permanent high tide
> Shrinks to puddles, in every sense.[130]

Cabral tended to associate the northeastern elite with qualities of gentleness and sweetness, as Freyre did; but where Freyre saw these as positive traits, Cabral reversed polarities. Far from being salutary aspects of Brazilian nationality, this placid amiability demonstrated a lack of consciousness of serious national problems. He saw the Northeast of these elites as a place where nothing significant happened; every important issue was papered over by fake smiles and puffs of rhetoric. He shared none of Freyre's or contemporary poet Manuel Bandeira's nostalgic fascination for the colonial underpinning of the region's port cities, such as Recife and its neighbor Olinda. Cabral saw them as growing too fast, sinking into the murk, losing their defined angles and lines. He felt that the traditionalists, in trying to suspend these cities between tradition and modernity, were consigning them to slow deaths. Meanwhile, polluted water everywhere was corrupting them from the inside out. They were becoming monuments to false progress, where the hastily laid concrete cracked too soon and the steel rusted, unable to contend with the rot exhaled by so many befouled rivers and polluted inlets. They were places where "everything seems to encourage the termites, whether sugarcane or sea. . . . Life is worm-eaten, the density of things digested away, all is weightless from disease."[131]

If he viewed cities with a melancholy eye, Cabral reversed the conventionally austere strategies for describing the sertão by adorning it with florid, ornate rhetoric. He cultivated the rugged backlands with bouquets of poetic words to bring it to life, even if the most life it could support was clutches of thorny cactus. In "Morte e Vida Severina" he adopted the form of a folkloric Christmas pageant to affirm not the spiritual hope for life after death, but the resolute hope for life here on Earth where conditions were severe, even antagonistic. He worked against the tradition of regional discourses that emphasized death, praising the vitality of life, the spirit of resisting against desperate physical conditions.[132]

Cabral's ancestors had owned sugar mills and had occupied the elite ranks of society in Paraíba and Pernambuco. He diverted from their traditions and assumptions of propriety, searching out the Northeast of the humble people who had captivated him with stories as a boy. As an adult he found himself, and his artistic path, with the sertanejos—the servants and ranch hands and peasants. His poetry was a sort of salvo intended to interrupt the complacent dinner parties of the great house by making explicit the alienation and misery of the cane workers. He repeated the idea that the sertão was a milieu of revolutionary potential capable of transforming the region's corrupt agricultural and coastal aristocracies. The cane worker became his symbol of the laborer in capitalist society, abused by crude and domineering bosses who also laid waste to nature.[133]

The industrial sugar mill was another potent symbol for Cabral of how a voracious capitalism was ingesting and dissolving the sugar zone, a destructive force, immense termites of steel eating away at the lands and lives of the Northeast. The system of industrial agriculture was turning men into savages, and substituting a struggle between man and nature for the real fight between people, between classes. Cabral responded by humanizing animals, plants, and other natural phenomena. The region's bright sunlight was leveraged to represent reason, illumination, the capacity to grasp the unity of what bourgeois rationality tries to disperse. Operating with an aesthetic based in Marxist dialectics, Cabral constructs opposites that circle or clash or reconcile in bursts of enlightenment. He wanted his images to shock and penetrate, to puncture both the real and the reader's consciousness.[134]

A central opposition in Cabral's work was the dynamic between time and space. Time was inconstant and knowable only in the pinprick of the present instant, whereas space was concrete, real, and measurable, and the continuity of society depended on it. Memory in his poetry was more spatial than temporal. Memory condensed space, making it more palpable, while memories themselves were corporeal, taking on solid forms. Memories were felt more than pondered. This was why he felt so keenly the forces threatening to dilute the diverse forms of regional geography. Where the traditionalists interpreted memory as subjective, sentimental, and nostalgic, Cabral took it as objective, rational, and antirhetorical. False memories, official memories, were those based in so-called temporal continuity. To Cabral memories were discontinuous, like seeds, fragmentary; they could be reordered in the present in the name of projects for the future.[135]

Cabral asserted that the class divides in northeastern society were resulting in a homogenization of exploitation, misery, and hunger from the coast to the interior. While he questioned the traditionalist view of the Northeast as idyllic and harmonious, he too rejected differentiation by painting the region as defined by drought and grief. The imposed nostalgic uniformity of the elite gaze was replaced by an imposed despairing, contentious uniformity from the Marxist gaze. Cabral saw plurality, as his poems demonstrate, but he insisted that it return to a focused, anguished unity. He operated with many of the standard images of drought and the sertão from traditionalist discourse, reinforcing the idea that it was all a desert that barely produced anything, where violence and hunger reigned. Its people shared a common denominator of sinewy strength, but also emptiness and want and sorrow.[136]

Cabral implemented a telescopic visibility of the Northeast, capturing details in a close-up that was possible only by severing them from their context. He prized essence over diversity and a distanced, bird's-eye view to perceive the synthetic whole of reality. He was aware of the social and political influences shaping how different people saw the Northeast, from nordestinos to businessmen in São Paulo, from the plantation owner to the illiterate cane cutter. But he regarded these as effects of ideology and the unconscious. He believed there was an objective way to see, in the manner of the sun, rational, objective, all encompassing. His skepticism of words was based in this, in his preference for and trust in seeing. It is not a coincidence that his aesthetic sensibility was shaped far more by painting and architecture than by poetry or literature.[137]

The prevalence of vision over speech is clear in a poetry that resolutely transformed words to images, and things are scraped down to expose their bones. He practiced a sort of cubist geometry, constructing the Northeast's spatiality by a critical redisposition of its figures, by deforming its traditional forms, by rationally organizing its manifestations. There is nothing ideal in his Northeast. It is poor and pungent, painful and antiromantic. Ultimately he took a position that was more ethical than political, since he never engaged in explicit militancy or used the stock verbiage of pamphlets to stoke ideas of disciplined revolution and future utopias. He presented the Northeast as a cruel, raw place that could and should affect human consciences on its own terms.[138]

The onset of a new future, he thought, would come with the destruction of the illusions of temporal memory and the affirmation of the transformational potential of the present. Space needed to be seen in clean Cartesian terms, with architectural specificity. Only then could northeastern lives begin to be changed through concrete action supported by the collective sensibility of Brazil in the wave of developmentalist optimism after World War II. The Northeast had as yet been excluded from these currents. It seemed locked into repetition and litanies of destruction, its abstract emptiness a rebuke to the rest of the country. It was internally unified by misery and an inescapable social hierarchy. Nature itself translated human misfortune, with the region's rivers as well as its people fleeing southward to avoid dying a dusty death.[139]

João Cabral de Melo Neto can be regarded, along with Guimarães Rosa, as perhaps the first to fundamentally explore the "deregionalization" of the region in terms of inventing a language intended to represent the region itself. He denounced earlier textualities and the mock-scientificism of naturalism, but he nonetheless remained imprisoned in the illusion that he could construct an image and text that would correspond fully to reality. The bitterness of his poetry was embraced and used by regionalists as a weapon in national politics, in the demand for assistance and the assertion of local identity. In concretizing the Northeast, in building a vision of it with the stoniness of his words and images, Cabral ultimately helped reinforce the discursive tropes of those in power. He had wanted to reconstruct the region, not destroy it through outright revolution. By not taking it as an abstraction in the service of a sector of enemy dominants; by not attributing blame and making an orthodox call to action, the poet, with his alternate vision, offered new forms for the agents of oppression to reproduce and articulate themselves. He stumbled on the very stones he hoped to place in the way of further domination.[140]

Perhaps Cabral's greatest and most dour message is that death offered no exit. He had much in common with the Brazilian left at the time, but he was not convinced by the salvationist tone of their militant discourse. He repudiated the nostalgic image of the Northeast spun by the traditionalists but could not escape the fact that in weaving the opposite of their designs he was trapped in conceptual frames that were identical to theirs, only reversed.[141]

Seeing through the Camera Eye

Brazil's national cinema faced considerable challenges in developing consistent levels of production, due not just to the popularity of imported fare but to the substantial and expensive industrial base required to make movies. In the 1930s there were some national films made that were of good quality, such as *Limite* (Mário Peixoto, 1930) and *Ganga Bruta* (Humberto Mauro, 1933), but they were isolated and barely received screen time. Before the 1940s, Brazilian reality had a very fleeting cinematographic presence.

But soon, with industrial advances in Brazil and the growth of a middle class interested in consuming culture, national film production took root, first in Rio de Janeiro (Atlântida) and later in São Paulo (Companhia Vera Cruz), although in a form heavily derived from Hollywood studio models. Everything was copied, from the stars' manner of speaking and walking to the color schemes, lighting, camera angles, and scenery. But because of the gulf in their circumstances of production, the resulting films often came across as mere low-budget caricatures of American films. The only Brazilian genre to find success in the period was the chanchada, a form that embraced the imperfect imitation of American cinema as a formula. It brought over many of its stars and scripts from radio and often-parodic urban popular theater (*teatro de revista*). Atlântida in particular became known for farcical films that copied American cinematographic conventions, sometimes mocking them, but regularly populating them unsympathetically with Brazil's own so-called "national types."[142]

Outside of cinema, other Brazilian art forms were researching and engaging national problems and national realities, but the movies were resistant, preferring to show a sort of internationalized world of illusion in their autonomous spaces of consumption. The settings of chanchadas were often ad hoc and secondary to the plot itself. Even something as genuine and potentially controversial as a shantytown was represented as a simply drawn, nonproblematized backdrop. This enhanced the theatrical stage quality of the productions. In general these films as well as national cinema as a whole were viewed by critics as poor copies of foreign movies. Audiences learned to think that movies were simple diversion where realism and actual tensions did not belong.[143]

That said, one element of national reality that did infuse Brazilian movies in the late 1930s and 1940s was carnival, but it was there for its celebratory and celebrity dimensions. Before the rise of auditorium programs and other radio events with a live audience, these films were the only way for adoring fans to see their radio idols in person—male and female entertainers who danced and sang their way happily on-screen through the intended hit songs of the upcoming carnival season. *Alô, Alô, Brasil!* (Wallace Downey and Alberto Ribeiro, 1933) and *Alô, Alô, Carnaval!* (Adhemar Gonzaga, 1936) can be regarded as the precursors of the chanchada genre, which many critics allege came into being with *Banana da Terra* (Rui Costa, 1939), featuring Rio's famous young singing duo, sisters Carmen and Aurora Miranda.[144]

The visibility of Brazil and its people elaborated in the chanchadas was full of ambiguities and contradictions, themselves characteristics of carnivalization. At the same time that they attempted to "read" Brazilian reality according to imported models from American cinema, and thus reveal national defects (whether deliberately or not), they provoked a new relativism in viewing the imported model that was being assumed as a reference. The sarcastic smile, the self-awareness of parody that characterizes all chanchadas but certainly those made by the 1950s, reflects both knowledge that an imitation is being created, and a critical distancing from the imposition of the "foreign," imported paradigm. One could consider the chanchadas to be a product of what Oswaldo de Andrade called Brazil's incapacity to copy well. But the chanchadas, in their fascinatingly awkward simulacra of Hollywood prototypes, generate an art form far more insightful and critical than the films made by Vera Cruz, for instance, that were intended as "serious" copies of European cinema.[145]

In 1952, participants of the first National Congress of Brazilian Cinema debated the problems of domestic cinema as well as how Brazilian films could be encouraged to deal more directly with issues facing the country and its people. The first bulletin published by the recently founded National Cinema Institute (Instituto Nacional do Cinema, INC) included a commitment to ensure that cinema would reflect the realities of national culture and the aspirations of the people, especially their desires for peace, progress, and liberty. Questions of how to compete with foreign cinema, the nature of the domestic market, and the complexities of production were widely discussed. The INC initiated a study of how international film aesthetics should be altered for the Brazilian context, and took the position that a film should be considered "popular" if it actually managed to conquer a share of the domestic ticket-buying public. Even with its profound industrial and consumer basis, cinema was thus part of the contested field of national and popular culture at the time. The bourgeois intellectuals in São Paulo who controlled INC were not averse to implanting mass culture in Brazil if it were definably national in content.[146]

The precarious status of early national cinema can be seen not only in its industrial deficiency and its subservience to an imported cinematographic regime, but in the fact that when the impulse came to deal with the reality of the country and its regions, Brazilian cinema had to scour the production of other cultural forms—literature, theater, radio, painting—for images and texts to use. Rather than explore the potential of the new medium in the contemporary context of national self-curiosity, Brazilian cinema resorted to a suite of previously crystallized tropes—many, ironically, from fiction—to achieve the "truth-effect" of audience recognition and acceptance. Films that took the Northeast as a setting, for instance, either developed straight adaptations of novels from the 1930s generation or simply mined those books for their most famous scenes and events. The exceptions to this rule were the films of Glauber Rocha and certain other films from the New Cinema movement (discussed later), which attempted to create a distinct cinematic identity for the region.[147]

In the 1940s, such well-known northeastern types as the unschooled migrant worker, white-suited coronel, bespectacled priest, and carbine-brandishing outlaw were among the cultural material that the chanchadas carried over from radio comedies to adapt to the big screen. The typical nordestino was depicted as a dimwitted hayseed, dusty and animal-like, lacking in both intelligence and teeth—the opposite of the polished, educated, civilized city dweller. In his physical and mental poverty he was the inversion of the urban cosmopolitan. He represented the weak and vulnerable side of Brazil. In the Hollywood parodies, with their industrialized settings, glamorous parties and elaborate musical numbers, the wide-eyed, confused nordestino seemed clearly not to belong, to be out of place. But the nordestino could also be leveraged as a figure of strong morals and sincerity, contrasted with the city's scheming bourgeois social climbers who fretted over appearances. His simplicity, translated to a sort of reflexive honesty, made the nordestino a fitting national adversary against the well-dressed foreigners who arrived in Brazil with trunks full of lies and imperialistic schemes.[148]

It was not until the 1950s that the Northeast became a cinematic theme in and of itself, starting with *O Canto do Mar* (Alberto Cavalcanti, 1953) and *O Cangaceiro* (Lima Barreto, 1953), the latter of which became Brazilian cinema's first international success. These two films, both made at Vera Cruz, became extremely influential visions of the filmic Northeast for cinematic production outside of New Cinema. They generated similar films throughout the 1950s and 1960s that also reproduced clichéd regional images and enunciations within a generally derivative model imported from the United States. As an ostensible way of seeing the Northeast anew this genre was doubly preconceived, in its borrowed aesthetics and its rehashing of regional signifiers.[149]

O Canto do Mar opens with a series of standard images to localize the film in a familiar Northeast—cactus, sun-bleached ox bones, dry earth ripped open by drought; the camera stoops to reveal what appears to be hastily improvised grave pits and reaches skyward to capture glowering vultures. In case these images were insufficient to evoke the region, a map appears centering on the states of Paraíba and Pernambuco. A disembodied narrating voice drives the point home: "It has not rained here for a long time. The ground splits in its thirst, begging for water. The sky is always, inescapably blue; families abandon what they have built, their loved ones dead." The use of an offscreen voice seems to denounce the filmmaker's dependence on literary images, and his own insecurity regarding the capacity of these images to express the totality of the drama. The instance suggests how, even beyond cinema, perhaps as a condition of Brazilian epistemology at the time, words were needed to explain the visible.

This film clearly attempts to mount a visibility and speakability of the Northeast that was constructed by novels, journalistic reports, and drought discourse. Its naturalist aesthetics contribute to loading the film with conventions, reproducing a reality that has already been seen and spoken. Made at a moment in which another drought was wracking the region, spurring another wave of migration to the South, the film contains images that its national audience will be anticipating, images that reinforce the identity of the region as a place of suffering and misery. For southern urban viewers, the main ticket-buying demographic, the contrast was obvious—the Northeast was a backward victim of nature, unlike the stalwart South, marvel of Brazilian development.

The problematic relation between rural and urban cultural values, another of the themes of the chanchadas, was also operant here through an urban gaze looking to reaffirm the primitive nature of the character of rural people. Various staged scenes render local culture inexplicable, if not ridiculous, such as the wake for a child attended by singing locals who carry gas lamps rather than candles; and the letter to God, written by the child's mother and placed resolutely in its wan hands, asking that His Heavenly Father take as good a care of the tot as she would. The film is saturated with such stilted depictions of regional folklore. They are detached from the plot and often come out of nowhere to serve as "cultural illustrations," not unlike the abrupt appearance of nordestinos singing in the chanchadas. Their effect here, in a film with such a melodramatic tone, calls into question the meaning of the entire project. How could it be, in a place that is defined by drought, misery, and pain, there are nordestinos playing music over here, dancing the carnivalesque *frevo* over there, and others singing contentedly on the beach? Characters, such as they are, are two-dimensional and believe fervently in the promised land of the South. One youth declares, "The good life is in the South. We'll go there to get away from all this. One day I'll come back with lots of money and help everybody, and we'll all be happy." The film drives home that the Northeast is underdeveloped not just because of drought but because of its primitive, irrational population with their archaic religious practices and tendency to sing all day. Their popular culture is colorful and rich but it serves as merely a temporary distraction from the wretchedness they face daily and participate in constructing. For director Alberto Cavalcanti, it was clearly the nordestinos as well as harsh nature that were responsible for the region's deplorable state.[150]

O Cangaceiro was extremely popular, and influential in fixing a certain image of the Northeast among Brazil's urban middle classes. Its principal thrust was to demonstrate the distance separating the primitive world of the sertão from the industrial city, but it relied more explicitly than *O Canto do Mar* on tropes from Hollywood westerns and their idea of a savage frontier threatening civilization. Thus the frontier/sertão represented an authentic historical stage of Brazilian development, but one that should have been already transformed and "pacified" by a modern society of law, order, and discipline. The film used mythic overtones to validate the society of the present and its codes of values. To construct a plausible Northeast in a film shot in São Paulo, the crew relied on regional stereotypes as well as visual signifiers of the American West. The opening scene places this combination on display: a line of horsemen, silhouetted against the setting sun, ambles along a mountain ridge, which is soon shown to contain the expected cactus, sharp stones, and jumbled bones that announce its northeastern location.

The perspective of Lima Barreto's film follows a political tack that had been developing at least since the 1930s—the idea that the nation could be constructed by absorbing its differences, which meant replacing traditional values and customs with generalized bourgeois ethics and social relations. Barreto introduces bandits without any sociological analysis, but as villains in a Manichean context of good versus evil. The simple people of the sertão deserved intervention and rescue because of their telluric identification with the land, even though they were sullen because the shiny benefits of civilization were out of reach. The myth of the sertanejo as a social element making up part of the core of Brazilian nationality is here reformulated according to the view that the nation's identity should be based on the urban sphere and industrial development.

Another film that framed the Northeast in southern sensibilities was *O Pagador de Promessas*, directed by Anselmo Duarte and based on a play by Dias Gomes. It was even more successful than the others in critical terms, winning the Golden Palm at Cannes in 1962. It brought a classical, naturalist perspective to the setting, referencing the interior with shots of dry earth or cactus and the littoral with images of coconut palms lining the beach. Constant focus on the feet of the pilgrims suggests the physical sacrifice of their journey. The dichotomy between rural and urban takes a slightly different form, with the innocence of the peasants contrasting with the calculations of the sly urbanites. The representation of rural people is paternalistic, even discriminatory. They are contextualized according to the delivery of the narrator, who emphasizes how strange their culture is (and implies they should strive to integrate into the nation's more advanced cultural spheres). In a manner similar to the chanchadas, this film regards the nordestinos with a sort of sanctimonious populism—guardedly welcoming them to the Brazilian nation on the condition that the more distinctive aspects of their popular culture be abandoned. Of course, distilling and institutionalizing popular culture was also an effective mechanism for removing its potential for contestation.

The film is subtle in showing how a series of discourses can transform one "fact" into many facts, depending on the meaning it receives from each of them; how popular culture can be understood and deployed by different actors from different positions of power; and how a simple, apparently primitive act of faith can turn into a gesture of rebellion, sacrilege, and subversion. The film also explores relations between popular and erudite culture, and popular and "national," experimenting with their boundaries but coming down on the side of a national culture that accepts the popular if it follows certain rules, dictated from above. The Northeast, especially Bahia, is shown in all its exoticism; the characters, such as Zé do Burro, appear resistant to reality-based interrogation in their dogged persistence of a promise made to a saint. The radical lack of dialogue between cultural codes effectively cleaves the nation into distinct spheres and rejects the possibility for generalizing the presumably advanced metropolitan paradigms across Brazil. The encounter between a "complex" urban sociability and the mysterious simplicity of the peasants causes a short circuit in national communication and understanding.

But that is not the entirety of the film's conclusion. It shows the northeastern city at first as predictably typical—the stone streets, the baroque churches. But the city becomes a stage for diverse Bahian popular cultural manifestations, independent and intermingling: vendors of food and cordel literature, *capoeiristas*, samba musicians, poker players, processions, Afro-Brazilian religious groups. It is a universe of people and practices that have not been part of the rationality and official proceedings of the city; manifestations unknown by the official institutions that look down on them from above. The film celebrates both the popular culture and its presence in the city, the slight but significant opening of the gates of official culture for the participation of the popular element viewed as more national and authentic. But to what end? This film expresses the populist illusion of the people's conquest of power through the permission of institutions, institutions that mask a recognition of their demands as a genuine popular coup. The great question the film poses has to do with the meaning of the limits of cultural difference, of the alterity between popular and official cultures as paths to liberation and national identity. It looks toward a day when it would no longer be deemed necessary to kill the people like Zé do Burro because they challenge the comprehension and assumptions of those in power, a day when it would not be deemed necessary to articulate a rationalizing discourse that encompassed and constrained all Brazilian popular culture. This Northeast was still an area that was culturally "primitive," that needed to be integrated into national culture, but without forsaking its innate potential and its elements of authentic Brazilianness. The lingering problem was how that was to be done, and who was to make the decisions.

This urban-industrial gaze on the Northeast would begin to be transformed only by New Cinema, a movement that explicitly rejected the productions of both Vera Cruz and Atlântida as alienated, colonized, and trivial appeals to bourgeois sensibility.

THE AESTHETIC OF HUNGER

There is debate regarding what constituted the beginning of New Cinema. Some observers cite Nelson Pereira dos Santos's films *Rio, 40 Graus* and *Rio, Zona Norte*, made in the 1950s. Others point out that the discussion of what Brazilian cinema was and what realities it should express actually began in 1960 with the showing of *Aruanda* (made that same year), Lindoarte Noronha's documentary on the Afro-Brazilian community of Paraíba's Olho D'Àgua da Serra do Talhado, at a Cinema Critics Convention in Rio de Janeiro. It is suggestive of the values that would guide New Cinema that two more documentaries are also often cited as fundamental predecessors: Luis Paulino dos Santos's *Um Dia na Rampa* (1957), showing the Afro-Brazilian culture in Salvador's Mercado Modelo market; and *Arrail do Cabo* (1959), by Paulo César Saraceni and Mário Carneiro, depicting a Rio de Janeiro fishing village. All three of these had in common a nonfictionalized focus on underdeveloped social systems and their relations of production. But the New Cinema movement would receive its name and initial recognition through a series of three articles published in the early to mid-1960s, one by Glauber Rocha in several Bahian papers (as well as the *Jornal do Brasil*), and two by Gustavo Dahl and Jean-Claude Bernadet in the *Estado de São Paulo*. In his piece, Rocha argued that true Brazilian cinema was inescapably new because the Brazilian people were new, Brazilian problems were new, even the light was new. These circumstances assured that Brazilian films would be different from European and American ones.[151]

It should also be noted that New Cinema originated in three different places: in Paraíba, with Lindoarte Noronha; in Bahia, with the circle united around the Cinema Club founded by Walter Silveira; and in Rio, with a group led by Nelson Pereira dos Santos. Although the movement's spokesmen characterized it as united in both politics and aesthetics, there was wide stylistic latitude given the freedom of creation that its members asserted as a defining value. New Cinema also drew from various international movements including Italian neorealism (especially the work of Antonioni), Russian revolutionary cinema (Eisenstein), American cinema (John Ford), and French new wave (Resnais, Godard). Other Brazilian influences included the modernist movement and 1930s fiction, especially where these touched on the troubled "social reality" of Brazil. In large part, the movement was an imagetic re-reading of Brazil and the Northeast in particular. The cinematic style latent in northeastern literature had already attracted the attention of film critic Flávio de Campos, who remarked in the 1930s that books such as Graciliano Ramos's *Vidas Secas* and José Lins do Rego's *Pedra Bonita* contained all the elements that a cinematographer required: "movement, typologies, vivid scenes, dramatic intensity, harsh beauty, and truth."[152]

One of the hallmarks of New Cinema was its modernist sensibility, introducing new ways of seeing to a national cinema whose construction of spatiality had been overwhelmingly based in naturalism. Still, while modernism had changed from a nonrealist aesthetic in the 1920s to a realist one later, New Cinema moved in an opposite direction: the realism it embraced early in the 1960s had been mostly abandoned by the end of that decade. It moved from a symbolic language to an allegorical one, in which rationalism gave way to a magical, mythical vision of the concrete. The first phase of New Cinema runs roughly from 1960 to 1964, just before the military coup. In this early period the national-popular discursive formation had not yet entered into crisis, and New Cinema worked intently on a range of related themes, concepts, and strategies. After the coup, and its ensuing social and cultural fractures, people both within and outside the movement began to call its precepts into question, and its production became more Tropicalist in nature.[153]

New Cinema first took up the modernist problematic of discovering Brazil's identity through confronting its roots, and assessing the national unconscious through its archetypes. Its next step would be the rather didactic move of teaching the people about their own country and how to resolve its socioeconomic morass (phrased as underdevelopment and foreign dependence). All the ideas at play were exceedingly difficult to balance. Leftist ideological blueprints mingled with firm nationalist sentiments. The movement proposed its production as a rhetoric of consciousness raising, of establishing what was truly national, of throwing off alienating colonial influences. Its leaders argued that Brazilian cinema must focus on national/popular themes that would demonstrate, realistically and pedagogically, the country's structural problems, "rationally discovering the most significant elements of social relations." To Nelson Pereira dos Santos, for example, mounting *Vidas Secas* on the big screen was intended to contribute to the contemporary debate of northeastern agrarian reform.[154] Unequal landholding and imperialism were two of the most formidable problems they cited as obstacles to the development of Brazilian autonomy.

The historical period that gave rise to New Cinema helped define its visions and ambitions. Leftists were increasingly embracing culture as one of the best means to transform reality, while anticolonial movements and the Cuban Revolution were appearing to redraw global maps and reframe power structures. The middle-class intellectuals behind New Cinema adopted political discourses and social strategies in which they tried to take the perspective of the laboring classes, and to position themselves as progressives against the reactionaries who denied the revolutionary potential of popular culture. They were paternalistic in believing they could create culture that would be both for, and by, "the people." They determined that their fundamental conservative enemies were the oligarchies, which in the Northeast appeared as coroneis. These were the face of Brazil's primitive social system, which needed to be exposed to the rest of Brazil. The considerable (and controversial) mobilizations around land rights in the Northeast seemed to progressive activists to foster an immanent Cuba-style revolution. For all these reasons, New Cinema's directors and film crews helped enshrine the Northeast as Brazil's most primitive, oppressed, and feudal region.[155]

Their productions *Cinco Vezes Favela* (1962) and *Bahia de Todos os Santos* (1960) demonstrate the contradictions in how the filmmakers reconciled leftist political strategies. Since the populist pact foresaw an approximation with the nationalist bourgeoisie, these films tried to avoid depicting problematic relations between bosses and underlings in the cities. The bourgeoisie should be part of the "people (povo)," a vague and mythic term, and help them transform the country. But the films accepted the dualism of developed and underdeveloped regions, regions of capitalism versus regions of feudalism. The Northeast would be one extremity and São Paulo the other. New Cinema thus gave fresh terminologies to a national dichotomy that had been established decades before, by the turn of the twentieth century. From São Paulo, from the South, the revolution would come; the Northeast would provide a reaction, once it had been properly enlightened. The cinematic archetype of the bandit as both source and signifier of popular rebellion only enhanced the region's appeal to these filmmakers.

New Cinema's approach to the world of work also reflected some of the ambiguity that characterizes Jorge Amado's writing. Its directors were attracted to characters who lived on the margins of "proper" employment, making their way informally through a range of survival tactics while embodying the Brazilian prototype of the rogue. Popular culture and the improvised artistry of daily life could thus be a means of resistance to bourgeois domination. But a rational work ethic and the assumption of identity as a laborer were basic dimensions of a Marxist ideological posture. The films often vacillated between championing the avoidance of labor as a rebuke to the bourgeoisie, and condemning it in the name of disciplined revolutionary socialism.[156]

This lack of fit between the "reality" captured and the filmmakers' political and sociological values was a persistent problem. Films that were intended to be straightforwardly antibourgeois, intended to politicize the viewing public and serve as vehicles for the liberation of the working classes, often focused on people living at the margins of market reality—constructing mythic types that were ostensibly trapped in a stagnant time outside of history and quite beyond the narrow claims of ideological coherence. The thick layers of alienation applied to some characters rendered them pathetic, even implausible, while conversely other characters were portrayed as grandiosely poor and innocent, the wrongs they suffered inflicted by a baroquely villainous society. The middle-class intellectuals behind New Cinema seemed trapped in their own guilt and the paradox of their own position. They adored these mythically humble people, revering, if not precisely reveling in, their misery and stalled development. A middle class facing its own crises and deterritorialization, a scattered bourgeoisie, a fragmented working class, and the lack of meaningful dialogues and projects among them led these leftist artists to turn their hopeful gaze back to the unorganized and deeply marginalized. The Northeast offered visions of the nation's primitive force, its rogues and wretches living in a state of implicit, instinctual rebellion. But New Cinema was also attracted by what seemed to be the passivity of these people (symbolized by the trope of messianism in particular), an inferred quality that could then be interpreted as a plea for outside intervention.[157]

Within the Brazilian context, New Cinema appeared at a moment in which national autonomy through industrial development programs under President Juscelino Kubitschek was still a widely accepted proposition. Cinema needed to participate in those efforts by placing optimism on-screen, avoiding or denouncing the depiction of realities that were not proper to a developed society. In fact cinema was regarded as a prized medium for the delivery of genuine and appropriate popular culture, according to groups as diverse as the establishment Higher Institute of Brazilian Studies (ISEB) and the Communist-linked Popular Culture Centers of the National Students Union (UNE). However, the latter organization cast a skeptical eye on New Cinema because of what it considered the movement's weak links with the people; the hermetic, inaccessible language of its films; and the individualist, auteur nature of the movement itself, driven by personalities and preconceived strategies. The UNE also critiqued New Cinema's "realism" as extremely simplified, with the result of its images and language being actually depoliticizing rather than consciousness raising. However, New Cinema did share with the Popular Culture Centers a sort of general third-world vision, in which class struggle is transposed to a struggle between colonized spaces and their colonizers. This brazenly homogenized the sociopolitical realities of each nation involved. The goal became a solidarity between colonized nations, including blanket assessments of their problems and solutions.[158]

New Cinema proposed to reveal the essence of reality, not invent abstractions, although its preferred cinematic language emphasized public impact and shock value. The films prized aesthetic violence—the clash of images, the starvation of narrative—as a means to stimulate enlightenment. But this predilection also encouraged a focus on rural areas and rural people, whose instinctive, "primitive" violence might be recuperated into a revolutionary project. If dominant discourse had been downplaying the popular violence of bandits and other regional phenomena for its own hegemonic reasons, New Cinema would reincarnate the myths, breathing a new life of revolution into them. *Os Fuzis* (Ruy Guerra, 1964) was an example of the type of film that actually offered a defense of violence, using firearms as symbols of the path to liberation, all in the context of decrying popular subservience to the abusive, personalized power of coroneis. The familiar themes from northeastern fiction were held up and reversed in order to show the negative image of what was ostensibly a developed, civilized country. It mattered little that such films wildly exaggerated the number and intensity of outlaws and religious groups in the Northeast at that time, or at any time; or that the coronel they constructed had long ago been transformed into a very different sort of authority. What mattered was deploying the Northeast's best-recognized myths according to a political strategy in order to call attention to the need for social transformation. Ideologically, it was necessary to demonstrate that nothing had changed in the region, nor would it, without intervention.[159]

If New Cinema had the goal of rousing Brazilian audiences from their slumber of passivity for their own good, with polemical films that could be challenging to watch and understand, they immediately had to contend with the realities of a cultural market in which even the most commercially successful domestic films achieved nowhere near the popularity of imported ones. The movement's great challenge would be to reach mainstream viewers who were not accustomed to seeing themselves on screen, who often rejected Portuguese-language films beyond the cloying chanchadas, and who did not deem portrayals of Brazil's social and economic inequality to be enjoyable entertainment. This led to numerous contradictions, embodied in the fact that Glauber Rocha (perhaps New Cinema's principal exponent) became an ardent supporter of the state film production and distribution company Embrafilme, created by the military regime in 1969. Among its actions, Embrafilme reserved a portion of the national market for domestic film production—a move welcomed by leftist nationalists. But Rocha praised the regime's initiative a bit too eagerly for some, and he was quickly criticized for appearing to be a hypocritical champion of the dictatorship itself. New Cinema had aspired to become Brazil's central political-cultural venue for express-ing and debating national problems, but although it attained significant international success it was received with mostly bored nonchalance at home outside of a narrow sector of urban middle-class political and ar-tistic sympathizers. Its leaders looked with disdain on "alienated" mass culture, seeming to scorn the orthodox measures of popularity they craved for their own work. They chafed the National Cinema Institute's filmmakers, who accepted box office receipts as the clearest index of pop-ularity while rejecting the idea that complicated political films intended to enlighten the masses could be truly "popular." The movement ultimately was unable to contend with the constantly evolving questions of aesthet-ics, politics, and commerce that cinema must engage to remain viable, especially a self-affirmedly "national" cinema that is nonetheless navi-gating international currents of economics, politics, and culture. Even with the protection given to domestic production by Embrafilme, even in the context of an undemocratic authoritarian regime, New Cinema was simply unable to attract a public in significant numbers.[160]

The movement's mission was to reveal Brazil's underdevelopment and misery, which would require avoiding the industrial models imported by Vera Cruz and Atlântida for more experimental techniques leading to the discovery of Brazilian authenticity. The result of Brazil finally seeing its own face, its own image, its own alienated soul on-screen would be a qualitative leap toward a future of political engagement. This required taking the country seriously, rejecting the superficial stereotypes in the chanchadas for an aesthetic of hunger and violence—stern reality, not glit-tery optimism. The gaunt, rough faces of the Northeast were deemed the ideal counter to the civilized, prettified Hollywood-type stars or the festive carnival masks in the films from Rio and São Paulo.

But underlying this project was a sense of political certainty that be-came increasingly shaken. The country and its people had appeared to possess a theoretically simple reality that would be straightforward to rep-resent cinematically. As they progressed in their work, however, the film-makers all encountered more complexity than they predicted—far more than could easily square with their literary and ideological preconceptions. Once they started to confront the multiplicity of realities, of social, politi-cal, and cultural circumstances in Brazil, their initial abstract geography fell to ruins. In a manner similar to the authors of 1930s fiction, they had scoured popular cultural production and folklore for material to use in communicating with the people. The Northeast was recognized as rich in traditional popular culture, but high in inequality and social misery, leading New Cinema to avidly explore its images and cultural wellsprings and repurpose them for developing a new national cinematic language. The films of Glauber Rocha exemplify this, in the pervasive influence of cordel literature on their narrative structure, themes, and hazy, magical atmosphere between reality and dreams. Metaphors from cordel seemed to offer the manifestation of a collective unconscious that could be targeted to the debates over the nature of national cinema and its relations between truth, image, and narrative style.[161]

Rather than examining the underdeveloped space from the perspective of the developed, New Cinema proposed the opposite (as Guimarães Rosa had also done), for example, considering the city from the point of view of the sertão. They wanted to examine Brazil not from the perspective of bourgeois urban-industrial society, the São Paulo of Vera Cruz or Praça Tiradentes of Atlântida, but from that of the Northeast. This would shift the positioning of the gaze to present the country backward, from the inside out. Technically its cinema would be imperfect and dissonant like the national sociology, and politically rebellious and aggressive like the vanguard. They hoped to invert the criteria of image production in Brazil, transcending the country's cultural inferiority complex and the dread of what holding a mirror up to its own face might reveal. The desired vision was more diachronic than synchronic, more representative than productive of reality.[162] Still, it was only in the late 1960s that New Cinema began to approach the realities of the country's urban centers, once they started to abandon the dualist vision that had oriented their earlier production. They began to reflect that underdevelopment was also apparent in the cities of the South, that Brazilian hunger and misery were not limited to the sunbaked fields of the Northeast. Even within the elite neighborhoods, among the elegant boutiques, could evidence of the national predicament be encountered.

The cinematic reality of the Northeast they constructed was marked by lack, by an absence of musicality or sounds or conversation. It was a desolate space, visually and aurally, penetrated by monotonous, wordless noises such as (in the film *Vidas Secas*) a discordant fiddle-like *rabeca* string or screeching ox-cart wheel. Even when it appeared as a space of dense verbosity, as in some of Glauber Rocha's pictures, its very grandiloquence indicated a problematic abundance of palaver without substance. Its world was black and white, overexposed to sunlight, contrasting the burnt or yet to be burnt. Nature in devastation was never mere background but always one of the main characters, while the films' various poor people—servile, humble, inarticulate, awkward—were not given the expected prominence of "protagonists." They embodied the dusty environment, emerging from it briefly only to fade into it again. The entire universe seemed to reel in its own insanity, explicitly challenging the viewer to accompany and impose sense on it. It was a mythic world, unmoored from history and temporal signposts. The sertão was the symbol and synthesis of underdevelopment, alienation, and submission to the brute reality of class difference.

New Cinema's Northeast was homogenized by poverty, drought, banditry, and messianism, but simultaneously it was an exemplar of Brazilian reality that was believed to be generalizable to anywhere in the third world. Its internal nuances and diversity were smoothed over in the construction of images and themes that made the Northeast a concentrated space of shock and dismay. It revealed national problems and at the same time suggested specific, if limited, solutions. When New Cinema affirmed the sertão as a place lacking logic and meaning, it was arguing that rationality and consciousness would come to it from outside, from the South, from the coastal cities. Its migrants trudged toward the South almost as an act of sheer instinct, seeking the truth.[163]

What New Cinema looked for in the Northeast, beyond the primitive roots of Brazilian nationality, was a national unconscious of disgust with domination, oppression, and colonization. These filmmakers wanted to awaken and restore the forces of rebellion that history had put to sleep, the bandits and the messiahs, to spark a new and greater effort to transform reality. According to the revolutionary theory that shaped how they interpreted reality, it would be the peasants, the poor and uneducated, who would lead the charge once they had been enlightened by an intellectual vanguard. But the Northeast continued to be understood and redeployed as a region of misery and desperation.

GLAUBER ROCHA

Glauber Rocha (1939–81) was born in Vitória da Conquista, Bahia, to a middle-class family of Presbyterians. His father was a merchant and roadway engineer, and it was on trips with his father to the interior that a young Glauber first came into contact with the environment that would serve as the location-theme for some of his films.

In the early phase of his work, before the coup and while he was still associated with the national-popular discursive formation, Rocha made two films: *Barravento* (1962) and *Deus e o Diabo na Terra do Sol* (1964). In *Barravento* he was concerned with the alienation present in popular culture and the fatalism of the poor, as well as the question of racial divisions in Bahian society. The film centers on the opposition between the characters of Firmino and Aruan. Firmino comes from outside, from the city, and is thus destabilizing to the relations of passive equilibrium in this society of fishermen. He is also unstable in his relationship to capitalism, since he is reluctant to integrate into his new milieu of popular tradition but also eschews salaried work for an improvised existence of roguery. Aruan, on the other hand, represents the possibility for continuity of that society with its forces of subordination. Tensions mount between these two forces, and Firmino attempts to interrupt the symbolic and economic continuity of the society in hopes that the misery of the exploited will ultimately trigger a revolt. Firmino, with his urban experience, is granted a sharper sense of vision and understanding. Rocha reaffirms the urban sphere as the source of rationality from which the seeds of social transformation will be dispersed to the alienated and primitive, those still locked into natural rhythms and the idle distractions of religion.[164]

The goddess Iemanjá is shown to be just as domineering and unpredictable a force as the businessman who owns the fishermen's nets and underpays them for their catch. The community suffers a double tyranny—that of earthly forces and that of the supernatural. The alienated rhetoric of the local characters is countered by images that seem to produce a second, more convincing discourse suggesting they are simply wrong and benighted. At the same time, the visual poetry of the images and the representation of the characters produces at least a temporary counterdiscourse of beauty to the film's ideological project with its valorization of revolution. Firmino attempts to provoke change, but he does so illicitly, and the true path to the future will only be assumed by Aruan when, at the end, he leaves the village to join the urban proletariat.

Deus e o Diabo na Terra do Sol opens with standard images of the sertão: drought, dying livestock, a wizened cowboy, a priest leading a flock of faithful as they pray for the miracle of rain. The nature of peasant life is presented rather selectively through the alienation of Rosa, and the deliriums of Manuel. It is a primitive life of claustrophobic misery, slow agony, and merciless domination. But this static world is rocked when Manuel, driven and exploited to his limits, attacks the cheating coronel. This violent act against his oppressor seems to restore his humanity. Ensuing events and the breaking of routine lead Manuel to seek a new meaning in life, including solidarity with some of the followers of the authoritarian priest Sebastião. However, the mythic, sacred world of religion might occasionally irk those in power but would not provide any real solutions; the landholders unite to hire a killer to deal with the upstart peasants.

Rocha makes Canudos leader Antônio Conselheiro's apocalyptic utterance "The sertão will become sea, and the sea sertão" a central metaphor for the film's meditation on the teleology of revolution and the transformation of humanity. While Rocha reproduces a traditional visibility and speakability of messianic movements, he is nonetheless able to derive new meanings from them. Sebastião is denouncing not only the lunacy of the past, but its continuity in the present, a present of myth and spirituality along with the material condition of brutal inequality. Ultimately, though, the film reveals its ambivalence toward popular culture, even after including admiring shots of the group's banners and flags. As a leftist intellectual, Rocha was fascinated by the rituals and artisanal splendor of popular culture, but he despised its logic; he was smitten with its forms and images but rejected its content.

The appearance of Antônio das Mortes, a character obviously sketched from Hollywood westerns, is a sort of third valence in an otherwise Manichean framework of good and evil, God and the Devil, rich oppressor and poor peasant, messianic priest and bandit. He is a revolutionary force with a complex human face. He embodies the potential to transcend closed dualities. His entrance also gives a helpful jolt to the film, which had been indulging in lengthy displays of Manuel's subservience to his new boss, the priest: ascending an endless staircase on his knees, carrying a stone on his head.

There is another shedding of blood, this time at the hand of Rosa, apparently the only character to have maintained rationality. By killing the priest, she makes the film's second violent gesture toward doing away with servility to the powerful and charismatic. As the antithesis of the godly figure of the priest, the devilish figure of Antônio now seems to the swooning Manuel to provide a path to follow. But the model of the bandit loses its luster for Manuel as an image of Corisco in trance babbles about being the representative of divine ire even as his violence is shown to be meaningless. The bandit, raised as the symbol of violence properly used against the unjust powerful, is at the same time demystified into a confused, raging man whose violence is not the beginning of a new and better world but a relic of the present awful one.

The dialectic between forces of good and evil is resolved by the assassination of each, and the appearance of Antônio das Mortes, who kills to free the sertanejos of their myths. But there is an uneasy subtext of the middle classes with a guilty conscience—people who have the capacity to understand the causes and mechanisms of exploitation but who maintain the status quo and continue to serve the elites. Manuel's dash to the sea concludes the metaphor that runs through the film. He finds a way out of his static, timeless space by heeding the transformative message from the coast. The ambiguity of the world depicted in terms of good/evil or violence/poetry becomes impossible for the filmmaker to resolve. Rocha was stuck between abandoning his ideological preconceptions and embracing fully the complexity he was discovering. His characters remained types, bound to dualities of hero versus antihero, the symbolic shadows of a theoretical posture. Perhaps that is why they seem flat and a bit gratuitous.[165]

Flexible temporality was one of Rocha's cinematographic characteristics. Not only his characters but the plots of his films oscillated between the discontinuous, multiple movements of history and the repetitive, cosmic cycles of myth. His dialogue, sounds, and narratives frame a periodization that is often contradicted by his images. If the former point to a specific time or era, his images jostle to be free of temporal bounds. But Rocha's interest in synthesis also contributes to a greater emphasis on continuity than on discontinuity. His characters typically seem imprisoned in a suffocating, repetitive chain of past and present that allows no hope of the future; but they finally intersect with history and find a way to a more alleviating future. In *Deus e o Diabo,* for instance, the temporalizing function of conscience is abandoned for the atemporal unconscious and the deep archetypes of nation and region. Rocha researched psychoanalysis for tools to artistically configure the ahistorical national character, as a product of patriarchal rural society in the sertão. He sought a time out of time, a moment that contained and channeled all possible realities. His totalizing ambition went beyond the nation to the conceptual geography of the third world. His films did not represent a time so much as invent an independent temporal frame that encompassed all the rest—memories and hopes alike.[166]

Rocha's spaces were also based more on myth than on history. They were closed off, their frontiers not implying an exteriority beyond the frame. Each filmic world was a concentrated summary of various spatialities and temporalities. He deployed emblematic images against each other to create a space of clashes and violent conflict. In this early phase of his work, his spaces were totalizing and densely rhetorical. Starting with *Terra em Transe* (1967), however, his approach to space grew more abstract. He seemed to give up on the use of any identifiable references or identity markers. His territories changed from being saturated with signifiers to realms of emptiness and dissolution, evoking the philosophical deterritorialization suffered by the director and his circle of progressives. The previously established parallels between natural environment, human characters, and narrative style were increasingly abandoned, resulting in a widening gulf between his characters and the spaces they lived in. Rocha's narrative technique also changed to reflect this deepening complexity, and the newly opaque interiority of his characters.[167]

Myth and history were two essential parameters of Rocha's films, not in the sense that measured proportions of each were applied recipe-like to each project; rather, they instituted a polarity or force field through which his films oscillate. On the one hand, Rocha utilized regional myths to impose on them a critique from the perspective of history. But in many cases his narrative approach and images concede to the myth such power that it generates a discourse in opposition to his declared ideological position. This contributes to the evaporation of linearity in his films' narratives, leading to ambiguity and confusion. Aspects of his popular characters' history and identities are rendered blank when Rocha lurches from affirming their human integrity and worldview to imposing an ideologically determined set of events and resolutions on their story. *Barravento* demonstrates this tension, as Rocha wants to construct a Marxist condemnation of candomblé in the fishing village but is simultaneously captivated by the beauty and collective force of the rituals. His ideology sought the end of history, but his films created a sense of enclosed totalities, rich in the continuity of popular culture, in which forces cancel each other out and movement is impossible. External force is required to introduce change to such mythic worlds—the instability brought by vanguard intellectuals, hoping to create momentum toward something like progress.[168]

Because Rocha wanted to reduce history to its essential pieces, his themes, processes, and characters tend to be emblems symbolizing social or class situations. The characters, in reaching universal significance, are distilled to transcend their immediate temporality. He sought to both discover and portray the origins of history and national culture, the national unconscious, in a drama of symbols. The essence of reality was beyond what could be shown, because realism was trapped in bourgeois appearances that needed to be unmasked. His goal was to reveal the inner truth of Brazilian society and the Brazilian people through popular myth, the use of which would be indispensable for social transformation because they metaphorically revealed the subterranean forces of revolt and liberation that those in power attempted to co-opt or deny. Rocha desired to free the country's unconscious powers of struggle and violence, through a project of mass psychoanalysis, against a stifling bourgeois conservatism. The myths of popular revolt would reveal the falsity of the official history of Brazil, a history paralyzed by the status quo and sterilized by rhetoric. At the same time, Rocha ambivalently recognized that there was a discrepancy between the reality constructed by myth and that constructed by history. The myths themselves were not sacrosanct and had to undergo an analysis of their own prevarications.[169]

To confront the myths within history would be to declare the death of myths, and the end of history itself as a myth. But myths keep alive the dream of changing history, including toward a revolutionary utopian future. They dialogue with deep-seated desires, passions, and anxieties, and thus would seem to have a place in a cinema that wanted to analyze history and construct a totalizing vision of Brazilian society's underdevelopment. Rocha had a clear political agenda in the early phase of his career, hoping to articulate a third-world aesthetic capable of conveying Brazilian truths and Brazilian hunger. When he dove into the search for primitive roots of the national unconscious in northeastern popular culture, he was taking up the modernist questions of Brazil's national and cultural identity. As he grew obsessed with finding the soul of the country, his discourse became entrenched in parameters of identity and nationalism that rejected mass culture as alienating, inauthentic, and destructive to the popular capacity for revolt. Such a quest for roots was

the product of a gaze cast downward and inward. It seemed to reproduce the Brazilian condition of a colonized people perpetually bent over,
scouring the country for clues of self-identity. As Brazilian historian and
cinema scholar Luiz Nazário observed, those who go trying to dig up
roots get themselves covered in dirt and muck. However, the inclination
driving great art is never down into roots, but up toward the stars. Rocha
persisted in his desperate search for the source of Brazilianness, for a
familiar face hazily glimpsed but always just beyond his grasp; and he
became quite muddy for his trouble.[170]

To create a cinematic language based on the misery and hunger of
Brazilian reality, Rocha believed it necessary not only to use the popular cultural forms of society's dispossessed, but to register a dialectical
critique of that culture as itself alienated, as a vehicle of domination.
To look at the world through a popular lens did not guarantee a gaze
opposed to that of the dominant, as the intellectuals linked to CPC and
UNE theorized. It was only the first step toward producing a revolutionary popular culture, and leftist intellectuals must be able to incorporate
criticisms of and improvements to the popular element. The doctrinaire
tone of Rocha's early characters follows this pedagogical function. But
his films contain a more profound populist contradiction. Rocha's ideology led him to look to the people for revolution and transformation, even
though his personal vision was rather more cynical: the people like to be
led; they love and respect a strong boss. Ostensibly to rouse them from
their alienated stupor (a state to which he felt mainstream cinema contributed), Rocha salted his films with scenes featuring characters staring at the camera, shattering the fourth wall, and hectoring the people
explicitly.[171]

Rocha's first two films participated in the general belief among Brazilian leftists in the early 1960s that social revolution was both inevitable
and immanent. The objective conditions were in place; all that was lacking were the subjective conditions of raising the people's consciousness,
and there was a role here for enlightened cultural production. His films
presented a schematic of the way things were supposed to proceed—from
a static state of confusion and subservience, a character or set of characters will advance on the path toward understanding, rationality, reality unmasked, and metaphysics forsaken. In practice the teleology that
guided his first two works unfolded into another sort of metaphysics in
which history becomes prophecy. Perhaps this salvationist current was a

lingering influence from his Protestant upbringing. History seems to be imposed on his characters rather than be made by them. Their lives, their world, the films themselves are all imprisoned in an evolutionist dialectic that should result in achieving illumination. From the sertão, overarching metaphor of alienation and exploitation, characters and viewers are carried to the sea—metaphor of the encounter with a transformed civilization. Liberation was a destiny from which characters could not flee. They were mere instruments for the stratagems of reason.[172]

At the start of the 1960s, extreme ideologues on both sides began to ponder, paternalistically, how to integrate the popular sectors into politics in a slow and controlled manner. Both sides assumed that space would be carefully conceded to the masses, not conquered by them. Popular participation had to be mediated, to obstruct change in the case of conservatives or to orient and guide change in the case of the leftists. If intellectuals on the right fetishized popular tradition, those on the left tended to interpret it as false consciousness. Their shared conception of politics focused on the actions of charismatic leaders who would anticipate the people, perform illustrious acts for them, point out the proper path forward, and utter truths for their edification. For their part the leftist vanguard believed themselves uniquely able to secularize popular customs, and reveal the relations of production as both the essence of exploitation and the source of all miseries and cruelties that victimized the poor. If the people did not understand the structural reasons for their hunger, if they were ostracized from the institutions of power, it was only revolution—led by a conscious vanguard—that would transcend this state of fragmentation. Revolution would retotalize the world, replacing delirium and alienation with meaning and understanding.[173]

Rocha's films were a product of these tensions and ambitions. They were ambivalently divided between defending traditional culture and militating for its elevation to more rational forms. He supported this popular culture to the extent that it was resistant to the invasion of industrial mass culture and was antithetical to bourgeois cosmopolitanism. It also furnished him with material and modes of expression distinct from (and more "authentic" than) the global cinematic language imported and re-created in the South. He was aesthetically drawn to violence, not order, as a means of establishing justice. Rebellion was imperative, so he did not condemn "evil" in the abstract but sought to explore the conditions that produced it in society. He sought the elements of resistance and revolt within popular culture, hoping to excavate from the layers of passivity their realization. He probed the people's morals and sentiments for political expression. Nonetheless, the people were always evading his gaze as he sought to materialize and comprehend them. He would meet them only in the utopian future, when they could slough off their alienation and take their revolutionary place in a time beyond history.[174]

The violence of the repressor was thought to be the starting point for a process of consciousness raising. The greater the violence of domination, the nearer the people were coming to the regeneration of revolution. Rocha believed that people should be capable of staring at death full-on and allow their convictions to transcend their fear of it, a view that explains in part his fascination with myths and archetypal forces. Revolutionary heroes would be cut from this cloth—men (nearly always men) willing to die for an idea, or for the cause that had driven their lives. Fear of death was an arm of manipulation leveraged by the dominant classes, who trembled at the thought of a mass insurrection. All these ideas drove Rocha to the Northeast, a space that had been crystallized as a milieu of violence and death. He combed the backlands for myths that would bring meaning and conviction to the struggle against unjust power relations. He believed that violence was the only form of expression left to the dominated, their only way out of the status quo. Violence was pedagogy, instructing in how to bring about change, and an aesthetic that conveyed cruel reality without relying on words. In Rocha's universe power was understood negatively, as the generator of misery and violence. Resistance and revolt were the opposite of power, they moved in the opposite direction, and only they could be used to combat power.[175]

His preoccupation that his aesthetic be an actual expression of reality led Rocha to foster a gaze that was objectifying, distancing, organizing, and analytical. He demanded that his cinematic language reflect the essence of the social processes they depicted. Improvised techniques such as holding the camera in hand and circling a character permitted a greater creative freedom that helped simulate the vertiginous lunacy experienced by the character. They also lent an illusion of movement to characters who were static in their lives and thinking. But the impulse was framed according to his vanguard notions of who ultimately is responsible for change and so came from outside the plebian characters who were themselves moved by it. His camera was guided by a defined, and defining, political posture, which is why his spaces and temporalities could be both deeply conceptual and hastily jumbled together. There was no naturalist or realist pretension in the cinematography. Entire scripts would be rewritten during filming. But these improvisations were countered by rigid editing, including careful choices of sound, determined by the ideological message a given film was constructed to deliver. Eisenstein's dialectical approach to montage, which Rocha ardently embraced, works to minimize the evidence of improvisation and spontaneity while affirming the presence of the director as the author of the whole final product. Only in *Barravento* is there some smooth editing between scenes that implies a certain visual harmony, a peaceful play of images that invites the viewer to enjoy the experience of watching. By *Deus e o Diabo* there are abrupt, jarring cuts to the film itself that reflect aspects of the plot.[176]

The handheld camera, wandering in disequilibrium, reveals the fact that someone is manipulating it. It is such vacillations around the characters and their spaces, framing disjointed perspectives, that ultimately affirm the multiplicity of points of view that composes history. Rocha wanted to not simply represent the real, but to break through the appearance of reality that he took as an ideological construction of the dominant class. His initial films are organized around the struggle between two opposing forces that winds up being resolved through the intervention of a third, different force, which puts an end to chaos and introduces rationality.[177]

Rocha's auteur cinema was intended to break with the narrative conventions of commercial cinema, to find other ways to represent a national reality he believed was still preindustrial. He emphasized shocking transitions, gaps, discontinuity, the odd fit between scenes, the presence of the camera rather than its invisibility. He assumed the fact that he was making a representation, a fiction, and he did not flee from accidents or improvisations. He seemed pleased that his films were barely controllable experiences. He also believed that the speakability of his work was able to articulate truths, unlike the pretty lies of commercial cinema. But this was another major contradiction in his filmmaking: he regarded the films as fiction but still believed they were vehicles of truth. His flash-style editing, seemingly done by hand as a traditional artisan would, obviously had cordel literature as an inspiration; and in *Deus e o Diabo* he sharpened the technique into one of the most successful attempts at a national cinematographic form in Brazilian history. The pulsation of that narrative reproduces the rhythms of characters, their slowness and exasperating repetitiveness as well as their quick actions. The film thus seems to breathe. It cycles through tension and distension. The interventions of history are jagged and unexpected, precipitating rapid change in an otherwise stagnant world. Immobility takes on the suggestive tone of patience, of accumulating energy before a leap into the future. The down time of inactivity is not pointless or neutral but is a phase of quiet, invisible intensity that gathers strength into readiness.[178]

In that film, too, the confluence of images, words, and didactically symbolic characters is invaded by a rending allegory of modernism, which lends further ambiguity to the meaning of the work. Rocha manages to combine elements of Greek tragedy and operatic stylization here, including the chorus that comments on or accelerates the action and a sense of the blind determinism of destiny. His dialogues were between characters, between characters and audience, between characters and the cinema, and ultimately between his cinema and the audience. He transposed the oral narrative of cordel literature and the sad, nasal song of northeastern singers into a new and sophisticated dramatic form with modern arrangements. He was inspired by his perception that the cordel storyteller was to a great degree a Brechtian actor, who did not just interpret history for the audience but was also its author, conductor, and fellow interlocutor.[179]

Rocha's early films centered on the battle between magical and materialist thinking, as he strove to create a language that could affirm the national and popular from the point of view of class struggle. In cordel he found the magical realism that helped him express the surrealism of national reality. By incorporating its myths he elaborated a highly inventive, antinaturalist space into which he projected his desire for the essential, eternal, and absolute. He used metaphor to magnify the real, reintegrating past, present, and future, the known and unknown, spaces of the present and future, into one totality. This totality had one primordial segmentation, represented by symbolic characters: on the one hand the bosses, the landowners, the power brokers; on the other the poor and submissive, who sought balm for their exploitation in mysticism. But alongside these a third force emerged, the enlightened revolutionary vanguard who would intervene to attempt to transform this desolate order. Those characters could represent monolithism or upheaval, just like the forces of society itself.[180]

Rocha declared in an interview that his interest in cinema came with the awareness of the basic regional problems of hunger and slavery. To show those problems, in all their ugliness and complexity, was his ultimate goal. In other words, his work begins already trapped in the same strategy of the numerous northeastern regionalist discourses examined in this book, to reveal misery and exploitation. Of course, Rocha had the Marxist ambitions of post–Cuban Revolution leftist intellectuals, and he created an iconoclastic set of discourses to try to achieve them. He focused on the Northeast but subordinated its regional spatiality to the global movement for revolutionary transformation of society. The Northeast was appealing as a means to address not only Brazilian reality, but also the reality of the entire third world. Rocha valorized popular culture to the extent that it was resistant to internationalization and opposed to the bourgeois logic of modernity, but his approach to it was contradictory. He fully accepted that the Northeast was magical, desperate, intense, and violent. He tried to retell its history through popular gazes, manifestations, and discourses, intending to challenge official history—even as he also wanted to demystify and comment sagely on the nature of the poor people's forms of seeing and speaking, on their customs and beliefs.[181]

In Rocha's films, regional memory revealed and questioned itself, finding a way to reelaborate itself from different points of view. Just as the diverse dimensions of his films (narration, sound, image, dialogue, musical commentary, the director's ideology, camera work, editing) were not producing a single coherent message in synchronicity, the works opened spaces for regional visibility and speakability to be rearranged in new perspectives. His films swung between rejecting the whole universe of images and enunciations that had constructed the received idea of the Northeast, and a complete identification with them. Whether seen from the right or from the opposite of the right, the Northeast appears as a unified world of burnt horizons, a place of the living dead where destiny is a condemnation. It was a scorched space of ruin, hunger, and misery, however one looks at it. Even inside out, the Northeast proved resilient—but this is another of its clichés.

In the end Rocha did not subvert but actualized the myths and themes of the Northeast, packaging them within a different political strategy for use as a denunciation of global capitalism and the global bourgeoisie. But he also saw the region as a space that was exciting because the future was overdue. It was the territory of revolt that had captivated Jorge Amado, and been dreamed of by Graciliano Ramos and João Cabral do Melo Neto. In the discourse of intellectuals on the left, the Northeast was locked into the same series of images and enunciations that the conservatives spun out of their nostalgia, their romanticism. The left repeated with mere repolarization the terms of desperation and misery used by local oligarchies to gain national pity and national contributions. They hauled the Northeast out with equal fervor as the place where national authenticity still existed, where traditions had best been preserved from cosmopolitanism and mass culture, where the struggle was greatest against values considered foreign and bourgeois. The Northeast was invented as the place in Brazil that rebelled against modernity, and begged for charity from the developed regions to keep the fight up. It was invented as a machine that ostensibly generates its own images and texts of stubbornness, tradition, squalor, and drought. Meanwhile, the Northeast itself remains mostly unknown.

CONCLUSION

The principal conclusion of this book is that, despite many appearances to the contrary, the Northeast is a recent invention in Brazilian history. The region must not be taken as an object of study without historicizing it, or the results will be anachronisms that falsely affirm it as an objectively natural and timeless cultural-geographical space. The idea of the Northeast was formed at the intersection of diverse regionalist practices motivated by particular conditions affecting the provinces of the older North region, at a moment when, after independence, elites around Brazil grew preoccupied with constructing a nation. Groups that were initially dispersed, focused only on particular local interests, increasingly came together to defend what they were perceiving as their shared space: a territory in economic and political decline that stood to benefit from state largesse. Diverse processes and practices—from drought policy to messianic movements, banditry to new regional political blocs, changing capitalist models to the attraction of Recife's intellectual life for sons of traditional landowners—all contributed to the consolidation of this novel concept of the Northeast. The region was cohering as a space of common references and concerns, both political and economic, bound together by history and culture. Congresses, symposia, scientific studies, political committees, novels, and movies would be among the products ultimately generated by this Northeast.

For such an accretion of commonsense reality to occur, regionalizing practices interacted with political and cultural discourses that transformed the place from being merely an area afflicted by periodic drought to a place with its own unique racial, economic, social, and cultural identity. Intellectuals, connected in various ways to the local dominant classes, were summoned to produce knowledge that would give breadth and depth and texture to the region, letting it speak and be seen with an increasingly assumed objectivity. They invented it in a particular way—as a region in decline compared to the rest of Brazil. It was with subtle artistry that these intellectuals, themselves linked to preindustrial socioeconomic models under threat, elaborated texts and images for the region that anchored it as defiantly backward-looking, even reactionary toward the changes affecting Brazil as a whole (which included a growing bourgeois sensibility expanding outward from the South). The invention of the Northeast also depended on a shift in how space was seen. No longer simply a natural or ethnic phenomenon, the region was demarcated by social and cultural traditions, values, and attitudes. The cohesion of the Northeast was a way to counter the processes of deterritorialization affecting social groups in the area, a circumstance provoked by their deepening subordination to the modernizing South and the spread of urban-capitalist sociabilities.

This book has not argued for the existence of an actual regional northeastern identity. Rather, it has tried to unearth the conditions that made the Northeast possible and plausible. It has endeavored to show how the Northeast became the most sophisticated elaboration of "region" in Brazil. Of course, the questions of regional and national identity are always interlinked and shape each other in dynamic ways. Regionalism and nationalism emerge together, like twins in a fraternal but competitive relationship from the moment of birth, each offering new potentialities for the other and lending special forms of credence to the other. The idea of nation that emerged in Brazil in the nineteenth century was interlaced with regionalisms; these preceded and created the regions that today can appear retroactively to explain and justify their existence.

Like Brazil's other component "regions," and indeed the whole tapestry of Brazil itself, the contemporary jigsaw puzzle of boundaries is not a product of natural geography, or of political or economic rationality. Each is a construct of images and discourses, a constellation of meanings. This book has attempted to reveal some of the ways Brazil and the Northeast have observed, heard, and read each other, and how their distinct meanings contributed to their mutual configuration in different ways. What seems to be an endless repertoire of signifiers is actually limited by the rules of meaning at any given time that inform what can be seen and spoken. Regions are given the symbolic weight of being the largest territorial bases that together inscribe the nation, but they are anything but solid. They are composed of sinuous threads of discourse, of carefully selected images and enunciations, of new music that comes to us as an evocative soundtrack for what always existed—in short, regions depend on all the mysterious arts that give contour and stability to what is intangible. To accept the premise that a region exists as a discrete entity is to perpetuate an identity forged narrowly, and dynamically, in processes of domination and resistance. Region should be understood as a historical construct that contains diverse temporalities and spatialities, whose various cultural elements along the axis of erudite and popular have been categorized as memory, character, tradition, soul, spirit, essence. Actually the "pure" Northeast exists in every corner of the region, and everywhere in the country, and nowhere at all, because it is a crystallization of stereotypes that is the product of a national dialogue. These institute a truth, or impose it, with such persuasive force that the multiplicity of regional images and voices is obliterated. The region can be grasped as such only by reducing it to a sheaf of clichés that are repeated ad nauseam by the vehicles of communication and the arts, by people from outside the region, and, most fundamentally, by people within it.

Structural prejudice toward the Northeast and its inhabitants (the "crooked gaze" of the media that Rachel de Queiroz denounced, but to which she nonetheless contributed) emerged from a given visibility and speakability of the region that was nourished not only outside of it but by it, by its own discourses, which were reproduced and advanced by the people living within it. This Northeast is nothing more than the normalization of certain themes, images, and texts that are repeated and reflected throughout the entire nation. If not to be too expansive and chaotic to comprehend, regional as well as national identity depends on the distillation of variations. But diversity is an inescapable fact of humanity. As Roberto de Matta has noted, formulations of Brazilian national identity pull in opposite directions. They vacillate between the acceptance and celebration of all-encompassing diversity as a unique Brazilian trait, and the naturalizing of an ostensibly nation-bound (or region-defined) human nature. The danger lurking in discourses of identity is that complex historicity can be elbowed aside by a reifying naturalism; aspects of social life are discursively frozen, removed from history, and reoriented along lines that are controlled to stay familiar.

Such discourses typically confuse the compilation of shared signifiers of identity with what "we really are," which results in a constant struggle to reconcile empirical beings with transcendental, categorical ones. Nation and region do have a real existence, a positivity, manifested in each attitude, articulation, or manifestation we make in their name. They exist as a language, but they are also produced when those in power and those they subordinate dialogue with each other in that language. Nation and region are spoken and seen distinctly depending on the place one occupies in society, and the particular webs of power and knowledge that one is connected with. This book has attempted to show how different subjects in different historical conditions, and occupying specific places in the fabric of power relations, produced different texts and images for the Northeast—and how what ostensibly is the "same" is actually heterogeneous. That should not be surprising, again given that contributions to solidifying the Northeast have come from so many different subjectivities and disciplines and creative endeavors over time. The Northeast invented within the sociological studies of Gilberto Freyre was taken up by writer José Lins do Rego, who in mirroring it also refracted it, introducing small dislocations and variations. Freyre also directly inspired Cícero Dias, whose paintings might be seen as inherently Freyrean images—or not, since Dias also had his own particular vision and his own artistic style.

In the same way, when diverse leftist intellectuals from the Northeast wanted to invert the official image of the region, they did so by attempting to show "the point of view of the people, those who are dominated." They also provoked a dislocation of the traditional images and texts linked to the region, but ultimately they stayed locked within a region whose established terms they could not help but reproduce since they never questioned the region's existence. Later, the Tropicalists would begin to ask some of those deeper questions, but only so far as to question the region's *mode* of existence, but not whether its reality should be interrogated. The left's imagination was imprisoned within national and nationalist boundaries. As early as the 1940s, Oswald de Andrade was calling attention to the fact that Stalinism and the theory of "revolutionary nationalism" was actually making frontiers more rigid, shored up by barrier walls and barbed wire and lines of watchful guards bearing carbines. What was tenuous became delineated explicitly by iron. By the 1960s, the reaction on the left was to regard nations as anachronistic. The nationalist dispositif went into crisis, associated with the rise of internationalist movements and the reflexive self-defense reactions by "historical nations." Regionalisms themselves were a conservative reaction to this process of globalization. Nationalisms and regionalisms both share a reactionary, anachronistic character, notwithstanding that at a certain historical moment they made possible important social and political conquests as well as providing incentives for artistic and cultural creativity. But their creative potential seems to have run dry, if we consider that they rather quickly fossilized into a basket of stereotypes and representative curios made up of stock images and enunciations, sounds and character types. As forms of knowledge they were facilitated and interpreted by interest groups in networks of power that wanted to perpetuate themselves as national defenders or regional embodiments.

Today it appears necessary to start over, to go beyond categories of nation and region, because both have turned into efficient machines for smothering the new and different. That is why they exist in states of crisis. Brazil has always lacked a nation, and the Northeast has been configured as a region completely defined by lack and need. With coups and dictatorships and the democracy that cycles in between, the winners always grow conciliatory in victory and promise to save both nation and region; but the desperation for both only worsens. Arguments regarding Brazil's dependency and colonial roots of exploitation have all been used to explain the state of the country/nation, and yet these too have little of merit to offer since they share the premise that victimization defines us, that others are always to blame for every aspect of our primitivity, hunger, and misery. The same could be said for arguments intending to denounce Brazil's "internal colonialism," the regional inequality deriving from one region exploiting another. These allegations repeat the logic of victimization that removes from the self any responsibility for past, present, or future conditions. The notion of regional inequality falsely presumes that one day there existed, or might possibly exist, regions that are completely homogeneous and equal. To imagine such a possibility is contradictory, since it suggests a reliance on naturalism and measurability that would undercut the discursive nature of the identity and coherence of the regions themselves. International relations of capitalism and imperialism are not external to the nation or the region; they intersect with us, align with us, prod us. They help constitute us and reproduce us. Even speaking of external and internal in this context is grossly misleading.

If this book has suggested that the Northeast is a circular concept, a knowledge based on self-definition and self-reflection, that does not mean the region's culture is a fraud—nor is it to suggest that to be genuine, culture must be connected to "tradition" and mechanically function as representative of a given space. The more interesting question is how culture is produced and recognized within a series of frames from the local and national to regional and international. We need to look critically at the conditions of production of culture and related knowledge in the country, in its diverse areas. We must be prepared to look back at that which gazes on us, and to speak dissonant truths back to the commanding voices that try to tell us what is so. The point is not to search for "true" national or regional culture, to finally discover our national identity (pulling it up, as it were, from the bottom of a stream bed or catching it in a butterfly net); but to seek out cultural difference, striving to be always different not only from others but from ourselves. Historians can contribute decisively to the collapse of the traditions and identities that imprison us, that reproduce us as a nation always looking for itself or a region always clamoring for charity. For this to happen it will be necessary that each historical work be as much a meditation on how history is written, its language and narrative and its ostensible relation with the "real," as on history itself as past issues and processes. The thrust of historical analysis should be on the present, discovering it in its multiplicity of spaces and temporalities, considering the various pasts that are in each of us and the diverse futures that may come to pass. We must always focus critically on how the past is narrated to us in the resources at our disposal—not as true or false representations, but as forms and forces that together participate in inventing the past for us. They are narratives that construct a given universe, a given memory, that continue operating in us, guiding our imaginations and our footsteps. We should try to free the images, texts, and sounds of the past from the cloak of present-day obviousness that hides their true nature from us.

This book demonstrates that the Northeast, which today appears obvious and is widely taken for granted, was configured during a certain historical era by many hands often working independently and unconsciously. Domination and struggle did more than attend its birth; they were the reasons for its creation, and they enter and reenter its stories in complicated ways. At no point in his writing did Graciliano Ramos explicitly set out to lend weight to an image and text of the region that reproduced, precisely, the patterns of domination that he despised and longed to extinguish. On the other hand, the critical assessment he brought to bear on the mechanisms of memory and language facilitate a radical new questioning of the creation of the Northeast itself. Ramos initiated in Brazilian literature the modern suspicion that there might not be a direct relation between words and things, that words and fixity are mortal enemies. He provided an elegant (if terrifying) way out from repetitive art and the brute power of custom.

The Northeast we confront is almost never the Northeast as it is, but the Northeast as it was made to appear. It has become a machine that mass produces texts and images. Responsibility for this cannot be placed at the feet of the dominant classes, because there is not a simple class logic involved. The high level of consensus surrounding these identity markers and the wide range of participants in their (re)production cause them to be perceived as "regional truths." It must be recognized that the region's class structure and nature of economic underdevelopment are not sufficient to explain the difficulties faced by those who tried to modernize it. This aversion to the modern pervades social groups and classes. The ideas, images, and enunciations that invented the Northeast and remain associated with it are a fundamental component of this "lack of modernizing capacity." What there seems to be is a lack of social legitimacy and value attributed to innovation, development, and change. But an accentuated valorization of old ways of doing things means that modernization acts in the Northeast to affect as lightly as possible the region's social relations, power relations, and cultural dynamics. It might be called "modernization without change": avoiding the necessity of individual independence and encouraging the acceptance of hierarchies and paternal systems of protection as weapons against meaningful transformation, even against basic citizenship. This broadly based social aversion to change renders the Northeast a place where the new is hobbled and emasculated. It serves not only the dominant sectors but the other classes as a convenient shield against the radical aspects of modernity, dulling the blades of novelty and innovation so they cannot affect social relations whose vulnerable traditional character must be protected.

The encroachment of mass culture and consumerism into the Northeast is given a different inflection by its coexistence with collective interests, which mobilize to block any of the positive aspects of modernity or capitalism and more deeply embed the region in underdevelopment. Codes of bourgeois individualization, with their depersonalized social relations, clash with rigid but subtle traditional norms that protect the group. Even the ideological energy of the dominant class is dissolved into a sort of obstinate collective pride pitting the Northeast against the rest of Brazil. But another perverse side of that corporate will against transforming social relations is the tendency for scattered interest groups to fight bitterly to conquer or preserve narrow advantages, helping ensure that no real progress in any direction will occur. Regionalism works to weaken the identity of groups and classes per se and advances by maintaining segmentary interests. The circulation of meanings in Brazilian society in general functions as a systematic obstacle to the development of more progressive social significations. By sacralizing the region, the nation, the people, order, family, or revolution, political discourses crystallize into doctrines and dogmas that undercut the potential for invention of new political configurations. The people, including in their lowest-common-denominator category of "citizens," are regarded by elites in Brazil as something as yet inexistent that needs to be brought into being through wise and generous intervention. From the heights of their wisdom, they will impose form on the amorphous mass. The real people in all their multiplicity and complexity are disdained, when not completely unrecognized, and understanding of them is substituted by abstract constructions that the elites want to declare into reality. This is another of this book's conclusions. Call them what you will, elites or dominant classes or "winners" on both the right and left in Brazil have, at least until now, shared an abstract and authoritarian vision of the people, reducing them to one homogeneous category or another (masses of poor, masses of potential criminals, masses of laborers)—a herd to be seen, organized, led, and improved by select others who are different from them and who "know what is best for them."

I have tried to sketch a vision, still rudimentary and mostly out of reach, of the basic problems surrounding present regional separatism and regional prejudice in Brazil. I was able to do little more than define the weak spots or structural supports in the webs of power that sustain regionalist practices and discourses regarding the Northeast, and through some tentative interpretation, suggest future possibilities for investigation and analysis. This book was never an attempt to invalidate "false" discourses and tyrannically impose a version of the truth against them. Authoritarianism and totalitarianism nourish themselves on claims of certainty that assuage all doubts, and they undermine any democratic perspective that is based on difference rather than the hierarchy of instituted identities. If this book can help stimulate a new form of relationship between Northeast and South—if it can help free our imaginations of these imposed boundaries and entrenched identities—it would have provided one step toward a liberating rejection of the hegemonic mechanisms of domination we have all learned and absorbed in Brazil. If I have been able to go deeply enough within the region of the Northeast to come out the other side, penetrating its familiarity and making it strange and distant; if I have shown how regional identity has limited us in Brazil as a curious fact of historical processes and not a dictate of teleology, then I have succeeded in everything I hoped to accomplish.

In this text I was not concerned with transcending modernity in the name of postmodernity. Rather, by pursuing modernity to its ultimate consequences I wanted to bring history back into a central place in our own epistemology. My focus was on applying history to what has taken on a supposedly impregnable sheen of naturalism, the objects and concepts that seem resistant to time's corrosions, the myths that sustain a particular construct of spatialities at the national level. The hierarchy of spaces in Brazil functions to reproduce a hierarchy of knowledges and powers, a hierarchy that distrusts the modern and invalidates difference— a political, social, and cultural regime that values the past more than the present.

What is commonly referred to today as "northeastern culture" to emphasize timelessness is historically dateable. It is the fruit of a political-cultural complex that tends to dilute the heterogeneity of the space in order to defend so-called northeastern interests and culture against national and international influences. Areas as diverse as the Bahian *reconcâvo*, the coasts of Pernambuco or Paraíba, the sertão of Ceará, and the Amazonian stretch of Maranhão came to be conceived as forming one entity, a geographic, ethnic, and cultural unit (that seems to disrespect state boundaries, although it also accepts them as indicative of a certain natural reality). This unit could be defended according to political strategies to counter its national disrepute, but it was also defined by its pleas for outside investment. The less "regional" the Northeast actually became, in terms of its economic, social, and cultural linkages, the more intransigently it bore down on reaffirming its pseudo-unity and pseudo-identity—even at one time suggesting with breathtaking ingenuousness that it might separate from the rest of Brazil to ease its people's exploitation and magically create new indexes of development and wealth. This book has argued that Brazil needs to renounce all of the continuities that we acritically receive and reproduce, above all those lodged in the terms of tradition, identity, national and regional culture, development, underdevelopment, and evolution, so that we can start to think and act differently.

It should be noted that there has been a surge in regionalist proclamations and cultural movements in recent years in Brazil. This book takes no part in them. It is not a manifesto championing northeastern identity and has tried to be consistently nonpartisan. Its concern was the mechanisms of knowledge and power that produced such regional fractures and gave them their distinctiveness. It has not attempted to defend nordestinos from the prejudice of the South, or claim one region has more integrity than another. Its goal was to question the existence of these regions at all, and how they are constructed in art, mass media, popular culture, academic production. My perspective as both (and neither) a nordestino and *sulista* inspired my efforts to dislocate the authorial tone from the gravitational pull of regional bases, which I regard as stultifying mechanisms of domination that prevent us from seeing other possibilities, other arts, other futures.

With this book I intended not to defend the Northeast, but attack it on a variety of fronts. I wanted to begin the project of disassembling its discursive and cultural capacity to reproduce the social, economic, and power relations that imprison its identity in poverty and misery. Even the "revolutionary" discourses that emerged to critique the condition of the Northeast took too much traditional logic for granted to allow a more complex, polymorphous reality to emerge. Why do we all perpetuate an idea of the Northeast that equates it to drought, violence, custom, fanaticism, and suffering? It is not enough to ease the misery we look for and find there, or to denounce it. New voices and gazes must complicate the region that we all seem to know too well. If the Northeast was invented as a space resistant to change, it must be destroyed to make way for new spatialities of power and knowledge.

For those of us with ties to the region, if we simply take on northeastern identity as it is, one based on exclusion and submission, we will continue to occupy the expected places in Brazilian hierarchies. Our voice will be only for begging and lamenting, our gaze only for bearing stoic witness and tearfully appealing to the consciences of faraway leaders. On the other hand, if we denounce the networks of power that marginalize and stereotype the great majority of people living in the Northeast, we must not fall into the trap of leveraging the identity of the region as inherently, collectively resistant and revolutionary. We should affirm all the ways we are not nordestinos at all, in the consecrated sense. The ways of being nordestino are innumerable and untold. We need to question the lenses through which nordestinos are seen and see themselves, as well as the words that circulate about them through the mouths and writings of nordestinos and non-nordestinos alike. Combating prejudice against the Northeast cannot be done through regionalist or separatist discourses that invert but maintain the terms, or by mounting counterattacks of prejudice against the southern "region" and those that live there. We must destroy the South as well as the Northeast, these abstractions mounted on preconceptions, if we are to truly get to know the national population and both understand and respect the differences we do find.

A place to start might be to criticize the mass media in Brazil, which saturates the country in northeastern references that rely on a negation of history. The media indulges in a visibility and speakability of the Northeast that amplifies it as a picturesque, arid place that never left the late nineteenth century. One might ask why the media shows the bandits, the droughts, the coroneis, apocalyptic priests and wandering peasants, but rarely anything else. These are cultural relics already devised as such when the Northeast was shaped out of its geographic and cultural ancestor, the North, in a particular historical and political era. Brazil at the time was widely viewed as polar, like a battery, with the North as negative and the South positive. The media repeats the hierarchies of space and identity, providing false context and justification for Brazil's social, economic, and cultural inequalities. It operates with received stereotypes and superficial, external differences, differences of "type" that are not investigated but affirmed. News reports on the Northeast are not undertaken to reveal in it something new, but to certify its established image—and thereby to reinforce the accepted image of São Paulo and Rio de Janeiro, of the South, and so on and on.

The pursuit of history has a fundamental human role to play here, not because it might discover reassuring certainties for us, but because it fosters doubt and new modes of inquiry. It offers no panacea. It should not be a ritual of pacification and the shoring up of truths; it should be voracious and restless, an exercise in dismembering. Like flame it reduces established truth to ash, but as it consumes and reprocesses its material it generates the sparks of new doubts, new problems to explore. Before we apply our theoretical resolutions to try to contain the flame and fashion a narrative from its embers, we must let our studies burn bright, to irritate and provoke. The history of the invention of the Northeast must be allowed to burn among us, to demand attention and interpretation—not just as an academic topic but as a question for human beings to ponder and reconstrue and configure into their art, in the name of love and the possible. There is little as inhuman as certainty, a kindred state of death. But art is a condition of life. It is possible that with art we can invent other Northeasts that will carry us beyond the prison walls that enclose the Northeast we are accustomed to.

NOTES

FOREWORD

1. Lincoln Gordon, interview by John E. Reilly, May 30, 1964, Kennedy Oral History Project, John F. Kennedy Library.

INTRODUCTION

1. ABC is a ring of communities around central São Paulo, including Santo André, São Bernardo do Campo, and São Caetano do Sul, an important industrial base. It has relatively high indices of income and literacy and played an important historical role in Brazil's modern labor movement.

2. Translator's note: *Nordestino* translates directly as "northeasterner," a word that in American English carries implicit but highly divergent cultural connotations (as well as referring also to a weather condition). For that reason in the text I have maintained the Brazilian Portuguese word *nordestino* in reference to people from or in Brazil's Northeast, while otherwise translating regional references.

3. The June festivals (*festas juninas*) derive from the colonial period and are held at the end of the rain season; the community celebrates the rain, as well as rural life and values more broadly, with events usually hinging around the Catholic holy days for Saint John and other saints.

4. Antônio Conselheiro was a religious leader who founded the village of Canudos in the interior of Bahia state in 1893. Conselheiro's preaching was often apocalyptical and in favor of the monarchy. He rejected taxes imposed by the new republic, ultimately making his alternative community a target for military action. He was killed in 1897.

5. Lampião (1897–1938) and his companion Maria Bonita (?–1938) led a band of outlaws in Brazil's Northeast in the 1920s and 1930s. His father had been killed by the police in 1919.

6. *Documento Especial*, Sistema Brasileiro de Televisão; *Programa Legal*, Rede Globo; telenovelas *Tieta do Agreste*, *Pedra sobre Pedra*, *Renascer*, Rede Globo; *Globo Repórter*, Rede Globo; Rachel de Queiroz, "Os olhos tortos da mídia," *O Estado do São Paulo* June 17, 1988.

7. Roberto da Matta, *O Que Faz o brasil, Brasil?*, 13; Dante Moreira Leite, *O Caráter Nacional Brasileiro*, 96; Roland Barthes, "A escritura do visível," in *O Óbvio e o Obtuso*, 9, and *Fragmentos de um Discurso Amoroso*, 24.

8. On the relation between power and knowledge see Michel Foucault, *História da Sexualidade 1 (A Vontade de Saber)*, 88.

9. For more on how I am defining power relations see Michel Foucault, *Microfísica do Poder*, 209–28.

10. On the concepts of visibility and speakability, see Gilles Deleuze, *Foucault*, and Michel Foucault, *A Arqueologia do Saber*.

11. I draw on the relation between discursive and nondiscursive practices in Foucault's work as analyzed by Roberto Machado, *Ciência e Saber (A Trajetoria da Arqueologia de Foucault)*.

12. Spatiality is explored further in Michel Foucault, "Sobre a Geografia," in *Microfísica do Poder*, 153–66; Eni Pulcinelli Orlandi, *Terra à Vista*, 55; Fernand Braudel, "O espaço e o tempo," *O Estado do São Paulo* July 29, 1947, 6.

13. Michel Foucault, *Microfísica do Poder*; Roland Barthes, *Fragmentos de um Discurso Amoroso*, 1; Haroldo de Campos, "Parafernália para Hélio Oiticica," *Folha de São Paulo* May 13, 1984 (insert), 11; Dominique Maingueneau, *Novas Tendências em Análise de Discurso*; Orlandi, *Terra à Vista*, 25–.

14. Paul Veyne, *O Inventário das Diferenças*; Luiz B. Orlandi, "Do enunciado em Foucault à teoria da multiplicidade em Deleuze," in *Foucault Vivo*, ed. Ítalo Tronca, 11–42.

15. See Margareth Rago, *Os Prazeres da Noite*, 23; Celina Albino and Nísia Werneck, "Anotações sobre espaço e vida cotidiana," in *Espaço e Debates* no. 17 ano 6, 33–43.

16. Foucault, "Sobre a Geografia," 153–66.

17. Foucault, "Sobre a Geografia."

18. On the relation between identity and difference, see Deleuze, *Diferença e Repetição*, 71 and 185; Luiz Carlos Maciel, "O esvaziamento da realidade," *Folha de São Paulo* February 27, 1977 (insert), 23.

19. Ademir Gebara, *História Regional: Uma Discussão*; Rosa Maria Godoy Silveira, *O Regionalismo Nordestino*; Francisco de Oliveira, *Elegia para uma Re(li)igião*.

20. The concept of referential illusion is explored by Paul Veyne, *Come se Escreve a História*, 11.

21. The method of interlacing enunciations and images was suggested by Roberto Machado, *Deleuze e a Filosofia*.

22. On the relation between subjects and conditions of historical possibility, see Michel Foucault, *As Palavras e as Coisas*, 384–90.

23. This approach drew inspiration from Jeanne Marie Gagnebin, "Origem da alegoria, alegoria da origem," *Folha de São Paulo* December 9, 1984 (insert), 8; José Américo Mota Pessanha, "Bachelard: as asas da imaginação," *Folha de São Paulo*, June 27, 1984 (insert), 9; Walter Benjamin, "As imagens de Proust," in *Magia e Técnica, Arte, e Política (Obras Escolhidas* vol. 1), 36.

24. Roland Barthes, "A escritura do visível," in *O Óbvio e o Obtuso*, 9; Scarlett Marton, "Foucault leitor de Nietzsche," in *Recordar Foucault*, ed. Janine Ribeiro.

25. Michel Foucault, *Microfísica do Poder*, 15; Roberto Machado, *Ciência e Saber (A Trajetoria da Arqueologia de Foucault)*.

CHAPTER ONE: GEOGRAPHY IN RUINS

1. Gilberto Freyre, "Vida social no Nordeste: Aspectos de um século de transição," in *O Livro do Nordeste*, 75.

2. "A Enciclopédia Brasileira," *O Estado de São Paulo* August 2, 1936, 4.

3. For an example of this, see Paulo Moraes Barros, "Impressões do Nordeste," *O Estado de São Paulo* August 15, 1923, 2.

4. Paulo Moraes Barros, "Impressões do Nordeste," *O Estado de São Paulo* August 10, 1923, 4.

5. "O Bloco Político do Norte," *O Estado de São Paulo* September 3, 1920, 4.

6. Oliveira Vianna, "Impressões de São Paulo" and Dionísio Cerqueira, "Impressões de São Paulo," *O Estado de São Paulo* February 17, 1924, 6.

7. Paulo Moraes Barros, "Impressões do Nordeste," *O Estado de São Paulo* August 16, 1923, 3.

8. João Lima Verde, "Impressões de São Paulo," *O Estado de São Paulo* January 14, 1925, 3; Oliveira Vianna, "Impressões de São Paulo," *O Estado de São Paulo* February 17, 1924, 6; Dionísio Cerqueira, "Impressões de São Paulo," *O Estado de São Paulo* October 28, 1923, 4.

9. "A colonização nacional em São Paulo," *O Estado de São Paulo* October 15, 1924, 4; "A São Paulo que desaparece," *O Estado de São Paulo* May 12, 1927, 4.

10. "Hoje, no Fênix," *O Estado de São Paulo* February 12, 1926, 14.

11. Chiquinha Rodrigues, "Cortando o Nordeste," *O Estado de São Paulo* November 16, 1941, 7.

12. Chiquinha Rodrigues, "Cortando o Nordeste."

13. For more discussion on the relation between the speakable and visible, power, and object and discourse, see Gilles Deleuze, *Foucault*, 57–78.

14. Mário de Andrade, *O Turista Aprendiz*; Raul Antelo, "A costela de Macunaíma," *O Estado de São Paulo* September 17, 1978 (cultural supplement), 3.

15. Roberto Ventura, *Estilo Tropical*, 67.

16. Sampaio Ferraz, *Cruzar e Nacionalizar*, 180; Mário de Andrade, "Oswald de Andrade," in *Brasil em Tempo Modernista*, 219; Graça Aranha, *Espírito Moderno*, 24.

17. Mário de Andrade, "O Movimento Modernista," *O Estado de São Paulo* March 15, 1942, 4; Carlos Berriel, "A Uiarra Enganosa," *Revista Ensaio* 17–18, 210; Maria Célia Leonel, "Antes que me falem d' A Bagaceira," *O Estado de São Paulo* September 17, 1978 (cultural supplement), 13.

18. João R. Pinheiro, *História da Pintura Brasileira*, 87.

19. Flora Süssekind, *O Brasil Não É Longe Daqui*, 187–221; Sérgio Miceli, *Intellectuais e Classe Dirigente no Brasil*, 1–56.

20. Antonio Candido, *Literatura e Sociedade*, 113.

21. Roberto Ventura, *Estilo Tropical*, 36–44; Eni Yatsuda, "O Caipira e os outros," in *Cultura Brasileira: Temas e Situações*.

22. Cyro T. de Pádua, "Aspectos da liderança de Antônio Conselheiro," *O Estado de São Paulo* October 22, 1942, 4; "Os Sertões," *O Estado de São Paulo* March 5, 1938, 4.

23. Paulo Dantas, "Os Sertões como tema literário," *Revista Brasiliense* 5 (May/June 1956): 86.

24. Monteiro Lobato, *Urupês*; Otávio Dias Leite, "Vidas Secas," *Revista Acadêmia* 34 (April 1938): 10.

25. Lobato, *Urupês*.

26. Mário de Andrade, "O Movimento Modernista," *Aspectos da Literatura Brasileira*, 236.

27. Mário de Andrade, "Departamento Municipal de Cultura" *O Estado de São Paulo* February 21, 1936, 3; Andrade, "O Movimento Modernista," 236.

28. See, for example, the paintings *Abaporu* (1928), *Lua* (1928), and *Distância* (1928).

29. Mário de Andrade, "O Movimento Modernista," 237 and 248.

30. Nina Rodrigues, *Os Africanos no Brasil*, 17–18.

31. Oliveira Vianna, *Raça e Assimalação* and *Evolução do Povo Brasileiro*; Dante Moreira Leite, *O Caráter Nacional Brasileiro*, 220–36.

32. Rodrigues, *Os Africanos no Brasil*, 261–.

33. Roberto Ventura, *Estilo Tropical*, 17–18; Graça Aranha, *Canaã*, 214.

34. Sampaio Ferraz, *Cruzar e Nacionalizar*, 25.

35. Durval Muniz de Albuquerque Jr., "Falas de Astúcia e de Angústia: A Seca no Imaginário Nordestino."

36. Gilberto Freyre, "Vida social no Nordeste: Aspectos de um século de transição," 75.

37. "O problema do nordeste," *Revista Spartacus* no. 1 (August 1919): 1.

38. Lourenço Filho, "Os Milagres," *O Estado de São Paulo* April 23, 1920, 4.

39. Lourenço Filho, "No Reino da insânia," *O Estado de São Paulo* November 25, 1925, 3 (emphasis added).

40. Lourenço Filho," Transpondo as trincheiras," *O Estado de São Paulo* November 19, 1925, 3.

41. "O banditismo no Nordeste," *O Estado de São Paulo* 15 June 15, 1927, 2; Célia Maria Marinho de Azevêdo, *Onda Negra, Medo Branco: O Negro no Imaginário das elites do Século* XIX.

42. See the series of articles entitled "O banditismo no Nordeste," *O Estado de São Paulo* June 15, 1927, 2; June 16, 1927, 5; June 22, 1927, 3; June 23, 1927, 2; July 11, 1927, 3; August 28, 1927, 3.

43. "O banditismo no nordeste," February 4, 1927, 6.

CHAPTER TWO: SPACES OF NOSTALGIA

1. On the problem of origin in history, see Süssekind, *O Brasil Não é Longe Daqui*, 15–21.

2. For more on the relation between economic and social crisis, politics, and regional elaborations, see Elide Rugai Bastos, "Gilberto Freyre e a Formação da Sociedade Brasileira." The sensations of fragmentation associated with modernity are explored by Lúcia Helena, *Totens e Tabus da Modernidade Brasileira*.

3. Gilberto Freyre, *Nordeste*, 5–6; Muniz de Albuquerque Jr., "Falas de Astúcia e de Angústia."

4. Oswald de Andrade's trip to Recife is discussed in Joaquim Inojosa, *Os Andrades e Outros Aspectos do Modernismo*, 259. On how São Paulo reacted to the droughts, including charitable campaigns, see the series "Pelas vítimas das secas" in *O Estado de São Paulo*: January 1–4, 6, 9, and 24, 1920.

5. "Pelas vítimas das secas," *O Estado de São Paulo* January 6, 1920, 4; January 9, 1920, 4.

6. Mário Pinto Serva, "As reivindicações do Norte," *O Estado de São Paulo* March 22, 1920, 5.

7. Muniz de Albuquerque Jr., "Falas de Astúcia e de Angústia."

8. Consuela Novaes S. de Quadros, "Formação do regionalismo no Brasil," *Revista do Centro de Estudos Baianos* 77: 5–13.

9. Albuquerque Jr., "Falas de Astúcia e de Angústia."

10. Albuquerque Jr., "Falas de Astúcia e de Angústia," 276.

11. A. de Limeira Tejo, "O Nordeste do senhor Palhano," *Revista de Antropofagia* 7 (November 1928): 2.

12. "O Bloco Político da Norte," *O Estado de São Paulo* September 3, 1920, 4.

13. Souza Barros, *A Década Vinte em Pernambuco*; Miceli, *Intellectuais e Classe Dirigente no Brasil*.

14. José Lins do Rego, *Meus Verdes Anos*, 125; Moema Selma D'Andrea, *A Tradição Redescoberta*, 49.

15. Gilberto Freyre, "Vida Social no Nordeste," in *O Livro do Nordeste*, 75; Mário Sette, *Senhora de Engenho*.

16. Joaquim Inojosa, *O Movimento Modernista em Pernambuco*, 208–9.

17. Inojosa, *O Movimento Modernista em Pernambuco*.

18. Gilberto Freyre, *Manifesti Regionalista*, 32; José Lins do Rego, *O Moleque Ricardo*. On the reaction of the paulista press to the Regionalist Conference, see Monteiro Melo, "Regionalismo ridículo," *O Estado de São Paulo* March 6, 1926, 3.

19. Cited by Souza Barros, *A Década Vinte em Pernambuco*.

20. Gilberto Freyre, *Sobrados e Mocambos* vol. 1.

21. Gilberto Freyre, *Região e Tradição*.

22. Lúcia Lippi Oliveira, "Repensando a tradição," *Ciência Hoje* 7 no. 38 (December 1987): 58.

23. On the invention of tradition, see Eric Hobsbawm and Terence Ranger, *A Invenção das Tradições*.

24. José Guilherme Cantor Magnani, *Festa no Pedaço*; Luis Felipe Baeta Neves, "Uma caçada no zôo: Notas de campo sobre a história e conceito de arte popular."

25. Arthur Ramos, *O Folclore Negro no Brasil*; Florestan Fernandes, "A burguesia, o progresso e o folclore," *O Estado de São Paulo* September 19, 1944, 4.

26. On the integrative function of folklore, see Florestan Fernandes, *Folclore e Mudança Social na Cidade de São Paulo*.

27. Manuel Bandeira, "Minha Terra" (*Belo Belo*), in *Poesias*, 340.

28. For more on the crisis of narrative in modernity and its traditionalist functions, see Walter Benjamin, "O narrador: Considerações sobre a obra de Nikolai Leskov," in *Magia e Técnica, Arte e Política*.

29. On the coexistence or linearity of temporalities, see Gilles Deleuze, *Proust e os Signos*, 83–93. On the emergence of history as a paradigm of the modern *episteme*, see Michel Foucault, *As Palavras e as Coisas*.

30. Ascensão Ferreira, *Catimbó e Outros Poemas*, 6–7.

31. Ascensão Ferreira, *Catimbó e Outros Poemas*.

32. José Lins do Rego, *Meus Verdes Anos*, 6.

33. José Lins do Rego, *Menino do Engenho*.

34. Jorge de Lima, "Passarinho encantado" (*Poemas Negros*), in *Obra Poética*, 237–38.

35. Rachel de Queiroz: "João Miguel," in *Três Romances*, 125; and "Mapinguari," in *Obras Reunidas* vol. 5, 136–37.

36. Luiz Gonzaga and Humberto Teixeira, "Qui nem Jiló," RCA, 1950.

37. Ariano Suassuna: *História do Rei Degolado nas Caatingas do Sertão*, xv; *O Santo e a Porca*; *A Pena e a Lei*.

38. Suassuna, *História do Rei Degolado nas Caatingas do Sertão*, 56–57.

39. Ariano Suassuna, *O Romance d'A Pedra do Reino*, xi–xiii.

40. Bezerra de Freitas, "O espírito modernista da literatura brasileira," *O Estado de São Paulo* July 20, 1941, 4; Antônio Salles, *Aves de Arribação (Romance Cearense)*.

41. Gilberto Freyre, *Nordeste*.

42. José Aderaldo Castelo, *José Lins do Rego: Modernismo e Regionalismo*, 105.

43. Gilberto Freyre, *Região e Tradição*, 20.

44. Castelo, *José Lins do Rego: Modernismo e Regionalismo*, 99; José Lins do Rego, "O escritor Antônio de Alcântara Machado," *Revista Travessia* 3, no. 5 (December 1982): 30.

45. Gilberto Freyre, *Região e Tradição*, 38–39 and 199. On the period critical concept of tradition see Silvio Castro, *Teoria e Política do Modernismo Brasileiro*, 97–104.

46. Castelo, *José Lins do Rego: Modernismo e Regionalismo*, 100–101 and 108; José Lins do Rego, *Presença do Nordeste na Literatura*, 25.

47. Castelo, *José Lins do Rego: Modernismo e Regionalismo*, 98.

48. Gilberto Freyre: *Sobrados e Mocambos* vol. 1; *Região e Tradição*; *Interpretação do Brasil*, 41–91.

49. Gilberto Freyre, *Sobrados e Mocambos* vol. 2, 424–89. He explains his distinction between modern and modernist in *Vida, Forma e Cor*, 99–115. His views on Portugal are in *Interpretação do Brasil*, 41–91.

50. Gilberto Freyre, *Vida, Forma e Cor*, 143–44.

51. Joaquim Inojosa, *O Movimento Modernista em Pernambuco*. Freyre, in his writing after 1940, rendered himself the merit of having called attention to the need to renovate national arts before 1920. Inojosa went back and surveyed Freyre's writing from the earliest days to the end of the 1920s and argued that Freyre did little more than heckle the modernists until after their victory, when he rewrote history to give himself undue prominence. Inojosa might also be critiqued, however, for overemphasizing his prestige in the northeast's modernist movement—a movement that Freyre accorded no importance. Inojosa went so far as to deny the very existence of Freyre's regionalist and traditionalist movement, citing the apparent fact that the 1926 Regionalist Manifesto, which Freyre claimed was read and approved at the Regionalist Congress, was written and published only in 1952. Joaquim Inojosa, "O movimento imaginário do Recife," *O Estado de São Paulo* June 25, 1972 (literary supplement), 4.

52. Noraldo Pontes, *Modernismo e Regionalismo*, 36.

53. In the newspaper *A Tarde*, October 30, 1922.

54. Pontes, *Modernismo e Regionalismo*, 22, 33.

55. Pontes, *Modernismo e Regionalismo*; José Américo de Almeida, "Reflexões de uma Cabra" in *Novelas*, 6.

56. Pontes, *Modernismo e Regionalismo*, 78–82.

57. Joaquim Inojosa, *O Movimento Modernista em Pernambuco*, 174–75, 182. Freyre published in the *Diário de Pernambuco* on April 22, 1923.

58. Pontes, *Modernismo e Regionalismo*, 26, 102, 121–22.

59. Sérgio Buarque de Holanda, "Modernismo, tradicionalismo, regionalismo," in *República das Letras*, 107; Gilberto Freyre, *Interpretação do Brasil* and *Região e Tradição*.

60. Herbert Baldus, "Ensaios sobre a história da etnografia brasileira," *O Estado de São Paulo* September 16, 1943, 4.

61. Leite, *O Caráter Nacional Brasileiro*.

62. Gilberto Freyre, *Interpretação do Brasil*; *Sobrados e Mocambos* vol. 1, 3–23.

63. Freyre, *Interpretação do Brasil*; *Casa-Grande e Senzala*.

64. Freyre, *Casa-Grande e Senzala*; *Sobrados e Mocambos* vol. 1, 173.

65. Freyre, *Casa-Grande e Senzala*; *Sobrados e Mocambos* vol. 2.

66. Freyre, *Nordeste*, 98–131.

67. On Freyre's use of images, see d'Andrea, *A Tradição Redescoberta*, 141–47. A helpful analysis of the difference between symbolic and allegorical images is in Walter Benjamin, "O Surrealismo," in *Os Pensadores* vol. 48, 84.

68. Freyre's method is explored in Mário Chamie, "Gilberto Freyre, o mago das recorrências," *O Estado de São Paulo* July 10, 1984 (literary supplement), 13.

69. Freyre: *Sobrados e Mocambos* vol. 1, 30–50; *Casa Grande e Senzala*, 288; *Vida, Forma e Cor*, 248–56.

70. Freyre, *Sobrados e Mocambos* vol. 2.

71. Freyre, *Sobrados e Mocambos* vol. 1 and vol. 2. For more on the thought process that operates by oppositions but denies difference to affirm identity, see Gilles Deleuze, *Diferença e Repetição*.

72. Leite, *O Caráter Nacional Brasileiro*; Gilberto Freyre, *Casa-Grande e Senzala*, 3–54.

73. Freyre, *Sobrados e Mocambos* vol. 1, 253, and *Vida, Forma e Cor*, 240.

74. Silveira, *O Regionalismo Nordestino*, 20.

75. Freyre, *Nordeste*, xi.

76. Freyre, *Nordeste*, xx.

77. Freyre, *Nordeste*, 16–37 and 43–58.

78. Freyre, *Nordeste*, 6.

79. Freyre, *Nordeste*, 91–138; *Sobrados e Mocambos* vol. 1, 152–234.

80. Roger Bastide, "Sociologia do folclore brasileiro," *O Estado de São Paulo* January 7, 1949, 4; Vicente Correia, "O progenitor do Sul e o progenitor do Norte," *O Estado de São Paulo* April 12, 1936, 4.

81. Freyre, *Casa-Grande e Senzala*, 217.

82. Freyre, *Casa-Grande e Senzala*, 188; Cassiano Rocardo, *Marcha para Oeste*.

83. Freyre, *Nordeste*, 164.

84. Oliveira Vianna, *Evolução do Povo Brasileiro*, 76–; Gilberto Freyre, *Interpretação do Brasil*, 91–139; Alcântara Machado, *Vida e Morte do Bandeirante*, 23–35.

85. Ricardo, *Marcha para Oeste* vol. 2.

86. Roger Bastide, *Brasil, Terra de Contrastes*.

87. Paulo Dantas, "Euclides e as dimensões sertanejas," *Revista Brasiliense* 19 (September/October 1958): 138; Aderbal Jurema, "Sobre os campos do Norte," *Revista Acadêmica* 10, no. 2 (April 1955): 4; Gilberto Freyre, *Vida, Forma e Cor*; Sérgio Buarque de Holanda, *Raízes do Brasil*, 117.

88. Joseph M. Luyten, "Desafio e repentismo do caipira em São Paulo," in *Cultura Brasileira: Temas e Situações*, 75; Gilberto Freyre, *Sobrados e Mocambos* vol. 1, 20.

89. Roger Bastide, *Brasil, Terra de Contrastes*.

90. Mário de Andrade, "Coreografias," *O Estado de São Paulo* March 5, 1938, 4; Oswald de Andrade, *A Utopia Antropofágica*.

91. Fernand Braudel, "Bahia," *O Estado de São Paulo* October 20, 1937, 4.

92. Oswald de Andrade, *Marco Zero I (A Revolução Melancólica)*, 125.

93. Amadeu Amaral. "Separatismo," *O Estado de São Paulo* September 30, 1920, 3.

94. Lúcia Lippi Oliveira, "Repensando a tradição," 64.

95. Viana Moog, *Uma Interpretação da Literatura Brasileira*; Cyro T. de Pádua, "Uma interpretação da literatura brasileira," *O Estado de São Paulo* April 28, 1943, 4.

96. Roger Bastide, *Brasil, Terra de Contrastes*; José Guilherme Merquior, "A caracterização do moderno," *O Estado de São Paulo* October 24, 1976 (cultural supplement), 4.

97. Oswald de Andrade, *Os Dentes do Dragão*.

98. Paulo Cavalcanti, "Romancista de um povo," *Para Todos* no. 33–34 (September–October 1957): 9; Cassiano Nunes, "Análise da problemática do romance nordestino," *Revista Brasiliense*, no. 14 (November–December 1957): 72.

99. Roger Bastide, *Brasil, Terra de Contrastes*, 195–; Moog, *Uma Interpretação da Literatura Brasileira*, 29; Rubens do Amoral, "Testamento de uma geração," *O Estado de São Paulo* January 25, 1942, 4.

100. Joaquim Inojosa, *Os Andrades e Outros Aspectos do Modernismo*, 70–; José Américo de Almeida, "Como me tornei um escritor brasileiro," *Revista de Antropofagia* ano 1 no. 1 (October 1928): 3; José Lins do Rego, *Usina*, xvii, lxiv; Viana Moog, *Uma Interpretação da Literatura Brasileira*.

101. Pierre Houcarde, "Tendências e individualidades do romance brasileiro contemporâneo, *O Estado de São Paulo* May 14, 1939, 6.

102. On the growth of the publishing industry in the 1930s, see Miceli, *Intellectuais e Classe Dirigente no Brasil*, 69–70.

103. The difference between monologic and dialogic is examined by Mário Chamie, *A Transgressão do Texto*.

104. Antonio Candido, *Literatura e Sociedade*, 109; Roger Bastide et al., *Jorge Amado: Povo e Terra, 40 anos de Literatura*.

105. Antonio Candido, *Brigada Ligeira*, 52–53; Bastide et al., *Jorge Amado*.

106. On the use of typical characters, see Umberto Eco, *Apocalípticos e Integrados*, 209.

107. Eco, *Apocalípticos e Integrados*.

108. Roberto Ventura, *Estilo Tropical*, 47–52.

109. Ventura, *Estilo Tropical*; José Antônio Pasta Jr., "Cordel, intelectuais e o divino Espírito Santo," *Cultura Brasileira: Temas e Situações*, 58.

110. José Lins do Rego, *Meus Verdes Anos*; Rachel de Queiroz, *O Quinze*; José Américo de Almeida, *A Bagaceira*.

111. José Aderaldo Costelo, *José Lins do Rego: Modernismo e Regionalismo*; Silviano Santiago, "Modernidade e tradição popular," *Folha de São Paulo* November 16, 1989 (literary supplement), 4.

112. Gilberto Freyre, *Vida, Forma e Cor*, 140–45.

113. On the tension between naturalist and modernist mimesis, see Lúcia Helena, *Totens e Tabus da Modernidade Brasileira*. The fight over land was an essential theme in Jorge de Lima's works, notably *Calunga*.

114. Luis Antônio Carvalho, "As pistas do moderno," *Revista Leia* May 1987, 22; Edgar de Decca, *O Nascimento das Fábricas*. On the equation of cities with perdition, see Amando Fontes, *Rua do Siriry* and *Os Corumbas*.

115. Sérgio Buarque de Holanda, "Modernismo, tradicionalismo, regionalismo?"; José Lins do Rego, *O Moleque Ricardo*, xvi–xlvi, and *Pedra Bonita*.

116. Ascenco Ferreira, "Cana-Caiana," in *Catimbó e Outros Poemas*; José Lins do Rego, *Meus Verdes Anos*, *Pedra Bonita*, and *Riacho Doce*; José Américo de Almeida, "Reflexões de uma Cabra" and "O Boqueirão" (in *Novelas*, 85); Rachel de Queiroz, "Caminhos de Pedras" in *Três Romances*, 327.

117. Ascenso Ferreira, "Minha Terra," in *Catimbó*, 68.

118. Ascenso Ferreira: "Os engenhos da minha terra," "A casa-grande de Megaípe," and "Trem das Alagoas," in *Cana-Caiana*, 91–92, 94–95, 127–29.

119. Jorge de Lima, "Banguê," in *Obras Poéticas*, 219–22; José Lins do Rego, *Meus Verdes Anos*, *Doidinho*, and *Fogo Morto*.

120. Ascenso Ferreira, "Sertão" and "Dor" in *Catimbó*; José Lins do Rego, *Pedra Bonita*, 330; Rachel de Queiroz, *Mapinguari*, 109; José Américo de Almeida, "O Boqueirão," 172, and "Coiteiros" in *Novelas*, 207.

121. José Américo de Almeida, "Coiteiros," 241. See also Almeida, *A Bagaceira*, xli.

122. On the links between language, vocabulary, and power, see Eni Pulcinelli Orlandi, *Terra à Vista*, 157–62.

123. Gilberto Freyre, *Vida, Forma e Cor*, 39; Freyre, *Casa-Grande e Senzala*, 463; José Lins do Rego, *O Moleque Ricardo*, xxxi.

124. Cyro T. de Pádua, "O dialeto Brasileiro," *O Estado de São Paulo* December 4, 1940, 4; Mário Marroquim, *A Língua do Nordeste*.

125. Marroquim, *A Língua do Nordeste*, 32, 37, 50, 67, 100.

126. José Lins do Rego, *Fogo Morto*, 98.

127. Gilberto Freyre, "Vida Social no Nordeste (Aspectos de um Século de Transição)," *O Livro do Nordeste*, 75–76.

128. José Lins do Rego, *Pedra Bonita*, 172, 211.

129. Rachel de Queiroz, *O Quinze*, 31–.

130. Rachel de Queiroz, *Mapinguari*, 3; "Lampião (Peça em 5 quadros)," *Obras Reunidas* vol. 2, 3. José Américo de Almeida, "Reflexões de uma Cabra," 59, 77; *A Bagaceira*, 3, 7.

131. Rachel de Queiroz, *O Quinze*; José Américo de Almeida, *A Bagaceira*; José Lins do Rego, *Fogo Morto*.

132. José Lins do Rego, *Usina*, xliii.

133. "There are many things to affirm / Celidônia, the lovely Yoruba woman / Who rocked me in the hammock / Who walked me to school / Who told me animal stories / When I was small, very small / . . . There are many things still to affirm / The pretty, the best house slave / The flesh abandoned, the night awhirl / Brunette rose, my first muse." Jorge de Lima, "Ancila Negra," in *Obra Poética*, 241–42. On the reaction to modern political ideologies, see José Lins do Rego, *O Moleque Ricardo*.

134. On the transformations of popular crime in modern society, see Michel Foucault, *Vigiar e Punir*. For more on the popular tradition of crime tales, see Foucault, "Os assassinatos que se contam" in *Eu, Pierre Riviére, que degolei minha mãe, minha irmã e meu irmão*, 211; Durval Muniz de Albuquerque Jr., "Mennochio e Riviére: Criminosos da palavra, poetas do silêncio," *Revista Resgate* 2: 48–55.

135. Michel Foucault addressed the changes to popular heroism in modernity in *Eu, Pierre Riviére*, 211.

136. José Lins do Rego, *Fogo Morto*, 58, 109, 207; *Cangaceiros*, 212, 240, 273; Rachel de Queiroz, *Lampião*, 7.

137. Roger Bastide, *Brasil, Terra de Contrastes*, 87–107; José Américo de Almeida, *Coiteiros*. See also "Lampião," *O Estado de São Paulo* April 19, 1931, 8.

138. José Lins do Rego, *Cangaceiros*, 179, 272, 359.

139. Rachel de Queiroz, *Lampião*, 8.

140. Frederick C. Glass, "As ruínas do reduto de Antônio Conselheiro," *O Estado de São Paulo* June 13, 1929, 9.

141. Roger Bastide, *Brasil, Terra de Contrastes*, 83–107.

142. Rachel de Queiroz, "A Beata Maria do Egito," in *Obras Reunidas* vol. 5.

143. José Lins do Rego, *Pedra Bonita*; Rachel de Queiroz, "A Beata Maria do Egito."

144. Heloísa Toller Gomes, *O Poder Rural na Ficção*.

145. Frederico Heler, "A grandeza do Capitão Vitorino: Aspectos sociológicos de Fogo Morto," *O Estado de São Paulo* April 27, 1944, 4.

146. José Lins do Rego, *Meus Verdes Anos*; *Menino de Engenho*; *Usina*. See also Gilles Deleuze and Félix Guattari, *O Anti-Édipo*.

147. Rego, *Usina*, 30; *Cangaceiros*, 429; *Menino de Engenho*. See also José Aderaldo Castelo, *José Lins do Rego*, and Moema Selma D'Andrea, *A Tradição Redescoberta*.

148. Citation from Flávio Campos, "Cinema e Literatura," *O Estado de São Paulo* June 27, 1938, 4. See also Mário de Andrade, "A psicologia em ação," *O Estado de São Paulo* November 19, 1939, 4; Rego, *Fogo Morto*, xvi; Rego, *Menino de Engenho*, xxxvi.

149. Rego, *Menino do Engenho*, xxxi; Rego, *Usina*, xx; Gomes, *O Poder Rural na Ficção*.

150. Gomes, *O Poder Rural na Ficção*, 47; Rego, *Usina*, 29; Rego, *Fogo Morto*.

151. Alfredo Bosi, *História Concisa da Literatura Brasileira*, 451; Rego, *Água Mãe*, xxi; Rego, *Fogo Morto*, 207.

152. Rego, *O Moleque Ricardo*, 101.

153. Rego: *Meus Verdes Anos*, 27, 53, 337; *Doidinho*, 54; *Menino do Engenho*, 8; *Cangaceiros*, 428.

154. Rego: *Menino de Engenho*, 11–64; *O Moleque Ricardo*, 138.

155. Rego: *Menino do Engenho*; *O Moleque Ricardo*, 41.

156. Rego, *O Moleque Ricardo*, 69, 119, 128.

157. Rego: *O Moleque Ricardo*, 18; *Fogo Morto*, 135.

158. Rego, *Menino de Engenho*, 11, 57 82–83, 92. See also Michel Foucault, *História da Sexualidade 1 (A Vontade de Saber)*.

159. Rego, *Usina*, 3, 282.

160. Rego, *Usina*, 3.

161. Rego, *Fogo Morto*. See also Nelson Werneck Sodré, "Fogo Morto," *O Estado de São Paulo* March 25, 1944, 4.

162. Rego, *Menino do Engenho*, 122.

163. José Américo de Almeida, *A Bagaceira*, lvi.

164. Maria Célia de Moraes, "Antes que me falem d'*A Bagaceira*," *O Estado de São Paulo* September 17, 1978 (cultural supplement), 13; Moema Selma D'Andrea, *A Tradição Redescoberta*, 176–96; Durval Muniz de Albuquerque Jr., "Falas de Astúcia e de Angústia," 218.

165. José Américo de Almeida, *A Bagaceira*, 5, 45, 49.

166. José Américo de Almeida, preface to *A Bagaceira*, 2; Fausto Cunha, "Regionalismo: Linguagem, criação, informação," *Folha da Manhã* December 15, 1957 (cultural supplement), 2.

167. Maria Célia de Moraes, "Antes que me falem d'*A Bagaceira*," 14.

168. Moema Selma D'Andrea, *A Tradição Redescoberta*, 174–96; Durval Muniz de Albuquerque Jr., "Falas de Astúcia e de Angústia," 221.

169. Almeida: *O Boqueirão*; *A Bagaceira*, 114.

170. Almeida, *A Bagaceira*, 45.

171. Almeida, *A Bagaceira*, 10. See also Silviano Santiago, "A Bagaceira: Fábula moralizante I," *Jornal Minas Gerais* August 17, 1974 (literary supplement), 4.

172. Moema Selma D'Andrea, *A Tradição Redescoberta*; Almeida, *O Boqueirão*.

173. Almeida, *O Boqueirão*, 85–119, 126.

174. Rachel de Queiroz, *Mapinguari*, 74.

175. Almir Andrade, *Aspectos da Cultura Brasileira*, 107.

176. Rachel de Queiroz, *Mapinguari*, 74.

177. Queiroz, *O Quinze*, 35, 103, 116; *João Miguel*, 125.

178. Queiroz, *Caminho de Pedras*.

179. Queiroz, *Caminho de Pedras*, 241.

180. Queiroz: *As Três Marias*; *Mapinguari*, 108–10, 124–26. See also Alfredo Bosi, *História Concisa da Literatura Brasileira*, 446–47.

181. Queiroz: *Mapinguari*, 24, 64; *Caminho de Pedras*; "Terra," *O Cruzeiro*, August 17, 1963, 130; "Mão-de-Obra," *O Cruzeiro* June 8, 1963, 130; "Nordeste," *O Cruzeiro*, May 20 1961, 129. See also Lausimar Laus, "O romance em Rachel de Queiroz," *O Estado de Minas*, October 11, 1975 (literary supplement), 11.

182. Queiroz, *O Quinze*, 121.

183. Quirino da Silva, "Lúcia Suané," *Diário de São Paulo*, October 16, 1955; João Ribeiro Pinheiro, *História da Pintura Brasileira*.

184. On representation and likeness, see: Michel Foucault, *Isto Não É um Cachimbo* and *História da Loucura*, 111–35; Gilles Deleuze, *Foucault*, 57–78.

185. Gilberto Freyre, *Vida, Forma e Cor*, 27–39, 156–61.

186. Freyre, *Região e Tradição*, 79–107.

187. Freyre, *Região e Tradição*; "Paisagem sexual," *Quase Poesia*, 21; *Manifesto Regionalista*, 66; "A pintura do Nordeste," *O Livro do Nordeste*.

188. Cícero Dias, *Família na Paisagem* (n/d); *Procissão* (1930); *Ano* (1933); *Composição Saudades* (1931); *Banho de Rio* (1931); *Vida* (1939); *Homem no Burrinho* (1930); *O Tirador de Coco* (1930s); *Paisagem com Figura* (1930); *Dançarina ou Mamoeiro* (1940s).

189. Freyre, "Cícero Dias, seu azul e encarnado, seu sur-nudisme," *Brasil e o 1° Tempo Modernista*.

190. Freyre, *Vida, Forma e Cor*, 170–79.

191. Lula Cardoso Ayres, *Vendedores de Rua* (1936); *Mulher e Mandacaru* (1938); *Tipos de Feira* (1942); *Caboclos Tuchaua—Carnaval do Recife* (1942); *Menino de Engenho* (1943); *Cabeleira no Carnaval* (1950); *Namoro de Ex-Votos* (1951); *Bichos de Festa Popular* (1952); *Bichos de Carnaval* (1954); *Ruína* (1966); *Grade e Sobrado* (1967); *Portão* (1969); *Cadeira* (1969); *Relógio* (1971).

192. Ayres, *Apresentação do Bumba-Meu-Boi* (1943); *Noivado na Casa de Engenho* (1943); *Retrato de Família* (1943); *Dando Cafuné* (1943); *Matheus e boi* (1945); *Capela Mal-Assombrada* (1945); *Cabriolet Mal-Assombrado* (1945); *Sofá Mal-Assombrado* (1945); *Vulto Branco* (1947); *Retirantes* (1947); *Cego Violeiro* (1947); *Cortadores de Cana* (1948); *Xangô* (1948). See also Joaquim Inojosa, *Os Andrades e Outros Aspectos do Modernismo*, 190–91; Quirino da Silva, "Lula Cardoso Ayres," *Diário da Noite* June 9, 1926, 7.

193. Antônio Risério, "Notas para uma antropologia do ouvido," *O Poético e o Político*, 143–52.

194. Arnaldo Contier, "Modernismo e Brasilidade: música, utopia e tradição," *Tempo e História*.

195. Mundicarmo Maria Rocha Ferretti, *Baião dos Dois*.

196. Ferretti, *Baião dos Dois*; José Nêumane Pinto, "Os marginais da música nordestina," *Sontrês* 23, 66.

197. Ferreti, *Baião dos Dois*, 45–55.

198. On hearing, see Roland Barthes, "O corpo da música," *O Óbvio e o Obtuso*.

199. Roland Barthes, "O sul da voz," *O Óbvio e o Obtuso*; Sérgio Cabral, "Getúlio Vargas e a MPB," *Ensaios de Opinião*; Alcir Lenharo, *Sacralização da Política*; N. Jahr Garcia, *Estado Novo, Ideologia e Propaganda Política*; José Miguel Wisnik, "Getúlio da Paixão Cearense (Villa Lobos e o Estado Novo)," *O Nacional e o Popular na Cultura Brasileira-Música*.

200. Ferretti, *Baião dos Dois*, 45–55.

201. José de Jesus Ferreira, *Luiz Gonzaga, O rei do Baião, suas vidas, seus amigos, suas canções*.

202. Arnaldo Contier, *Música e Ideologia no Brasil*, 37; Barthes, "O sul da voz," 217.

203. Alfredo Bosi, "Cultura e Desenraizamento," *Cultura Brasileira: Temas e Situações*, 26.

204. On the relation between music and the perception of urban space, see Fátima Amaral Dias de Oliveira, "Trilha Sonora," and Risério, "Notas para uma antropologia do ouvido," 143–53.

205. Consider the representative songs "Numa Sala de Reboco" (Gonzaga and José Marcolino, RCA, 1968); "Feira de Gado" (Gonzaga and Zé Dantas, RCA, 1954); "Acauã" (Zé Dantas, RCA, 1952); "O Jumento é Nosso Irmão" (Gonzaga and José Clementino, RCA, 1968); "O Tocador Quer Beber" (Gonzaga and Carlos Diniz, RCA, 1961).

206. Dias de Oliveira, "Trilha Sonora"; Genival Sá, *O Sanfoneiro do Riacho da Brígida*.

207. "A Volta da Asa Branca" (Zé Dantas and Gonazaga, RCA, 1950).

208. For instance, "São João Antigo" (Zé Dantas and Gonzaga, RCA, 1957); "Juazeiro" (Gonzaga and Humberto Teixeira, RCA, 1949); "No Meu Pé de Serra" (Gonzaga and Teixeira, RCA, 1946); "Estrada de Canindé" (Gonzaga and Teixeira, RCA, 1950).

209. "Noites Brasileiras" (Zé Dantas and Luiz Gonzaga, RCA, 1954); "Xote dos Cabeludos" (José Clementino and Luiz Gonzaga, RCA, 1955).

210. "Riacho do Navio" (Zé Dantas and Luiz Gonzaga, RCA, 1955).

211. Arnaldo Contier, *Música e Ideologia no Brasil*, 39.

212. José Nêumane Pinto, "Semeando ventos de caatinga," *O Estado de São Paulo* December 6, 1986 (section 2), 2. Gonzaga's linguistic approach was modern and inventive, particularly in the use of onomatopoeia, relating phonetic sound to meaning, such as his heavy use of the "x" sound (*xaxado, xote*) implying the sweeping movement of dancers' feet; and the alternation of song and spoken narrative, including musical breaks to allow space for digression.

213. "Algodão" (Zé Dantas and Luiz Gonzaga, RCA, 1953); "Paulo Afonso" (Zé Dantas and Luiz Gonzaga, RCA, 1955); "Nordeste pra Frente" (Gonzaga and Luis Queiroga, RCA, 1968); "Sertão Setenta" (José Clementino, RCA, 1970).

214. In "Nós num Have" (Zé Dantas, Odeon, 1957). Gonzaga rhetorically confronts an urban lad who, speaking broken English with the learned accent of a "gringo," asks him whether he likes rock and roll. Gonzaga replies that his *baião* is both more profound and more irresistible on the dance floor.

215. Ariano Suassuna, *Auto da Compadecida*, 9–14; "Subvenção do governo ao teatro," *O Estado de São Paulo* April 10, 1937, 7; Hermilo Borba Filho, "Um teatro brasileiro," *Revista Brasiliense* 12 (July–August 1957): 180.

216. Borba Filho, "Um teatro brasileiro."

217. Ariano Suassuna, *História do Rei Degolado nas Caatingas do Sertão*, 43–58, 59–64.

218. Suassuna, *História do Rei Degolado*, 116–22.

219. Suassuna: *Romance d'A Pedra do Reino*, 3–6; *História do Rei Degolado*, xv; "O Rico Avarento," *Seleta de Prosa e Verso*.

220. Suassuna: *Romance d'A Pedra do Reino*, 193–210; Roger Bastide, *Imagens do Nordeste Místico*; Maria de Graça Rios de Melo, "Literatura Oral e Teatro Popular," *O Estado de Minas* November 29, 1975 (literary supplement), 4.

221. Suassuna: *Auto da Compadecida*; *O Santo e a Porca*.

222. Suassuna: *Auto da Compadecida*; *O Santo e a Porca*; *A Pena e a Lei*; *Romance d'A Pedra do Reino*, 347–52.

223. Sábato Magaldi, "Auto de Esperança," *O Estado de São Paulo* May 23, 1964, 10; Ariano Suassuna, "Torturas de um Coração," *Seleta de Prosa e Verso*; Suassuna, *O Castigo da Soberba*.

224. Suassuna: *Auto da Compadecida*; *Uma Mulher Vestida de Sol*; *Farsa da Boa Preguiça*; *O Romance d'A Pedra do Reino*; "Notas sobre o romanceiro popular do Nordeste," *Seleta de Prosa e Verso*, 162.

225. Suassuna: *História do Rei Degolado*, 97; *O Romance d'A Pedra do Reino*, 172–77; *Farsa da Boa Preguiça*; "Em busca do populário religioso" and "O homem da vaca e o poder da fortuna," *Seleta em Prosa e Verso*.

226. Suassuna: *O Casamneto Suspeitoso*; *Uma Mulher Vestida do Sol*; *Torturas de um Coração*; *História do Rei Degolado*, 64–69; *O Romance d'A Pedra do Reino*, 118–22, 143–51, 606–17.

227. Suassuna, *História do Rei Degolado*, 10–14, 54–59, 88–93.

228. Suassuna: *Romance d'A Pedra do Reino*, 599–607, 504–15; *História do Rei Degolado*, 79–83; *Auto da Compadecida*.

229. Suassuna: *História do Rei Degolado*, 5–10; *Romance d'A Pedra do Reino*, 3–6.

230. Suassuna: *História do Rei Degolado*, 59–64, 93–98, 102–7.

231. Suassuna: *O Homem da Vaca e o Poder da Fortuna*; *O Rico Avarento*; *A Pena e a Lei*; *Auto da Compadecida*. See also Melo, "Literatura Oral e Teatro Popular."

232. "Ariano Suassuna, o Rei Degolado," *Folha de São Paulo* (insert) June 19, 1977, 12.

CHAPTER THREE: TERRITORIES OF REVOLT

1. Jorge Amado, *Cacau*, 187.

2. Statements based in Marxist philosophy are common in Jorge Amado's *Jubiabá*.

3. On the messianic vision of Marxism, see Oswald de Andrade, "A crise da filosofia messiânica," *A Utopia Antropofágica*; Nelson Brissac Peixoto, *A Sedução da Barbárie*, 28–36.

4. Gilles Lipovetsky, *O Império do Efémero*; Cornelius Castoriadis, *A Instituição Imaginária da Sociedade*, 19–88. On the Marxist distrust of words, see Jorge Amado, *São Jorge dos Ilhéus*, 203.

5. Castoriadis, *A Instituição Imaginária da Sociedade*, 54.

6. André Malraux, "O homem e a cultura artística," *O Estado de São Paulo* June 20, 1945, 11; Oswald de Andrade, "Uma geração se exprime," *O Estado de São Paulo* June 29, 1943, 4.

7. Nelson Werneck Sodré, "Formação da sociologia brasileira," *O Estado de São Paulo* June 15, 1941, 4 (emphasis added).

8. Sodré, "Formação histórica do Brasil," *O Estado de São Paulo* December 31, 1942, 4; Caio Prado Júnior, *Formação do Brasil Contemporâneo*; Antônio Piccarolo, "Interpretações econômicas da história do Brasil," *O Estado de São Paulo* February 11, 1942, 4; "Uma Sociedade Etnográfica," *O Estado de São Paulo* April 10, 1943, 7; "Sociedade de Sociologia de São Paulo," *O Estado de São Paulo* August 12, 1937, 5; "Fundação da Sociedade de Estudos Econômicos," *O Estado de São Paulo* October 27, 1937, 1.

9. George Gurvitch: "A crise da sociologia contemporânea," *O Estado de São Paulo* April 2, 1949, 5; "A atual vocação da sociologia," *O Estado de São Paulo* August 23, 1947, 4 (emphasis added).

10. Francisco Weffort, "Problema nacional no Brasil," *Revista Anhembi* no. 119 vol. 2 (October 1960): 350.

11. Nelson Werneck Sodré, "Quem é o povo no Brasil?" *Cadernos do Povo Brasileiro* no. 2; Randal Johnson, *Macunaíma: Do modernismo na literature ao Cinema Novo*.

12. On history's sacrificial character see Friedrich Nietzsche, "Considerações Extemporâneas," *Obras Incompletas*; Michel Foucault, "Nietzsche, a genealogia e a história," *Microfísica do Poder*, 15–38.

13. Alfredo Bossi, *Reflexões sobre a Arte*.

14. Georg Lukács, *A Teoria do Romance*, 85; Roger Bastide, *Arte e Sociedade*.

15. Bastide, *Arte e Sociedade*; Graciliano Ramos, "O fato econômico no romance de trinta," *Linhas Tortas*.

16. Mário de Andrade, *O Turista Aprendiz*.

17. Graciliano Ramos, *Infância*, 26.

18. A cinematic genre known as "Nordestern," suggesting a hybrid of nordestino and western, addressed conflicts between civilization / barbarism and order / disorder through such films as *Corisco, o Diabo Loiro* (Carlos Coimbra, 1969) and

O Cangaceiro Sem Deus (Osvaldo de Oliveira, 1969). An early example was *O Cangaceiro* (Lima Barreto, 1954).

19. Ismail Xavier, *Sertão Mar*; the film *O Cangaceiro Sanginário* (Osvaldo de Oliveira, 1969); Paulo Dantas, "Nordeste, 1917," *Revista Brasiliense* no. 3 (January/February 1956).

20. Jean-Claude Bernadet, *Brasil em Tempo de Cinema*, 13–17.

21. Willis Leal, *O Nordeste no Cinema*, 17–27.

22. Examples of the manipulation of northeastern myths as symbols of subaltern rebellion can be found throughout the works of Jorge Amado: *Capitães da Areia*, 211; *Seara Vermelha*; *São Jorge dos Ilhéus*. On the popular culture movement, see Vivian Schelling, *A Presença do Povo na Cultura Brasileira*.

23. Schelling, *A Presença do Povo na Cultura Brasileira*; Graciliano Ramos, *Infância*, 126, 131–37, 156. See also the film *Cangaceiros de Lampião* (Carlos Coimbra, 1967).

24. Jorge Amado: *Suor*; *Mar Morto*. Graciliano Ramos, *Angustia*.

25. See the film *Maioria Absoluta* (Leon Hirzman, 1964); Roger Bastide, *Brasil, Terra de Contrastes*; Schelling, *A Presença do Povo na Cultura Brasileira*.

26. For different takes on the South as promised land, see Amado, *Seara Vermelha* and *Gabriela, Cravo e Canela*; Willis Leal, *O Nordeste no Cinema*, 59–67; Jean-Claude Bernadet, *Brasil em Tempo de Cinema*, 111–16.

27. Graciliano Ramos, *Vidas Secas*, 12, 26, 99, 108; Jorge Amado, *Suor* and *Jubiabá*; Ismail Xavier, *Sertão Mar*; the film *Vereda da Salvação* (Anselmo Duarte, 1966).

28. Graciliano Ramos, *Linhas Tortas*, 32.

29. On the image of horsemen in Brazilian fiction, see Mário Chamie, "O cavalo e o crucifixo," *A Linguagem Virtual*. For a typical chanchada portrayal of nordestinos see the film *Fogo na Canjica* (Luis de Barros, 1947).

30. See the profile of the coronel type in Graciliano Ramos, *São Bernardo*; the film *O Cangaceiro Sem Deus* (Osvaldo de Oliveira, 1969); Jorge Amado, *Terras do Sem Fim*, *Gabriela, Cravo e Canela*, and *Seara Vermelha*.

31. Oswald de Andrade, "A crise da filosofia messiânica," *A Utopia Antropofágica*.

32. Jorge Amado, *Cacau*; "Dispersão de grupo de fanáticos pela polícia do Ceará," *O Estado de São Paulo* September 15, 1936, 1; the film *Vereda da Salvação* (Anselmo Duarte, 1966).

33. All these stereotypes are present in the film *Vereda da Salvação* (Anselmo Duarte, 1966).

34. Graciliano Ramos, "Pequena história da República," in *Alexandre e Outros Heróis*, 161–62; Ramos, *Viventes das Alagoas*, 147; Jorge Amado, *Seara Vermelha*, 236, 245; the film *O Cangaçeiro Sem Deus*.

35. Graciliano Ramos, *Viventes das Alagoas*, 135, 142, 149–54; anonymous, "Uma descrição de Lampião," *O Estado de São Paulo* April 23, 1931, 5; the film *O Cangaceiro Sangiunário* (Osvaldo de Oliveira, 1969).

36. *Corisco, o Diabo Loiro* (Carlos Coimbra, 1969).

37. Willis Leal, *O Nordeste no Cinema*, 89–97. See the films *Cangaceiros de Lampião* and *Lampião, Rei do Cangaço* (Carlos Coimbra, 1963, 1967); *Entre o Amor e o Cangaço* (Aurélio Teixeira, 1960); *Memórias do Cangaço* (Paulo Gil Soares, 1965); *A Morte Comanda o Cangaço* (Carlos Coimbra, 1960); *Nordeste Sangrento* (Wilson Silva, 1963); *O Lamparina* (Glauco Laurelli, 1966).

38. Jorge Amado: *Jubiabá*, 289–90; *Capitães da Areia*, 157–61, 175.

39. Graciliano Ramos, *Viventes das Alagoas*, 128–34, 147–49.

40. Graciliano Ramos, "O romance de Jorge Amado," *Linhas Tortas*, 92–96.

41. Renato Ortiz, *A Moderna Tradição Brasileira*, 22; Antônio Candido, *Literatura e Sociedade*, 122.

42. Roberto Simões, "Ficção nordestina: diretrizes sociais," *Revista Brasiliense* no. 41 (May–June 1962): 172; Edgard Cavalheiro, "O drama do café e o romance brasileiro," *O Estado de São Paulo* March 9, 1941, 4; Lúcia Helena, *Totens e Tabus da Modernidade Brasileira*, 90–101; Graciliano Ramos, *Caetés*, 152.

43. Sérgio Milliet, "O moderno romance brasileiro," *O Estado de São Paulo* October 20, 1937, 4.

44. Roberto Simões, "Ficção nordestina: Diretrizes sociais"; Adhemar Vidal, "O romance do Nordeste," *Revista Acadêmica* 11 (May 1935): 7.

45. Roger Bastide, "Bahia de Todos os Santos," *O Estado de São Paulo* October 20, 1945, 4.

46. Jorge Amado: *Suor*, 250–54; *Jubiabá*, 53–63; *Capitães da Areia*, 158–59.

47. Amado: *Suor*; *O País do Carnaval*.

48. Jorge Amado, "Discurso de posse na Academia Brasileira de Letras," in Bastide, *Jorge Amado: Povo e terra*, 3–22.

49. Bastide, *Jorge Amado: Povo e terra*, 54.

50. Pièrre Houcard, "Tendências e individualidades do romance brasileiro contemporâneo," *O Estado de São Paulo* March 14, 1939, 6; Lúcia Helena, *Totens e Tabus da Modernidade Brasileira*, 102; Jorge Amado, *Cacau*.

51. Bastide, *Jorge Amado: Povo e terra*; Amado, *Gabriela, Cravo e Canela*.

52. Roger Bastide: *Brasil, Terra de Contrastes*, 202; *Jorge Amado: Povo e terra*, 59. Jorge Amado: *Mar Morto*, 21; *Capitães da Areia*.

53. Bastide, *Jorge Amado: Povo e terra*, 59.

54. Oswald de Andrade, "Fraternidade de Jorge Amado," *Ponta de Lança*, 55–57.

55. Jorge Amado, *O País do Carnaval*, 98.

56. Amado, *São Jorge dos Ilhéus*, 295; *Capitães da Areia*, 227; *Seara Vermelha*, 270.

57. Amado, *Tenda dos Milagres*, 318.

58. Amado: *Cacau*, 131; *Jubiabá*, 23; *Tenda dos Milagres*, 215. See also José Guilherme Merquior, "Em busca de uma definição para o estilo modernista," *O Estado de São Paulo* May 14, 1972.

59. Amado, *Capitães da Areia*; *São Jorge dos Ilhéus*; *Tereza Batista, Cansada de Guerra*.

60. Amado, *Terras do Sem Fim*, 191; Roger Bastide, *Jorge Amado: Povo e terra*, 62.

61. Amado, *São Jorge dos Ilhéus*; *Gabriela, Cravo e Canela*; *Tereza Batista, Cansada da Guerra*, 99.

62. David Brookshaw, *Raça e Cor na Literatura Brasileira*; Sérgio Milliet, "O cancioneiro de Dorival Caymmi," *O Estado de São Paulo* November 21, 1947, 6; "Linha de cor," *O Estado de São Paulo* May 6, 1947, 1; Dorival Caymmi, *Cancioneiro da Bahia*, 7–11.

63. Jorge Amado, *Bahia de Todos os Santos*; Dorival Caymmi, "Você Já Foi à Bahia?"

64. Roger Bastide, *Imagens do Nordeste Místico*; Viana Moog, *Uma Interpretação da Literatura Brasileira*; Caymmi, *Cancioneiro da Bahia*, 7–11.

65. Jorge Amado, *Bahia de Todos os Santos*.

66. Amado, *Bahia de Todos os Santos*, 19, 135.

67. Suggestions of the collapse of Bahia's traditional world are in such works as *São Jorge dos Ilhéus* and *País do Carnaval*.

68. David Brookshaw, *Raça e Cor na Literatura Brasileira*; Jorge Amado, *O País do Carnaval*; *Capitães de Areia*; *Tenda dos Milagres*.

69. Amado, *Tenda dos Milagres*, 164, 282.

70. Brookshaw, *Raça e Cor na Literatura Brasileira*.

71. Amado, *Tereza Batista, Cansada de Guerra*.

72. Amado: *Cacau*; *Terras do Sem Fim*, 209; *São Jorge dos Ilhéus*.

73. Jorge Amado, *Terras do Sem Fim*.

74. Amado: *Cacau*, 164; *São Jorge dos Ilheus*, 39; *Tereza Batista, Cansada de Guerra*; *Mar Morto*, 107; *Capitães da Areia*, 63.

75. Nestor Perlonguer, "Territórios Marginais," *Papéis Avulsos*, no. 6; Jorge Amado: *Suor*; *Jubiabá*; *O País do Carnaval*, 21.

76. Amado, *Jubiabá*.

77. Note the similarity in the relations between humans and nature in Caymmi's songs "É Doce Morrer no Mar," "Itapoan," "Noites de Tempestade," "Saudade de Itapoan," and "Seria," and in Amado's novels: *Mar Morto*, *Capitães da Areia*, and *Seara Vermelha*.

78. Amado: *Cacau*, 121; *Mar Morto*, 20–21; *Capitães da Areia*, 211; *Terras do Sem Fim*; *São Jorge do Ilhéus*; *Bahia de Todos os Santos*, 25, 69, 191; *Tenda dos Milagres*.

79. Letícia Malard, *Ensaios da Literatura Brasileira: Ideologia e Realidade em Graciliano Ramos*; Silvio Castro, *Teoria e Política do Modernismo Brasileiro*, 10; Graciliano Ramos, *São Bernardo*.

80. Graciliano Ramos: *Infância*; *Alexandre e Outros Heróis*. See also Jorge Coli and Antônio Seel, "Duas visões de Graciliano Ramos," document in Graciliano Ramos folder, Arquivo CEDAE, UNICAMP.

81. On the relation between language, speech, silence, and power, see Eni Pulcinelli Orlandi, *Terra à Vista*.

82. Graciliano Ramos, *São Bernardo*; *Vidas Secas*. See also Coli and Seel, "Duas visões de Graciliano Ramos," and Flávio Campos, "Cinema e Literatura."

83. Ramos, *Linhas Tortas*, 35, 42; *Viventes das Alagoas*; *Insônia*, 171; *Alexandre e Outros Heróis*, 11; *São Bernando*; *Caetés*.

84. Roger Bastide, "O mundo trágico de Graciliano Ramos," *O Estado de São Paulo* March 30, 1947, 4.

85. Ramos, *São Bernardo*; *Angústia*, 9. See also Sérgio Miceli, *Intellectuais e Classe Dirigente no Brasil*.

86. Ramos, *Angústia*; *Infância*, 69–77, 126–38; *Alexandre e Outros Heróis*, 139.

87. Ramos, *Angústia*; Letícia Malard, *Ensaios da Literatura Brasileira*.

88. Ramos, *Vidas Secas*, 128; *São Bernardo*, 189. See also Otto Maria Carpeaux, "Visão de Graciliano Ramos," document in Graciliano Ramos folder, Arquivo CEDAE, UNICAMP.

89. Ramos, *Caetés*; *São Bernardo*, 10.

90. Ramos, *Infância*. See also Coli and Seel, "Duas visões de Graciliano Ramos"; Flávio Aguiar, "A grande fome do romance brasileiro," *Revista Leia*, July 1988.

91. Ramos, *Memórias do Cárcere* vol. 1, 7–30; *Caetés*; *Angústia*, 163–64, 175. See also Almir Andrade, *Aspectos da Cultura Brasileira*, 96–100; Antônio Candido, *Brigada Ligeira*; Dênis de Moraes, *O Velho Graça*.

92. Ramos, *Linhas Tortas*, 194–96 and 116; *Angústia*, 134. See also Malard, *Ensaios da Literatura Brasileira*; Dênis de Moraes, *O Velho Graça*.

93. Ramos, *São Bernardo*; *Caetés*.

94. Ramos, *Vidas Secas*; *Infância*; *Insônia*. See also Coli and Seel, "Duas visões de Graciliano Ramos"; Dênis de Moraes, *O Velho Graça*.

95. Ramos, *Caetés*, 43.

96. Ramos, *São Bernardo*; *Angústia*, 161–62.

97. Ramos, *Infância*, 263; *Vidas Secas*, 99–108.

98. Ramos, *São Bernardo*; *Angústia*, 163–64; *Vidas Secas*; *Viventes das Alagoas*, 124.

99. Ramos, *São Bernardo*.

100. Ramos, *São Bernardo*; *Angústia*.

101. Ramos, *São Bernardo*, 184; *Infância*, 27, 88, 247.

102. Ramos, *Angústia*; Coli and Seel, "Duas visões de Graciliano Ramos."

103. Ramos, *Viventes das Alagoas*, 86–90; *São Bernardo*, 117; *Caetés*, 60; *Angústia*. See also Roger Bastide, *Brasil, Terra de Contrastes*, 195.

104. Ramos, *Angústia*, 131, 137; *Viventes das Alagoas*, 18, 70, 114–18; *Vidas Secas*, 17–26; *Infância*, 138; *Linhas Tortas*, 51.

105. Carlos Zilio, *A Quarela do Brasil*; André Breton, *Manifesto do Surrealismo*; André Breton and Louis Aragon, *Surrealismo frente ao Realsimo Socialista*.

106. Aracy de Abreu Amaral, *Arte para Quê? A Preocupação Social na Arte Brasileira (1930–1970)*; Sérgio Milliet, *Tarsila do Amaral*, 41; Carlos Zilio, *A Quarela do Brasil*; Carlos Zilio, "A dificíl histórial da arte brasileira," *Folha de São Paulo* (Folhetim) October 2, 1953, 4.

107. Carlos Zilio, *A Quarela do Brasil*, 107; Aracy de Abreu Amaral, *Arte para Quê?*

108. Aracy de Abreu Amaral, *Arte para Quê?*

109. Sérgio Milliet, "Artistas de nossa terra: Di Cavalcanti," *O Estado de São Paulo* May 13, 1943, 4.

110. Ibiapaba Martins, "Notas de arte: Internacionalismo e nacionalismo na arte," *Correio Paulistano* June 21, 1948, 6; Luis Martins, *Emiliano di Cavalcanti*; Aracy de Abreu Amaral, *Arte para Quê?*

111. Emiliano de Cavalcanti, *Viagem de Minha Vida*, 109; Carlos Zilio, *A Quarela do Brasil*, 85.

112. Carlos Zilio, *A Quarela do Brasil*, 85–90.

113. Jorge Amado, *O Capeta Carybé*; Quirino Silva, "Caribé," *Diário da Noite* May 25, 1955. See also images by Carybé: *A Morte de Alexandrina* (1939); *Lampião* (1940); *Pensão São Bento* (1940); *Carnaval* (1944); *Retirantes* (1945); *Bahia* (1951); *Vaqueiros* (1953); *Os Pescadores* (1955); *Cangaceiros* (1962); *Lampião ou A Assombração do Cangaço* (1968); *Vaqueiros na Caatinga* (1969); *Nordeste* (1972).

114. Carlos Zilio, *A Quarela do Brasil*, 105–13.

115. Mário Pedrosa, *Dos Murais de Portinari aos Espaços de Brasília*, 7–25; Mário de Andrade, *O Baile dos Quatro Artes*, 128–29; Aracy de Abreu Amaral, *Arte para Quê?*, 103.

116. João Cândido Portinari, *O Menino de Brodósqui*.

117. André Vieira, "Cândido Portinari: Pintor da véspera," *Revista Acadêmica* no. 12 (July 1935): 10; Sérgio Milliet, "A paisagem da moderna pintura brasileira," *O Estado de São Paulo* March 26, 1941, 3; the film *Viramundo* (Geraldo Sarno, 1965).

118. Portinari, *Retirantes* (1945); *Enterro na Rêde* (1944); *Menino Morto* (1944); *Cabeça de Cangaceiro* (1952).

119. From João Cabral de Melo Neto, "Tecendo a Manhã," *Poesias Completas (1940–1965)*, 19–20.

120. Carlos Nejar, "João Cabral: os favos do deserto," João Cabral folder, Arquivo do CEDAE, UNICAMP; João Alexandre Barbosa, *A Imitação da Forma*.

121. Barbosa, *A Imitação da Forma*, 129–57; Mário Chamie, *A Linguagem Virtual*.

122. Barbosa, *A Imitação da Forma*, 129–57.

123. Barbosa, *A Imitação da Forma*; Carlos Felipe Moisés, "João Cabral: Poesia e poética II," *O Estado de São Paulo* September 3, 1966, 7; João Cabral de Melo Neto, "Graciliano Ramos," *Terceira Feira*, 54; Haroldo de Campos, "Arte pobre, tempo de pobreza, poesia menos," *Novos Estudos CEBRAP* July 1982, 63.

124. Sérgio Buarque de Holanda, *Cobra de Vidro*, 29–45; Sérgio Milliet, "Dados para a história da poesia modernista," *Revista Anhembi* 2, no. 4 (March 1951): 26; João Cabral de Melo Neto, "A educação pela pedra," "Catar feijão," "Uma faca só lamina," "Cemitério pernambucano," and "O cão sem plumas," in *Poesias Completas*.

125. João Cabral de Melo Neto, "O cão sem plumas" and "O sol em Pernambuco," *Poesias Completas*; Barbosa, *A Imitação da Forma*; Nejar, "João Cabral: Os favos do deserto"; Carlos Felipe Moisés, "João Cabral: Poesia e poética I," *O Estado de São Paulo* September 27, 1966; Adélia Bezerra Menezes, "A alquimia da pedra," *Folha de São Paulo* (Folhetim) November 11, 1984, 9; Mário César Carvalho, "João Cabral explica como construir poemas," *Folha de São Paulo* May 24, 1988, 31.

126. João Cabral de Melo Neto, "O cão sem plumas," "Lição de poesia," "Graciliano Ramos," and "Morte e Vida Severina" in *Poesias Completas*; Moisés, "João Cabral: Poesia e poética I."

127. Modesto Carone, "Severinos e comendadores," *Os Pobres na Literatura Brasileira*, 165; Antônio Rangel Bandeira, "A poesia como conquista da razão," *O Estado de São Paulo* November 9, 1947, 6; Jean-Paul Rebaud, "Tradição literária e criação poética em Morte e Vida Severina," *Folha de Letras*; Silviano Santiago, "Cultura brasileira: Tradição e contradição," *Jornal da Tarde* March 29, 1986.

128. Interview with João Cabral de Melo Neto, *Revista Pau-Brasil* November–December 1986; Barbosa, *A Imitação da Forma*, 157–211; Carone, "Severinos e comendadores," 167; Alfredo Bosi, *História Concisa da Literatura Brasileira*.

129. João Cabral de Melo Neto, "Morte e Vida Severina," and "O alpendre do canavial," *Poesias Completas*; Moema Selma D'Andrea, *A Tradição Redescoberta*.

130. Cabral, "Velório do comendador" and "O aplendre do canavial," *Poesias Completas*.

131. Cabral, "Duas faces do jantar dos comendadores," "Festa na casa-grande," and "Paisagem com cupim," *Poesias Completas*.

132. Cabral, "Cemitério paraibano," "O rio," "Psicologia da composição," and "Congresso no Polígono das Secas," *Poesias Completas*; Menezes, "A alquimia da pedra"; Rebaud, "Tradição literária e criação poética em Morte e Vida Severina."

133. Cabral, "Festa na casa-grande," "O ovo da galinha," and "Poema da cabra," *Poesias Completas*; Marly Oliveira, "Rápida visão da obra de João Cabral de Melo Neto," *Revista Nicolau*, document in João Cabral folder, Arquivo CEDAE, UNICAMP.

134. Cabral, "O rio" and "O cão sem plumas," *Poesias Completas*; Menezes, "A alquimia da pedra."

135. Cabral, "Bifurcados de 'Habitar o Tempo,'" "Habitar o tempo," "Coisas de cabeceira," "Escritos com o corpo," and "Infância," *Poesias Completas*.

136. Cabral, "Morte e Vida Severina," "O cão sem plumas," and "Pregão turístico do Recife," *Poesias Completas*; D'Andrea, *A Tradição Redescoberta*.

137. Cabral, "De um avião" and "A voz do canavial," *Poesias Completas*; Barbosa, *A Imitação da Forma*; Carvalho, "João Cabral explica como construir poemas."

138. Barbosa, *A Imitação da Forma*; Bosi, *História Concisa da Literatura Brasileira*, 525; Carone, "Severinos e comendadores."

139. Cabral, "O sol de Pernambuco" and "Morte e Vida Severina," *Poesias Completas*; Sérgio Buarque de Holanda, *Cobra de Vidro*.

140. Cabral, "O rio"; Barbosa, *A Imitação da Forma*; Mário de Andrade, *Aspectos da Literatura Brasileira*.

141. Cabral, "Congresso no Polígono das Secas," "Morte e Vida Severina."

142. Bernadet, *Brasil em Tempo de Cinema*, 11–25; Augusto, *Este Mundo É um Pandeiro*.

143. Bernadet, *Brasil em Tempo de Cinema*, 11–25.

144. Augusto, *Este Mundo É um Pandeiro*.

145. Augusto, *Este Mundo É um Pandeiro*; Oswald de Andrade, *A Utopia Antropofágica*. See also the Brazilian Hollywood parodies *Nem Sansão e Nem Dalila* (Carlos Manga, 1954) and *Matar ou Correr* (Carlos Manga, 1954).

146. *Boletim Noticioso* no. 1, Comissão Permanente de Defesa do Cinema Brasiliero, 1952.

147. Leal, *O Nordeste no Cinema*, 17–27.

148. See, for example, the character of the colonel Fulgêncio in *Fogo na Canjica* (Luis de Barros, 1947), or the taxi driver in *Rico Ri à Toa* (Roberto Farias, 1957).

149. Leal, *O Nordeste no Cinema*, 47–59.

150. *O Canto do Mar* (Alberto Cavalcante, 1953). Owing to the significant popular success of the *baião* as a national music alongside samba in the 1940s and 1950s, and the wave of northeastern migrants attending movies in the South, northeastern songs (often by Luiz Gonzaga and Dorival Caymmi) were common features in the films. See *Este Mundo É um Pandeiro* (Watson Macêdo, 1946), with Gonzaga singing "Que Mentira que Lorota Boa," and *Abacaxi Azul* (Wallace Downey, 1944), with Caymmi performing "Acontece que Eu Sou Baiano."

151. Cláudio Bueno Rocha, "Cinema Novo: O que é, quem faz, para onde vai," *O Cruzeiro* June 30, 1965, 13; Paulo Emílio Sales Gomes, "Perfis baianos," *A Tarde* (Salvador) April 20, 1962, 2; Arquivo Glauber Rocha (AGR), Cinemateca Brasileira, Cx. BA 1, doc. 13; Maurice Capovilla, "Cinema Novo," *Revista Brasiliense* no. 4 (May–June 1962): 182; Glauber Rocha, *Revolução do Cinema Novo*, 15.

152. Campos, "Cinema e Literatura."

153. Castro, *Teoria e Política do Modernismo Brasileiro*; Johnson, *Macunaíma: Do Modernismo na Literature ao Cinema Novo*.

154. Chamie, *A Linguagem Virtual*; Capovilla, "Cinema Novo"; Johnson, *Macunaíma*.

155. Johnson, *Macunaíma*; Bernadet, *Brasil em Tempo de Cinema*, 35–39.

156. Bernadet, *Brasil em Tempo de Cinema*, 29–31; Roger Bastide, "O Brasil em Andreza," *Revista Anhembi* no. 65 (April 1956): 27; Augusto, *Este Mundo É um Pandeiro*. See also the films *Cinco Vezes Favela* (Maros Farias, Miguel Borges, Carlos Diegues, Joaquim Pedro de Andrade, Leon Hirzman, 1962) and *Bahia de Todos os Santos* (Triguerinho Neto, 1960).

157. Bernadet, *Brasil em Tempo de Cinema*, 67–72, 112–17.

158. Rachel Gerber, *Glauber Rocha*, 14–15.

159. José Guilherme Corrêa, "Cinema brasileiro sincrônico," *Correio da Manhã* June 26, 1968, 4; Rocha, *Revolução do Cinema Novo*, 109.

160. Jean-Claude Bernadet, "A origem e a utopia," *Folha de São Paulo* (Folhetim) August 22, 1982, 9; *Revolução do Cinema Novo*.

161. Johnson, *Macunaíma*; Xavier, *Sertão Mar*, 89–94; interview with Glauber Rocha in *Status* n.d., Arquivo Glauber Rocha, Cx. GR1, doc. 21.

162. Rocha, *Revolução do Cinema Novo*; Rachel Gerber, "Glauber Rocha e a busca da identidade," Arquivo Glauber Rocha, Cx. GR 2, doc. 4; Miriam Chnaiderman, "Nelson e Graciliano: Memória do Cárcere," *Folha de São Paulo* (Folhetim) September 2, 1984, 11.

163. *Vidas Secas* (Nelson Pereira dos Santos, 1963); *Grande Sertão* (Gilberto e Renato Santos Pereira, 1965).

164. Bernadet, *Brasil em Tempo de Cinema*, 58–67; Caetano Veloso, "Um filme de montagem," Arquivo Glauber Rocha, Cx. BA3, doc. 30.

165. Maurício Jonas Leite, "Violência e coragem na terra do sol," *Tribuna da Imprensa* March 24, 1964, Arquivo Glauber Rocha, Cx. DE2, doc. 3; s/n, "Nova face da mística nordestina," *Diário de Pernambuco* September 6, 1964, 15; Mário Chamie, "As metáforas da transigência," *O Estado de São Paulo* July 8, 1967 (literary supplement), 4; Rocha, *Revolução do Cinema Novo*; Orlando Senna and Glauber Rocha, *Roteiros do Terceiro Mundo*.

166. Xavier, *Sertão Mar*, 69–82; Glauber Rocha, "A miséria de uma filosofia," Arquivo Glauber Rocha, Cx. GR1, doc. 10; Rachel Gerber, "Glauber Rocha e a busca da identidade"; Gerber, *Glauber Rocha*.

167. Xavier, *Sertão Mar*, 43, 54, 94–102.

168. Xavier, *Sertão Mar*, 39–43; "Barravento no cinema brasileiro" (interview with Glauber Rocha), Arquivo Glauber Rocha, Cx. BA3, doc. 19.

169. Xavier, *Sertão Mar*, 72–121; Gerber, "Glauber Rocha e a busca da identidade"; Glauber Rocha, *Revisão Crítica do Cinema Brasileiro*, 69–70; Zulmira Ribeiro Tavares, "Os confins da ignorância," *O Estado de São Paulo* (literary supplement) July 26, 1969, 4.

170. Glauber Rocha, "As aventuras de Antônio das Mortes, o matador do sertão" (initial film script), Arquivo Glauber Rocha, Cx. DR1, doc. 1; Bernadet, "A origem e a utopia."

171. Xavier, *Sertão Mar*, 17–21; Bernadet, "A origem e a utopia"; Glauber Rocha, "A Ira de Deus" (initial script for *Deus e o Diabo na Terra do Sol*), Arquivo Glauber Rocha, Cx. DD1, doc. 1.

172. Xavier, *Sertão Mar*, 102–6; Senna and Rocha, *Roteiros do Terceiro Mundo*.

173. Xavier, *Sertão Mar*, 183; Bernadet, *Brasil em Tempo de Cinema*, 85; Glauber Rocha, "La Estética de la Violencia," Arquivo Glauber Rocha, Cx. DE7, doc. 6; Rocha, *Revolução do Cinema Novo*, 65; Rubens Machado Jr., "O espaço de Terra em Transe," *Folha de São Paulo* (Folhetim), August 22, 1981, 10; Eduardo Peñuela Canizal, "A função política no Cinema Novo," *O Estado de São Paulo* April 24, 1977, 3; Bruno Torri, "Poesia e Política nel Cinema Novo Brasiliene," *Formazioni Cinematografichi* April 1969, Arquivo Glauber Rocha, Cx. DE7, doc. 11.

174. Xavier, *Sertão Mar*, 94–102; Rocha, *Revolução do Cinema Novo*, 31; Gerber, *Glauber Rocha*.

175. Xavier, *Sertão Mar*, 153–67; José Wolf, "Morrer como poeta," *Jornal do Comércio* May 28, 1967, 6; Rocha, "A Ira de Deus"; Torri, "Poesia e Política nel Cinema Novo Brasiliene"; Gerber, *Glauber Rocha*.

176. Xavier, *Sertão Mar*; Capovilla, "Cinema Novo."

177. Rocha, *Revolução do Cinema Novo*; Xavier, *Sertão Mar*, 82–87; Gerber, "Glauber Rocha e a busca da identidade"; Gerber, *Glauber Rocha*.

178. Xavier, *Sertão Mar*, 74–86.

179. Xavier, *Sertão Mar*, 94–102; anonymous, "Arte popular no cinema do Brasil com Deus e o Diabo," *Diário de Notícias* March 25, 1964, Arquivo Glauber Rocha, Cx. DE2, doc. 4; Rachel Gerber, "Glauber Rocha e o cinema brasileiro hoje," *Folha de São Paulo* (Folhetim) August 22, 1982, 6.

180. Gerber, *Glauber Rocha*.

181. Xavier, *Sertão Mar*; Bernadet, *Brasil em Tempo de Cinema*, 25–29; Glauber Rocha, "A Ira de Deus"; Carlos Alberto Silva, "Meu sol, teu diabo, vosso senhor, nosso Nordeste," *Debate* ano 2 (October 1964): 16.

BIBLIOGRAPHY

LIBRARIES AND ARCHIVES

Arquivo Edgar Leuenroth, Campinas, UNICAMP.
Arquivo Glauber Rocha, Cinemateca Brasileira, São Paulo.
Arquivo Mário de Andrade, Instituto de Estudos Brasileiros (IEB), USP, São Paulo.
Arquivo Oswald de Andrade, Centro de Documentação Alexandre Eulálio (CEDAE), Campinas, IEL, UNICAMP.
Biblioteca Central (Coleções Alexandre Eulálio, Sérgio Buarque de Holanda, Obras Raras), Campinas, UNICAMP.
Biblioteca da Casa Mário de Andrade, São Paulo.
Biblioteca da Cinemateca Brasileira, São Paulo.
Biblioteca da Escola da Comunicação (ECA), USP, São Paulo.
Biblioteca da Pinoteca do Estado, São Paulo.
Biblioteca do Centro de Estudos Migratórios (CEM), São Paulo.
Biblioteca do Instituto de Filosofia e Ciências Humanas, Campinas, UNICAMP.
Biblioteca do Instituto dos Estudos Brasileiros, São Paulo.
Biblioteca do Memorial da América Latina, São Paulo.
Biblioteca do Museu de Arte Moderna (MAM), São Paulo.
Biblioteca do Museu Lasar Segall, São Paulo.
Museu da Imagem e do Som (MIS), São Paulo.
Museu de Arte Contemporânea, São Paulo.
Museu de Artes de São Paulo (MASP), São Paulo.
Museu do Estado de Pernambuco, Recife.
Pinacoteca do Estado de Pernambuco, Recife.

BOOKS AND ARTICLES

Albuquerque, Durval Muniz de, Jr. "Falas de Astúcia e de Angústia: A Seca no Imaginário Nordestino (1877–1922)." Master's thesis, UNICAMP, 1988.
Albuquerque, Durval Muniz de, Jr. "Mennochio e Riviére: Criminosos da palavra, poetas do silêncio." *Resgate*, no. 2 (1991).
Albuquerque, Durval Muniz de, Jr. "Vidas por um Fio, Vidas Entrelaçadas: Rasgando o pano da cultura e descobrindo o rendilhado das 'trajetórias culturais.'" *História e Perspectiva*, no. 8 (1993): 87–96.
Albuquerque, Durval Muniz de, Jr. "Violar Memórias e Gestar a História: Abordagem de uma problemática fecunda que torna a tarefa do historiador um 'parto difícil.'" *Clio (Série Nordeste)*, no. 15 (1994): 39–52.
Almeida, José Américo de. *A Bagaceira*, 26th ed. Rio de Janeiro: José Olympio, 1988.

Almeida, José Américo de. *O Boqueirão (Novelas)*. Rio de Janeiro: Civilização Brasileira, 1979.

Almeida, José Américo de. *Coiteiros (Novelas)*. Rio de Janeiro: Civilização Brasileira, 1979.

Almeida, José Américo de. *Reflexões de uma Cabra (Novelas)*. Rio de Janeiro: Civilização Brasileira, 1979.

Amado, Jorge. *Bahia de Todos os Santos*, 19th ed. São Paulo: Martins, 1970.

Amado, Jorge. *Cacau*, 47th ed. Rio de Janeiro: Record, 1987.

Amado, Jorge. *O Capeta Carybé*, 6th ed. São Paulo: Berlendis and Vertecchia, 1986.

Amado, Jorge. *Capitães da Areia*, 57th ed. Rio de Janeiro: Record, 1983.

Amado, Jorge. *Gabriela, Cravo e Canela*, 40th ed. São Paulo: Martins, 1970.

Amado, Jorge. *Jubiabá*, 48th ed. Rio de Janeiro: Record, 1987.

Amado, Jorge. *Mar Morto*, 26th ed. São Paulo: Martins, 1970.

Amado, Jorge. *O País do Carnaval*, 25th ed. São Paulo: Martins, 1970.

Amado, Jorge. *São Jorge dos Ilhéus*. São Paulo: Martins, 1970.

Amado, Jorge. *Seara Vermelha*, 42nd ed. Rio de Janeiro: Record, 1983.

Amado, Jorge. *Suor*, 24th ed. São Paulo: Martins, 1970.

Amado, Jorge. *Tenda dos Milagres*, 5th ed. São Paulo: Martins, 1970.

Amado, Jorge. *Tereza Batista, Cansada de Guerra*. São Paulo: Martins, 1972.

Amado, Jorge. *Terras do Sem Fim*. São Paulo: Circulo do Livro, n/d.

Amaral, Aracy de Abreu. *Arte Para Que? A Preocupação Social na Arte Brasileira (1930–1970)*. São Paulo: Nobel, 1984.

Andrade, Almir. *Aspectos da Cultura Brasileira*. Rio de Janeiro: Schmidt Edito, 1939.

Andrade, Mário de. *Aspectos da Literatura Brasileira*, 5th ed. São Paulo: Martins, 1974.

Andrade, Mário de. *O Baile das Quatro Artes*. São Paulo: Martins, 1975.

Andrade, Mário de. *O Turista Aprendiz*. São Paulo: Duas Cidades, 1976.

Andrade, Oswaldo de. *Os Dentes do Dragão*, 2nd ed. São Paulo: Globo, 1990.

Andrade, Oswaldo de. *Marco Zero I (A Revolução Melancólica)*. São Paulo: Globo, 1991.

Andrade, Oswaldo de. *Ponta de Lança*. São Paulo: Globo, 1991.

Andrade, Oswaldo de. *A Utopia Antropofágica*. São Paulo: Globo, 1990.

Aranha, Graça. *Canaã*. Rio de Janeiro: F. Briguet e Cia., 1949.

Aranha, Graça. *O Espírito Moderno*, 2nd ed. São Paulo: Cia. Ed. Nacional, n/d.

Augusto, Sérgio. *Este Mundo é um Pandeiro*. São Paulo: Cinemateca Brasileira, 1989.

Azevedo, Célia Maria Marinho de. *Onda Negra, Medo Branco: O Negro no Imaginário dos Elites*. Rio de Janeiro: Paz e Terra, 1987.

Bandeira, Manuel. *Poesias*. Rio de Janeiro: José Olympio, 1955.

Barbosa, João Alexandre. *A Imitação da Forma*. São Paulo: Duas Cidades, 1975.

Barthes, Roland. *Fragmentos de um Discurso Amoroso*, 10th ed. Rio de Janeiro: Francisco Alves, 1999.

Barthes, Roland. *O Óbvio e o Obtuso*. Rio de Janeiro: Novas Fronteiras, 1990.

Bastide, Roger. *Arte e Sociedade*, 2nd ed. São Paulo: Cia Ed. Nacional, 1979.

Bastide, Roger. "O Brasil em Andreza." *Revista Anhembi* 22, no. 65 (April 1956): 27.

Bastide, Roger. *Brasil, Terra de Contrastes*, 2nd ed. São Paulo: Difel, 1964.

Bastide, Roger. *Imagens do Nordeste Místico*. Rio de Janeiro: Empresa Gráfica O Cruzeiro S/A, 1945.

Bastide, Roger. *Jorge Amado: Povo e Terra, 40 Anos de Literatura.* São Paulo: Martins, 1952.

Bastos, Elide Rugai. "Gilberto Freyre e a Formação da Sociedade Brasileira." Ph.D. diss., Pontifícia Universidade Católica de São Paulo, 1986.

Batista, Martha Rossetti, ed. *Brasil em Tempo Modernista (1917–1929).* São Paulo: IEB, 1972.

Benjamin, Walter. *Magia e Técnica, Arte e Política (Obras Escolhidas* vol. 1). São Paulo: Brasiliense, 1985.

Benjamin, Walter. "O surrealismo." In *Os Pensadores,* vol. 48. São Paulo: Abril Cultural, 1975.

Bernadet, Jean-Claude. *Brasil em Tempo de Cinema,* 2nd ed. Rio de Janeiro: Paz e Terra, 1976.

Bernadet, Jean-Claude. "A origem e a utopia." *Folhetim* (São Paulo), August 22, 1982, 9.

Berriel, Carlos Eduardo O. "A uiara enganosa." *Revista Ensaio* (São Paulo), no. 17/18: 210.

Bosi, Alfredo. *Cultura Brasileira: Temas e Situações.* São Paulo: Ática, 1987.

Bosi, Alfredo. *História Concisa da Literatura Brasileira,* 3rd ed. São Paulo: Cultrix, 1990.

Bosi, Alfredo. *Reflexões sobra a Arte,* 3rd ed. São Paulo, Ática, 1989.

Breton, André. *Manifestos do Surrealismo.* Lisboa: Moraes Editores, 1976.

Breton, André, and Aragon, Louis. *Surrealismo Frente ao Realismo Socialista.* Barcelona: Tusques Editor, 1973.

Brookshaw, David. *Raça e Cor na Literatura Brasileira.* Porto Alegre: Mercado Aberto, 1983.

Cabral de Melo Neto, João. *Poesias Completas (1940–1965).* Rio de Janeiro: Ed. Sabiá, 1968.

Cabral de Melo Neto, João. *Terceira Feira.* Rio de Janeiro: Editora do Autor, 1981.

Campos, Haroldo de. "Arte pobre, tempo de pobreza, poesia menos." *Novos Estudos CEBRAP* (São Paulo) July 1982, 63.

Campos, Haroldo de. "Parafernália para Hélio Oiticica." *Folhetim* (São Paulo) May 13, 1984, 11.

Candido, Antonio. *Brigada Ligeira.* São Paulo: Martins, 1961.

Candido, Antonio. *Literatura e Sociedade,* 7th ed. São Paulo: Ed. Nacional, 1985.

Canizal, Eduardo Peñuela. "A função política no Cinema Novo." *O Estado de São Paulo* April 24, 1977, 3.

Capovilla, Maurice. "Cinema Novo." *Revista Brasiliense* no. 4 (March–June 1962): 22.

Carvalho, Luis Antônio de. "As pistas do moderno." *Revista Leia* May 1987, 22.

Castelo, José Aderaldo. *José Lins do Rego: Modernismo e Regionalismo.* São Paulo: Edart, 1961.

Castoriadis, Cornelius. *A Instituição Imaginária da Sociedade.* Rio de Janeiro: Paz e Terra, 1982.

Castro, Josué de. *Geografia da Fome.* Rio de Janeiro: Antares, 1980.

Castro, Silvio. *Teoria e Política do Modernismo Brasileiro.* Petrópolis: Vozes, 1979.

Caymmi, Dorival. *O Cancioneiro da Bahia.* São Paulo: Martins, 1947.

Chamie, Mário. "Gilberto Freyre, o mago das recorrências." *Suplemento Literário de O Estado de São Paulo* no. 209 (June 10, 1984): 13.

Chamie, Mário. *A Linguagem Virtual.* São Paulo: Edições Quíron, 1976.

Chamie, Mário. "As metáforas da transigência." *O Estado de São Paulo* July 8, 1967 (literary supplement), 4.

Chnaiderman, Miriam. "Nelson e Graciliano: Memória do cárcere." *Folhetim* (São Paulo), September 2, 1984, 11.

Contier, Arnaldo. "Modernismo e brasilidade: Música, utopia e tradição." In *Tempo e História,* edited by Adauto Novaes. São Paulo: Companhia das Letras, 1992.

Contier, Arnaldo. "Música e ideologia no Brasil." *Coleção Ensaios* no. 1 (1978): 37.

Corrêa, José Guilherme. "Cinema brasileiro sincrônico." *Correiro da Manhã* June 26, 1968, 4.

D'Andrea, Moema Selma. *A Tradição Re(des)coberta.* Campinas: Ed. da UNICAMP, 1992.

Dantas, Paulo. "Euclides e as dimensões sertanejas." *Revista Brasiliense* no. 19 (September–October 1958): 138.

Dantas, Paulo. "Os Sertões como tema literário." *Revista Brasiliense* no. 5 (May–June 1956): 86.

Decca, Edgar Salvatori de. *O Nascimento das Fábricas.* São Paulo: Brasiliense, 1979.

Decca, Edgar Salvatori de. *O Silêncio dos Vencidos.* São Paulo: Brasiliense, 1986.

Deleuze, Gilles. *Diferença e Repetição.* Rio de Janeiro: Graal, 1988.

Deleuze, Gilles. *Foucault.* São Paulo: Brasiliense, 1986.

Deleuze, Gilles. "Pensamento nômade." *Folhetim* (São Paulo) February 8, 1985, 4.

Deleuze, Gilles. *Proust e os Signos.* Rio de Janeiro: Forense-Universitária, 1987.

Deleuze, Gilles, and Félix Guattari. *O Anti-Édipo.* Rio de Janeiro: Imago, 1976.

Di Cavalcanti, Emiliano. *Viagem da Minha Vida I (O Testamento da Alvorada).* Rio de Janeiro: Civilização Brasileira, 1955.

Dória, Carlos Alberto. "1930: Romance e revolução." *Folhetim* (São Paulo) June 14, 1981, 4.

Eco, Umberto. *Apocalípticos e Integrados.* São Paulo: Perspectiva, 1970.

Ellis, Alfredo, Jr. *Capítulos de História Psicológica de São Paulo.* São Paulo: USP, 1945.

Fernandes, Florestan. *Folclore e Mudança Social na Cidade de São Paulo,* 2nd ed. Petrópolis: Vozes, 1979.

Ferreira, Ascenso. *Catimbó e Outros Poemas.* Rio de Janeiro: José Olympio, 1963.

Ferreira, José de Jesus. *Luiz Gonzaga, o Rei do Baião, sua vida, seus amigos, suas canções.* São Paulo: Ática, 1986.

Ferretti, Mundicarmo Maria Rocha. *Baião dos Dois.* Recife: Fundarj, 1988.

Fontes, Amando. *Os Corumbas.* Rio de Janeiro: Livraria Schmidt, 1933.

Fontes, Amando. *Rua do Siriry.* Rio de Janeiro: José Olympio, 1937.

Foucault, Michel. "Ariane enforcou-se." *Livros* (São Paulo) August 13, 1988, 4.

Foucault, Michel. *A Arqueologia do Saber,* 2nd ed. Rio de Janeiro: Forense Universitária, 1986.

Foucault, Michel. *As Palavras e as Coisas.* São Paulo: Martins Fontes, 1985.

Foucault, Michel. *Eu Pierre Riviére, que degolei minha mãe, minha irmã e meu irmão,* 2nd ed. Rio de Janeiro: Graal, 1982.

Foucault, Michel. *História da Loucura.* São Paulo: Perspectiva, 1978.

Foucault, Michel. *História da Sexualidade I (A Vontade de Saber),* 4th ed. Rio de Janeiro: Graal, 1977.

Foucault, Michel. *Isto Não É Um Cachimbo*. São Paulo: Brasiliense, 1989.

Foucault, Michel. *Microfísica do Poder*, 4th ed. Rio de Janeiro: Graal, 1984.

Foucault, Michel. *Vigiar e Punir*. Petrópolis: Vozes, 1984.

Freyre, Gilberto. *Casa-Grande e Senzala*, 21st ed. Rio de Janeiro: José Olympio, 1981.

Freyre, Gilberto. *Interpretação do Brasil*. Rio de Janeiro: José Olympio, 1947.

Freyre, Gilberto. *Manifesto Regionalista*, 4th ed. Recife: Instituto Joaquim Nabuco, 1967.

Freyre, Gilberto. *Nordeste*, 5th ed. Rio de Janeiro: José Olympio, 1985.

Freyre, Gilberto. *Quase Poesia*. Recife: Edições Pirata, 1980.

Freyre, Gilberto. *Região e Tradição*. Rio de Janeiro: José Olympio, 1941.

Freyre, Gilberto. *Sobrados e Mocambos*, 5th ed. 2 vols. Rio de Janeiro: José Olympio, 1977.

Freyre, Gilberto. *Vida, Forma e Cor*, 2nd ed. Rio de Janeiro: Record, 1987.

Freyre, Gilberto. "Vida Social no Nordeste (Aspectos de um Século de Transição)." *Diário de Pernambuco*. 1925.

Gagnebin, Jeanne Marie. "Origem da alegoria, alegoria de origem." *Folhetim* (São Paulo) December 9, 1984, 8.

Garcia, N. Jahr. *Estado Novo, Ideologia e Propaganda Política*. São Paulo: Loyola, 1982.

Gebara, Ademir, ed. *História Regional: Uma discussão*. Campinas: Ed. da UNICAMP, 1987.

Gerber, Raquel. *Glauber Rocha*. Rio de Janeiro: Paz e Terra, 1977.

Gerber, Raquel. "Glauber Rocha e o cinema brasileiro hoje." *Folha de São Paulo* (Folhetim) August 22, 1982, 6.

Gil, Gilberto, and Antônio Risério. *O Poético e Político*. Rio de Janeiro: Paz e Terra, 1988.

Gomes, Helena Toller. *O Poder Rural na Ficção*. São Paulo: Ática, 1981.

Guattari, Félix. "Impasse pós-moderno e transição pós-mídia." *Folhetim* (São Paulo) April 13, 1986, 2.

Hansen, João Adolfo. "Terceira margem." *Folhetim* (São Paulo) November 20, 1987, 2.

Helena, Lúcia. *Totens e Tabus na Modernidade Brasileira*. Rio de Janeiro: Tempo Brasileiro, 1985.

Hobsbawm, Eric, and Terence Ranger, eds. *A Invenção das Tradições*. Rio de Janeiro: Paz e Terra, 1984.

Holanda, Sérgio Buarque de. *Cobra de Vidro*, 2nd ed. São Paulo: Perspectiva, 1978.

Holanda, Sérgio Buarque de. *Raízes do Brasil*, 15th ed. Rio de Janeiro: José Olympio, 1976.

Inojosa, Joaquim. *Os Andrades e Outros Aspectos do Modernismo*. Rio de Janeiro: Civilização Brasileira, 1975.

Inojosa, Joaquim. *O Movimento Modernista em Pernambuco*. 3 vols. Rio de Janeiro: Gráfica Tupy Editora, 1969.

Johnson, Randal. *Macunaíma: Do Modernismo na Literature ao Cinema Novo*. São Paulo: T. A. Queiroz, 1982.

Laus, Lausimar. "O romance de Raquel de Queiroz." *Suplemento Literário de Estado de Minas* October 11, 1975, 11.

Leal, Willis. *O Nordeste no Cinema*. João Pessoa: Ed. Universitária, 1982.

Leite, Dante Moreira. *O Caráter Nacional Brasilerio*, 2nd ed. São Paulo: Pioneira, 1969.

Leite, Otávio Dias. "Vidas secas." *Revista Acadêmica* no. 34 (April 1938): 10.

Lenharo, Alcir. *Sacralização da Política.* Campinas: Papirus, 1986.

Lima, Jorge de. *Calunga.* Porto Alegre: Ed. Livraria Globo, 1935.

Lima, Jorge de. *Obra Poética.* Rio de Janeiro: Ed. Getúlio Costa, 1949.

Lipovetsky, Gilles. *O Império do Efêmero.* São Paulo: Companhia das Letras, 1989.

Lobato, Monteiro. *Urupês,* 13th ed. São Paulo: Brasiliense, 1966.

Lopez, Telê Ancona, ed. *Macunaíma: A Margem e o Texto.* São Paulo: Hucitec, 1974.

Lucas, Fábio. "Vanguarda literária e ideologia." *Encontros com a Civilização Brasileira* (Rio de Janeiro) no. 3 (September 1978).

Lukács, Georg. *Teoria do Romance.* Lisboa: Presença, n/d.

Machado, Alcântara. *Vida e Morte do Bandeirante.* São Paulo: Martins, n/d.

Machado, Roberto. *Ciência e Saber (A Trajetória da Arqueologia de Foucault).* Rio de Janeiro: Graal, 1981.

Machado, Roberto. *Deleuze e a Filosofia.* Rio de Janeiro: Graal, 1990.

Machado, Rubens, Jr. "O espaço de Terra em Transe." *Folha de São Paulo* (Folhetim) August 22, 1981, 10.

Maciel, Luiz Carlos. "O esvaziamento de realidade." *Folhetim* (São Paulo) February 27, 1977, 23.

Magnani, José Guilherme Cantor. *Festa no Pedaço.* São Paulo: Brasiliense, 1984.

Maingueneau, Dominique. *Novas Tendências em Análise de Discurso.* Campinas: Pontes, 1989.

Malard, Letícia. *Ensaio de Literatura Brasileira: Ideologia e Realidade em Graciliano Ramos.* Belo Horizonte: Itatiaia, n.d.

Marroquim, Mário. *A Lingua do Nordeste,* 3rd ed. São Paulo: Cia. Ed. Nacional, 1945.

Martins, Luis. *Cândido Portinari.* São Paulo: Gráficos Brummer Ltda., 1972.

Martins, Luis. *Emiliano Di Cavalcanti.* São Paulo: MAM, 1953.

Matta, Roberto da. *Carnavais, Malandros e Heróis.* Rio de Janeiro: Zahar, 1979.

Matta, Roberto da. *O Que Faz o brasil, Brasil?* Rio de Janeiro: Salamandra, 1984.

Melo, Maria das Graças Rios de. "Literatura oral e teatro popular." *Suplemento Literário do Estado de Minas* November 29, 1975, 4.

Menezes, Adélia Bezerra de. "A alquimica da pedra." *Folhetim* (São Paulo) November 11, 1984, 9.

Menezes, Djacir. *O Outro Nordeste,* 2nd ed. Rio de Janeiro: Civilização Brasileira, 1972.

Miceli, Sérgio. *Intelectuais e Classe Dirigente no Brasil (1920–1945).* São Paulo: Difel, 1979.

Miceli, Sérgio. *Tarsila do Amaral.* São Paulo: MAM, 1953.

Milliet, Sérgio. "Dados para a história da poesia modernista." *Revista Anhembi* 4 vol. 11 (March 1951): 26.

Moog, Viana. *Uma Interpretação da Literatura Brasileira.* Rio de Janeiro: Casa de Estudante do Brasil, 1943.

Moraes, Dênis de. *O Velho Graça.* Rio de Janeiro: José Olympio, 1992.

Naxara, Márcia Regina Capelari. "Estrangeira em sua Própria Terra." Master's thesis, UNICAMP, 1991.

Neves. David E. *Cinema Novo no Brasil.* Petrópolis: Vozes, 1966.

Nietzsche, Friedrich. *Obras Incompletas.* 2 vols., 5th ed. Text selection by Gerárd Lebrun. São Paulo: Nova Cultural, 1991.

Novaes, Adauto, ed. *Tempo e História.* São Paulo: Companhia das Letras, 1992.

"Nova face da mística nordestina." *Diário de Pernambuco* September 6, 1964.

Oliveira, Fátima Amaral Dias de. "Trilha Sonora." Master's thesis, UNICAMP, n/d.

Oliveira, Francisco de. *Elegia para uma Re(li)gião,* 2nd ed. Rio de Janeiro: Paz e Terra, 1977.

Oliveira, Lúcia Lippi. "Repensando a tradição." *Ciência Hoje* 7, no. 38 (December 1987): 58.

Orlandi, Eni Pulcinelli. *Terra à Vista: Discurso do confronto: Velho e novo mundo.* São Paulo: Cortez, 1990.

Ortiz, Renato. *A Consciência Fragmentada.* Rio de Janeiro: Paz e Terra, 1980.

Ortiz, Renato. *Cultura Brasileira e Identidade Nacional,* 3rd ed. São Paulo: Brasiliense, n/d.

Ortiz, Renato. *A Moderna Tradição Brasileira,* 3rd ed. São Paulo: Brasiliense, 1991.

Pedrosa, Mário. *Dos Murais de Portinari aos Espaços de Brasília.* São Paulo: Perspectiva, 1981.

Peixoto, Nelson Brissac. *A Sedução da Barbárie.* São Paulo: Brasiliense, 1982.

Perlonguer, Nestor. *O Negócio do Michê,* 2nd ed. São Paulo: Brasiliense, 1987.

Perlonguer, Nestor. "Territórios marginais." *Papéis Avulsos* (Rio de Janeiro) no. 6, 1989.

Pessanha, José Américo Mota. "Bachelard: As asas da imaginação." *Folhetim* (São Paulo) June 10, 1984, 9.

Pignatari, Décio. "Cultura Brasileira Pós-Nacionalista." *Folhetim* (São Paulo) February 17, 1985, 6.

Pinheiro, João Ribeiro. *História da Pintura Brasileira.* Rio de Janeiro: Casas Luiznijer, 1931.

Pinto, José Nêumane. "Os marginais da música nordestina." *Somtrês* no. 23 (1980): 66.

Pontes, Neroaldo. *Modernismo e Regionalismo.* João Pessoa: Secretaria da Educação e Cultura da Paraíba, 1984.

Portinari, João Cândido. *Portinari: O Menino de Brodósqui.* Rio de Janeiro: Livroarte Editora, 1979.

Prado, Caio, Jr. *Formação do Brasil Contemporâneo,* 18th ed. São Paulo: Brasiliense, 1983.

Quadros, Consuelo Novaes S. de. "Formação do regionalismo no Brasil." *Revista do Centro de Estudos Baianos* no. 77 (1977): 5–13.

Queiroz, Rachel de. *Caminho de Pedras.* Rio de Janeiro: José Olympio, 1948.

Queiroz, Rachel de. *João Miguel.* Rio de Janeiro: José Olympio, 1948.

Queiroz, Rachel de. *Mapinguari (Obras Reunidas* vol. 5). Rio de Janeiro: José Olympio, 1989.

Queiroz, Rachel de. *O Quinze.* Rio de Janeiro: José Olympio, 1948.

Queiroz, Rachel de. *As Três Marias,* 3rd ed. Rio de Janeiro: José Olympio, 1956.

Rago, Margareth. *Os Prazeres da Noite.* Rio de Janeiro: Paz e Terra, 1991.

Ramos, Arthur. *O Folclore Negro no Brasil,* 2nd ed. Rio de Janeiro: Livraria Editora da Casa do Estudante do Brasil, 1954.

Ramos, Graciliano. *Alexandre e Outros Heróis*, 24th ed. Rio de Janeiro: Record, 1982.
Ramos, Graciliano. *Angústia*, 27th ed. Rio de Janeiro: Record, 1984.
Ramos, Graciliano. *Caetés*, 20th ed. Rio de Janeiro: Record, 1984.
Ramos, Graciliano. *Infância*, 19th ed. Rio de Janeiro: Record, 1984.
Ramos, Graciliano. *Insônia*, 19th ed. Rio de Janeiro: Record, 1984.
Ramos, Graciliano. *Linhas Tortas*, 11th ed. Rio de Janeiro: Record, 1984.
Ramos, Graciliano. *Memórias do Cárcere*, 17th ed. 2 vols. Rio de Janeiro: Record, 1984.
Ramos, Graciliano. *São Bernardo*, 42nd ed. Rio de Janeiro: Record, 1984.
Ramos, Graciliano. *Vidas Secas*, 52nd ed. Rio de Janeiro: Record, 1984.
Ramos, Graciliano. *Viventes das Alagoas*, 14th ed. Rio de Janeiro: Record, 1984.
Rebaud, Jean Paul. "Tradição literária e criação poética em Morte e Vida Severina." *Folha das Letras* (Maceió), 1986.
Rego, José Lins do. *Àgua Mãe*, 8th ed. Rio de Janeiro: José Olympio, 1976.
Rego, José Lins do. *Cangaceiros (Romances Reunidas)*. Rio de Janeiro: José Olympio, 1961.
Rego, José Lins do. *Doidinho*, 30th ed. Rio de Janeiro: José Olympio, 1991.
Rego, José Lins do. *Fogo Morto*, 6th ed. Rio de Janeiro: José Olympio, 1965.
Rego, José Lins do. *Menino do Engenho*, 16th ed. Rio de Janeiro: José Olympio, 1971.
Rego, José Lins do. *Meus Verdes Anos*. Rio de Janeiro: José Olympio, 1981.
Rego, José Lins do. *O Moleque Ricardo*, 8th ed. Rio de Janeiro: José Olympio, 1970.
Rego, José Lins do. *Pedra Bonita*, 11th ed. Rio de Janeiro: José Olympio, 1986.
Rego, José Lins do. *Presença do Nordeste na Literatura*. Rio de Janeiro: Serviço de Documentação, 1957.
Rego, José Lins do. *Riacho Doce*, 5th ed. Rio de Janeiro: José Olympio, 1969.
Rego, José Lins do. *Usina*, 7th ed. Rio de Janeiro: José Olympio, 1973.
Ribeiro, Renato Janine, ed. *Recordar Foucault*. São Paulo: Brasiliense, 1985.
Ricardo, Cassiano. *Marcha para Oeste*. 2 vols. Rio de Janeiro: José Olympio, 1942.
Risério, Antônio. "A dupla modernista e as realidades brasileiras." *Caderno Letras da Folha de São Paulo* May 26, 1990, 7.
Rocha, Glauber. *Revisão Crítica do Cinema Brasileira*. Rio de Janeiro: Civilização Brasileira, 1963.
Rocha, Glauber. *Revolução do Cinema Novo*. Rio de Janeiro: Alhambra, 1981.
Rodrigues, Nina. *Os Africanos no Brasil*, 6th ed. São Paulo: Ed. Nacional, 1982.
Rolnik, Suely. *Cartografia Sentimental*. São Paulo: Estação Liberdade, 1989.
Roncari, Luiz. "O lugar do sertão." *Folhetim* (São Paulo) December 16, 1964, 3.
Sá, Genival. *O Sanfoneiro do Riacho da Brígida*. Fortaleza: Edições A Fortaleza, 1966.
Salles, Antônio, *Aves de Arribação*, 2nd ed. São Paulo: Cia. Ed. Nacional, 1929.
Salles Santiago, Haroldo. "Teatro e nacionalismo." *Revista Brasiliense* no. 23 (January–February 1960): 186.
Santiago, Silviano. "A Bagaceira: Fábula Moralizante I." *Suplemento Literário do Estado de Minas*, August 17, 1974, 4.
Santiago, Silviano. "Modernidade e Tradição Popular." *Folha de São Paulo (Caderno Letras)* November 16, 1989, 4.
Santos, Luis Antônio de Castro. "O espírito da aldeia." *Novos Estudos* CEBRAP no. 27 (July 1990): 45.

Schelling, Vivian. *A Presença do Povo na Cultura Brasileira*. São Paulo: Campus: Ed. da UNICAMP, 1990.

Schnaiderman, Boris. "Modernismo: Literatura e Ideologia." *Movimento* no. 9 (September 1, 1975): 3.

Schwarz, Roberto. *Os Pobres na Literatura Brasileira*. São Paulo: Brasiliense, 1983.

Secchin, Antônio Carlos. *João Cabral: A Poesia do Menos*. São Paulo: Duas Cidades, 1985.

Senna, Homero. *República das Letras*. Rio de Janeiro: Gráfica Olímpica Ed., 1968.

Senna, Orlando, and Glauber Rocha. *Roteiros do Terceyro Mundo*. Rio de Janeiro: Alhambra, 1985.

Sette, Mário. *Senhora de Engenho*, 5th ed. São Paulo: Ed. Fagundes, 1937.

Silva, Carlos Alberto, "Meu sol, teu diabo, vosso senhor, nosso nordeste." *Debate* (Salvador) ano 2 (October 1964).

Silva, Quirino da. "Caribé." *Diário da Noite* (São Paulo) May 25, 1955.

Silveira, Rosa Maria Godoy. *O Regionalismo Nordestino*. São Paulo: Moderna, 1984.

Simões, Roberto. "Ficção nordestina: diretrizes sociais." *Revista Brasiliense* no. 41 (May–June 1962): 172.

Sodré, Nelson Werneck. "Quem é o povo no Brasil?" *Cadernos do Povo Brasileiro* (Rio de Janeiro) no. 2, 1967.

Souza Barros. *A Década Vinte em Pernambuco*, 2nd ed. Recife: Fundação de Cultura da Cidade do Recife, 1985.

Squeff, Enio, and José Miguel Wisnik. *Música (O Nacional e o Popular na Cultura Brasileira)*. São Paulo: Brasiliense, 1982.

Suassuna, Ariano. *História do Rei Degolado nas Caatingas do Sertão*. Rio de Janeiro: José Olympio, 1977.

Suassuna, Ariano. *Romance d'A Pedra do Reino*, 4th ed. Rio de Janeiro: José Olympio, 1976.

Suassuna, Ariano. *Seleta em Prosa e Verso*. Rio de Janeiro: José Olympio, 1974.

Subirats, Eduardo, *Da Vanguarda ao Pós-Moderno*, 3rd ed. São Paulo: Nobel, 1987.

Süssekind, Flora. *O Brasil Não é Longe Daqui*. São Paulo: Companhia das Letras, 1990.

Tavares, Zulmira Ribeiro. "Os confines da ignorância." *O Estado de São Paulo* July 26, 1969 (literary supplement), 4.

Tronca, Ítalo, ed. *Foucault Vivo*. Campinas: Pontes, 1987.

Ventura, Roberto. *Estilo Tropical*. São Paulo: Companhia das Letras, 1991.

Ventura, Roberto. "Saudades do engenho e a nostalgia dos escravos." *Caderno B da Folha de São Paulo* May 13, 1988, 15.

Veyne, Paul. *Como se Escreve a História*. Brasília: Ed. da UnB, 1982.

Veyne, Paul. *O Inventário das Diferenças*. São Paulo: Brasiliense, 1989.

Vianna, Oliveira. *Evolução do Povo Brasileiro*, 4th ed. Rio de Janeiro: José Olympio, 1952.

Vianna, Oliveira. *Populações Meridionais do Brasil*, 5th ed. Rio de Janeiro: José Olympio, 1952.

Vidal, Adhemar. "O romance do Nordeste." *Revista Acadêmica* no. 11 (May 1935): 7.

Vieira, André. "Cândido Portinari: Pintor da véspera." *Revista Acadêmica* (Rio de Janeiro) no. 12 (July 1935): 10.

Weffort, Francisco. "Problema Nacional no Brasil." *Revista Anhembi* 11 no. 119 (October 1960): 350.

Wisnik, José Miguel. "Estado, arte e política em Villa-Lobos, Vargas e Glauber." *Folhetim* (São Paulo) June 20, 1982, 6–8.

Wolf, José. "Morrer como poeta." *Jornal do Comércio* May 28, 1967, 6.

Xavier, Ismail. *Sertão Mar (Glauber Rocha e a Estética da Fome)*. São Paulo: Brasiliense, 1983.

Zilio, Carlos. "A difícil história da arte brasileira." *Folhetim* (São Paulo) October 2, 1983, 4.

Zilio, Carlos. *A Quarela do Brasil*. Rio de Janeiro: Funarte, 1982.

Zilio, Carlos, João Luiz Lafetá, and Lígia Chiappini Moraes Leite. *Artes Plásticas e Literatura (O Nacional e o Popular na Cultura Brasileira)*. São Paulo: Brasiliense, 1982.

ICONOGRAPHY

Amaral, Tarsila do. *Abaporu*. 1928.

Amaral, Tarsila do. *Distância*. 1928.

Amaral, Tarsila do. *Lua*. 1928.

Amaral, Tarsila do. *Paisagem*. 1925.

Ayres, Lula Cardoso. *Apresentação do Bumba-meu-Boi*. 1943.

Ayres, Lula Cardoso. *Bichos do Carnaval*. 1954.

Ayres, Lula Cardoso. *Bichos de Festa Popular*. 1952.

Ayres, Lula Cardoso. *Cabeleira no Canavial*. 1950.

Ayres, Lula Cardoso *Caboclos Tuchauas. Carnaval do Recife*. 1942.

Ayres, Lula Cardoso. *Cabriolet Mal-Assombrada*. 1945.

Ayres, Lula Cardoso. *Cadeira*. 1969.

Ayres, Lula Cardoso. *Capela Mal-Assombrada*. 1945.

Ayres, Lula Cardoso. *Cego Violeiro*. 1947.

Ayres, Lula Cardoso. *Cortadores de Cana*. 1948.

Ayres, Lula Cardoso. *Dando Cafuné*. 1943.

Ayres, Lula Cardoso. *Grade e Sobrado*. 1967.

Ayres, Lula Cardoso. *Matheus e Boi*. 1945.

Ayres, Lula Cardoso. *Menino de Engenho*. 1943.

Ayres, Lula Cardoso. *Mulher e Mandacaru*. 1938.

Ayres, Lula Cardoso. *Namoro de Ex-Votos*. 1951.

Ayres, Lula Cardoso. *Noivado na Casa de Engenho*. 1943.

Ayres, Lula Cardoso. *Portão*. 1969.

Ayres, Lula Cardoso. *Relógio*. 1971.

Ayres, Lula Cardoso. *Retirantes*. 1947.

Ayres, Lula Cardoso. *Retrato de Família*. 1943.

Ayres, Lula Cardoso. *Ruína*. 1966.

Ayres, Lula Cardoso. *Sofá Mal-Assombrado*. 1945.

Ayres, Lula Cardoso. *Tipos de Feira*. 1942.

Ayres, Lula Cardoso. *Vendedores de Rua*. 1936.

Ayres, Lula Cardoso. *Vulta de Branco*. 1947.

Ayres, Lula Cardoso. *Xangô.* 1948.

Carybé. *Bahia.* 1951.

Carybé. *Cangaceiros.* 1962.

Carybé. *Carnaval.* 1944.

Carybé. *Lampião.* 1940.

Carybé. *Lampião* or *A Assombração do Cangaço.* 1968.

Carybé. *A Morte de Alexandrina.* 1939.

Carybé. *Navio Negreiro.* 1965.

Carybé. *Nino Gafieiro.* 1940.

Carybé. *Nordeste.* 1972.

Carybé. *Pensão São Bento.* 1940.

Carybé. *Os Pescadores.* 1955.

Carybé. *Retirantes.* 1945.

Carybé. *Vaqueiros.* 1953.

Carybé. *Vaqueiros na Caatinga.* 1969.

Dias, Cícero. *Amizade.* 1928.

Dias, Cícero. *Amo.* 1933.

Dias, Cícero. *Banho de Rio.* 1931.

Dias, Cícero. *Casas.* 1939.

Dias, Cícero. *Composição Saudades.* 1931.

Dias, Cícero. *Dançarina ou Mamoeiro.* 1940.

Dias, Cícero. *Eu Vi o Mundo . . . Ele Começava no Recife.* 1931.

Dias, Cícero. *Ex-Voto.* 1970.

Dias, Cícero. *Família na Paisagem.* N/d.

Dias, Cícero. *Homem no Burrinho.* 1930.

Dias, Cícero. *Igreja.* 1930.

Dias, Cícero. *Jangadinha.* 1930.

Dias, Cícero. *Lavouras.* 1930.

Dias, Cícero. *Mocambos.* 1930.

Dias, Cícero. *Mormaço.* 1940.

Dias, Cícero. *Olinda.* 1935.

Dias, Cícero. *Paisagem com Figura.* 1930.

Dias, Cícero. *Porto.* 1930.

Dias, Cícero. *Procissão.* 1930.

Dias, Cícero. *Recife.* 1930.

Dias, Cícero. *Terra Chão.* 1940.

Dias, Cícero. *Tirador de Coco.* 1930.

Dias, Cícero. *Vida.* 1939.

Dias, Cícero. *Vista do Engenho Noruega.* 1930.

Di Cavalcanti, Emiliano. *Arlequins.* 1940.

Di Cavalcanti, Emiliano. *Baiana com Charuto.* 1970.

Di Cavalcanti, Emiliano. *Baianas e Frutas.* 1957.

Di Cavalcanti, Emiliano. *Bumba-meu-Boi.* 1959.

Di Cavalcanti, Emiliano. *Carnaval.* 1973.

Di Cavalcanti, Emiliano. *Cenas da Vida Brasileira.* 1950.

Di Cavalcanti, Emiliano. *Figuras.* 1957.

Di Cavalcanti, Emiliano. *Morro*. 1930.
Di Cavalcanti, Emiliano. *Mulher*. 1952.
Di Cavalcanti, Emiliano. *Mulher*. 1970.
Di Cavalcanti, Emiliano. *Músicos e Mulatas*. 1972.
Di Cavalcanti, Emiliano. *Natureza Morta*. 1958.
Di Cavalcanti, Emiliano. *Pescadores*. 1940.
Di Cavalcanti, Emiliano. *A Quitanda da Rosa*. 1952.
Di Cavalcanti, Emiliano. *Retrato de Maria*. 1927.
Di Cavalcanti, Emiliano. *Samba*. 1925.
Di Cavalcanti, Emiliano. *Três Mulheres Sentadas*. 1961.
Di Cavalcanti, Emiliano. *Varanda na Bahia*. 1961.
Portinari, Cândido. *Baianas*. 1940.
Portinari, Cândido. *Baiana com Crianças*. N/d.
Portinari, Cândido. *Cabeça de Cangaçeiro*. 1952.
Portinari, Cândido. *Carnaval*. 1940.
Portinari, Cândido. *Enterro na Rede*. 1944.
Portinari, Cândido. *Retirantes*. 1944.
Portinari, Cândido. *Futebol*. N/d.
Portinari, Cândido. *Índio*. N/d.
Portinari, Cândido. *Menino Morte*. 1944.
Portinari, Cândido. *Mestiço*. N/d.
Portinari, Cândido. *Mulata e Índia*. N/d.
Portinari, Cândido. *Mulher Imigrante*. 1935.
Portinari, Cândido. *Retirantes*. 1936.
Portinari, Cândido. *Retirantes*. 1945.
Portinari, Cândido. *São João*. N/d.

AUDIO RECORDINGS: ORAL STATEMENTS / LECTURES

Castilho, Almira. São Paulo: MIS, July 7, 1983.
Chamie, Mário. Seminário sobre a Semana de 22. São Paulo: MIS, May 1972.
Ferreira, Edgar. São Paulo: MIS, July 11, 1983.
Xavier, Ismail. "O Cinema e a Ficção em Oswald de Andrade." Campinas, UNICAMP, CEDAE, April 4, 1990.

PLAYS

Queiroz, Rachel de. *A Beata Maria do Egito* (*Obras Reunidas*, vol 5). Rio de Janeiro: José Olympio, 1989.
Queiroz, Rachel de. *Lampião* (*Obras Reunidas*, vol 5). Rio de Janeiro: José Olympio, 1989.
Suassuna, Ariano. *Auto da Compadecida*, 21st ed. Rio de Janeiro: Agir, 1985.
Suassuna, Ariano. *O Casamento Suspeitoso*. Recife, Editora Igarassu, 1961.
Suassuna, Ariano. *O Castigo da Soberba*. Deca (Recife) 2, no. 2, 1960.
Suassuna, Ariano. *Farsa da Boa Preguiça*. Rio de Janeiro: José Olympio, 1974.
Suassuna, Ariano. *A Pena e a Lei*. Recife: Imprensa Universitária, 1964.

Suassuna, Ariano. *O Rico Avarento*. In *Seleta em Prosa e Verso*. Rio de Janeiro: José Olympio, 1965.

Suassuna, Ariano. *O Santo e a Porca*. Recife: Imprensa Universitária, 1964.

Suassuna, Ariano. *Torturas de um Coração*. In *Seleta em Prosa e Verso*. Rio de Janeiro: José Olympio, 1965.

Suassuna, Ariano. *Uma Mulher Vestida de Sol*. Recife: Imprensa Universitária, 1964.

DISCOGRAPHY

Caymmi, Dorival. *Todo o Dengo da Bahia*. História da Música Popular Brasileira no. 3. Abril / RCA Victor, 1970.

Gonzaga, Luiz. *Os Grandes Sucessos de Luiz Gonzaga* vol. 1. RCA Victor, 1982.

Gonzaga, Luiz. *Os Grandes Sucessos de Luiz Gonzaga* vol. 2. Magazine, 1983.

Gonzaga, Luiz. *A História do Nordeste na Voz de Luiz Gonzaga*. RCA Victor, 1955.

Gonzaga, Luiz. *Luiz Gonzaga Canta seus Sucessos com Zé Dantas*. RCA Victor, 1959.

Gonzaga, Luiz. *Luiz Gonzaga*. RCA Victor, 1967.

Gonzaga, Luiz. *Luiz Gonzaga e Humberto Teixeira*. RCA Victor, 1969.

Gonzaga, Luiz. *Luiz Gonzaga e Zé Dantas*. RCA Victor, 1968.

Gonzaga, Luiz. *Luiz Gonzaga. Sua Sanfona e Sua Simpatia*. RCA Victor, 1966.

Gonzaga, Luiz. *O Nordeste na Voz de Luiz Gonzaga*. RCA Victor, 1962.

Gonzaga, Luiz. *O Reino do Baião*. RCA Victor, 1957.

Gonzaga, Luiz. *O Sanfoneiro do Povo de Deus*. RCA Victor, 1968.

Gonzaga, Luiz. *A Triste Partida*. RCA Victor, 1964.

FILMOGRAPHY

Barreto, Lima. *O Cangaceiro*. 1953.

Barros, Luiz de. *Fogo na Canjica*. 1947.

Cavalcanti, Alberto. *Canto do Mar*. 1953.

Coimbra, Carlos. *Cangaceiros de Lampião*. 1967.

Coimbra, Carlos. *Corisco, O Diabo Loiro*. 1969.

Coimbra, Carlos. *Lampião, Rei do Cangaço*. 1963.

Coimbra, Carlos. *A Morte Comanda o Cangaço*. 1960.

Costa, Rui. *Banana da Terra*. 1939.

Diégues, Carlos. *Cinco Vezes Favela*. 1962.

Downey, Wallace. *Abacaxi Azul*. 1944.

Downey, Wallace, João de Barros, and Alberto Ribeiro. *Alô, Alô, Brasil!* 1933.

Duarte, Anselmo. *Vereda da Salvação*. 1966.

Duarte, Anselmo, and Dias Gomes. *O Pagador de Promessas*. 1962.

Farias, Edmundo. *Terra Violenta*. 1948.

Farias, Roberto. *Rico Ri à Toa*. 1957.

Gonzaga, Adhemar. *Alô, Alô, Carnaval!* 1936.

Guerra, Ruy. *Os Fuzis*. 1965.

Hirszman, Leon. *Maioria Absoluta*. 1964.

Laurelli, Glauco. *O Lamparina*. 1966.

Lima, Walter, Jr. *Menino de Engenho*. 1965.

Macêdo, Watson. *Este Mundo É um Pandeiro*. 1946.
Manga, Carlos. *Matar ou Correr*. 1954.
Manga, Carlos. *Nem Sansão e Nem Dalila*. 1954.
Neto, Triguerinho. *Bahia de Todos os Santos*. 1960.
Oliveira, Osvaldo de. *O Cangaceiro Sanguinário*. 1969.
Oliveira, Osvaldo de. *O Cangaceiro Sem Deus*. 1969.
Pereira, Gilberto, and Renato Santos. *Grande Sertão*. 1965.
Rocha, Glauber. *Barravento*. 1962.
Rocha, Glauber. *Deus e o Diabo na Terra do Sol*. 1964.
Santos, Nelson Pereira dos. *Vidas Secas*. 1963.
Silva, Watson. *Nordeste Sangrento*. 1963.
Soares, Paulo Gil. *Memória do Cangaço*. 1965.
Teixeira, Aurélio. *Entre o Amor e o Cangaço*. 1960.

INDEX

Klaxon, 58
Kubitschek, Juscelino, 123, 203

labor, 99–100; New Cinema and, 202
labor leaders, 43
labor movement, 107–8, 150–51
O Lamparina, 149
Lampião, 1, 91, 141, 150
language: Afro-Brazilian contribution
  to, 84; Cabral's use of, 184–87, 190;
  northeastern dialect, 1, 84–86; power
  and, 4–5; Ramos's use of, 75, 184–85;
  Suassuna's use of, 130
Law of the Free Womb, 32
Leftists, 133, 136, 140–41, 142; Amado's
  critique of, 157–58, 163; appropriation
  of bandit myth, 150–51; characterization of Northeast for political
  purposes, 141, 143–45; inversion of
  Northeast, 13; poverty and, 147; rejection of naturalism/fatalism of, 143;
  religiosity and, 147–48; as warrior/
  savior, 146
Lima, Jorge de, 51, 78
A Língua do Nordeste (Marroquim), 84–85
literature, regionalist: aesthetic shift in,
  151–52; as antimodern, 53–54; bandits
  in, 90–93; character types in (*see*
  character types); childhood gaze in,
  50; cinema adaptation of, 194; class
  conflict in, 90–91; *coronelismo* in,
  94–95; drought in, 87–88; growth
  as an industry, 76–77; language of,
  84–86; as "literary province," 74–76;
  messianism in, 93; narrative structure of, 79–81; naturalist nostalgia
  of, 78, 81–83; New Cinema and, 200;
  origins of, 25–29; patriarchy/planta-
  tions in, 89–90; Ramos's criticism
  of, 175–76; realist, 152–53; *sertão* in
  (see *sertão*); societal stimulation of,
  76; themes, 77, 86; transformation
  to national, 74
Lobato, Monteiro, 27–28
Lourenço, José, 147
Lukács, Georg, 137

Machado, Alcântara, 70
Macunaíma (Andrade), 21, 24
madness, in Rego's works, 101
Magalhães, Agamenon, 44
malandro, 166
The Mansions and the Shanties (Freyre),
  65–66
Mar Morto (Amado), 158
Marroquim, Mário, 84–85
Martins, Ibiapaba, 179
Martins, Wilson, 59
Marxism: Amado and, 151, 156, 157, 167;
  art in, 137–38; banditry and, 141;
  coronelismo and, 145; development in
  Brazil, 132–39; messianism and, 141;
  in New Cinema, 202; Queiroz and,
  107; Ramos and, 151, 174; religion in,
  147–48; Sodré on, 134
The Masters and the Slaves (Freyre),
  65–66
Matta, Roberto de, 222
Maurras, Charles, 60
media stereotypes, 1–2, 16, 230
memory, 45–46, 48–54, 189–90
Menezes, Djacir, 135
Menino Morto (Portinari), 182
Menotti del Picchia, 71
Merquior, José Guilherme, 75
messianism, 23, 32–33, 41, 93, 146–47
mestiço: in Amado's works, 166–67; as
  inferior, 30–31, 35; in Rego's works,
  98; as superior, 62, 162
Milliet, Sérgio, 153, 179
miscegenation: as beneficial, 61–62,
  162; as detrimental, 102; Rego on,
  98, 101. See also *mestiço*
mixed-race. *See* mestiço; miscegenation
Modern Art Week (1922), 56, 58
modernism, 19; aversion to, 226; Brazilian vs. European, 24; identity and,
  23, 24; naturalist regionalism vs.,
  28–29
modernist fiction, 56
modernist regionalism: traditionalist
  vs., 54–60
O Moleque Ricardo (Rego), 43, 99

Monteiro, Joaquim do Rego, 60
Monteiro, Vicente do Rego, xi, 60
Moog, Vianna, 74
A Morte de Alexandrina (Carybé), 181
Movimento Cultura Popular, 142, 203
Municipal Culture Department, City of
  São Paulo, 28–29
muralists, Mexican, 178, 179, 182
music, popular: Dorival Caymmi, 159,
  160; commercial nature of, 119; José
  (Zé) Dantas, 47, 116, 119; genesis of,
  115–16; Luis de Gonzaga, 116–24; as
  participatory, 118
"My Land" (Bandeira), 48–49
mysticism, 51, 93, 163

Nabuco, Joaquim, 79
nation: Andrade on, 21; as homogenization, 22–23; as regional pact, 66
National Cinema Institute (INC), 194
National Congress of Brazilian Cinema,
  193–94
National Department of Works against
  the Droughts, 43
nationalism: as reactionary, 223–24;
  regionalism and, 221
National Liberator Alliance, 152
national-popular discursive formation, 8
National Students Union (UNE), 203
naturalism: in Amado's works, 158, 166;
  in Ayres's works, 112; in Gonzaga's
  works, 124; in painting, 109–10; in
  Queiroz's works, 108; realist fiction's
  view of, 154; in Rego's works, 98–99;
  rejection by leftists, 143; in Suassuna's
  works, 128
naturalist regionalism: contribution to
  idea of Northeast, 29–30; decline of,
  45; in literature, 78, 81–83; modernism vs., 28–29
Nazário, Luiz, 213
Nazism, influence on art, 178
New Cinema: authenticization of,
  205–9; commercial success of,
  204–5; didactic tone of, 201; first
  phase, 200–201; Leftists and, 201–3;

Northeast as seen by, 138; origins
  of, 199–200; revolutionary goals of,
  203–4, 207; use of bandits, 145
New York Times, ix–x
nomadism, 69
O Nordeste, 43
Nordeste (Freyre), 66
nordestern, 149
nordestinidade, 3
nordestino (dialect), 1, 84–85
nordestino (person): invention of, 11;
  political views of, 142; racial inferiority of, 18; stereotypes of, 1–2; as
  threat, 145
Noronha, Lindoarte, 199, 200
North: as barbaric, 34; as decadent, 31;
  as desert, 35; as synonymous with
  Northeast, 38
Northeast: as barbaric, 92; definitions
  of, 37–38, 40; as having always
  existed, 44; as obstacle to development, 142; as preserver of traditions,
  72–73; as synonymous with North,
  38; as ubiquitous, 222; as victim of
  capitalism, 152–54
Northeastern Regionalist Center, 42–43,
  54, 59
Northern bloc, 40
nostalgia, 36–37, 46, 52, 122
novelists. *See* literature, regionalist

Olho D'Àgua da Serra do Talhado, 199
Olinda, 188
Oliveira, Osvaldo de, 149
Onça Caetana, 128
Order and Progress (Freyre), 65–66
origin myths, 69
orixás, 163
"other," 39, 68–73, 141
O Outro Nordeste (Menezes), 135

Padre Cicero, 33, 141
Pádua, Cyro T. de, 74
O Pagador de Promessas (Duarte), 197–99
painters/painting, 25, 109–14; Amaral, 29; Di Cavalcanti, 179–80, 181;

nationalism of, 178; Northeast as theme, 179; Cândido Portinari, 180–84; realist, 177–79; as transformational act, 176–77

O País do Carnaval (Amado), 155

Palanquim Dourado (Sette), 60

Paraíba: Afro-Brazilians in, 199; Inojosa's reception, 59; New Cinema origins in, 200; *O Canto do Mar*, 195; stereotypes, 3

A Paraíba e Seus Problemas (Almeida), 59

Parliament: Northern bloc, 40; response to 1877 drought, 39–40

patriarchy: Amado on, 164; Freyre on, 64–65; Gonzaga on, 124; in Northeastern literature, 77, 89–90; stability of, 70, 89

Paulicea Desvairada (Andrade), 28

paulistas, 26–27; racial superiority of, 18

Peasant Leagues, 142

Pedra Bonita (Ramos), 200

Pernambuco: as core of national identity, 69; Dutch influence, 44; Freyre's praise of, 59–60; modern art in, 58; sugar production in, 65–66

physiognomy: Brazilian, 63; mixed-race, 64; *nordestino*, 127; Northeastern, 66–67; Northern, 31

Picturesque Brazil—Journeys of Cornélio Pires to the North of Brazil, 20

Pires, Cornélio, 19–20

plantations, 13, 67, 70; Amado on, 156; Ayres on, 112; in Northeastern literature, 80, 81, 82–83; realist fiction's view of, 154; in regionalist painting, 110; Rego on, 99–101

Popular Culture Movement, 142, 203

Portinari, Cândido, 13, 180–84

Portugal, as model for Northeast, 57

Portuguese language, 85–86

poverty: bourgeois view of, 147; in Cabral's works, 186–87; leftist view of, 147; in Queiroz's works, 108; in Rego's works, 99

Prado, Caio, Jr., 134

Prado, Paulo, 63

O Primo do Cangaceiro, 149

proto-regionalism, 16

publishing industry, 76–77

puppetry, 125, 127

Queiroz, Rachel de: analysis of literary oeuvre, 105–8; geographic focus, 78; on media's treatment of Northeast, 2, 222; as *nordestinidade*, 3; *sertão*'s importance for, 88–89; time/space dichotomy, 51–52; traditionalism of, 13, 47; youth, 105

O Quinze (Queiroz), 106–7

radio, 114–15, 118

Rádio Nacional, 115, 116, 117

Rádio Record, 117

Ramos, Graciliano: *Angústia*, 171; on bandits, 149; bourgeois society and, 140; *Caetés*, 173; Campos on, 200; challenge to idea of Northeast, 225–26; on Conselheiro, 148; criticism of regionalist fiction, 175–76; decline/instability as theme, 170–71; on exaggeration of Northeast's ills, 145; inversion of traditionalist Northeast, 13, 138–39; language/silence as theme, 167–70; Marxism of, 151; memory/history as theme, 171–72; modernism and, 173–74; *São Bernardo*, 173, 174; use of language, 75, 184–85; *Vidas Secas*, 170, 173; youth, 167

Ramos, Guerreiro, 135

realist fiction, 152–54

realist painting, 177–79

Recife: Agricultural Congress, 38; Andrade on, 38; Cabral's view of, 186; as cultural center, 16; higher education in, 41; as journalism locus, 41; in *O Moleque Ricardo*, 99–100; Regionalist Conference (1926), 42–43

Recôncavo, 160, 164

Reflexões de uma Cabra (Almeida), 59

region: defined, 7, 9, 12; as precursor to nation, 45

regionalism: aesthetic, 24; modernist vs. traditionalist, 54–60; nationalism and, 221; as obstacle to progress, 227–28; as perpetuation of victimhood, 229–30; as precursor to nationalism, 24; proto-, 16; as reactionary, 223–24; of 1920s, 15, 21–22

Regionalist Conference (1926), 42–43, 44, 54, 59

regionalist discourse, 23–24

regionalist gaze, 15–21

regional psychology, 50

Rego, José Lins do, xi, 223; analysis of literary oeuvre, 96–101; bandits in works of, 91; on *Book of the Northeast*, 42; Campos on, 200; *coronel* character type, 94; criticism of Andrade, 55–56, 57; on *Diário de Pernambuco*, 41; dissolution as theme, 89; Freyre's influence on, 56, 223; geographic focus, 78; *O Moleque Ricardo*, 43; narrative voices of, 80–81; on Northeastern dialect, 84; Northeast in decline, 48; personal identification with Northeast, 50–51; traditionalism of, 13, 47; youth, 95

O Rei Degolado nas Caatingas do Sertão (Suassuna), 125–26

religion: Marxist view of, 147–48; in Suassuna's works, 125, 126–27

religious extremism, 33

Representação do Bumba-Meu-Boi (Ayers), 113

Os Retirantes (Portinari), 182, 183, 184

Revista Mauriceia, 59

"Riacho do Navio" (Gonzaga), 123

Ribeiro, João, 25

Ricardo, Cassiano, 70–71

Rio de Janeiro: Agricultural Congress, 38; Amado's view of, 161, 165; as discursive center, 16; Lobato on, 28; New Cinema origins in, 200; theatrical tradition, 124

Rocha, Glauber, xi; *Barravento*, 208, 211; cinematographic techniques, 215–17;

cordel's influence on, 206; *Deus e o Diabo na Terra do Sol*, 150, 208–10, 216–17; Embrafilme and, 204; history/myth as theme, 211–12, 215; on newness of Brazilian cinema, 199–200; populist goals of, 194, 213–15, 217–18; *Terra em Transe*, 211; use of time, 210–11; youth, 207–8

Rodrigues, Chiquinha, 20

Rodrigues, Nina, 30–31

Romero, Silvio, 79

Rosa, Guimarães, 187, 191, 206

rural vs. coastal polarity, 27

rural vs. urban motif, 81–82, 89–90, 145, 196, 197–98

Salvador, 160, 161

samba, 120

O Santo e a Porca (Suassuna), 127

Santos, Luis Paulino dos, 199

Santos, Nelson Pereira dos, 199, 200, 201

São Bernardo (Ramos), 173, 174

São Jorge de Ilhéus (Amado), 159

São Paulo: Amado's view of, 161, 165; Amaral on, 73; aristocracy of, 70–71; artistic autonomy from, 56, 58; Braudel on, 73; as center of national culture, 16, 28–29, 72; as core of national identity, 69; Cunha on, 26–27; Freyre and, 59; literature of, 75; response to autonomist movement, 43; superiority of, 18–19; theatrical tradition, 124

Saraceni, Paulo César, 199

Sarno, Geraldo, 184

saudade, 36, 46

Seara Vermelha (Amado), 159–60

sedentariness, 70

Senhor de Engenho (Sette), 42, 60

sertanejo, 26, 102, 108, 142, 170, 188, 197

sertão, 27–28, 53; Almeida's use of, 102, 104; Cabral's use of, 187–88, 189; in cinema, 196–97; Conselheiro's prediction, 209; Gonzaga's use of, 121–23; in Northeastern literature generally, 83–84, 88–89; as part of